Governed by a Spirit of Opposition

STUDIES IN EARLY AMERICAN ECONOMY AND SOCIETY
FROM THE LIBRARY COMPANY OF PHILADELPHIA

Cathy Matson, *Series Editor*

Governed by a Spirit of Opposition

*The Origins of American Political Practice
in Colonial Philadelphia*

JESSICA CHOPPIN RONEY

Johns Hopkins University Press
Baltimore

© 2014 Johns Hopkins University Press
All rights reserved. Published 2014
Printed in the United States of America on acid-free paper

2 4 6 8 9 7 5 3 1

Johns Hopkins University Press
2715 North Charles Street
Baltimore, Maryland 21218-4363
www.press.jhu.edu

Library of Congress Cataloging-in-Publication Data

Roney, Jessica C. (Jessica Choppin), 1978–
Governed by a spirit of opposition : the origins of American political practice in
colonial Philadelphia / by Jessica C. Roney.
pages cm. — (Studies in early American economy and society from the Library
Company of Philadelphia)
Includes bibliographical references and index.
ISBN 978-1-4214-1527-7 (hardcover : acid-free paper) — ISBN 1-4214-1527-5 (hardcover :
acid-free paper) — ISBN 978-1-4214-1528-4 (electronic) — ISBN 1-4214-1528-3
(electronic) 1. Philadelphia (Pa.)—History—Colonial period, ca. 1600-1775.
2. Philadelphia (Pa.)—Politics and government—17th century. 3. Philadelphia (Pa.)—
Politics and government—18th century. 4. Political participation—Pennsylvania—
Philadelphia—History. 5. Municipal government—Pennsylvania—Philadelphia
—Citizen participation—History. 6. Civic leaders—Pennsylvania—Philadelphia
—History. 7. Associations, institutions, etc.—Pennsylvania—Philadelphia—History.
8. Community life—Pennsylvania—Philadelphia—History. 9. Democracy—
Pennsylvania—Philadelphia—History. 10. Political culture—Pennsylvania—
Philadelphia—History. I. Title.
F158.4.R66 2014
974.8'11—dc23   2014004990

A catalog record for this book is available from the British Library.

The maps on pages 12 and 132 appear courtesy of the
Library Company of Philadelphia.

*Special discounts are available for bulk purchases of this book. For more information, please
contact Special Sales at 410-516-6936 or specialsales@press.jhu.edu.*

Johns Hopkins University Press uses environmentally friendly book materials,
including recycled text paper that is composed of at least 30 percent post-consumer
waste, whenever possible.

For Adam

CONTENTS

Series Editor's Foreword   *ix*
Acknowledgments   *xi*

Introduction   1

1 "Named Before Thou Wert Born":
A City Imagined and Realized   11

2 Intoxicated with Power: *Chartering the
Philadelphia Corporation*   38

3 For a General Benefit: *Developing Popular
Voluntary Associations*   59

4 Amidst "Rancour and Party Hatred":
Association by Exclusion   80

5 Lending in Plain Sight:
Covert Banks   104

6 Private Men Interfering with Government:
Taking Over from the State   131

7 Mars Ascendant: *The Military Association and the
Reconstitution of Government*   158

Epilogue   183

Notes   *189*
Essay on Sources   *239*
Index   *245*

In this addition to Studies in Early American Economy and Society, a collaborative effort between Johns Hopkins University Press and the Library Company of Philadelphia's Program in Early American Economy and Society (PEAES), Jessica Roney takes us into the world of colonial Philadelphia's economy and politics. *Governed by a Spirit of Opposition: The Origins of American Political Practice in Colonial Philadelphia* begins with the origins of the city's capacious and orderly design and quickly informs us that the men and women who came to Philadelphia followed a dramatically different plan that suited the ideals of an ambitious people. After just two decades the Quaker meetinghouse, setpiece of Penn's plan for an ideal city, had fallen into disrepair. Thereafter, the means by which city dwellers shaped their governing bodies mirrored this early demise of an ideal. Caught between the world of British governing practices and the potential for creating their own distinctive institutions, Philadelphians moved through successive phases of trial and error to define the powers by which they would be governed. Moreover, residents learned early and often that their struggles to define property rights, civic responsibilities, and a workable public good would be circumscribed by a cacophony of shifting private and group interests. As Roney compellingly insists, the rights and responsibilities of inhabitants would be molded by the pragmatic needs of a young city trying to find its way in the Atlantic world and at the edge of a volatile frontier.

Local governing bodies found it hard to identify, let alone address, the pragmatic needs of a diverse urban community. But as Roney shows, scholars have cast too small a net to capture an understanding of how Philadelphians actually did meet those pragmatic needs. She moves us far beyond the typical views of residents casting votes in elections, petitioning authorities, engaging in rational-critical discourse in places like taverns, writing for the newspapers, and even rioting. The reality of political practices was, she argues, not a straightforward democratizing process. It was at once more local, more ordinary, and more shifting than previous analyses allow. "A dispute over a public wharf contained within it a fight over the grounds of private property ownership in the city.

Fights over mandatory duty as a night-watchman turned into a contest over men's civic duties and the limits of executive power. The founding of a hospital became a weapon with which to champion the representative legislature at the expense of the authority of the Penn family. The need to defend the city from invasion provoked a debate about the nature and basis of citizenship and civil rights." Civic life in Philadelphia was both ordinary and transformational. Inhabitants regularly moved between the poles of mundane decisions about the size of market stalls and the imperative to found an enduring educational system.

Just as importantly, Philadelphians' political practices flowed through discussions on the street and in printed exchanges, as the work of ordinary men and women striving for governance over their economy and society without the authoritarian structures of a central government. The governing authorities they created evolved slowly, through informal but enforceable decisions from the bottom up. Yet Philadelphia's political economy and culture did not emerge as a haphazard pastiche created by random interpersonal arguments about what was best for their collective advancement. It emerged through a widely accepted model of civic participation, classes intermingling on the governing boards and local committees that established food markets, served the poor, fought fires, sheltered the sick, regulated construction, and much more.

This model of civic participation did not meld differences into a homogenous body of imperial subjects or like-minded locals. In fact, it encouraged the wide distribution of power and a contentious hubbub of discussion spilling from one new institution to another. It was a bold new step in early modern governance, argues Roney. Elsewhere in the British empire, conformity and quashing of cultural and economic opposition was the norm, especially when the eruption of violence threatened.

At the center of Roney's argument is a brand of "civic technology" that privileged voluntary associations for economic regulation as well as sociable, charitable, and civic gatherings that slowly evolved into more permanent organizations. These associations—some sixty were created before the North American Revolution, involving some twenty percent of adult white males—were built by daily give and take among interested individuals, and they provided the multiple new sites for creating rules by which Philadelphians could live together and pursue opportunities for mutual development. As a result, with the advent of the American Revolution, myriad city inhabitants were not faced with a sudden watershed in which they radically transformed the civic engagement of ordinary while males; rather, they carried forward their decades of local practice.

Cathy Matson
Professor of History, University of Delaware
Director, Program in Early American Economy and Society

When I began this project a decade ago now, I originally thought it was going to be about eighteenth-century constructions of friendship. In an effort to pare down such a vast topic into something more discrete and manageable, I found myself in the membership rolls of Philadelphia voluntary associations and that led me in rather different directions from those I had originally imagined. But the project began in an interest in friendship and networks; it was sustained through its evolution by many friends and by the especially vibrant and generous networks of early American scholarship of which I am privileged to be a part.

Foundational to my education and early career was my time at Johns Hopkins University, where I was particularly influenced by the Early American History Seminar on Monday nights run by Jack P. Greene, Philip D. Morgan, and Toby L. Ditz. Each week the talented scholars who assembled for this seminar modeled how to ask good questions, construct strong arguments, offer criticism, and navigate disagreement. It was a heady, if sometimes daunting, place to be a graduate student, and I wish to thank all its participants and particularly its conveners. CVP, where we recovered afterwards, deserves special mention as well. I was extremely fortunate to work with Jack, a formidable role model and mentor, and have Toby and Phil as sort of academic godparents.

Philadelphia itself is the other core academic influence in my scholarly life. The interdisciplinary community that gathers around the archives and the programs through the American Philosophical Society, Program in Early American Economy and Society, Library Company, and above all the McNeil Center for Early American Studies have taught and continue to teach me so much. I was particularly fortunate to return to Philadelphia as a postdoctoral fellow at the McNeil Center in 2011-12. My brilliant, madcap cohort of fellows at the Center showed me the true meaning of fellowship. It is a testament to the many regular participants and particularly to Daniel K. Richter that the McNeil Center is such a challenging, energizing, and welcoming place to congregate. My thanks as well to Patrick and Laura Spero, who made it possible for me to spend that year living in the eighteenth-century Man Full of Trouble Tavern, a stimulating (in both senses of the word) place to write and think about early Philadelphia. My thanks to Adam for always keeping it well stocked with the Colony in Schuylkill's recipe for Fish House Punch.

I owe Dan Richter another debt of gratitude for facilitating as part of my fellowship a book workshop in 2011. I cannot thank enough my readers, all of whom slogged through the whole manuscript draft: Wayne Bodle, Candice L. Harrison, C. Dallett Hemphill, Susan Klepp, Cathy Matson, Matthew Öhman, Daniel Richter, Aaron Tobiason, and Nic Wood. I must thank separately the two outside readers, Patrick Griffin and Johann Neem, who flew in for the event and bore the brunt of the heavy lifting of the workshop; I am profoundly indebted to them both. Adam Choppin generously took notes. These readers' careful reading of the entire manuscript and subsequent suggestions and interventions transformed this work profoundly, reconfiguring its core question and narrative arc and therefore its argument. John Brooke read the entire manuscript and many subsequent revisions. His timely encouragement and advice were critical, and I thank him for both. I presented chapters at the McNeil Center, Omohundro Institute Colloquium, Ohio Early American Seminar, Kentucky Early American Seminar, Washington Early American Seminar, and at the "Alternative States" seminar at UC Berkeley. I thank the many participants for their questions and suggestions.

Cathy Matson, my editor, mentor, and friend, has been my rock and my role model for many years now. Her penetrating questions, support, and tireless vitality drive me forward. To emulate her example as a teacher, mentor, and colleague is a lifelong goal. Ronald Hoffman, Fredrika J. Teute, and Michael Zuckerman have each been generous and demanding mentors to me since early graduate school.

I was privileged to write about the "Athens of America" from the Athens of Ohio. The Ohio University History Department was a generous and invigorating place for a young scholar and I am tremendously grateful to all my colleagues. I must single out for special thanks Patrick Barr-Melej, Michele Clouse, Mariana Dantas, Jill Ingram, Brian Schoen, Kathleen Sullivan, and Ingo Trauschweizer. Robert Ingram started poking his head through my door in my first week asking "Is the book finished yet?" He is a model of what the university should be about: high standards, strong work ethic, tough questions, and informed dialogue between dissenting standpoints. No one has been more generous with their time or done more to help me navigate the shoals of the early career years, and I value his friendship tremendously.

The research and writing of this book was made possible by an Andrew Mellon research fellowship at Johns Hopkins University, the Albert M. Greenfield Foundation Fellowship at the Library Company of Philadelphia, a Program in Early American Economy and Society fellowship, the Barra Foundation Post-

Doctoral Fellowship at the McNeil Center for Early American Studies, and through the Ohio University History Department. In Philadelphia the staffs of the Historical Society of Pennsylvania, Pennsylvania Hospital Archives, American Philosophical Society, Library Company of Philadelphia, and the Quaker and Special Collections at Haverford College were invaluable. Jim Green of the Library Company and Stacey C. Peeples of the Pennsylvania Hospital were especially generous in their assistance. Jim St. Bishop of the St. Andrew's Society of Philadelphia very kindly allowed me access to the extensive papers of that organization.

In the decade that it took to write this book, many fellow travelers and friends helped shape my thoughts, listened to arguments, offered suggestions, and generally kept me grounded. I would like to thank Joseph Adelman, Sari Altschuler, Jane Calvert, Kenneth Cohen, Pamela Edwards, Cassandra Good, Glenda Goodman, Katie Gray, Emma Hart, Amanda Herbert, Rachel Herrmann, Albrecht Koschnik, Nenette Luarca-Shouf, Will Mackintosh, Simon Middleton, Catherine Molineux, Amanda Moniz, Katherine Moran, Dael Norwood, Matthew Osborn, Ken Owen, Christopher Parsons, Christopher Pearl, Seth Perry, Justin Roberts, Leonard Sadosky, Jessica Stern, Phil Stern, and Molly Warsh. Susan Lin, Aparna Kumar, and Jonathan Vogan put me up in Philadelphia on many occasions and provided sustaining friendship. They and Shirin Ali, Julie Levin Russo, Kate Moran, Rachel Rusch, and Molly Warsh have gone above and beyond as friends.

My family has provided love and support through every stage of this journey. I have been blessed along the way to include in my family Bakows, Choppins, Davises, Farmers, Llobreras, Roneys, and Shapels, enriching my life with each new addition, particularly the most recent arrival, Melanie Llobrera. Kristen and Joseph bring love, laughter, and good food into my life. My grandmother, Mabel Smith, grounds and inspires me with her own remarkable story. My parents, Milt and Lisa Roney, have given so much of themselves to make my dreams possible. Along with Kristen and Joseph, their unconditional love, commitment to family, and support make me who I am. Lexi Byrd Roney Choppin arrived just in time to supervise and distract from the finishing stages of this book—the most delightful and demanding taskmaster of any so far.

Adam Clark Roney Choppin has taught me more about partnership than anyone I know. Through his perpetual energy, relentless questioning of everything (exasperatingly so sometimes!), hard-nosed common sense, unflagging generosity, brash confidence, quieter courage, and above all his deep love, he nurtures and pushes me every day to be a better scholar and a better person. This book and this author would not be here today without him. I dedicate the book to him—a small token. The author is already and always will be his.

Governed by a Spirit of Opposition

Introduction

Philadelphia began with an act of imagination. Before William Penn ever laid eyes on the site where his capital city would be built, the eager proprietor sketched out a handsome, proportional city with streets laid out in an orderly grid, leaving plenty of space for private gardens, orchards, and four graceful public squares in each quadrant. The centerpiece of the city was a fifth square, the Center Square, which Penn intended to be the political, religious, social, and economic center of the city. Equidistant between the Delaware and Schuylkill Rivers, which bounded the city, the Center Square emanated the interlocking authority of the institutions that ordered society: state, church, and marketplace.[1]

But Penn was not the only founder of Philadelphia. The men and women who flocked to a city till then only sketched on paper left their own indelible marks on the physical shape of the city and in so doing influenced the kind of community it would be. They never acceded to Penn's plans. The Center Square was a full mile away from the Delaware River, the economic and residential core of the city. The only major building ever to be constructed there as Penn had wished was the Quaker Meeting House, and that because Penn wheedled and strong-armed his coreligionists into building it. Friends complained perpetually about the tedious mile-long walk to the Center Meeting House for worship and often refused to go altogether, building more convenient meetinghouses closer to home. By 1702 the Center Meeting House suffered from such disuse and disrepair that it was in danger of collapse. Ever practical, Friends dismantled the lone public building in Center Square and used the salvageable material to reconstruct a new "great" meetinghouse by the Delaware. The attempt to create a physical center for Philadelphia had early and resoundingly failed.[2]

Just as Philadelphia's physical layout—streets, wharves, and city lots—had to be demarcated on the ground, the practices and processes by which the community would be governed had to be worked out. Who would exercise which powers and bear which responsibilities? Through what structures and offices would they operate? What, if any, checks would operate on the exercise of secular and religious authority? How would the public good be defined, and where would the boundaries of public good versus private right be delimited? These issues of governance raised questions about the origins or foundation of residents' rights, privileges, and duties. On what basis did individual or collective rights depend? That is to say, what rights did Philadelphians have, either as individuals or corporately as a community, and upon what basis did they hold those rights?

These were questions at the highest level of importance but also of abstraction. Most Philadelphians grappled with them not through the articulation of highbrow political rhetoric but in the day-to-day operations of community life. A dispute over a public wharf contained within it a fight over the grounds of private property ownership in the city. Fights over mandatory duty as a night-watchman turned into a contest over men's civic duties and the limits of executive power. The founding of a hospital became a weapon with which to champion the representative legislature at the expense of the authority of the Penn family. The need to defend the city from invasion provoked a debate about the nature and basis of citizenship and civil rights.

This is a book, then, about everyday community problems. It is about road maintenance, building houses of worship, providing for the poor, firefighting, ensuring the safety of property and lives, educating children and expanding the intellectual and civic horizons of adults, protecting bodies from illness, and stimulating local economic growth. The debates around these and other questions, from the most mundane to the transformational, drew ordinary men and sometimes women into civic life. The decisions consciously and less consciously reached about how to organize and authorize residents to address these problems gave them power, experiences, and a language that could be translated into the ability to affect the very small (the location of market stalls) and the enormous (the outcome of the French and Indian War or the unfolding of the American Revolution). Critically, Philadelphia residents empowered themselves to act on their own account, not only through intermediaries, representatives, or elites. By the same token, they did not act only or even usually through the state.

This book examines the colonial origins of American political practice through a close consideration of how residents addressed those everyday problems in Philadelphia between 1682 and 1776. It presents a fundamentally different bottom-up perspective on political engagement by ordinary men in the hundred years before the American Revolution, arguing for a more capacious understanding of individual participation and popular mobilization. It argues that in part by choice and in part by a series of circumstances Philadelphia evolved without strong central government. Instead, white men of all walks of life created a flexible, decentered system of local governance which dispersed authority for policy and services broadly among a number of governmental commissions, churches, and private civic associations, each with varying degrees of accountability to the public. Through these bodies ordinary white men became involved on an intimate and daily basis in vital civic and policy questions in their communities. Merchants, shopkeepers, carpenters, brewers, shoemakers, and silversmiths served as churchwardens, visiting Friends, street commissioners, constables, and overseers of the poor. They volunteered to fight fires, organized relief for the needy, contributed money toward the care of the sick, shouldered arms in defense of the community, raised capital for local lending, and even interjected themselves in Indian diplomacy. Through myriad institutional avenues, men from many social strata engaged in long-term, sustained forms of civic and political participation that shaped their community in direct and lasting ways.

The system of dispersing power among various governmental bodies, commissions, churches, and associations allowed, and even encouraged, considerable room for difference. Power diffused widely among various bodies that operated independently—or sometimes in outright opposition—of one another. These institutions had overlapping, sometimes competing, and even conflicting responsibilities, objectives, and tactics. Through them various constituencies vied to implement their own vision of the public good, sometimes to the outrage of others who disagreed with them. Philadelphia evolved as a city that operated not by unity and consensus, and certainly not based on homogeneity, but by means of differences negotiated through broad (if sometimes apparently byzantine) distribution of power in a variety of governmental, quasi-governmental, and nongovernmental bodies that appealed to and included a diverse range of constituencies. Philadelphia's culture of expansive political inclusion and mobilization, then, not only affected the political capacities and engagement of individuals but also structured in innovative ways mechanisms whereby the larger political community could accommodate and even foster difference while maintaining peace.[3]

Such an accomplishment was by no means common in the late seventeenth and early eighteenth centuries, when city residents first haltingly worked it out. At the time Philadelphia was founded, contemporary English town and city dwellers emphasized unity over disagreement and continually engaged in rounds of purge and counterpurge to remove opponents from office. New England communities, in a similar vein, excluded altogether those who did not fit. The Chesapeake, by contrast, had in the late seventeenth century just undergone a contentious armed uprising that exposed the problem of unequal access to political and economic power. Philadelphians pioneered ways of living together that did not insist on unity and yet managed to prevent tensions from spilling over into violence. In common with every other British community, Philadelphia's public forum almost entirely ignored and excluded women and people of color. Among the white men thought to constitute the legitimate members of the body politic, however, the civic life of the city relied on the sometimes cacophonous input of many different groups at the same time.[4]

Philadelphians thus contributed toward the development of what might be understood as a new civic technology: the voluntary association. In this innovation they participated in a wider British Atlantic phenomenon taking place in the seventeenth and eighteenth centuries with the rise of sociable, charitable, and civic clubs and associations. Philadelphia organizers drew as well from collaborative economic models such as joint-stock companies and even churches. The civic technology of formal voluntary associations they developed did not spring forth fully formed but emerged over time through trial and error. Once the earliest organizations had been established on strong foundations, others built on their experiences, adopting similar organizational tactics, rules, and economic strategies. Some moved from this foundation to assert an increasingly assertive role in public life and policy formation. Taken together, civic voluntary associations provided a new vehicle for individuals to express their opinions and shape both policy and events. Alongside formal government and churches, individuals gained a new site with different rules, possibilities, and limitations on which to meet and organize for sustained action.[5]

Most scholarship on American voluntary life has focused on the period after the Revolution, ignoring almost entirely what came before. Alexis de Tocqueville's fascination with the civic and partisan organizations he saw in his 1832 tour of the United States has drawn historians' gaze to the postrevolutionary world of voluntary association, though Tocqueville himself recognized roots that extended into the colonial period. The assumption common to these works is that the genesis of American civic and voluntary life lay in the years after the Revolution. In this light, though the voluntary associations of the 1790s represented, as one scholar has called it, "the final fluorescence of a long tradition" stretching back into the colonial era, the transforming hand of the Revolution wrought powerful change. It swept away a relatively unitary, consensual, and hierarchical public sphere, to be replaced by one that was oppositional, equalitarian, and radical. Voluntary associations and incorporated institutions became central, if contested, elements of the new Republic. All the important changes, according to this scholarship, came after—and to a large degree because of—processes unleashed by the American Revolution. No basis exists for historians to make these claims or any pre- and postrevolutionary comparison because they have not fully explored the colonial context, stereotyping it as being characterized by constrained political participation by the masses, limited popular mobilization, and a unitary, consensual public sphere.[6]

Colonial Philadelphians were enthusiastic associators. They formed at least sixty formal associations before the American Revolution. By 1770 at least one in five white men in the city belonged to one or more of them; in 1748 that number may have been as high as one in two. Philadelphia thus boasted levels of civic engagement rarely if ever matched in later urban environments. Volunteer firefighters in twenty separate fire companies protected property by combating fires and rescuing people and property from burning buildings; the Library Company provided books otherwise unavailable to an eager reading public; the College of Philadelphia established the first nonsectarian college in North America; the Pennsylvania Hospital provided health care for poor Philadelphians; and the Contributors for the Relief of the Poor took over all public poor relief in the city, supplanting the state altogether.

This study thus reorients scholarship on early American political practice away from the limited catalogue of political behaviors normally attributed to nonelite white men. Most scholars focus only on a limited range of political behaviors by nonelite people in colonial America: casting votes in elections, petitioning authorities, rioting, and engaging in rational-critical discourse in places such as taverns or through the press. These are all important avenues of participation. However, Philadelphians did not only talk; they acted. Rarely did they riot; commonly they created organizations with rules, membership, and financial clout that took the long view. They did not merely vote once a year for their socioeconomic "betters"; they took matters into their own hands. Political engagement by ordinary men, then, was more varied and extensive than most scholarship has previously appreciated. This study suggests a more capacious understanding of the ways in which ordinary men in Philadelphia, through a rich array of state, religious, and voluntary endeavors, made claims to authority and shaped vital local matters. In the process, they contributed to evolving definitions of the rights and duties of male citizens, as well as the basis on which they held those rights and duties. Often this discourse occurred in the context of pushing back against the assumptions and desires of the proprietary Penn family, but always it was a local conversation as well, pitting local constituencies against one another in defining and authorizing who held what civil rights and duties.[7]

An appreciation for the extent of engagement by ordinary white male Philadelphians in turn disrupts a straightforward narrative of evolving American representative democratic institutions. Pennsylvania has been heralded as foundational to American political culture; it had the broadest franchise in British America and boasted one of the most powerful legislatures vis-à-vis its executive. The provincial government lay lightly upon the people, legislating less than most colonial assemblies and requiring little in the way of taxation. Pennsylvanians were quick to champion their legislature against attempts to weaken or control it, and their hearty defense has occupied much fine scholarly attention.[8] However, from the perspective of the political participation of ordinary men, focusing on this narrative alone limits our understanding of their political behaviors. Though as much as 75 percent of the adult white male population was eligible to vote, Pennsylvania yet had a closed, oligarchic government, little influenced by elections or ordinary voters. Voter interest and turnout remained low apart from a few extraordinary elections. Usually no more than a quarter of eligible voters turned out in Philadelphia, a percentage that actually declined over the course of the eighteenth century. When they did vote, consistently Pennsylvanians chose affluent men of standing in the community to represent them, bestowing a "virtual monopoly" on what has been described as an exclusive Quaker oligarchy. Thus, at the provincial level Pennsylvania, celebrated for its relatively broad franchise, produced a closed political system that constrained flexibility or access. This tendency was further exacerbated by unequal representation for the growing city of Philadelphia or the western counties. Certainly, in Philadelphia voting for assemblymen meant little to the day-to-day running of the city. Philadelphians needed and gradually developed a complicated set of accommodations at the local level to answer pressing community needs. These accommodations yielded a political culture that did not fit easily in the category of either democracy or republicanism.[9]

Because Philadelphia evolved with no strong center, but instead dispersed power over local matters broadly among many institutional avenues, policy decisions did not rest exclusively in the hands of elites or even necessarily in the hands of the majority. In critical moments in Philadelphia's history nonelites and nonmajorities would force their vision on the rest of the community, as in 1747 and 1775 when lower-class men formed powerful militias against the wishes of elites, or in 1756 when a small group of Quakers hijacked Indian diplomacy, in opposition to both imperial policy and overwhelming popular opinion. These groups acted without having to obtain consensus among disparate factions; they simply left out those who disagreed. The larger public had no say and no recourse to stop them. Vital policy making in Philadelphia, in short, was not democratic. Indeed, it was the opposite of democratic; it was exclusive and exclusionary.

If democracy (the expression of majority will) did not pertain in Philadelphia, neither did republicanism—the concept that elected representatives would legislate on behalf of others. Time and again Philadelphians acted not through a few select intermediaries, but instead chose to represent themselves. They acted on their own behalf at sociable tavern meetings, at rain-drenched outdoor gatherings, drilling through the military manual of arms, and going door-to-door soliciting contributions. They signed their names to membership lists, pledged subscriptions of money, and gave their time and labor in tasks from the mundane to the extraordinary (usually the former). This self-representational voluntary culture does not mean that leaders did not emerge who dominated the origins and trajectory of these civic projects. They did. Benjamin Franklin especially is synonymous with Philadelphia civic participatory culture. Moreover, elites disproportionately participated in and dominated Philadelphia's organizational life because they had the leisure time and money, and they were the most integrated into dense and powerful social, economic, and political networks. But many of Philadelphia's most important and transformative civic projects relied on large-scale organization, widespread monetary backing, and boots on the ground. Neither patronage nor top-down dictates proved effective. Elite patronage, a very successful model in England, never took root in Philadelphia. The one attempt at an endowed institution—the Loganian Library, given to the city in James Logan's will—was a dismal failure and eventually folded into the broad-based Library Company of Philadelphia. Successful Philadelphia institutions and projects would time and again rely not on elites but on large-scale mobilization, commonly involving "middling" white men, as well as, in critical moments, white men deemed to belong to the "lower sorts."[10]

The inadequacy of oligarchy, democracy, or republicanism to explain Philadelphia's political culture, combined with the absence of a unified governing center, necessitates a reframing of the civic and political options available to early American actors in how they navigated pluralism and difference, how they negotiated access to authority and power. In the first near century of the city's history, Philadelphians created accommodations that accepted fragmentation and disagreement rather than insisting on a unitary public culture. The city's polycentric form of local governance pertained in Philadelphia because in its earliest founding no strong governing center emerged, a problem that only became exacerbated over time, as Philadelphia became one of the most heterogeneous polities in the British Atlantic world. Philadelphians engineered resourceful accommodations to provide services that otherwise would have been lacking. In the process they created a decentered power structure that facilitated a relatively stable and peaceful community. The system operated through a bewildering warren of mandates, powers, and responsibilities. Multiple institutions jostled to fulfill their duties and assert their authority. They acted sometimes in concert, sometimes in competition, and at still other times in total ignorance of one another. Through the eighteenth century, then, Philadelphia had little coherence as a political community. Its most important boundaries were articulated not by some sense of corporateness or unity but only by territorial limits. Community functioned not by finding common ground but by allowing disparate clusters to claim power and authority over particular patches and then work together or not as they saw fit. This strategy, however, facilitated a relatively stable and peaceful community, channeling differences through institutional mechanisms rather than violent outbreaks, which were quite rare in Philadelphia. Moreover, it simultaneously galvanized and restricted broad participation, absorbing the energy and loyalty of many Philadelphians even as it prevented them from restraining the activities of those with whom they disagreed. The lack of a center could be exploited by state and private actors, opening up all kinds of possibilities, up to and including the demise of the entire political system in 1776.[11]

Chapters 1 and 2 explain the origins of Philadelphia's decentered civic culture and the limits of state power, examining respectively the founding of the city in 1682 and its charter of incorporation in 1701. In chapter 3 I demonstrate the possibilities and limits of denominational organization and chart the rise and adaptation of a new and widely accepted civic technology: voluntary associations. With chapter 4 the book moves forward in time, showing how newly hardening political cleavages transformed civic organizations to be associated with opposing camps, making them less bridging institutions and more into exclusive and exclusionary groups answering only to specific constituencies. I argue in chapter 5 that certain of the larger voluntary associations quietly moved beyond their publicly stated aims to act as major lenders of capital in a local economy denied banks by English law and yet desperate for sophisticated financial services, particularly large loans. Chapter 6 shows how during and just after the Seven Years' War Philadelphians began to use their exclusive voluntary associations to supplant and usurp powers that belonged to the state: military defense, Indian diplomacy, and public-tax-supported poor relief. Finally, chapter 7 demonstrates how Philadelphians built on a long evolution of decentralization and wide latitude for private organization first to form a powerful extralegal militia and then to use it to supplant the state, collapsing the old civic accommodations and introducing a new rhetoric of a unitary polity with a new emphasis on apparently transparent democratic practices, but in fact predicated on exclusion and depriving important constituencies their full civil rights.

The American Revolution did not, as is often argued, effect a radical transformation of the civic capacities or engagement of ordinary white male Philadelphians, who in fact had long practice in state, quasi-state, private, and even extralegal organizations. The nonelite white men who came to dominate Patriot organizing were not "new men" freshly empowered or awakened after the Stamp

Act Crisis in 1765. They had long engaged deeply in politics and the negotiation of power through local institutions. The rapid extralegal military mobilization after 1775 in Pennsylvania did not represent, as one historian has termed it, "the first step in the transition from crowd activity to organized politics" or a "school of political democracy" for lower-class Philadelphians. Rather, it represented the outgrowth of nearly a century of active civic and political engagement by a range of nonelites, usually, but not exclusively, white men. Indeed, independence-minded radicals deliberately capitalized on Philadelphia's multinodal form of local government, undermining and ultimately abolishing the existing government in the process.[12]

Nor did the Revolution usher in a new dawn of democratic inclusion—indeed, quite the opposite. Instead, the Revolution introduced a new insistence on a unitary public sphere during the exigencies of wartime, leaving no room for dissent or difference. Revolutionaries mobilizing in 1775 and 1776 built upon the model of previous civic associations, a major reason they were so spectacularly and rapidly successful. However, they drew on earlier precedents as well in that their 1776 revolutionary government operated without reference to the opinions of those who disagreed. Revolutionaries established Pennsylvania's new state on their own authority and initiative, never allowing it to be voted on through any form of popular referendum. Despite this nondemocratic foundation, they moved quickly and harshly against anyone perceived to oppose or even insufficiently support the new regime, particularly Loyalists and pacifist Quakers, mobilizing the might of public shaming and their new state institutions to stamp out even tacit signs of disapproval or resistance. Caught up in the exigencies of war, revolutionaries claimed they did not have the luxury of allowing the kind of latitude that had throughout the city's history characterized its political and civic culture. Revolutionaries withdrew the franchise from all who would not swear allegiance to the United States and then moved to attack their property and their very bodily freedom—in the most egregious example imprisoning and deporting twenty Quakers without charges or trial. In the midst of a dangerous civil war, revolutionaries insisted upon a unitary public culture in Philadelphia and harshly curtailed the previous tradition of local governance by plural and even conflicting bodies controlled by various constituencies.[13]

The Revolution in Philadelphia tied definitions of citizenship and full political participation to a willingness to bear arms in defense of the community. In so doing, it merely introduced a different basis for civic inclusion and exclusion, now denying full civil rights to anyone who disagreed or conscientiously refused to bear arms. Pennsylvania's new political regime masked its exclusivity by staking its claims to legitimacy on an apparently unitary representative democracy, which, however, merely replaced the previously imperfect form of inclusion with a new one. The city's civic culture would never be the same again. It would take decades for the emphasis on unity to give way to greater acceptance of so-called self-created societies, whether they be partisan political groups or incorporated banks.[14]

Eighteenth-century British North American cities, among them Philadelphia, have been characterized as "crucibles," a metaphor that evokes transformation through fire. In this metaphor, the Revolution is the fire; the city is the crucible, the vessel that can withstand a heat so high that its contents liquefy and alter. In other words, the city is a glorified melting pot. Philadelphia was in this sense never a crucible, and the Revolution was not the fire through which its contents changed. It had long harnessed and thrived off of the opposition of its constituent parts. If the city was a vessel, its contents did not meld together, but smashed into and reacted off of one another, retaining their distinctiveness, their individual trajectories. Philadelphia was a city born and governed not out of brotherly love but a vigorous spirit of opposition.[15]

CHAPTER ONE

"Named Before Thou Wert Born"
A City Imagined and Realized

Philadelphia got its start not on the banks of the Delaware, but in Penn's fertile brain back on his estate in England. With provincial charter in hand by the spring of 1681, the new proprietor eagerly envisioned a stately port capital that would project the order, harmony, prosperity, and peace of Pennsylvania. His "great Towne" would be bounded on the east by the Delaware and on the west by the Schuylkill River. Midway between them, at the intersection of the major thoroughfares, Broad and High Streets, would sit a central square where all the public buildings and functions would cluster together: state house, court, marketplace, mercantile exchange, religious meetinghouses, even schools. Streets intersected at right angles on a methodical grid. Each quadrant of the city would boast large, open squares, and, to add to the verdure, householders' lots would be capacious enough for them to plant gardens and even orchards brimming with nutritious produce. With no concept of the realities on the ground, Penn had drawn an urban plan that beautifully balanced the river commerce that would be the city's lifeblood with a vibrant town center that concentrated together the critical functions of community: religion, law, education, and marketplace.[1]

If William Penn deserves recognition as the founder of Philadelphia, it is not because he got the charter for Pennsylvania that made the city possible, it is not

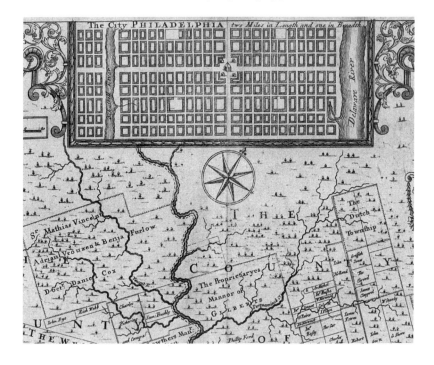

because he financed the construction of the city (which he did not), and finally it is not because of his own extensive personal labor or direction (he stayed in his colony only a short time, from 1682 to 1684, and then again from 1699 to 1701); it is because Penn was the one to imagine a great cosmopolitan port on the Delaware and the one to set in motion the labor and ingenuity of others to begin laying it out. Philadelphia began as an act of imagination—that was Penn's critical contribution, with far-reaching consequences, because settlers could never entirely escape the vision Penn had conjured.

The work to translate a city imagined into a city realized came through the efforts of hundreds and eventually thousands of men and women, each founders in his or her own right, and each with his or her own aspirations, fears, and plans—at odds not only with Penn's ideal but often with the ideas of their new neighbors. The most dramatic population buildup in English colonial history had by 1684 swelled Philadelphia to at least eight hundred residents intent on fashioning a town out of the swamp and forest they found when they first arrived. These were the men and women who would clear the land, construct the houses, and build the intangible but no less critical civic infrastructure of community. Most of them were used to urban life: three-quarters of the Quakers Penn recruited to come to his province came from towns or cities in England.

The majority of Philadelphia's adult male founders worked as artisans, representing an extraordinary diversity of trades. They found immediate and sustained employment in a city under construction. A smaller but vital class of wealthy merchants also came to the city, many of them successful Quaker merchants from other Caribbean and North American mainland colonies, attracted by the prospect of religious freedom. Philadelphia was conceived through imagination, but brought to life through their hard work, negotiation, and competition.[2]

The themes of space and ownership twine like crimson threads through these early struggles. In fighting over the physical layout of the city, Philadelphians and Penn battled over the nature and basis of property ownership—and through property ownership over the nature and basis of political rights, those held collectively by a community and those of an individual. Most new Philadelphians resisted Penn's plans for the city layout, refusing to live, trade, and worship where he hoped they would. In the process they partially (but never entirely) remade the city to fit their needs and asserted their rights against the pretensions of the proprietor.

Philadelphia's many founders operated in an environment quite new to them. The "wilderness" that they perceived all around them in the Delaware valley represented only one element of what was new. Of lasting importance to the religious, political, civic, and social evolution of Philadelphia and all of Pennsylvania was William Penn's critical pair of decisions: first, to practice religious toleration; and second, to have no established church. These commitments shifted the ground on which both church and state stood, requiring adaptations in the way that each acted as agents of local community and governance. It has long been understood that European settlers could rarely if ever transplant Old World institutions to the New without modifications. The particular character of those alterations—and the reasons behind them—in Philadelphia produced an urban infrastructure that, against the hopes and intentions of its founders, lacked a strong, coherent center. Instead, both the physical and the civic framing of the city came to be characterized by multiple, often competing, nodes jostling noisily for position and power.[3]

Penn witnessed this process with consternation. He set sail from Philadelphia in August 1684 with a heavy heart, called back to England to protect at court the interests of his colony. "Thou, Philadelphia," he lamented, "the virgin settlement of this province, named before thou wert born, what love, what care, what service, and what travail has there been, to bring thee forth, and preserve thee from such as would abuse and defile thee! Oh," he prayed, "that thou mayst be kept from the evil that would overwhelm thee." As Penn himself admitted, Philadelphia—the City of Brotherly Love—had been named before it had been "born." As with all his other grand plans for the colony, the birth had been far messier than he had foreseen—the reality so much farther from what he had imagined. In the spring before he left, Penn seemed to become increasingly vexed, prone to "strong and impressive sighs" in Quaker meetings, convinced that "the true Philadelphia and brother love is not to be met with as freely in this our Philadelphia as he on his part desires." Philadelphia, it turned out, drawn before it had been settled and named before it had been born, was not going to live up to its name.[4]

A City with No Center

When Penn and his fellow travelers arrived in the ship *Welcome* in November of 1682, surveyors had only begun marking out streets and lots the previous summer. A few rudimentary structures, including a tavern, and a small Swedish settlement just to the south were the only signs of European habitation on a swampy landscape so "overgrown with woods" that it was said a pair of horses lost in the woods that winter could not be found again for several months, despite having been hobbled together. Still, the Quaker settlers shared Penn's optimism. They recorded matter-of-factly that "a multitude of Friends arrived here and erected a city called Philadelphia." The "city" they "erected" consisted that first autumn of hastily built log huts and caves dug into the sandy river banks for shelter against the approaching winter. The caves were supposed to be temporary, but five years later many "loose" inhabitants still lived in them. The concerned proprietor and council each attempted to order those that "yet remain Contemptuously in Caves" into more appropriate habitations. Erecting a city, it turned out, was not so instantaneous as Friends' confident assertion implied; it was a slow and soon enough an acrimonious process.[5]

William Penn advocated a detailed physical plan for Philadelphia which, while never realized, shaped profoundly the kind of city that its settlers could build. In part his plans suffered from lack of knowledge on the ground—the geographic location and extent of the city layout, for example—but to a critical degree, the plans suffered from the expectation that top-down planning could work with little attention to local conditions or input from the residents themselves. The men and women pouring into the new "city" were less concerned with the aesthetic order and balance that so stimulated Penn. They wanted to build a home that answered their needs, and based on where they were willing to live, it quickly became apparent that those who chose to be urban residents were determined to obtain a prime location for trade. To that end, they quarreled with Penn over the layout of the city and the way that city lots would be allocated to householders. In the process, they opened a debate about the nature of property ownership itself in Philadelphia which called into question the basis of the rights of its inhabitants and those of the proprietor himself.

Penn's extensive plans for the city ran into two problems. The first had to do with the city layout itself. The balanced grid the proprietor had hoped for proved a nonstarter for his settlers, who clung stubbornly to the banks of the Delaware and refused to occupy the lots farther west or along the Schuylkill. The town grew rapidly, with fresh faces arriving on forty-three ships in the first two years alone. About one-fifth of the three thousand newcomers stayed in Philadelphia and began building. By 1690 Richard Morris found "improvements (beyond my Expectation) to Admiration," but he noted that "Bank and River-Street is so filled with Houses, that it makes an inclosed Street." To accommodate the high demand for housing near the river, residents carved unauthorized lanes or alleys and filled them with "very good Buildings" between the gridded streets Penn had so carefully planned—right through land that should have sustained gardens and orchards. Penn's "very fair Plan" was falling apart. "If it was all built," one observer thought, it "would make a great and beautiful City" spanning from river to river. Instead, Philadelphia was rapidly on its way to becoming the most congested city in British North America, with houses packed one upon another. The gardens and orchards failed to appear, and in desperation in 1700 Penn and his council shepherded through a law that required each householder to plant a single tree in their yard so that the town might be "well shaded from the violence of the sun in the heat of summer and thereby be rendered more healthy." Decades later in the middle of the eighteenth century, it was easy to forget that Penn's plan had ever had much force. One observer scoffed, "That this town should ever have such extent [to the Schuylkill] is almost impossible; it does extend one third of the way."[6]

Some of Philadelphia's founders explicitly challenged Penn. In 1684 Anthony Weston and several associates met to discuss their disagreements with elements of Penn's plan. They knew that the time for any difference of opinion or revision was drawing rapidly to a close. New settlers were rapidly acquiring property and building houses along Penn's grid, in the process inscribing into what had been merely imaginary lines the force and authority of property law, one of the most powerful forces in English law or society. Weston and his associates knew that unless they acted quickly, the city's layout would be established beyond the possibility of change. The time to voice objections was now. They gathered in a tavern to discuss the plans handed down by William Penn and draw up their own proposals.[7]

Unfortunately, the exact nature of Weston and his associates' proposals is unknown, but many townspeople particularly opposed the central square— literally the centerpiece of Penn's plan. A mile from the waterfront, the square was much too far out of the way. Philadelphians wanted to be on the water, the critical zone of news and economic transaction. When Penn pressed Quakers to build a meetinghouse in the center, the first step toward realizing his vision, Friends dragged their heels. When they finally did build a meetinghouse in the center in 1685, they simultaneously erected another one of nearly equal dimensions on Front Street, ostensibly "for an evening meeting," but then proceeded to transact most worship and business there. Soon enough Friends grumbled that the Center Meeting House was useless, "built very much to their Charge, Inconveniency and Damage." Penn and his supporters continued to try to make the Center Square a focal point. In 1688 the Provincial Council decreed that the annual fair be held at the Central Square, only to be presented with a "Comptemptuous Printing paper" signed by numerous townspeople who protested "against Keeping ye fayre at ye Center."[8]

Penn, however, remained from the first adamant that "so necessary and good a design be not spoiled." He and his closest supporters did not take at all kindly to any of these critiques. The furious proprietor interpreted Anthony Weston's meeting as representing "great presumption and Contempt of this Government, and authority." Each participant in the offending group was made to put up bonds for his future good behavior, while Weston, the ringleader, was sentenced to be whipped in the public marketplace, ten lashes each on three separate days, a clear warning to others who might presume to meddle with Penn's plans. The signers of the "Comptemptuous Printing paper," meanwhile, were hauled in front of the Provincial Council, which ultimately pardoned them but refused to move the location of the fair. Penn, it turned out, was as unbending as his city grid.[9]

Flog or bully whom he might, however, Penn could not in the end dictate the shape his city would take. The public whipping of Anthony Weston laid bare the tension between plans and enactment, between central planning and scattered individual initiatives, between a city imagined and a city made real. Penn's harsh reaction to townspeople like Weston can be read as an attempt to invest power in a center—both in the form of a physical city square and in his own authority and status as proprietor. In both he failed.

Praised by scholars as "a pioneer in the field of city planning," Penn created a plan that in fact sabotaged its own objective. Because he privileged birds-eye-view aesthetics over practicalities on the ground or the needs and input of residents, Philadelphians would never embrace it, even as they could not escape or overthrow it. Because of the grid, no new center could grow organically somewhere more convenient. In spite of William Penn's best efforts—or, perhaps more precisely, *because* of them—Philadelphia evolved as a town without a center. His grid depicted an imagined ideal, never the reality of Philadelphia—not in 1683 when the survey was published or indeed at any point in the following century. It would remain so for its entire provincial history.[10]

Settlers resisted putting important buildings or functions in the Central Square; by the same token, many balked at receiving lots along the Schuylkill River. Penn had hoped that the Schuylkill waterfront would be just as built up as that of the Delaware. He even went to the extent of trying to convince one credulous "First Purchaser" that the Schuylkill was "where he intended the chief Settlement of the City should be." This plan ignored the fact that while the Delaware was calm and deep, the Schuylkill was rocky, shallow, and treacherous to navigate—closed to ocean-bound vessels and therefore to Atlantic commerce. Those unlucky enough to receive Schuylkill lots soon enough realized their disadvantage. In 1690, the same year the town limits were admitted to extend only as far as Broad Street, six property owners—four men and two women—petitioned to exchange their worthless lots on the Schuylkill for smaller but more valuable ones on the Delaware side. Most of the Schuylkill purchasers were not so fortunate, however. Authorities sanctimoniously advised them they were "obliged to bear" their "Disappointment" even though their lots had "become of little or no value, tho' the contrary was at first expected."[11]

From the beginning, then, the city did not look as Penn had intended, reshaped to fit the needs and desires of its residents. They were constrained by Penn's dictates to a point, because they purchased or were granted city lots according to his plan and could not build on space designated for streets. However, economic imperatives moved them out of those carefully balanced lots and to the Delaware riverbank. Atlantic trade influenced the commercial and residential patterns of Philadelphia to a greater extent than William Penn ever could. Beginning in 1682 and extending through the eighteenth century, Philadelphians would live, work, trade, worship, and socialize within sight and sound of wharves, commercial vessels, and mercantile warehouses on the Delaware. The interior of the "city" became farmland and sheep pasturage.[12]

The state, civic, economic, and religious functions Penn had hoped to see grouped together in his central square dispersed instead along that waterfront. Economic transactions centered on the wharves all along Front Street, but particularly near Dock Creek (1684), or at the market on High Street (1693). Disputes over economic transactions could be decided at the Court House built at the head of permanent market stalls on High Street in 1709. Meanwhile, townspeople could choose to worship at a Quaker meetinghouse on Front, just north of Arch (1685), or at Second and High (1696); a Baptist Meeting at Second and Walnut Streets (1688); the Church of England at Second and High (1695); or a Presbyterian Church at High Street and Bank Alley (1704). As the final insult, in 1702 Quakers dismantled the rarely used Center Meeting House and used the materials to reconstruct a new "great" meetinghouse by the river.[13]

The decentralization of the city was further defined not only by what was there but by what was not. Philadelphians never built a mercantile exchange building, though many contemporary European port cities boasted them and Penn had hoped for such a facility in his commercial entrepot. Instead, merchants exchanged news and conducted business in one of at least twenty taverns operating all over the city by 1693. Meanwhile, the legislature would not have the wherewithal to build a house of assembly for half a century. Legislators met instead in private houses, in the Quaker meetinghouse, or in the municipal Court House. No town common or city square existed where men could collect together in monthly militia musters, which in any case did not occur in a pacifist colony. Even death and grieving did not unite the townspeople: Philadelphians were buried in graveyards according to their religious affiliation, or, after 1705, if they were poor, African American, or "Strangers," they were laid to rest in Potter's Field on the edge of town.[14]

In addition to strong disapproval of Penn's town grid, the second pressing problem had to do with the allocation of city lots to new settlers. The city, once its site was chosen and its bounds surveyed, proved to be too small (or "short of our expectations," as one settler grumbled) for Penn to keep all the promises he had made to the "First Purchasers" back in England. Penn had always planned that a "great town" would be the commercial center of his province; he hoped too that it would be the seat of power in a highly hierarchical (and therefore he hoped orderly) polity. To that end, he promised city lots to those First Purchasers who bought substantial property, thus concentrating together in his "great town" the economic and social elites of the province. Initially Penn promised that any purchaser of five hundred acres in the new colony would receive a bonus ten-acre lot in the city. Soon enough, he revised this ratio upward: now only purchasers of five thousand acres would be guaranteed city lots, and these would come in parcels of one hundred acres. Then it turned out that the site on which the city had been surveyed was not large enough to accommodate these plans. Purchasers of five thousand acres now could only expect to receive one acre in the city; the remainder of the promised acreage was reduced to eighty acres and would be given them in the form of rural land in the "Liberties" just north of the city: here grandees could build comfortable country estates near the commercial capital of the colony.[15]

Not all city lots were created equal, however. The pressing problem from the beginning revolved around how these finite properties would be allocated. Penn decided to reward his most important economic and political backers by assigning them the most valuable properties. Half of the biggest spenders would get lots along the mile-long Delaware waterfront, the other half along the Schuylkill; other smaller purchasers would get interior lots. He gave first choice to the Society of Free Traders, a joint-stock company he had chartered in 1682 to encourage investment in the colony. Penn believed the society "most capable and likely to improve and render any part of the Town Valuable," so when he chose the next lots (for himself and his family members) he chose sites near what would come to be known as "Society Hill." He tried to make the northern sector on the Delaware attractive as well by locating the market there and convincing prominent investors to accept lots there. (In the long run those investors had the last laugh: the Society of Free Traders never flourished and by 1712 was complaining about its lots and unsuccessfully petitioning for land nearer the market.) The need to convince investors to accept lots may help explain why Penn was so committed to his balanced city grid, singing the praise of properties in the "Center" and on the Schuylkill long after it had become clear they were not in equal demand in a desperate attempt to placate disgruntled settlers who had not been fortunate enough to gain lots on the Delaware.[16]

The struggles and resentments about the city layout and allocation of city lots were concrete problems that spoke to more abstract but no less fundamental concerns. What were the terms upon which city residents held their land—by a contractual relationship with Penn worked out in England before he and his settlers sailed, or by the proprietor's gift? The distinction mattered because it dictated the relative privileges, duties, and powers of city property owners vis-à-vis Penn. If Philadelphia belonged to Penn, if it was his gift, then he had the right to apportion the city as he wished, to withhold unsettled land to sell later for his own profit, and to charge quitrents—a kind of property tax—on city lots. If, however, as the settlers maintained, the city had been erected on a contractual basis to reward substantial investors with valuable urban property and all settlers with a vital economic center, the nature of the city changed: Penn as proprietor could oversee its layout and the distribution of lots, but he could not charge quitrents; he did not own unclaimed land, which instead belonged in common to the city; and finally, he must immediately grant the city a charter, incorporating it as an independent entity and securing the rights and privileges of its citizens (that is to say, those city residents eligible for full political rights).

Town residents presented Penn with a remonstrance setting forth their objections to his policies in 1684, shortly before he was set to return to England, and the Provincial Council even appointed a committee "to draw up a Charter for Philadelphia to be made a Burrough." Penn bitterly refused the justice of the petitioners' claims, cited the costs and effort he had expended in setting up the city, and departed without resolving the matter. The Provincial Council dropped the idea of incorporating Philadelphia for the time being. The political and property rights of Philadelphians remained undefined for more than fifteen years, provoking anxiety and resentment that undermined many settlers' original faith in Penn and contributed to a rancorous political climate, pitting the rights of inhabitants against those of the proprietor.[17]

"Raised by Voluntary Contributions among Themselves": Religious Societies

For all the acrimony around the laying out of the city and the basis for property rights in it, Philadelphians appreciated much about Penn's plans for government in his new colony. Among the most popular was Penn's policy of religious toleration. However, in ways that neither Penn nor his settlers quite appreciated at the outset, toleration made Pennsylvania a very different place to try to replicate Old World religious structures. Congregations became voluntary associations, unhelped and unhindered by the state, in a new world where they needed to build everything. If the clergy eventually reasserted religious hierarchies that they could dominate, the earliest years were characterized by a high degree of negotiation and compromise with a laity well aware of their own clout. Historians have focused on the Keithian Schism of the early 1690s as a moment of intense challenge against Quaker structures of authority. It certainly was. But the schism was merely the most dramatic, not the only way in which rank-and-file laypeople pushed back against clerical authority and asserted their own voice.[18]

In his 1683 *Frame of Government*, Penn guaranteed that "all persons . . . who confess and acknowledge the one Almighty and eternal God . . . and that hold themselves obliged in conscience to live peaceably and justly in civil society, shall, in no ways, be molested or prejudiced for their religious persuasion, or practice, in matters of faith and worship." This was the religious toleration for which Pennsylvania became so famous. Penn's decision to guarantee freedom of religion generated denominational diversity, manifested through the numerous and competing churches that sprouted up in the first decades of settlement: Quakers, Presbyterians, Baptists, Anglicans, and a number of smaller sects. But Penn's clause went further: "nor shall they be compelled, at any time, to frequent or maintain any religious worship, place or ministry whatever." In other words, Pennsylvania would have no established church.[19]

Most of Europe and the English-speaking world had an established church. In most of the British Isles and its colonies, the established church was the Church of England; in Scotland, it was the Presbyterian Church; and in New England (outside of Rhode Island), it was the Congregational Church. The established church performed a number of explicit and implicit functions. As a part of government, the established church received taxes, structured local poor relief, delimited political membership for adult males (in most places church membership was one necessary component for full political rights), and in some places had say over local governance, policy issues, or ecclesiastical courts. Implicitly, an established church provided a central locus for worship, communion, and socializing. Dissenting churches, while not illegal, faced restrictions, and their membership often enjoyed fewer political and legal rights than "Churchmen."[20]

Penn's commitment to religious toleration eliminated the formal privileging of one church over others, transforming the relationship of all churches to the state. By foreclosing a formal state relationship with religion, Penn converted denominations in Pennsylvania into purely voluntary associations, unsupported but also unhindered by the state. Communities of believers would be left to themselves to determine their own theology, style of worship, and institutional structures. Pennsylvania's religious landscape was thus characterized by circulation and competition. The absence of religious persecution was at once freeing and potentially alarming. Without external pressures to encourage solidarity, formerly persecuted religious communities faced the possibility that lay folk might stray from strict orthodox beliefs, fragmenting into various strains of heterodoxy. Conversely, religious circulation and competition might lead to stronger identification within a church, particularly if that identity went hand in hand with aversion to another church—a critical element, for example, for the fledgling Church of England, horrified by Quaker ascendancy. With no state arbiter determining the primacy of one religion over another or maintaining it financially, however, all were at least theoretically on an even playing ground.[21]

The promise of religious freedom paired with the absence of establishment meant that after 1682 as religious societies sought to lay foundations in Pennsylvania, they faced a daunting task. They had literally to build everything from the ground up—not only the physical structure but also their religious infrastructure and hierarchy. "Our first concern" in 1682, Quaker Richard Townsend recalled, "was to keep up and maintain our religious worship." Before any other task, even building houses, Friends began holding "several meetings" that increased the "love and goodwill in our hearts to one another," and "after our meeting was over, we assisted each other in building little houses for our shelter." Quakers, like all the other denominations first setting up in Philadelphia, started with the raw materials at hand in the American landscape and the religious beliefs, customs, and structures they brought with them from Europe. Jon Butler has stressed this European connection, arguing that the foundations of religion in the Delaware valley were not democratic but decidedly hierarchical, drawing on familiar religious patterns from home. However, in the short term at least, because religious societies were voluntary associations, because they had no reserve of funds on which to draw, and because their immediate infrastructure needs were so pressing, the relationship between the clergy and laypeople depended intensely on negotiation and cooperation.[22]

Because they operated as a voluntary association, as Quakers sought to root their denomination in the New World, they had to rely on their own personnel and economic resources. Here they had a tremendous advantage in the first decades of settlement over every other religious group. Famously the proprietor himself was a Friend. Though he did not establish Quakerism as a state religion, he founded his colony with Quaker values at heart, and with the express intent to provide a safe haven for his coreligionists from the persecution of England. To that end, he donated land and building materials for a meetinghouse in Philadelphia (the one in the Center, as per his own agenda and city plan). Moreover,

Quakers had the advantage of numbers. The vast majority of new settlers were Friends; most of them came from the middling or artisanal classes in England, and a substantial minority arrived as wealthy merchants. Most of them could contribute something toward setting up their faith in Pennsylvania, and some of them could give quite a lot. Finally, because plainness was one of the foundations of their faith, Quakers formed "relatively inexpensive communities of the Holy Spirit." Still, the building of meetinghouses and establishing of programs such as relief of poor Friends and education of children quickly added up.[23]

At first, Quaker leaders in the Monthly and Quarterly Meetings seemed to have no idea how to get funds. They voted for their first major expenditure in the summer of 1683—£60 toward the construction of a meetinghouse—but did not specify where the money would come from. That winter they were still trying to "Contrive a Method for the Raising of a Stock in order to Defray all Publique Charges relating to ye Service of ye Church." When they needed to pay a clerk or to fence in the Quaker burial ground the next year, they still had no plan and could only lamely order that "ye next Monthly Meeting take Care how" these things "shall be paid for." But the Quakers could only float their debts for so long. Friends had to come up with a way to finance two meetinghouses and a burial ground and to pay for religious books and social services important to them, such as poor relief and education.[24]

Ultimately, the Monthly Meeting had to solicit contributions directly from the individuals in the congregation. "Subscriptions" became a constant source of funds for the Monthly Meeting. In the fall of 1684 they urged Philadelphia Friends to contribute money toward "the p[res]sent & Urgent Occation" of a number of their poor brethren. By February of 1685 Friends took on a more systematic approach, urging members to subscribe on paper a sum that the Monthly Meeting would thereafter collect monthly toward the relief of poor Quakers and "for other Concerns of truth." Later that spring the Monthly Meeting began another desperately needed subscription for the Center Meeting House, to pay the workmen, whose wages were overdue.

Quakers enhanced their spiritual communion through the very act of subscribing and collecting subscriptions. The physical buildings rose by virtue of the goods and labor purchased with financial contributions. "Holy conversation," meanwhile, was strengthened by the giving of many small and large subscriptions, material manifestations of communal purpose and consensus. Friends could expect to be approached about these subscriptions both in and out of Meeting. Repeatedly the Monthly Meeting appointed prominent Quakers to visit Friends to encourage those who had not subscribed to do so and those who had subscribed to pay up. These house-to-house visits paralleled closely the rounds of visiting common among Quakers to monitor one another's behavior and exhort one another to a godly life. By asking congregation members to sign public documents promising money, and by going door-to-door to check up on those who had and had not subscribed, the leadership of the Monthly Meeting exerted considerable pressure on the rank and file to make what were ostensibly voluntary contributions. To be a good Christian, a good Quaker, was "Cheerfully to Contribute."[25]

The subscription model placed decision making and therefore power in the hands of rank-and-file Quakers. Even as a hierarchical Quaker meeting structure akin to that in England was reproduced in Pennsylvania, ordinary Friends retained a powerful voice about what they valued through the constant demand on their pocketbooks. This power became especially evident in times of tension. One early "Cause of Strife amongst the lords People" revolved around Penn's insistence that the meetinghouse and burial ground be in the Center Square. With Penn gone after 1684, it was left to Quaker elites to carry on his plans, but they ran up against resistance. In 1685 "Many Good ffrds" expressed their "Disatisfaction" with this plan to such an intense degree that at last reconciliation could only be reached by agreeing that while Sunday morning meetings would happen at the Center, the afternoon and other meetings would be held near the Delaware River. Just over a year later, most business meetings were being held at the Front Street Meeting House—and in winter Friends stopped using the Center Meeting House altogether because of the distance and poor roads.[26]

In the 1690s Philadelphia Quakers suffered internal debates so acrimonious that it led to religious schism. The schism centered on theological matters, but its partisans enacted their esoteric disagreements through a more down-to-earth attempt to control the physical space—and therefore the authority—of the denomination. The Keithian Schism began when George Keith, a writer and schoolmaster, challenged the basis of Pennsylvania Quaker ministers' authority, arguing that they had strayed from true Christianity by an insufficient belief in the historical Jesus and too much emphasis on the saving grace of the Inner Light. The ensuing debate turned the colony on its ear for two years, leading to struggles over Meeting protocol, the printing press, the role of magistrates, and the public spaces of the city. Historians have focused on the theological and political aspects of the schism, casting it convincingly as a challenge to the Quaker hierarchy.[27]

The schism was not only concerned abstractly with authority and control; its most dramatic episode centered on control of an actual place: the Front Street Meeting House. Keith and his followers were among those who wanted to discontinue use of the Center Meeting House and have all meetings at Front Street. In 1692 when the Monthly Meeting decided after the winter was over to resume Sunday meetings at the Center, they refused. At first they met at Keith's house, but soon enough they attempted to meet in the empty Front Street Meeting

House, only to find it locked against them. Furious, the Keithians declared this affront a major reason for their "Separation" from other Quakers. Keithians felt they had just as much right—if not more by virtue of their (alleged) majority status—to the physical spaces held in common by the Society of Friends. The Monthly Meeting moved to secure its own claims to the building with a list of the subscribers to the construction of the two meetinghouses, "that it may be seen, who therein is chiefly concerned." The implication was that elites, who mostly opposed Keith and who had done the most to foot the bill for building the meetinghouses, in fact had superior right to those spaces, whatever numbers Keith might be able to muster, and could lock out the troublesome Keithians if they chose. Subscriptions became a way to justify one group's control of the meetinghouse. In this instance, subscriptions acted not to help build spiritual communion or equality, but instead as ammunition to justify fracturing it—a way for one internal, elite party to claim ownership and practical control over the church.[28]

Soon enough the meetinghouse would be not only metaphorically but literally fractured. Keith and his followers never conceded that their opponents could control the meetinghouse. In January of 1693 they made a new attempt to assert their own control by reshaping its interior. Many had long objected to the raised gallery on one end of the meetinghouse, reserved for influential "Public Friends," who thereby had a privileged position from which to declaim to the assembly below. One Sunday, during service, Keith's followers attacked it, hewing it with axes and bringing it down. No people were hurt in the commotion, but the unity of Friends had been rent asunder, much like the splintered interior of their meetinghouse. Elites might point to any subscription list they liked, but Keith and his followers challenged their authority over either the tangible or intangible church.[29]

One last coda remained in the struggle over the Front Street Meeting House. After the affair with the axes, the two sides split irrevocably. Unable to assert their control over the denomination or the meetinghouse, Keithians withdrew themselves and their economic resources from the fold. They "raised by voluntary Contributions among themselves" enough money to purchase their own meetinghouse, where they continued to meet as the "Society of Christian Quakers." This created an awkward problem for the Society of Friends because one of the defectors was Robert Turner, one of the wealthiest and best-connected men in the city. He was a member of the Provincial Council, a justice of the peace, a powerful commissioner of property, and—this was the part that was awkward—a trustee for the Front Street Meeting House. Even though Turner had been one of those wielding axes to bring down the offending gallery and had since left the denomination, he retained his legal authority as a trustee. Friends went to herculean lengths to reconcile with him. The concern and attention lavished on

Turner's defection laid bare the dependence the Society of Friends—indeed all Pennsylvania's denominations—had on their membership for funds and manpower. Turner, however, remained defiant, asserting "that he had allways a Testimony against gallerys in meeting houses, and that he was well satisfied with what he had done," leaving Friends no choice but to disown him. Years later when the old meetinghouse was "much decayed & in great danger of falling down," the members of the Monthly Meeting decided to sell it, but they had to "give Robert Turner notice thereof." He did nothing to hinder the sale, though legally he could have. Denominational authority and ownership sometimes flew not to abstraction but plodded the path of the practical.[30]

Shocked by the schism, Quakers intensified the internal ties binding Friends to one another—and to the faith. If the denomination was a voluntary association, then Friends reinvigorated the definitions of who was in and who out. They effected this delineation of boundaries physically with the construction of a fence. As early as 1689, before George Keith had set foot in Pennsylvania, some Friends "being disatisfyed that the Burying Place is made to[o] Common," proposed a separate Quaker burial ground, but nothing came of it. By 1694 circumstances had changed. In the wake of the hurtful division with Keith and other Friends, the matter of the burial ground returned, and the Monthly Meeting decided "with all expedition" that it "be appropriated to the service of friends only" and be fenced in. The exclusion presumably meant little to the dead, but a great deal to the living.[31]

Quakers, moreover, created a new layer of institutional power, in which "weighty" Quakers of both sexes policed the boundaries of the congregation. The Yearly Meeting in 1695 renewed attention to the comportment of Friends, charging local Meetings to appoint "Two or more Friends, Men & Women" to oversee the behavior of other Friends, "admonish" them where necessary, and report back to the Meetings. Overseers inquired into Friends' clothing, financial transactions, tobacco and alcohol consumption, meeting attendance, child rearing, and tendency to gossip. In 1696 the Yearly Meeting instituted quarterly Youths Meetings to instill in Quaker children the principles and discipline that would make them good—and loyal—members of the congregation. By 1705 the Yearly Meeting disseminated codified guides of "Discipline" to the Monthly and Quarterly Meetings, making clear the standards for membership in the spiritual communion of Friends. The Keithian Schism—and with it the loss of both middling and more substantial members like Robert Turner—had emphasized to the Quaker hierarchy the importance of solidarity. Friends enforced this solidarity through an increasingly dense and institutionalized system of oversight.[32]

Lay Quakers continued to support the society with their subscriptions, but as time passed they exercised less power through them. The meetinghouses were now constructed, the hierarchy set in place and reinforced through overseers and a more careful attention to the everyday behavior of Friends. The power Quakers held through their financial clout became proportionately less as the tangible and intangible infrastructure of the denomination solidified. Thousands of small voluntary contributions had created for some time a way for ordinary Quakers to voice their opinions; now those contributions collectively began to undermine that power by creating a fund large enough for the weighty Friends in the Monthly, Quarterly, and Yearly Meetings to begin to invest and collect interest. By 1699 the Monthly Meeting could order disbursements "out of the Stock," rather than relying on subscriptions for every little expense. Moving forward, the religious hierarchy would operate with increasing financial independence and therefore greater strength.[33]

If the early years of instituting a Quaker Meeting in Pennsylvania demonstrated the difficulty in immediately reproducing familiar European religious hierarchies, denominations with less strength in numbers faced even greater challenges. As Churchmen (Anglicans), Baptists, and Presbyterians began to build their own tangible and intangible church structures, they had to operate without anything like the numbers or the wealth of Quakers.[34] In all three denominations laypeople began meeting together for years before ordained clergy reached them. Baptists began formally to organize church government around 1695, the Presbyterians received their first minister in 1698, and Anglicans had to wait until 1700 for a permanent minister.

All of the ministers struggled with their new parishioners over social and economic control. As long as laypeople held the purse strings, they held a certain degree of power over their ministers, particularly in the first decades when everything had still to be built. Jedediah Andrews, the Presbyterian minister, found Philadelphia too "quiet" and threatened to go home, but another clergyman exhorted him instead to "bring them [his parishioners] to a better subscription," arguing that their "self interest" in retaining Andrews would encourage more substantial contributions. Andrews was also unhappy about the practice of Philadelphia Presbyterians sharing their meeting space with Baptists. Since 1694 the tiny congregations of Presbyterians and Baptists had banded together, sharing a single building, "the Barbadoes storehouse," for their services, one sect meeting in the morning and the other in the afternoon. At the time neither congregation had a regular minister, but relied on visiting clergy. When regular minister Andrews arrived in 1698, he became convinced that this sharing of space represented a direct threat to his authority and the congregation's integrity, but at first he proved reticent to do anything about it. A fellow clergyman "upbraided" him for allowing it, but remarked sadly, however, that he "could not spur" Andrews to action. Perhaps Andrews met too much resistance initially from his congregants who had long shared amicably with the Baptists. In the long run, Andrews did prevail and barred the Baptists from further access to

their makeshift meetinghouse. Andrews's frustration over his salary and difficulty ejecting Baptists from Presbyterian meeting spaces demonstrated both the
power of his parishioners and his own acute awareness of that power.[35]

The Church of England also had to rely heavily on parishioners. Accustomed
to state support, Churchmen were not used to having to raise money to finance
their church. When they built their first church in 1695, it cost the enormous
sum of £600. Anglicans, unlike Quakers, did not have a wide membership on
which to draw, and so the cost "lay only upon some particular persons," and
particularly the generosity of Francis Nicholson, the governor of Virginia, who
contributed heavily. Anglicans more than some other sects placed great value
not only on the church building but on the "Plate for the communion Table"
and other accoutrements necessary for their religious rituals. They also wanted
a library of religious books to help them combat what they saw as the dangerous tenets of Quaker faith. Unable to afford these items in the early years, they
petitioned Governor Nicholson and the bishop of London to assist them. Their
petitions, along with those of other Anglican congregations, would eventually
effect great changes in the Church of England's Atlantic organization with the
rise of the Society for the Propagation of the Gospel, which would shift profoundly the financial strategies and fortunes of local congregations.[36]

In the meantime, every church member (and particularly the wealthy ones)
mattered, sometimes to the great frustration of the clergy. Minister Thomas
Clayton understood himself to be in direct competition with Presbyterian minister Andrews for some of their congregants. One particular "advantage he has
got on me," Clayton fumed, was that "Madam Markham and her daughter . . .
frequently leave my Church and countenance their [the Presbyterians'] Meeting." The wife and daughter of William Markham, cousin to William Penn, and
at that time deputy governor of Pennsylvania, were indeed important congregants to retain, for their social prestige, their economic clout, and their potential
influence over the governor, who, though himself a Churchman, kept aloof
from the congregation. Why did the Markham women leave Clayton's meeting? Clayton thought it was "because I cannot be so servile as to stoop to their
haughty humors." He seemed particularly galled that two prominent women
presumed to pass judgment on his clerical performance by leaving his church
altogether when it suited them. He dismissed them as possessing "neither good
breeding, reason, nor religion," but he knew nonetheless that he depended for
his livelihood on the approval of women like Joanna and Ann Markham. Clayton's successor, Evan Evans, complained bitterly about his "subsistence, and
Livelyhood . . . more or less depending upon the Bounty of the People, by
Contributions." While he relied on his parishioners, he could never combat
the "Adultery, and Polygamy, Incest, and A Thousand other Crimes" he saw all
about him, "for to touch the more Topping, and Considerable men of them,

either in Publique or Private is to draw the fury of the whole Congregation upon
the Missionary, and to deprive himselfe of that Salary, or maintenance which
he has from them."[37]

The founding of religious faiths in Philadelphia (and the greater Delaware
valley) has been characterized as reproducing closely the hierarchical models
with which settlers had been familiar back in Europe. This approach focuses
on the theology and intangible hierarchy of religious bodies, which did indeed
begin to become more tightly controlled by clergy over time. However, this approach elides the economic dimensions of religious corporate identity. Churches
relied on laypeople to contribute money, time, and materials to construct the
infrastructure and spaces of religious worship. Churches were built with and
through subscriptions. These sites gave physical expression to a community of
worshippers and were often the settings of contest over religious identity and
the literal and metaphorical ownership of the church. Through their subscriptions laypeople (and particularly elites named as overseers or trustees of the buildings) acted not as passive flocks subject to ministerial oversight, but as owners—
literally—of their churches. Ministers of congregations other than the Quakers
struggled with the fact that their congregations were small and therefore less
able to provide a stable economic base. As a result, Church of England and
Presbyterian ministers felt themselves beholden to their parishioners, a position they deplored. Parishioners held power, moreover, not only through
their vital financial backing, but because they had the power of choice among
competing churches. They could leave, just as Robert Turner and the Keithians did from the Quakers, or they could threaten to leave, as Joanna and Ann
Markham aggravated their minister by doing. The same city residents who
refused to abide by Penn's city layout could similarly exert pressure on church
hierarchies through the power or refusal of their purses and their presence on
Sunday.

"Effectually Regulated": Urban Government

For all William Penn's loving attention to the layout of his capital city, he arrived
with no plans at all for how Philadelphia would be governed, apart from the
suggestion inherent in its name that the city be governed first and foremost by
brotherly love. Orderly streets and prosperous gardens might advertise the kind
of settlement he envisioned, but he neglected to frame the vital institutional
infrastructure that would give social and political coherence to the new community. By 1700 Philadelphia, with twenty-two hundred residents, was already
the size of an English commercial town and the second-largest urban area in
British North America. Despite its rapid growth and projected grandeur, before
1701 Philadelphia had no city government.[38]

Contemporaries advocating for municipal government wanted it to solve two quite different sets of problems. The first set concerned the provision of civic services such as poor relief; basic civil functions such as recording births, marriages, and deaths; and infrastructural services such as the maintenance of public goods like marketplaces and wharves. In most of the English-speaking world, poor relief and record keeping would have been performed or assisted by the state church, which often provided a first layer of local government. Without an established church, local government in Philadelphia faced an unexpected hurdle in how to provide, pay for, rationalize, and centralize civic services. In the meantime, denominations filled the void, but by definition they were parochial, serving only congregants, not the entire urban community. The services provided by churches, particularly the Quaker Meeting, met immediate needs but in the long term blunted the impetus toward a coherent local government. In the meantime, services never provided by churches—the regulation of markets, streets, wharves, and other public goods—became an increasingly pressing problem.

The second set of problems meant to be addressed by setting up an independent city government stemmed from struggles over political power and authority. Going back to the laying out of the city and the allocation of city lots, Philadelphia residents had butted heads with Penn over their property rights, which in turn formed the basis for their political rights. Increasingly those concerned about both communal and individual rights came to advocate for a municipal government that would not only provide services but act as a shield against the overreach of the proprietor. Penn and his supporters, in turn, understood the ways in which a city charter might be deployed against proprietary prerogative, and resisted it.

William Penn's decision not to have a state church has long been understood to have affected the practice and organization of denominational life in Philadelphia; less appreciated have been the ways in which this decision shaped profoundly the practice and organization of the state and local governance as well. On a practical level local government found itself deprived of institutional support and personnel. In England most of the contact ordinary men and women had with the state came through their parish church. In addition to a state-mandated obligation to attend church (at least nominally), every household owed tithes to maintain the parish priest and church. The parish held the official records of births, marriages, and deaths; those records in turn were used by parish officers to assess and collect taxes for poor relief. In incorporated towns and cities the relationship between parish officers and city magistrates was close; parochial officers acted "as *de facto* representatives of the corporation" in some cases, while in other cities magistrates oversaw their work and set poor rates. In other words, priests, churchwardens, and overseers served as a layer of bureaucracy at the local level which counted, assessed, and taxed parishioners, as well

as interacting with them regularly and sometimes passing on state pronouncements from the pulpit. Similarly in English America, established churches
received taxes, structured local poor relief, and delimited political membership
for adult males because in most places church membership was one necessary
component for full political rights. The state church, in short, structured and
expanded the scope of what was possible for local governments in most of the
English Atlantic.[39]

Philadelphia's government had to rely on the work of non-state actors,
specifically churches, to perform some of its most basic functions even in the
absence of religious establishment. Two state entities had oversight over the city:
Philadelphia County and the Provincial Council. The county government had
little power or resources, and the Provincial Council admitted its own inability
to operate without assistance, for which it turned to local churches. In 1690 it
passed a law that the registry books of all churches, recording the births, marriages, and burials of inhabitants, "shall be held Authentick, & shall be allowed
of upon all occasions." In so doing, the council admitted that state authorities
had to rely on nongovernmental organizations—churches—for basic knowledge
about the numbers and composition of the households within their jurisdiction.
Church registry books would become the basis for determining residence and
marital status—all with implications for taxation, naturalization, poor relief,
and voting. Legally disconnected from the state by a policy eschewing establishment, churches nonetheless had work to do on behalf of local government.[40]

Local authorities in Philadelphia struggled to implement poor relief and other
services without clerical bureaucratic support. County officials were ostensibly
empowered and responsible for poor relief and other local services, but by 1688
the Provincial Council noted that the counties did not have "sufficient Power to
Raise money for a Stock to Defray necessary Charges of their Respective Counties." The council proposed a bill to strengthen the counties, but nothing came
of it and the counties remained so weak that local inhabitants often bypassed
them altogether to petition the Provincial Council for help instead, which itself
could do little to help. In 1693 Jacobus Fabricius did exactly this. The elderly
and nearly blind minister of the Swedish congregation was "reduced to that
poveritie that hee had not whereupon to Live." The Provincial Council could
only angrily summon the wardens of his church to explain why they were not
caring for him. Rather than offer much in the way of poor relief, state officials
had again to rely on churches.[41]

Quakers, as the largest denomination, dominated poor relief in the earliest decades. Because of their strong subscription model, they were powerfully
positioned to provide services for the poor. However, they did not extend their
charity to "any poor," but only to "such as walk according to truth," which is to
say, other Quakers. Historians have cast seventeenth- and eighteenth-century

Quakers as "clannish" or "tribalistic." Friends' approach to poor relief reflected these exclusionary tendencies; they wanted to help their own. Yet even membership might not be enough to receive aid. Friends agreed that preferential treatment should go to "the faithfull and honest" over "such as walk disorderly." Within these bounds Quakers took seriously their Christian duty to aid the poor. They hoped their efforts would ensure that there "may not be a beggar amongst us nor any Justly to Complain In our Streets but that Our Bowls may be open to them for their Relief."[42]

For those who qualified, the poor relief meted out by the Monthly Meeting acted as a relatively comprehensive safety net. Some needed and received assistance upon first arriving in Pennsylvania. Other families with male heads needed help because of some calamity such as sickness or fire. When Edward Josmins fell ill, the Meeting paid his medical expenses. When fire destroyed the homes of John Carnes in 1692 and Joseph Phips in 1695, Friends took up subscriptions to assist them. Phips received one of the largest disbursements of the period, £32 to rebuild and get back on his feet. Clearly Phips was one of those "faithfull and honest" members the Meeting most wanted to help, but Quakers helped as well those who were less thrifty and industrious. They helped John Gardner and his family, for example, but only with £5, and dispensed the money themselves, never trusting him directly with it. Quakers gave counsel in lieu of money in some cases, appointing weighty Friends to "speak to poor ffrds that are like to be in want & that they advise them the proper way of the Getting of a livelyhood." Finally, the Meeting might loan money, as in the case of Daniel Smith, who received a loan of £20 in 1697 "in order that he may carry on some trade to maintain him and wife," and when that sum proved insufficient, the Meeting stood security to any other Friend willing to lend him another £25.[43]

Widows and orphans found themselves especially vulnerable to economic hardship, and they figured prominently among the poor that the Meeting assisted. The Monthly Meeting helped many widows with funds, medicine, and sometimes with loans, such as the £4 Katherine Morgan received in 1691. Other women received vital goods, such as clothing for Elinor Lewis and her children, or, in the case of Widow Libby, a cow. Quakers were concerned to help orphaned children and keep them in Quaker families. When Widow Ratchford died, leaving behind five children, the Meeting appointed a Friend to meet with her creditors and negotiate to try to preserve something of the estate to be passed on to her children. The Ratchford children were then apprenticed into good Quaker homes. One boy was only four years old and apprenticed until the age of twenty-one to weaver Thomas Hood to learn his trade in addition to reading, writing, and basic accounting. The Meeting instructed Friends to set up indentures for Quaker children before they could come before county officials at the Orphans Court. Friends wanted to be sure children born into

Quaker households would be raised by Quakers; they went to magistrates only after they had internally worked out their plans for orphans.[44]

The Quakers had decided to aid only their own, but by doing so they provided a strong safety net—and one that in the earliest decades of Philadelphia's founding applied to the majority of the town's population. However, their insistence on exclusive internal aid and on placing orphaned children in strong Quaker families underscored the reality that in the long run neither the Society of Friends nor any other religious society could take the place of state-run poor relief.

As with poor relief, the powerful engine of the Quaker Meeting usurped initiative on education. In 1689, Friends, "being willing to encourage a School in this town," started a subscription and hired a schoolmaster who received a substantial annual salary in return for agreeing to teaching poor children for no fee. In 1698 Quakers wished to put their school on stronger legal ground. They approached the governor and Provincial Council, mindful that only the council had the legal authority to "establish" schools. They asked to be incorporated into a discrete legal body, with the privileges of limited liability and the ability to hold and pass on property. The "Free School," as it came to be known, received a formal charter that was further supplemented in October of 1701.[45]

Originally Penn had intended that the Provincial Council and governor would encourage education. The 1682 charter and earliest laws made provision for schools, giving the governor and Provincial Council the power to "erect and order all public schools." As early as 1683 the council took "into their serious Consideration the great Necessity there is of a Scool [*sic*] Master for ye Instruction & Sober Education of Youth in the towne of Philadelphia" and employed Enoch Flower to open a school, funded primarily by fees charged to students. The school apparently did not flourish, and the council did nothing more to oversee or fund it. The only way the council asserted its power over education was to berate Thomas Makin in 1693 for keeping a school without a license. The council instructed him to get credentials from a number of respected townsmen immediately. By 1700 the state had no role in education, and when Penn issued a new charter in 1701, he no longer assigned the state any responsibility for schools.[46]

More so than poor relief, education represented a sensitive and politically fraught social service. Quakers who in 1682 might have agreed with Penn's utopian vision of state-supported schools by 1700 had turned away from this possibility because they believed powerfully that young people's faith could only be inculcated in carefully controlled learning environments. The same impulse that led them to place orphans in committed Quaker families led them also to wish to send children to their own schools. Quakers throughout the Atlantic world shared this belief. The 1690 London Yearly Meeting epistle warned against sending Quaker children to others' schools where children might pick up "the corrupt ways, manners, Fashions and Language of the World and of the Heathen in their authors and names of heathenish gods & goddesses." Quakers wanted tight control of their schools, not management by state authorities in a polity committed to religious toleration. Meanwhile, other religious groups interpreted the founding of a strong Quaker school as a dire threat. John Arrowsmith, a Churchman, kept his own school for the children of Anglicans or other sympathetic families, and in the absence of an ordained minister, Arrowsmith also served as a kind of religious leader for the small Anglican community. He worried mightily about the newly endowed Quaker school, fuming that it had been founded "in effect to blast my endeavors" and provide a platform for spreading dangerous "Quakerisms." Education was going to be not only a parochial but a divisive service in Philadelphia in the years to come.[47]

By investing in and using their religious societies to provide poor relief and education, Philadelphians expedited necessary community services but impeded the formation of strong institutions of local government. Like a muscle that gets stronger as it gets used but atrophies with inactivity, Philadelphia local government (or the impetus to create one) was not helped but weakened by the laudable desire of churches to help their own. Because poor relief and education were being met through other venues, Philadelphians did not put pressure on any of the officials with jurisdiction over the town—including William Penn, the Provincial Council, or the county justices of the peace—to provide them. In turn, that meant that local officials did not need to formulate a cohesive system for raising funds, building infrastructure, keeping records, or employing tax collectors, overseers of the poor, schoolmasters, or other functionaries. As long as Philadelphians focused their time, energy, and money on their own churches and used those institutions to meet pressing community needs, local government would have neither the need nor the ability to exert itself.[48]

One arena, however, went beyond the scope of church structures and defied parochialism because it dealt not with social services but with the common spaces of the town. The one set of problems that inhabitants put consistent and increasing pressure on local officials to solve had to do with the town's streets, marketplace, and—of particular concern—public wharves. The Provincial Council, moreover, controlled who could operate privately owned enterprises seen to have public utility, such as ferries over the Schuylkill and Delaware Rivers, local taverns, and the commerce in the market. But who had responsibility for other critical public goods was often unclear.

The Provincial Council and Philadelphia County officials both held jurisdiction over the town, and often they themselves could not decide who had power or responsibility in particular cases. In September 1686, for example, resident Henry Jones complained to the Provincial Council about the "badness" of the road between Philadelphia and Moyamensing, a township just south of the town. The council referred the matter to the Philadelphia County magistrates, "who," they thought, "it's presumed has power to appoynt Roads." Two months later, however, the council reversed itself and assumed jurisdiction over Philadelphia streets when it collaborated with officials from both Philadelphia and Bucks Counties to improve the route to the Delaware Falls from Broad Street. By the 1690s many of the town streets were in a terrible state of disrepair, eroded by or flooded with water. The Commissioners of Property, a board of three men appointed by Penn to allocate city lots and manage other property matters in his stead, were galled in 1691 by the "decayed" state of the bank beside Sassafras Street, which was falling into the street. Even though they did not have jurisdiction over streets, the commissioners nevertheless ordered that "forthwith publick Notice be given to the Magistrates and Inhabitants of Philadelphia that they Support and Maintain the Same, and where it has Broaken into the Front Street it be Repaired, Otherwise," they threatened (without any clear authority for doing so) that they would "grant it unto Such as will perform the same." No hierarchy made clear which body should regulate streets, leading to confusion and poor roads, which, in turn, led to complaints from residents and inhibited local commerce.[49]

In some cases town residents took matters into their own hands. For example, in 1691 the Commissioners of Property granted timber to "some persons" who requested it to repair a bridge on Chestnut Street. "Several of the Inhabitants" petitioned the Provincial Council for permission to construct a public wharf at the end of Walnut Street. Within months "John Delavall and others (the overseers for the Building of ye Wharf against Walnut Street)" were collecting supplies and beginning work. In 1693 a grand jury issued a presentment to the Provincial Council about the immediate need for a shallow channel in the area around Front Street to carry off water and prevent flooding. The council had no choice but to call the householders of that street in for a conference and convince them to deal with the "nusance" themselves. The cost of the work would be borne "equallie & proportionablie [by] the freeholders on each side" of the affected streets. Soon the council and legislature formalized this kind of arrangement, setting up a system whereby the governor and council would appoint a committee to regulate urban streets, but the law did not include a way to raise communal funds. Rather, street residents themselves would pay for repairs, a solution that cast streets not as a public good, a thoroughfare shared by all townspeople, but as the responsibility of the particular people who lived on that street. The law did not function very well. By 1701 inhabitants complained that Front Street was "almost impassible . . . and becom Dangerous." They demanded speedy redress, which, however, was not forthcoming. Officials estimated that it would take £500 to complete the necessary repairs. Such a tremendous sum could not be raised only from the residents of that street; a tax would have to be assessed and collected, an undertaking that would stretch the power of the government as it then stood, not only because of the effort entailed but also because it advanced the recognition of streets as communal property—and a communal responsibility.[50]

Responsibility for the town watch and military defense caused similar confusion and contention. As early as 1683 the Provincial Council began handing down orders to city constables to preserve order in local taverns, but two years later it drew up a bill dismissing control of the town watch into the hands of county officials. Apparently that grant of power was not enough because within five years, the county justices of the peace approached the council "ffor a ffurther Strengthening of ye Authority of ye watch," which it was struggling to maintain.[51]

Of far greater weight were concerns over military defense because the Crown and other colonial officials expected Pennsylvania to bear its share of the cost of imperial defense, particularly after the outbreak of King William's War in 1689. Throughout the 1680s and 1690s governors called repeatedly on the Provincial Council and assembly alike to put the colony in a state of military preparedness by organizing a militia and raising funds. Strict Quakers avowed again and again that their religious beliefs would not permit them to authorize military measures. The Provincial Council and assembly refused to raise a militia, even when non-Quaker inhabitants petitioned for one, focusing their efforts instead on Indian diplomacy. Non-Quakers, particularly Churchmen, reacted with outrage at the refusal of local authorities to organize some kind of mechanism for defense.[52]

The refusal to raise a militia occurred at the provincial level, but it had local effects, contributing in increasingly diverse Philadelphia to the lack of a center in the community. Already religion parceled men and women into separate religious spaces for worship. Social services likewise dispersed among churches that served only their own. Meanwhile responsibility for infrastructure and public spaces was uneasily and mostly ineffectively dealt with between the Provincial Council and county officials. Religion and state services thus did little to unify Philadelphians as one community. The absence of a militia exacerbated the lack of common civic rituals. It deprived the town of common ground (literally) that could be shared by all adult white men as they gathered for periodic musters and drills. For most of Philadelphia's history, the militia would shape the community by its absence rather than its presence.

Philadelphia evolved around another pointed absence: the lack of a strong economic or financial center. Penn had hoped to build a mercantile exchange to assist business transactions and the flow of information, but this did not come to pass until after the American Revolution. Some Philadelphians themselves

had an even more extensive plan in mind. In 1689 six of the town's most prominent merchants petitioned the governor and council for "a bank ffor money,
&c." Chronically short of currency, all the colonies struggled to find a sufficient medium for local exchange. The merchants wanted a bank on the model
of contemporary institutions in England which could issue and honor bills of
exchange. Bills of exchange could circulate much like currency and would facilitate trade and financial transactions in specie-poor Pennsylvania. In response
to the petition for a local bank, Governor John Blackwell replied vaguely that
he thought that Penn might be contemplating something of the sort and that
they would all hear from him through the mail in the near future. Blackwell
encouraged the merchants meanwhile to feel free to circulate their own personal
bills of credit, which could circulate as money "as merchants usually did bills of
Exchange" in England, but acknowledged that this could be a risky endeavor
because of the danger of counterfeited bills. Penn never did send instructions
to charter a bank, and the matter dropped. Philadelphia, well on its way within
decades of its first founding to being one of the busiest North American ports,
would not have the benefit of strong local financial institutions.[53]

Philadelphia entered the eighteenth century with a confused and weak system of
local government which allowed and even encouraged direct action by residents
themselves. Endowed by Penn and the earliest constitutions with little coherent
structure, the authorities charged with town government had difficulty performing a number of basic tasks, such as record keeping, poor relief, and education, their problems exacerbated by the absence of the clerical bureaucracy that
would have come with a state-established church. Local government authorities
—either the Provincial Council or Philadelphia County justices of the peace;
it was never entirely clear which—were responsible for the infrastructure and
public spaces of the community, but here too government often accomplished
little, relying on the efforts of townspeople instead. Philadelphians rushed into
the void. Through their churches, they ensured that at least the needs of their
own coreligionists would be met. They aided newly arrived immigrants, victims
of fires, widows, and orphans; they taught young boys and girls to read; and
they recorded the vital statistics of the community in births, marriages, and
deaths. They acted independently or semi-independently to rebuild bridges,
repair roads, and construct public wharves.

   All this commendable work helped build Philadelphia into a thriving commercial center, but it also shaped the civic community into something quite
different than had been originally envisioned by Penn and the other founders
of the city. Civic life did not revolve around a central authority, a common
space, or shared activities and rituals. Instead, civic life fragmented into many
independent venues, each reflecting separate interests, objectives, and strategies.

Religious societies served as particularly important sites of building discrete subcommunities. The absence of a unitary religious community meant serious differences about the ways and means of government—indeed, of community itself. Without an established church, Philadelphia lacked a major site of common rites, beliefs, and activities which might help unite a community. Churches themselves became contested spaces rather than immediately reconstituting the hierarchical forms of religious life in Europe. Laypeople asserted their opinions and ownership through the donation or withholding of financial contributions. Other institutions that might have provided common rituals or services across the community regardless of religious persuasion—such as a militia or a bank— could not be founded in the circumstances of colonial Pennsylvania.

The city imagined in 1682 was by 1700 a real town, well on its way to being a city. But by 1700 it had become clear that Philadelphia could not continue to limp along without some more coherent civic and government structure to manage local concerns. Philadelphia's civic structures were about to be overhauled, but like the grid that rigidly configured the city and prevented the creation of a new central square closer to the waterfront, attempts to remake government and centralize authority could not depart from but only build up from the existing infrastructure of civic life. The foundation laid in the 1680s and 1690s proved unstable ground on which later to attempt strong centralization.

CHAPTER TWO

Intoxicated with Power
Chartering the Philadelphia Corporation

"If anyone were to see Philadelphia who had not been there" before, wrote Swedish minister Andreas Rudman in 1700, "he would be astonished beyond measure [to learn] that it was founded less than twenty years ago." The transformation had been made possible, as another commentator noted, by "the Industrious (nay Indefatigable) Inhabitants." Out of what they had perceived to be wilderness, Philadelphia's founders had carved streets, built churches, and initiated enthusiastic participation in Atlantic commerce. They had moved beyond temporary shelter in riverbank caves to build "Noble" houses and stores along a handful of streets closely paralleling the Delaware. Two congregations, the Quakers and Church of England, had custom-built meetinghouses in the town, and others, among them the Keithians, Baptists, and Presbyterians, had regular spaces of their own as well. Small though it still was, Philadelphia was already the second-largest urban settlement in British North America.[1]

Philadelphia looked nothing like anyone had imagined in 1682. It had no center, no balance, and none of the "peaceableness" that the proprietor had so encouraged. The town had evolved with its most important institutions and functions dispersed, a fractured and fractious community with nothing resembling a unified public culture. Religious life and social services dispersed among churches; political life was entangled with accusations and counteraccusations by Quakers, Keithians, and Churchmen alike of religious persecution (threatened or perceived to have already occurred); and little existed in the way of common rites and activities that drew community members together—no church services together, no musters on the town green for militia practice. In 1701 broad political reform would reshape the civic landscape of the city, introducing a municipal corporation based on medieval and contemporary English precedent. Whether it would provide a strong center for the community remained to be seen.

"Secure and Defend Us": The Origins of Incorporation

In December 1699 as much as half the population of Philadelphia thronged the waterfront, eager to catch a glimpse of a momentous occasion: the return at last of William Penn. He had come back, this time he hoped permanently. As proof of his intent, he brought his family, including his very pregnant wife, with him. His son John was born the following month, always to enjoy a particular local popularity for being the only Penn born in Pennsylvania. William Penn, meanwhile, was impressed and pleased with the "Surprizing Improvement in Town & Country" he found and took it as "a Proof of the Power of Industry and Sobriety." However, his mission there was not to admire but to whip into shape. English authorities had expressed deep concern about the fractious colony, and Penn himself was no less concerned at how his proprietary prerogatives had been ignored while he was away. He had returned to bring his colony in line with imperial policy, particularly as regarded piracy and the Navigation Acts, and to stave off his own financial ruin by a vigorous effort once and for all "to put the colony on a paying basis."[2]

The initial joy Philadelphians had demonstrated on the Penn family's arrival quickly took a colder turn as the townspeople feared that Penn's intended reforms imperiled their property and political rights. Philadelphians had for some time been concerned about the status of their collective and individual liberties and began to press for codification of their rights, pressing ultimately for a charter creating a municipal corporation that would protect Philadelphia from proprietary overreach. However, their agitation by no means represented a united front. Various constituencies in the city identified different threats to their liberties. Elite Quakers focused on encroachments on collective and individual property rights in the city, while other factions, particularly the growing community of Churchmen and others such as the old Keithians who opposed elite Quaker rule, saw greater threats looming over their representation and political rights.[3]

A pitched battle began in 1700 over a private wharf built on the Delaware River, swirling into a reaching debate about property rights. Opponents debated the definition of "public" or "common" property and argued about the rights of individual ownership against the communal rights of the town. In the early 1690s Henry Elfreth had begun to build on valuable waterfront land just north of Dock Creek by the old Blue Anchor Tavern. In the summer of 1691 Philadelphia justices of the peace put an abrupt stop to his construction and claimed the land "for the use of the Publick" as a wharf or landing place. Perhaps because of the upheaval of the early and mid-1690s, it took Elfreth until 1700 to bring his case before the Provincial Council, but when he did, he met immediate and loud public resistance. A petition signed by thirty-two of the most substantial men in the community declared that "no p[er]son for private gains or Intrest may Incomode the Publick Utility of a whole City." They argued that the contested site had been used "w[i]thout any Interruption" as a common landing place since the first English arrived in 1682, and that Penn's original charter had guaranteed them a capital city with "the most Convenient Landing places." The allusion to Penn's charter took the debate to a new level, connecting the petitioners' demands with not just convenience or the public good but contractual obligations worked out between Penn and his settlers before they had left England. Elfreth protested that it could not be proved that the contested property had ever been granted to the town, and moreover that he had suffered substantial financial damage. Penn and the council tried to mediate, but the inhabitants "shew'd no inclination to comply," insisting that though the public wharf had never been delineated, "ye Town had always claimed it," and they were shocked that Elfreth had the presumption to build on it for himself. In frustration Penn ordered that the land should be left vacant until he had decided what to do and in the meantime Elfreth would be reimbursed for his losses.[4]

This expression of "ye Town" as a discrete political and economic entity with rights that needed to be protected melded with an increasingly articulated set of concerns that neither their individual nor their collective property rights were secure in Philadelphia. Some Philadelphia householders began to detect in Penn's actions a concerted threat to their property and therefore their rights and liberties. They objected to annual quitrents charged by Penn on their individual property and were horrified by Penn's move to create a "Court of Inquiry" that would investigate the legitimacy of all land titles and ensure payment of all quitrents. Moreover, they began to demand that communal property (like the wharf discussed above) that they believed belonged to the town be secured more effectively. Their agitation struck a blow to Penn, who was by then locked in an acrimonious debate with his colonists over the constitution and provincial government. Many Philadelphians believed that Penn had trespassed on their rights by renting city land that had been intended to remain common, and they insisted that the land by the Blue Anchor Tavern (the land on which Elfreth had tried to build) and also by the Penny Pot Tavern be secured for the use of all the residents of Philadelphia.[5]

While some worried about property rights, others had become increasingly worried about local political rights, particularly under the new provincial constitution, the Frame of 1696. In April 1693 Pennsylvania came briefly under royal control, at which time the original 1683 Frame of Government had been abrogated. When proprietary government resumed in the spring of 1695, Penn and his appointed lieutenant-governor, William Markham, assumed that the original charter came back into effect. However, the assembly had other plans and passed in 1696 a new frame that enhanced its own power. The assembly forced reluctant Markham to accept the new Frame of 1696, in return for appropriations for military defense. The assembly and council then operated under the terms of the 1696 Frame even though Penn and many Pennsylvanians objected to it. A vocal group of Philadelphians in particular opposed the Frame of 1696 because it reduced the number of councilmen and representatives and made it harder for city dwellers to vote by mandating higher property requirements and insisting on two years' residency. Opponents interpreted the changes of the 1696 Frame as a deliberate attempt to consolidate the power of Quaker elites and inhibit the political influence of Philadelphia because of its rising populations of Churchmen and other non-Quakers.[6]

The antipathy between supporters of the old and more liberal 1683 Frame and the newer and more restrictive 1696 Frame came to a head in the election of 1697. Refusing to recognize the legitimacy of the other, each group set up their own polling place on Election Day. However, the group that clung to the 1683 Frame was unable to make the results of its election stick. They were forced to accept the outcome of the election under the 1696 Frame, even as they argued it had been an illegitimate election and one in which they had not participated. Their defeat meant the demise of the original frame and forced them to accept the higher property and residency requirements for voting enshrined in the 1696 Frame. They were not happy about it. They wrote Penn in deep consternation that their rights were being violated, pointing out that they had never agreed to the changes. They affirmed their stalwart defense of "the peoples Libertys and the Old Charter" and deplored the abridgement of their ability to vote and the number of their representatives. Robert Turner bemoaned "the loud Cry of Oppression from Philadelphia" and believed that the persecution there exceeded even that in New England.[7]

These two sets of imperatives—the desire to secure communal property and combat quitrents on individual property, and the desire to protect Philadelphians' political influence against the provincial assembly and Quaker elites—framed the debate and range of possibilities when in September of 1701 Penn announced that, against his original intentions, he needed to return to England. He charged Pennsylvanians to "review again your Laws, propose New ones that may better your Circumstances," but cautioned, "what you do, do it quickly."

Penn would sail within weeks before the weather became too dangerous to cross the Atlantic, for he had once again to return to England as soon as possible to protect his charter. With his back against the wall—or in this case the wharf—Penn found himself having to make extreme concessions.[8]

The ensuing month and a half brought tremendous change to Pennsylvania, culminating in Penn's signing the Charter of Privileges just before he sailed. The Charter of Privileges guaranteed the two central and enduring elements of Pennsylvania government in the colonial period: liberty of conscience and the supremacy of a popularly elected legislature. Much of Pennsylvania's later economic and demographic success would be predicated on these two tenets. However, Penn signed this charter against his will and under substantial duress. He had originally intended a hierarchical provincial government that would be dominated by his representative, the governor, and an appointed provincial council; the representative legislature would serve primarily in an advisory role. However, two decades of contention and political upheaval had by now left Penn's vision in shambles. In what one historian has summarized as nothing less than "a peaceful coup d'etat," the Charter of Privileges that Penn's colonists forced him to sign stripped power from the executive and the Provincial Council and vested that power instead in the hands of the popularly elected legislature. This move drastically undercut Penn's authority and made the Pennsylvania Assembly among the most powerful of all colonial legislatures in America. It also aligned Pennsylvania government more fully with Quaker ideals of governance, which stressed the equality of all members and bottom-up government. The Charter of Privileges reconstituted Pennsylvania's body politic, vesting the bulk of the power in the hands of the people's popularly elected representatives.[9]

The Charter of Privileges also, for the first time, gave the city of Philadelphia its own representation in the assembly, answering to some degree concerns about representation and political rights in the city. Henceforth, city residents would annually elect two men to represent them in the House of Representatives. In 1701, with about 10 percent of the population, Philadelphia thus had a little less than 8 percent of the representatives in the assembly. However, the Charter of Privileges made no provision for adjusting the number of seats elected by Philadelphia or the counties as population shifted. Within twenty years Philadelphia accounted for 13 percent of the population but still had 8 percent of the seats in the House. As new counties were added to the colony and began sending their representatives to the assembly, Philadelphia's share of government would continue to shrink, even as its population boomed. By 1752, when the last two counties of the colonial period were added, Philadelphia had 12 percent of the population but only 5 percent of the representation in the assembly. The Charter of Privileges, then, may have done much to set Pennsylvania on the path toward strong representative government, but it did not spread that representation equally. The counties to join later always complained (with justification) that they were underrepresented to allow for a Quaker majority in the assembly. By a similar token, heterogeneous Philadelphia within a very short time also found its political clout undermined at the provincial level.[10]

Simultaneously with the drafting of the Charter of Privileges, the long-discussed project of securing municipal government for Philadelphia inched toward reality, but here economic and property considerations trumped concerns about political rights or representation, which proponents did not even mention. "A Considerable Number of the Inhabitants" asked for "an Instrument" that would "absolutely secure and defend us in our Estates and Properties, from [Penn], his heirs and assigns for ever" and a guarantee that any seizure of property would go through a court of law. The inhabitants stipulated that Penn formally (and finally) recognize that Philadelphia had been "a free gift" to his settlers and would no longer be "clogg'd with divers Rents and Reservations, Contrary to the first design and grant, & to the Disatisfaction of the Inhabitants." The petitioners moreover wanted all unsettled land within the bounds originally conceived for Philadelphia (two miles in length from the Delaware to the Schuylkill and one mile wide) to be declared common property belonging to the city and that Penn and his heirs would neither sell, lease, nor enclose any of that land. They demanded free wharf access at the sites of the Blue Anchor and Penny Pott Taverns and control over the regulation of their streets. They also made a series of requests relating to transparency of government, desiring officials with "integrity," a clear schedule of fees for government services, the preservation and consolidation of public documents, and timely patents for property. A committee of the assembly gave the petition the weight of its recommendation as well, an indication that these petitioners' aims were in harmony with those of prominent provincial politicians.[11]

Penn reacted with frustration, asserting multiple times that the petitioners were "under a great mistake" in the assumptions that guided their requests. He defended his prerogative to charge quitrents and his sole ownership of the unallotted land in the city, grumbling moreover about the "great abuse done me in my absence by Destroying of my Timber and Wood," for which he deserved monetary compensation. However, Penn asserted himself open to an "accommodation," and he was under enormous pressure, both in his negotiations over the Charter of Privileges with the assembly and because he needed so desperately to set sail soon.[12]

The strenuous petition from the "Considerable Number of the Inhabitants" had its intended effect: it forced Penn to incorporate the city, giving it powers and protecting its common property. In light of the political fights leading up to the 1701 charter, it has been interpreted not only as a reaction to the growing size of the town but also as a political weapon designed to undermine Penn.

The so-called Lloydian faction, led by David Lloyd (and before him his brother Thomas), had been working assiduously to curtail Penn's property rights and political power for years. Incorporating Philadelphia would create yet another political entity through which to protect settlers' rights and to needle Penn. This interpretation almost certainly gets at the motivations of most of the sixty-nine petitioners in 1701 (of which David Lloyd was one), but not the concerns or motivations of all Philadelphians.[13]

Distinct interest groups in the city had differing agendas for what municipal government might mean. Some, like those who had worried in the 1697 election that Philadelphia's political clout was being undermined, continued to be concerned not by the overreach of Penn but by that of elite orthodox Quakers and politicians like David Lloyd. Members of the Church of England in particular felt shut out of the political process. Robert Suder, for example, asserted that one Quaker had been "heard to say he would sooner take a Negroe that is a heathen's word before a Church of England man's oath." An émigré from Jamaica, Suder found Quakers' "prejudice" and "malice" toward his coreligionists boundless. He articulated the feelings of many when he complained that Churchmen had no freedom of religion, no ability to defend themselves through a legally constituted militia, and no opportunity for fair trials because Quakers did not allow sworn testimony (it being against Quaker beliefs to swear or give oaths). Robert Quarry, perhaps the most politically active Churchman in Philadelphia, summarized Quakers as "Invaders of our Estates, liberties and properties." Ruling Quakers brushed aside these deeply held concerns in the Anglican community and did nothing to include them in the process of eliciting either the provincial or city charters. No prominent Churchmen signed the 1701 petition for city government, and only four men who had signed the petition complaining about electoral abuse in 1697 signed the 1701 petition. The opinions voiced by Churchmen and other Philadelphians disaffected by the ruling elite therefore did not play into the settlement of 1701, but their desire to use city government as a bulwark not so much against Penn but against elite Quakers did not die away. Within a few decades their children and grandchildren would try to use city government exactly with that aim.[14]

The drive for local governmental reform in 1701 in many ways reflected how divided Philadelphia itself had become over the previous twenty years. The petitioners who set the process in motion represented one part of the population: the kind of structure they wanted for local government was tailored to protect a particular set of interests, specifically the concerns of Quaker elites against Penn. The reform they advocated both in the city charter and in the Charter of Privileges focused on one threat: proprietary prerogative. To defend against that evil, the Charter of Privileges set up a powerful assembly, and the city charter established a bulwark meant to protect Philadelphians' property rights, the basis of their economic power and political rights. The petitioners did not represent the full spectrum of opinion in the city, however, and they took no steps to address concerns held by certain segments of the population about threats other than Penn to political and property rights, or to find a way to include or assuage those constituencies.

"One Body Corporate & Politick": The Philadelphia Corporation

In late October 1701 the fate of Pennsylvania and its capital changed dramatically, and all because William Penn was in a hurry. In a flurry of business in the final days before he sailed, Penn signed three charters apportioning power at the local level. Though they were signed within days of one another, the political and economic communities constituted by these charters could not have been more different. The most famous by far was the Charter of Privileges, discussed above.

The other two new charters Penn signed in that fateful month have received less scholarly attention: they incorporated two towns, Philadelphia and the rural town of Chester. In part these charters have garnered less notice because they dealt with smaller polities, but more importantly, they shared none of the radicalism of the Charter of Privileges, none of the ingenuity and care that Penn had manifested even in drawing the physical layout of his capital city. Penn had seized the opportunity of founding Philadelphia to rethink what an urban space could be. But in pushing the bounds of urban layout, and in the midst of being pushed by his fractious colonists to reconsider the role of provincial government, Penn applied neither set of lessons or innovations to city governance. Instead, he and the residents of Philadelphia and Chester settled on the standard language and format of medieval, English corporate charters.[15]

English municipal charters had stemmed out of the unique needs of towns in the medieval era, lonely centers of commerce set amid a largely agricultural landscape. Town charters exempted members from service to local lords and conveyed particular privileges to help the small commercial classes survive. In general, in order to be a freeman, a man needed to have lived in the town a year and a day—thus proving no lord had claim over him—and he needed to have served an apprenticeship in a trade or hold a certain amount of property. The city charter set up a governing structure that regulated the marketplace. English town corporations owned and operated the markets and fairs; controlled prices; monitored weights, measures, and quality; and prevented non-freemen from trading in the town. Dominated at first by successful artisans, over time town government became riven by partisan battles and "undoubtedly oligarchic," though always subject to the acquiescence of town residents. Already by 1689, when many town charters were reissued in the reign of William and Mary, the old model no longer answered the needs of urban governance; but rather than wholesale reform (which would not come until the nineteenth century), authorities set up ancillary bodies that supplemented or bypassed altogether the existing structure.[16]

The Philadelphia charter resembled closely the bulk of English municipal charters. It set up the requirements for freeman status, though it divorced craft status from the prerequisites, insisting only that to be admitted a man must own at least £50 in property and have lived in the city two years. By the terms of the charter, only freemen could practice trades in the city, eliminating competition from non-freemen. The city's official structure would consist of a mayor, a recorder, eight aldermen, and twelve common councilmen. Penn appointed the initial officers; thereafter, the body was self-perpetuating. Officers would be chosen by the existing office holders only; they did not answer to freemen. The charter made this group into "one Body Corporate & Politick . . . by the Name of the Mayor & Comonalty of Philadelphia." Incorporation gave the body legal personality—that is to say, it could hold, buy, or sell property, and it could sue and be sued—the right of perpetual succession, and the use of a common seal that acted like a person's signature on legal documents. The mayor, recorder, and aldermen would act as local judges and maintain the court of record, a place for Philadelphians to record legal obligations like debts. The corporation would oversee the city's markets, wharves, and run two annual fairs. It was responsible, moreover, for setting and enforcing prices and measurements for bread, wine, beer, wood, and other goods.[17]

Chester, a small county town, received similar privileges though on a smaller scale. It had a high constable and four burgesses responsible for local justice, running a market once a week, and two annual fairs. In contrast to the Philadelphia councilmen, these burgesses met not in isolation but in a general "town meeting," and they passed ordinances in conjunction with the meeting's input. Moreover, officer selection was much more open: all "freeholders" in the town annually elected officers.[18]

These charters have often been misinterpreted as setting up local government. They did not. The Philadelphia charter claimed to be for "the more Immeadiate & Intire government of the said Town," but it was the Chester charter that more exactly identified what incorporation accomplished: the confirmation and bestowal of "additional privileges . . . for the better encouragement of the settlers and regulations of trade therein." The municipal corporations of Philadelphia and Chester (as with all their English counterparts) were not constituted by the contract or consensus of the people, nor were they constituted by law: they were constituted by charter, a very specific legal instrument that conveys privileges and responsibilities to one man or body of men, not all men. Indeed, no difference existed between town charters and other kinds of corporations. English political theorist Thomas Hobbes argued that a charter is not law but an *exemption* from law applicable only to some. The exemptions and privileges thought vital for urban residents in the medieval period continued to be applied in the early modern period, even though the feudal system that had provided the context for those privileges no longer prevailed. Philadelphia's charter was never intended to set up comprehensive government; instead, it bestowed particular privileges on a small group.[19]

The "Comonalty" the charter created remained a small, exclusive body throughout the colonial period, consisting of the common councilmen, aldermen, mayor, and recorder. In the fifty years before the American Revolution only 112 men sat on the Common Council. The vast majority of them were merchants, and three-quarters were related to at least one other member by blood or marriage. The first four mayors, serving a total of five terms, were all in the same family, a fact that worried critics of the corporation. This small, closed body did not purport to legislate on behalf of all the residents of the town or even to be directly answerable to them. The mayor, aldermen, and common councilmen were not responsible even to those men who by coming forward to qualify formally as "freemen" were technically part of the corporation. Indeed, freemen played "no perceivable part" in corporation activities.[20]

The reasons that propelled Quaker elites to seek a municipal charter in Philadelphia were linked closely to the original reasons medieval cities had pursued them. It would serve as a bulwark against the prerogative of the lord, or, in this case, the proprietor, and it would shore up the political and economic power of a small group. The model pioneered by feudal English town corporations proved an effective vehicle for this purpose. However, it also shaped, even blinkered, the ways Philadelphians thought about the possibilities for local governance. Certainly, with their eyes on the ultimate prize, the Charter of Privileges, Quaker elites did not deploy for city government the creativity and attention that characterized their pursuit of popular representation and legislative supremacy at the provincial level. They accepted an existing format, only mildly modifying it to fit local needs.[21]

The focus on checking Penn's power shaped the kind of institution the charter created. Oriented toward the dangers represented by Penn, the city government set up by Quaker elites failed to delineate clear boundaries or carve out power away from the provincial assembly or from the Philadelphia County government—both of which would turn out to meddle much more and share murkier boundaries with Philadelphia municipal government. If the primary purpose of the charter was to defend against Penn, then it achieved that goal, but it did so at the cost of effective protections against other layers of local government. Given that the major objective of the Charter of Privileges of 1701 had been to make the assembly the most powerful entity in Pennsylvania politics, this oversight fits with the prevailing tenor of the political reforms of 1701. The same men who sought incorporation for Philadelphia believed in the supremacy of the legislature; they did not see it as ever presenting a problem to local government, and they saw no reason to limit its reach.

In addition, the structure set up by the charter did not create an effective system to deal with local infrastructure and services—critical matters such as poor relief, street maintenance, the town watch, or the regulation of public spaces like the market. In some respects, this omission seems surprising. It happened for two reasons. First, the overwhelming objective of the municipal charter was to protect individual and communal property against Penn; other considerations therefore took a back seat. Second, by 1701 Philadelphians had gone without centralized municipal services for nineteen years. They had found other ways of dealing with matters such as record keeping, poor relief, and education, primarily through their religious societies, especially the powerful Quaker Meeting. Even some street repair had been undertaken by independent actors. These mechanisms were not always ideal, particularly in the upkeep of common property such as wharves and markets, but on the whole elite Quakers were satisfied with the dispersed provision of services that already existed. They retained more power and could tailor social services as they wanted through their own efforts, rather than ceding all power for social services in city government. Their determination not to yield to government responsibility for at least one service, education, became enshrined in one of the other charters Penn signed dockside just before leaving: a charter incorporating the Quaker Free School forever as "the Overseers of the Publick School founded in Philadelphia at the Request Cost and Charges of the Pepole [*sic*] of God Called Quakers." The Philadelphia Corporation would never in its history have a direct hand in local schools, though this was a service that many contemporary English towns and cities did provide.[22]

That the Philadelphia Corporation was never set up or expected to provide substantial public services is made most clear in the fact that its charter did not give it the clear power to tax. Technically, the Philadelphia Corporation had the power to make "so many good & Reasonable Laws . . . [as] shall seem Necessary & Convenient for the Government of the said city," which might be interpreted to include taxation. However, without an explicit grant in its charter, the corporation never felt empowered to take this step. In 1706, five years after incorporation, the freemen recognized the weakness of the corporation and petitioned William Penn, the assembly, and Provincial Council to strengthen the corporation and give it increased power to repair streets and wharves, regulate building, control stray animals and slaughterhouses, suppress vice, and, most importantly, "rate and levy such Taxes as shall be needful for that Service." Despite a promise to do so, the assembly never acted to strengthen the corporation or give it the power to tax.[23]

The explicit revenue powers given the corporation included membership fees for becoming a freeman/woman, rents from a twice-weekly market and a biannual fair, rents from public wharves, wharfage (only to be charged nonresidents, and set at one shilling per ton), and the right to impose fines on lawbreakers. The bulk of the waterfront was to "be Left open & common" with all residents retaining the "Liberty to Digg Docks and make Harbours." Moreover, the charter mandated that all vacant land in the city limits "remain open as a Free Common of Pasture for the use of the Inhabitants of the said City until the same shalbe gradually taken in order to Build or Improve thereon." Over time the city did gain monopolies over three ferries over the Schulykill and Delaware Rivers. These revenues, though not insubstantial, paled in comparison to those of many other cities, like Bristol or New York City, whose municipal corporations were able to provide extensive services or use their capital as collateral to raise loans for still more services.[24]

The Philadelphia Corporation was the brainchild of a constituency most concerned about protecting property rights and standing against Penn; accordingly, they created it in the pattern of medieval English town corporations carving out rights against a local lord. The authors of the city charter deliberately created a body that could stand against proprietary overreach but that would not be invested with power that might allow it to stand against the assembly. They endowed the corporation with limited economic clout, which in turn hampered its ability to oversee or compete with those social services to which local churches and particularly Quakers had already taken a hand. As a result, the corporation stood well positioned to withstand challenges from the executive branch, but not to resist other layers of government or to provide local services. Its long-term power and authority suffered as a result.

"To Serve in ye Militia": Contests over Duty and Authority
James Logan did not count himself a fan of the new Philadelphia Corporation. Penn's secretary and most trusted counselor and advocate in Pennsylvania, Logan reported early and often to his patron the "intrigue" perpetrated by the corporation. "This town's charter," he complained, "which should bind the people to thee, sets them so much for themselves, that there is too little regard paid thee, and scarce any to thy interest." It was intended instead, Logan thought, "to confuse all our courts and their proceedings" and put a stop "to the administration of justice." He fretted that the Mayor's Court claimed precedence over Philadelphia County judges and claimed that all fines, which formerly had gone to the proprietor, must now go to the city. A few years later his alarm had increased: "pray either destroy or humble the Corporation," he urged, "[they are] thy most backward friends in the Government."[25]

The fights over provincial rights and proprietary prerogative had by no means ended with the Charter of Privileges and Philadelphia Corporation Charter of 1701; the contest had merely changed in character. Now the new entity of the Philadelphia Corporation could participate in the fray—or find itself a football between partisans. Philadelphia witnessed passionate struggles over the power and rights of the governor vis-à-vis both the legislature and the new municipal corporation. Successive governors wanted to assert their primacy over a number of issues, including military defense, local police powers, judicial appointments, and the collection of taxes and fines. Equally intensely, Quaker elites mobilized their political institutions—now including the Philadelphia Corporation—to thwart executive power. The charter privileges bestowed on the corporation here proved a strong ground upon which to challenge Penn and his lieutenant governors.

The corporation spent much of its earliest years in a pitched battle—at one point literally—with the newly arrived governor, John Evans. Only twenty-six when he arrived in 1704, with no government experience, and a staunch Churchman, Evans was never likely to be popular among Quaker political elites, but Penn's supporters were at first impressed with his maturity, "beyond what could possibly be expected from his years," Logan thought. Very quickly, however, Evans would prove the reverse of what his allies had hoped: impetuous, fitful, and impolitic.[26]

Evans moved immediately "with all vigor" to institute a militia as both the English Board of Trade and William Penn himself had urged. England was by then two years into Queen Anne's War, and questions of imperial defense were pressing. When the war began, Pennsylvania's previous governor had attempted, with little success, to form a militia. Evans would surpass earlier efforts, which, however, would put him in direct conflict with Philadelphia's new corporation and trigger a debate about the nature of masculine rights and duties. Evans sought to build up the militia by offering Philadelphia volunteers exemption from the corporation's mandatory service in the city watch. This particular civic obligation of "watching" was irksome; often the corporation had to prosecute men for failing to take their turn keeping watch on the dark and often cold streets through the night. Corporation councilmen took Evans's promised exemption from the city watch as a direct affront to their authority and charter-given privileges, and they opposed it vigorously. The governor had no ability to relieve Philadelphia residents of their civic duty. The councilmen threatened to haul those who "Contemtuosly" refused to take their turn on the city watch—whether or not they were militiamen—before the Mayor's Court. "Under such discouragements" the next muster day saw few militiamen in the field. Evans responded furiously that "To serve in ye Militia is much more ye duty of ye subject than to watch." In this assertion, Evans drew on long-standing political theory that linked full political rights with a man's ability and willingness to bear arms in defense of his community. The city watch, while also a form of civic protection, could not compare with the venerable institution of the militia, believed by many to be the bulwark of English rights. Evans believed that militia volunteers should be rewarded, rather than forced to carry a "double Burthen" of service. Therefore, in defiance of the corporation, he convinced the Provincial Council to issue a proclamation repeating and reinforcing the exemption. By the summer, "three good companies" of militia were drilling in the city, but in protest, many Quakers refused to serve in the city watch as long as some men were exempted from the obligation.[27]

Tensions mounted still higher between governor and corporation in early fall as partisans on either side turned to physical violence. On September 1, 1704, Enoch Story's tavern witnessed a barroom fight over whether the governor could exempt men from their turn in the city watch. When the city watch itself arrived on the scene to keep the peace, the watchmen instead fell into an outright brawl with the tavern's well-heeled clientele, most of whom were supporters of Governor Evans. Adding to the scandal, the proprietor's own son William Penn Jr. was involved in the brawl. The younger Penn was visiting the province with an eye to moving there permanently, but after this event he disgustedly decided against it and also left the Society of Friends for good measure. The Mayor's Court attempted to back its watchmen by pressing charges against Enoch Story and his tavern patrons, including young Penn himself, but Story was able to petition the Provincial Council that the evidence against him had not been sworn on oath,[28] and Governor Evans accommodatingly invalidated the case.[29]

This disturbance of the peace, however, paled before the "great fray" that occurred two months later, again at Enoch Story's tavern. A city watchman tried to disperse after-hours drinkers at the tavern and began to beat those who were too sluggish or drunk to move quickly. Unfortunately for the watchman, a man named Solomon Cresson, Governor Evans was himself one of the late-night drinkers, and the outraged governor returned Cresson's blows and tried to march him off to jail. Runners must have alerted corporation officials of the altercation because suddenly the mayor, recorder, and one of the city aldermen burst onto the scene to defend the hapless Cresson. Rather than a peaceful resolution, the City of Brotherly Love was treated to the spectacle of an undignified and violent melee involving the governor, the city mayor, and their various supporters in which "several persons [were] injured." The next day the Provincial Council tried to dismiss the altercation as quietly as possible, ruling that the mayor, recorder, and alderman had acted only to "quell the disturbance," and hoping thereby to defuse a potential powder keg.[30]

The corporation refused to back down, however, and the next summer issued a public proclamation in the marketplace that every man must serve his time in the city watch without exemption. Angrily, Governor Evans called the mayor and aldermen before the Provincial Council, where, however, they stuck to their original proclamation. Evans responded by trying to use intimidation in the election that fall, marching his militiamen "with their Arms Drums and Colours" through the streets of the city to the polling place where the militia "treated [the voters] very rudely severall of them having their swords in their hands to the great terror and disturbance of the peaceable people there present." The result was a disputed election of the sheriff. The contest of wills continued that winter as the corporation constables went ward by ward, indicting at least forty men and two women who refused to serve in the city watch.[31] James Logan worried that all these altercations served to help the corporation, which he thought was winning ground and growing "very strong" through its stand against the governor.[32]

Evans, in the meantime, was losing ground through his own follies. He was determined at any cost to whip up support for his militia, which by the summer of 1706 was languishing for lack of volunteers—most of them scared off by the harsh actions of the corporation. He made one last desperate gamble to prove that Quakers' hostility to the militia stemmed from self-interest and cowardice. He arranged for two false reports (which he himself forged) to arrive in Philadelphia with news that French ships were sailing up the Delaware River and that they had already put the town of Lewes to the torch. In the midst of this manufactured crisis, Governor Evans "rode about the town with his sword drawn," urging men to arm themselves and muster together at Society Hill, the highest point in the town. The townspeople did not respond as he had hoped. Instead of arming themselves, they panicked. Residents tried to flee the city with their loved ones and possessions, only to find themselves blocked by Evans's partisans, who called them cowards. Others threw their possessions down wells "and all manner of holes, greatly to their damage," to protect them from theft by the imaginary marauding French. Meanwhile, the biannual fair, "which has become a general time for payments, was utterly discomposed," harming the local economy and causing "many private damages [that] will be long remembered." When residents discovered the ruse, as they very shortly did, the entire town united in their disgust of Evans. Even the militiamen themselves refused to serve in future, furious at being used as his dupes.[33]

The demise of the militia represented a victory for pacifist Quakers and for the corporation, which Evans had unwisely challenged by framing militia service as an exemption from service in the city watch. Evans had championed a militia, not only as a strategy toward defense, but as a way to build a base for his own political power, mobilizing and galvanizing a small but growing non-Quaker urban constituency. Moreover, he combined his attempts with an explicit effort to undermine the power and authority of the corporation, a snake's den of anti-proprietary agitation in his opinion. His disastrous attempts at a militia ended for forty years any attempt at military organization in Philadelphia; and not for another ten years after that would the government itself try its hand again at a militia, and only then under the gravest threat the colony had faced since its founding.

The defeat of a local militia, however much it might have been regarded as a triumph by some, had long-term consequences that went beyond defense or military preparedness. Evans had recognized the potential inherent in a militia for institution building, creating a power base outside the sway of local churches or the formal, Quaker-controlled political machinery of legislature, corporation, and courts. He would have used it for his own political ends, but the larger insight remained that a militia might provide a common space, a common rite for adult white men otherwise splintered among different religious and ethnic groups. Pennsylvania and Philadelphia alike boasted few common or centralizing rites or institutions. The shared service of the city watch might have served a similar function, but it had none of the history and tradition associated with militias.

Militia service formed the very basis of citizenship as understood by most contemporary Englishmen, and its absence in Pennsylvania called into question precisely what united political community. Theorists agreed that militias served a vital political function: protecting the people from the tyrannical overreaching of government at the expense of the liberties of the people. Moreover, militias proved the individual and collective virtue of male citizens willing to take up arms in defense of their community. In most of early America militias played a central role in defining a man's full civic participation in a community. As an institution, it served as a centralizing force, one that drew a community together. But in Pennsylvania, without a militia, and with a large Quaker population explicitly opposed to martial activity, male residents had no similar avenue to perform and express either civic virtue or their participation in a collective endeavor or identity.[34]

The defeat of Evans and his militia, then, represented a victory for pacifist Quakers and in the short term for the power and authority of the corporation, but its absence deprived the city of an institutional common ground. When matters of local defense became pressing decades later, military service would become the major flash point in debates about duty, rights, and citizenship; the city would divide sharply and painfully over an institution that in every other English colony functioned as an accepted part of public life.[35]

The corporation proved capable of withstanding the challenge Evans posed through his attempts at a militia for three reasons. First, its charter had been crafted with the limitation of executive power in mind; in its first test, the corporation had lived up to that promise and withstood a governor's attack on its privileges. Second, the corporation acted with and represented the interests of Quaker elites and the assembly, giving it critical clout. Third, and not least important, Evans helped considerably by alienating friend and foe alike. Although the corporation persevered in this fight, it was not as well equipped for other challenges to its powers or privileges because it had not been designed to be.

The Limits of Corporation Power

The corporation began with every intention of manifesting its organization and power. Among its earliest recorded business was an intention to draw up ordinances for the carters within the city, regulate the night watch, and oversee the infrastructure of the city wharves and streets. The aldermen took measures to determine the "true bounds" of the city and divided the inhabited area into ten wards for easier and better administration. They intended to erect such necessary public accommodations as a burial ground and "a pair of Stocks with a Whipping post & pillory."[36]

The mayor and aldermen moreover strongly asserted their judicial powers, particularly in matters pertaining to the regulation of taverns, the maintenance of streets, and public peace. The Mayor's Court arraigned three men for fighting in the streets in 1702 and two men and two women for cross-dressing publicly in the city streets at Christmastime (and John Simon for allowing them to revel at his tavern). The grand jury brought to the attention of the court such problems as boys stealing fruit from orchards, butchers throwing their offal in the streets, barbers cutting hair on Sundays, local dogs running loose to the danger of sheep, and "the Ill Consiquences of the great multtitudes of negros who commonly meet together in a Riott & Tumultios manner" on Sundays. The court inquired into the actions of Alexander and Mary Paxton for renting a house to John Lobot, "he being a Stranger," without ensuring that he had given the required security to the corporation for his good behavior while resident. The court moved to prevent five householders, one of them himself an alderman, from "making Incroachm[en]ts" on city streets. And the corporation supervised closely the licensing of tavern keepers, hauling a number of would-be tavern keepers into the Mayor's Court for operating without a license or in one case for "selling Rum to Negros & Others."[37]

The corporation's assumption of judicial powers did not go unchallenged. Governor John Evans, in addition to his machinations for a local militia, sought to undermine the corporation in favor of county officials, over whose appointment he had some control. In the fall of 1704 the county court saw fit to hold court in the city of Philadelphia, holding its session in the tavern of none other than Enoch Story, the governor's longtime supporter, hearing cases that should have come under the jurisdiction of the Mayor's Court. The Philadelphia Corporation protested the county justices' "interfering" and making "Incroach-

ments upon our ffranchise." The assembly came to the defense of the corporation in a related matter, resolving that only the city magistrates, and not county
justices, had the power to oversee local tavern licenses.[38]

Quickly the assembly emerged as the dominant local power broker. If the
assembly was disposed to back the corporation in judicial matters, and particularly in its fight with Governor Evans, elsewhere it siphoned powers away from
Philadelphia's municipal corporation. The assembly was little more answerable
to the residents of Philadelphia than was the closed and self-selecting corporation. Only two of its members represented the city; the rest answered to the
rural counties. Benjamin Franklin later ran up against this problem when he
and others petitioned the assembly for funds for a hospital in 1751. "The Country Members," he remembered, "did not at first relish the Project. They objected
that it could only be serviceable to the City, and therefore the Citizens should
alone be at the Expence of it." Legislators spent time in the capital city and were
not insensitive to its needs, but their first responsibility always remained their
own tax-averse constituents. These considerations affected their treatment of
Philadelphia, causing them to hesitate or refuse to spend funds at all, as Franklin found in 1751, or to massage legislation in other ways. For example, in 1762,
when the assembly finally set up street paving in Philadelphia, it mandated that
Philadelphia taxpayers foot the bill for the expensive project, but also directed
that the first roads to be paved should be those "that are most used by the country in bringing in their produce and effects to market." The assembly asserted its
power early by carving powers up among different bodies, all of which had jurisdiction in the same city. Two of the earliest of these commissions gained some of
the economic power the corporation itself lacked and so desperately wanted.[39]

Very early the Philadelphia Corporation's limited formal revenue streams
proved inadequate to its needs. In 1710 when the corporation decided to build
a new marketplace, it had to rely on contributions that would later be repaid
with interest out of the rents from the market stalls. But as this building project
demonstrated, the lack of reliable income hampered the ability of the corporation to act. The city needed a workhouse, a courthouse, wharf maintenance,
road repair—these could not be financed by the paltry city funds or by loans
without some clear strategy of how to repay investors. The city marketplace
might raise money, but a workhouse or wharf repair almost certainly would not.
For example, a proposal in 1713 to collect subscriptions for a public jail failed
utterly—it was not a good investment that would attract subscribers, and public
spiritedness could go only so far.[40]

The corporation petitioned the assembly for the ability to tax city residents
directly, but instead in 1712 the legislature set up a separate commission to han-
dle taxes. The assessors, as the tax collectors were called, had originally been set
up in 1700 before the city had been incorporated, to operate at the county level.

In 1712 the assembly extended the assessors to the city as well. Charged with assessing and collecting each resident's taxes, the six city assessors were elected annually. Unlike the corporation, with whom they worked closely, the assessors thus answered directly to city voters. By 1712 the number of men qualifying themselves as freemen (and thus part of the Philadelphia Corporation) had already dropped precipitously—within five years no one would qualify as a freeman who had not been appointed to the council. Perhaps taking note of this trend, the assembly refused to vest the power to assess taxes in a body so utterly divorced from public oversight. The city assessors were charged with meeting with the mayor and aldermen annually and together deciding what the expenses for the coming year would be and what taxes should be charged—but it was up to the assessors to determine how much each household owed and to collect it. This responsibility explains why it was so important that they be elected officials rather than part of the closed corporation. If residents felt they had been unfairly assessed, they could elect new men the following year.[41]

The assembly passed another bill for the entire province in 1706 setting up Overseers of the Poor in Philadelphia and each of the counties to administer poor relief. The overseers had the power to decide who was and was not eligible for poor relief, and in order to meet their expenses, they too received the power to tax local residents. Despite this power to tax (which they would do with increasing frequency as the century progressed and the poor rolls ballooned), the overseers were appointed, not elected, to their positions. On balance the assembly seems to have decided that in order to fulfill their responsibilities, these officials would be better off *not* answerable to their neighbors. In the counties local magistrates named them, but in Philadelphia the mayor and aldermen held that power. Still, once appointed, these officials acted relatively independently. The corporation retained the power to audit their accounts and had to be consulted on some matters, but overwhelmingly the overseers remained independent and increasingly powerful over time, eventually taking over control of the city almshouse in 1749 and wresting from the corporation any control over the poor in the city. Already in 1718 the assembly had incorporated a separate body to run the city's public workhouse rather than leave that power with the corporation. Parceling out to independent commissions responsibility for local poor relief diminished the role for the Philadelphia Corporation in everyday local governance, just as it was starting out.[42]

While the assembly reduced the corporation's power from above, the householders of Philadelphia themselves reduced its authority from below by refusing to participate in it. To qualify as a freeman in the Philadelphia Corporation, a man had to be over twenty-one, a free denizen of the province, with property exceeding £50, and a resident of the city for two years. Conversely, he could purchase his freemanship directly from the corporation. The charter did not specify that women could apply for free status, but in the earliest years a few single female heads of household did so, probably to take advantage of the economic privileges that were supposed to (but never did) come with it. Stemming from medieval tradition, only freemen had the right to set up shop or sell their wares within city or town limits.[43]

After the corporation's first decade, it became clear that no commercial privileges or protections accompanied freeman or freewoman status. Quite simply, the corporation had no ability to enforce an economic monopoly for freemen. Increasingly inhabitants refused to apply for or purchase freeman status or respect the special privileges of those who had done so. After a concerted membership campaign by the corporation in 1717, no evidence exists for new freemen joining unless they had been elected to the Common Council and had to become a freeman retroactively to qualify to hold the office. For the rest of the corporation's history, the city's freemen were coterminous with the Common Council. There was thus no separate body of freemen to which the corporation could answer had it chosen to do so. The decisions of the corporation would affect all residents, whether freeman or "inhabitant," particularly through the regulation and fees for the market and wharves, but no sense prevailed that inhabitants should therefore have input; they were not party to the privileges of corporate membership.[44]

This general indifference to participating in the Philadelphia Corporation created something of an impasse in local government. The city founders had crafted a municipal corporation for which the vast majority either did not qualify or simply did not care to join. As a result, the corporation, which might otherwise have been more representative, foundered. It had a grant of authority from its charter, but no legitimacy from below. The corporation was thus limited in its ability to resist the assembly parceling out to other commissions responsibility for tax collection, poor relief, and the local workhouse. Over time the assembly would insert itself increasingly in local city affairs and siphon off still more powers to newly created commissions. Whatever ambition the early corporation members had manifested to govern matters from road maintenance to the prices charged by carters, they found themselves powerless to resist the encroachment of the assembly without clearly delineated charter rights to assist them or a sustained groundswell of local support to press home their claims against a legislature gifted with both a strong charter and popular legitimacy.

"Charters here have been . . . of fatal consequence," James Logan complained in 1704; "some people's brains are as soon intoxicated with power as the natives are with their beloved liquor, and as little to be trusted with it." Logan, a devout proprietary supporter, understood that the Philadelphia Corporation was set up in 1701 mainly as a bulwark to withstand proprietary privilege and executive power. In that capacity, it worked. It proved more than capable of putting up a rousing fight with Governor John Evans over the matter of a militia. It also successfully defended its charter privileges of local magistracy and judicial control over the city, dispensing justice and ensuring that no appointees of Penn or his governors meddled in the Mayor's Court's jurisdiction. However much its origins shaped and empowered the corporation in these matters, in other ways the corporation found itself sharply limited by the kind of institution it had been created to be. From its origins it had ignored the concerns of a vital, if minority, constituency that worried not so much about defending property rights from Penn as about defending political rights from a powerfully entrenched Quaker political elite. Set up to defend against the executive, the Philadelphia Corporation contained no clear boundaries against intrusion by the powerful assembly, which soon enough asserted its supremacy by delegating local powers to separate commissions. With limited economic resources and no ability to tax, the corporation was never set up to govern comprehensively. It could not provide necessary local services, which undermined its connection and legitimacy with local residents, who very quickly stopped participating in the corporation even through the limited capacity of freeman or freewoman. The lack of a political base in turn further weakened the corporation's ability to assert itself against the assembly.[45]

The origins, creation, and rapid political decline of the corporation after its first fifteen years left Philadelphia with a gaping hole not unlike the one in the city "center" so assiduously promoted by Penn in the 1680s. The urban map could not be changed; it included a city center that the people of Philadelphia themselves never used, but the streets still led there all the same. By the same token, the city charter of 1701 mapped out the urban civic landscape but placed at its center the Philadelphia Corporation, an institution without the capacity or economic resources to govern but still vested with responsibility for vital urban infrastructure such as the wharves, ferries, markets, and local administration of justice. Already before the beginnings of the corporation, other entities, namely, churches, had carved out places for themselves on this civic map, providing services otherwise unmet. Shortly after the creation of the corporation, new institutions filled out the landscape, empowered by the assembly to take over responsibilities the corporation found itself unable to fulfill. In the following decades, as an act of necessity and stemming from a strong tradition that went back to the first founding, an increasing number of voluntary associations would join churches and state-created organizations, altering and decentering Philadelphia's civic landscape still further.

CHAPTER THREE

For a General Benefit

Developing Popular Voluntary Associations

On a cold Sunday morning in October 1723, the history of Philadelphia took an unexpected but decisive turn. A teenager, exhausted and bedraggled, stumbled from the waterfront into the city, in search of food and lodging. His entrance caused little notice, though his future wife would always remember the bizarre figure he cut in his filthy clothes, with a puffy loaf of bread tucked under each arm and devouring a third loaf as he wandered along the unfamiliar streets. Benjamin Franklin had arrived in Philadelphia. He may have entered with little fanfare at the age of seventeen, but within a few decades he would be his adopted city's and then his nation's most famous resident. Franklin changed Philadelphia indelibly. As a printer, as a civic organizer, as a politician, even as a scientist, he did more than any other individual in his generation to shape the city.[1]

If Franklin's arrival in Philadelphia that October morning changed the city forever, his new home changed him too. As important as Franklin was to Philadelphia, Philadelphia was vital to shaping Franklin's life and opportunities. In contrast to Boston, where his older brother had already once fallen afoul of authorities through his printing activities, or crowded London, where Franklin also traveled and which had a much more established civic infrastructure, Philadelphia proved to be the place where Franklin's civic spirit could effect real change, where he could apply his talents and innovations to pressing local problems, where his ideas met a receptive audience and inspired collaboration.[2]

Franklin landed in Philadelphia, moreover, at a particularly propitious moment, amid intense change as Philadelphia grew from a town into a city—soon to be the largest in British North America. The community that Franklin meandered through in 1723, munching his bread, had nearly doubled in one decade, growing from 2,465 in 1709 to 4,885 in 1720. Then it nearly tripled by 1751 to almost fourteen thousand residents. "Wherever I went," one visitor commented, "I found everything come up to, or rather exceed the Character I had often heard of Philadelphia." Another marveled at the rate of growth in the city, noting the rapid construction of new houses, and concluding that the city was "likely to increase in inhabitants every day." Yet another observer thought that Philadelphia "surpasses belief (when we consider that there were scarce any houses there about 90 years ago)." The population growth did not, however, dramatically change the physical contours of the city. Newcomers like Franklin were no more willing than older residents to live more than a few blocks away from the vital Delaware River. Instead, they squeezed themselves into the existing footprint, making the tiny settled space of the city intensely crowded, with "buildings as close together as in most places in *London.*" In 1748 alone one visitor estimated that 120 new buildings had been jammed in "between dwelling-houses, warehouses, and store-houses."[3]

The population growth and physical compactness of the city demanded innovative solutions to civic problems. By the second quarter of the eighteenth century Philadelphians focused their attention on three: poor relief, educational opportunity, and fire protection. Existing state and church infrastructure proved unable to meet these needs, so Philadelphians pioneered a new civic technology that could: voluntary associations.

Through their civic voluntary associations men created a formal mechanism to pool their collective energies toward education and fire prevention in the city. They did not invent their associations from scratch, but built upon British models and Quaker religious structures. Philadelphia organizations, moreover, depended on trends that made voluntary association popular in the eighteenth-century British Atlantic world, including urbanization, cosmopolitanism, and the consumer revolution. However, as much as their civic associations moved in tandem with a larger British fashion of club sociability, Philadelphians exercised tremendous innovation in both the form and function of their organizations. They created something new: a fresh set of tools, skills, and practices through which to organize men (and tangentially women) to shape public affairs in a long-term, systematic way outside of either church or state. They were both pushed into and able to engage in this new collaborative mechanism because the decentered nature of Philadelphia governance left at once many civic needs unmet and a great deal of latitude for nongovernmental activity. Having long ceded substantial responsibility for social services to religious organizations, the formal state did not interfere when nondenominational voluntary associations also stepped into the void. And as long as voluntary associations pursued projects that boasted broad public consensus, like fire protection or the foundation of a library, government authorities, clergy, and Philadelphians in general not only allowed but celebrated their activities.[4]

The Limits of State and Church

Neither the structures of formal government nor the numerous religious organizations in Philadelphia could provide a central, all-encompassing framework to address local needs for services. As detailed in the previous chapter, the municipal corporation, which in other British towns and cities might play an active role in local affairs, in Philadelphia could not effectively wall off its powers and prerogatives from the provincial assembly. Within a decade the assembly had already hived off numerous responsibilities among a number of government commissions, a trend that would only continue as the century progressed. The corporation's weakness was moreover exacerbated by its lack of basic economic powers, such as the ability to tax and the absence of legitimizing grassroots support from below. Every religious denomination except the Quakers, meanwhile, was at this time too preoccupied in building the tangible and intangible infrastructure for their churches; they had few resources left over for social programs. The Society of Friends, by contrast, had extensive power to provide a range of services, but they sharply restricted their resources to their own membership. Even if any of these religious groups had attempted greater outreach to help people of other faiths, interdenominational suspicion and hostility would have limited the reach of their efforts.

The shortcomings of the existing infrastructure were cast in sharp relief by the provision of poor relief, an essential local service. Haphazard administration and overlapping authority by various governmental bodies hampered the state's efforts. The Overseers of the Poor, first set up in 1696 to assist the needy, faced serious limitations. The assembly did not originally give it sufficient funds. By 1700 the overseers complained they were "out of Purse" £42 and needed to be reimbursed. Five years later they had no money at all and city mayor Griffith Jones had to supply money "out of his pocket" to cover immediate expenses. Finally, in 1706 the assembly gave the overseers the power to assess taxes for poor relief and distribute funds to the needy. Now the overseers possessed many of the responsibilities that would have belonged to town selectmen in Boston or parish vestrymen in Virginia, yet the law limited them to giving money or goods directly to the poor, and only those poor first certified by corporation magistrates as being truly in need.[5]

The overseers, moreover, lacked an essential power: they did not administer the institutions that were soon built to house paupers. Contemporary poor relief practice dictated against the distribution of money and goods alone, known as "outdoor relief," and emphasized instead the importance of putting the poor into institutions—workhouses if they were able-bodied, almshouses if not. Philadelphians endorsed this kind of thinking and demanded such institutions, but once they were built, the Overseers of the Poor administered neither. The municipal corporation first moved to provide for a workhouse as early as 1712. However, five years later the assembly supplanted the corporation when it passed a law requiring the city and counties to build workhouses paid for by public taxation. Each locality would choose a president, treasurer, and assistants who would be legally incorporated and henceforth entirely responsible for the workhouse. The assembly gave the officers of the workhouse corporations the ability to direct local assessors to collect taxes. In Philadelphia, moreover, to defray costs, the assembly assigned to the workhouse corporation all revenues arising from a new ferry between the city and New Jersey. When it came time to build and administer an almshouse, however, the assembly again passed over the overseers and assigned responsibility to the municipal corporation. In 1729 the assembly loaned the corporation the extraordinary sum of £1,000 to build an almshouse, which was accomplished by 1734. However, the corporation aldermen, saddled now with an enormous loan they had no immediate or foreseeable ability to repay, lamented that the new almshouse had "in nowise contribute[d]" to reduce the cost of poor relief.[6]

As a result of this division of labor, a fair amount of confusion reigned about precisely which government bodies were responsible for which aspects of poor relief. In 1734, when the corporation members complained about the "Excessive Charge" of poor relief, they were in charge of the almshouse, but they had no idea how many poor people were on the public poor rolls. Only the Overseers of the Poor had that information, and they alone determined whether the poor should get outdoor relief or be forced to go into the workhouse or almshouse, which most people resisted. The overseers, meanwhile, spent money, but they were not obligated to raise it or to deal directly with grumpy taxpayers. That duty belonged to the assessors, who in consultation with the corporation found themselves saddled with the task of raising funds whenever the overseers indicated they needed more. The assessors and corporation had no say in dispensing these funds—indeed, only the overseers even knew the status of their accounts. The corporation thought that putting more of the poor in the almshouse would reduce costs, but it could not compel the overseers to do so.[7]

The divergence between the corporation officers and the overseers about how best to relieve the poor may have arisen from their different class backgrounds. The aldermen and common councilmen of the corporation numbered among the wealthiest and most prestigious men in the city. Overwhelmingly, they were merchants from prominent, well-connected families. The overseers, who were appointed by the corporation, were, on the other hand, mostly artisans and came from much farther down the social scale, with tax assessments that ranked them as "substantial, but not wealthy" men of the middle class. The disparity in their social status may have led the corporation members and overseers to a very different evaluation of how best to relieve the poor. The middle-class overseers were perhaps more sympathetic than corporation officials to the desire of impoverished people to avoid the degradation of confinement in the almshouse. Whatever the cause of their difference of opinion, because of their separate grant of power, the Overseers of the Poor were able to resist the cost-cutting reforms of the corporation, even though they had been initially appointed by that body.[8]

Part of the reason that governmental poor relief remained so unsystematic in Philadelphia was that the Society of Friends answered the needs of most of Philadelphia's needy, keeping them off public poor rolls altogether. The number of poor on public relief was quite small. In 1709 only fourteen "regular clients" received public aid on a weekly basis. Fifteen years later one resident boasted that "there are people who have been living here for 40 years and have not seen a beggar in Philadelphia."[9]

Friends could provide more comprehensive assistance to their impoverished members than was possible from the Overseers of the Poor, the municipal corporation, or the workhouse corporation. Quakers had a strong financial base thanks to regular subscriptions from its membership, a growing stock of money from bequests and other charitable contributions, and, increasingly, rents from various property holdings. Moreover, Friends boasted a powerful and interlocking meeting structure and a culture of visiting one another that allowed them to monitor members' behavior and circumstances closely. Quakers in good standing with the Meeting faced much less of a hurdle in requesting aid than did applicants for poor relief through formal government channels, where applicant and official were less likely to know one another or be connected through a dense personal and spiritual network. When Widow Griffith sustained considerable losses from a fire, others brought her case before the Quaker Monthly Meeting, which immediately determined to give her the considerable sum of £5 and commissioned two Friends to "Enquire into her Condition" and report back how she was at the next meeting. When William Southbee brought the news that John Sopas, "an aged poor man, that usually came amongst friends, was in great want," Quakers moved immediately to assist him. Moreover, the Meeting structure remained active in assisting widows to place their children in apprenticeships in good Quaker homes.[10]

The Society of Friends could by no means be characterized as a soft touch, however, and strictly limited its assistance to Friends in good standing. The

Monthly Meeting decided, for example, that Widow Finley did not "properly belong to us to be maintained," and moreover that she was "a healthy Woman & Able to work." Paul Sanders, his wife, and family of small children could expect no help until he produced a certificate from his previous Meeting attesting to his credentials as a good Quaker. Sanders did eventually obtain a loan from Friends, but he died without repaying it. Friends noted that Widow Sanders was "very poor" but still decided to confiscate her meager household effects to make up part of the outstanding debt, noting that she was known for "her disorderly walking and accompanying with another womans husband." They declared her "to be no member of our Religious community." Her small children merited no further mention in the meeting minutes and no further aid.[11]

Friends soon moved beyond traditional outdoor relief, establishing the first almshouse in Philadelphia. In 1702 John Martin, a tailor of modest means, left his house on Walnut Street to the Society of Friends for the use of the poor on the condition that the society would care for him in his old age. By 1706 the Monthly Meeting was allowing poor Friends a room in the house, and by 1713 the original house and a few other structures on the same property opened as an almshouse. Friends began contemplating building a new structure for an almshouse in 1727 and, with the aid of subscriptions and bequests, opened it in 1729, the same year the corporation began to think about building an almshouse of its own. Poor Quakers, often the elderly, could find refuge here, and instead of being divided into separate apartments for men and women, as was common in most almshouses, families could live together in private rooms. They were encouraged to continue to live good lives according to Quaker standards, working and attending religious meeting. Through the rest of the eighteenth century, Quakers in need could use this exclusive almshouse.[12]

Quakers hoped to forestall poor relief altogether with another program: the extension of small, interest-free loans. The practice had been used sporadically before but began to become more regular around 1712 when the Monthly Meeting loaned £6 to Mary Davis, who was in distressed circumstances, and £7 to Thomas Speakman to pay for his recent passage from Great Britain. The Meeting did not keep regular accounts of these loans, so it is difficult to gauge their full extent, but at least fifteen Quakers (three women, ten men, and one married couple) received loans between 1712 and 1730, usually from £1 or £2 to around £20. Often the Monthly Meeting extended smaller loans to Friends who suffered from poverty or sickness, but in some cases the loans were intended to help men set up their trades, such as Thomas Cannon, who received a loan in 1713 to establish a candle-making business, and Dennis Rachford, who got a loan a year later to set up his trade as a potter. A man appropriately enough named Robert Borrow received the largest loan of £22 to repay his creditors. The terms of the loans were never clearly articulated in the minutes, but it appears that though the Monthly Meeting expected to be repaid, it did not charge interest for these loans. Moreover, it rarely specified time limits for the loan, and even when it did, it did not press the issue. When Evan Thomas and his wife first arrived from Europe in 1719, they received a loan of £12 due after one year; only a full nine years later did the Monthly Meeting begin to talk of pressing the couple to get the money repaid. The Meeting urged tardy borrowers to pay their debts, so that they might recycle the funds into new loans "for ye use of other poor friends." The record of repaid loans, however, is scant, either because of lax accounting in the minutes, or because borrowers did not in fact repay their loans. Of the fifteen loans in this period, only two were definitely repaid: Hugh Clifton repaid within a year a small loan he received while he was sick, and, as discussed above, the Monthly Meeting seized some household effects of Widow Sanders to make up part of a loan given to her husband three years before, a move evidently more provoked by disgust at her personal behavior than motivated by financial considerations. Whether those other loans ever were repaid or represented a face-saving form of charity cannot be determined from the available records.[13]

Quaker organizational and economic strength allowed active investment in education as well, a project aimed at improving and protecting the next generation and giving the children of poor Quakers the tools they would need to provide for themselves one day. Friends had begun a school in 1689 and gained a charter for it just before Penn sailed in 1701, with the intention that it be free for the poor. Here they could ensure the "more pious & select education of the youth" in a carefully controlled environment and shield their children from "corrupting Connection[s]" with non-Quaker children. In 1702 Friends took steps to put their school on a more permanent setting. They started an ongoing subscription first to pay for a schoolhouse and thereafter to fund it. The same year they acquired a lot on High Street and erected a schoolhouse. By 1709 they had raised enough money for thirty nonpaying pupils of poor parents. In subsequent years, they would boast of the benefit of the school for the children of poor Friends and even admitted "as many of the Children of poor People of other Perswasions as our Stock will permit," though the Monthly Meeting expressed some concerns about mixing Quaker and non-Quaker children in the same classroom.[14]

Other religious denominations, though growing, could not match the strength and organization of Quakers, or provide anything like their social services. Churchmen in particular looked with jaundiced eyes on the extent of Quaker influence through their social programs. George Keith, now a minister in the Church of England, wrote bitterly of Quaker organizational and economic strength, seeing in them the ability to spread their religious message and bring "many poor People to their way, by their Charity." The Church of England was adding members rapidly but continued to rely on the largesse of a few individuals even as smaller contributions from large numbers of believers began to increase. Keith and others did not seek to reproduce the interlocking Quaker system of meetings that did so much to fund poor relief and education, but instead implored English clergy to supply Pennsylvania with more trained ministers and religious books with which to combat Quaker heresies. By 1703 the assistant minister, Mr. Thomas, had set up a school that a fellow Church-man described as a "very good success," but it had nothing like the number of pupils or the broad community support of the Quaker Free School.[15]

Rather than seeking to cultivate local sources of support, Churchmen looked back to England and the newly created Society for the Propagation of the Gospel in Foreign Parts (SPG). The spread and growth of Church of England congregations in the Delaware valley relied heavily on funds from the SPG, which had the unintended consequence of discouraging congregations from supporting their own ministers. Philadelphia Churchmen never established a strong local mechanism for enforcing internal discipline and doctrine, an institutional home in which ministers or vestrymen could gather to support one another and perhaps establish on a stronger basis services such as poor relief or education. Instead, Church of England elites endlessly petitioned the SPG and the archbishop of Canterbury to appoint a bishop to America who they hoped could bring about the order and strength they so palpably lacked.[16]

Baptists and Presbyterians were no more successful in competing with Quaker social services, but went considerably further toward creating local institutions that facilitated religious cohesion. The tiny Philadelphia Baptist Church could devote almost no resources to social services. Denominational organization focused instead on creating greater coherence and harmony within and among Baptist congregations in the Delaware valley. Baptists in 1707 formed the Philadelphia Baptist Association "for their mutual strength, counsel, and other valuable advantages." Formed along the lines of similar English organizations, the Philadelphia Baptist Association consisted of ministers, deacons, and elders, who determined the suitability of ministers, settled disputes, raised funds for ministerial education and for poor congregations, and maintained a religious library. It would have tremendous influence on Baptist congregations throughout the colonies. However, the scope of its activities would remain firmly doctrinal; it could never match the wealth, organization, or social programs of Quakers.[17]

Presbyterian organization in the early decades of the eighteenth century focused on internal doctrinal matters and creating an economic resource for religious personnel; only in a very limited fashion did Presbyterians pursue social programs akin to those of the Quakers. Presbyterian congregations in Philadelphia and the Delaware valley increased rapidly thanks to immigration, particularly from Scotland and Ireland. The Philadelphia congregation found itself on a more stable footing after it welcomed its first permanent minister in 1698, Jedediah Andrews, who would serve for nearly fifty years. In 1704 Presbyterians built their first church on the corner of Market and Bank Alley, which they would enlarge in 1755 and 1761. In 1706 to promote "the nearest Union & Fellowship" and address the "perishing Condition as to Spiritual things," ministers and elders formed the Philadelphia Presbytery, and then in 1716 in response to the proliferation of Presbyterian congregations they created the overarching Synod of Philadelphia. Unlike the Philadelphia Baptist Association, the presbytery and then the synod had direct governing power over the congregations in its domain. The presbytery and synod entered into minute and continual investigation of ministers to ensure doctrinal consistency and discipline, imposing a hierarchical organizational model on the denomination. Harmony prevailed through the 1720s because the synod never defined too precisely its theology, but controversy broke out after 1729 when one faction pushed through the Westminster Confession, a formal subscription of articles of faith to which another faction bitterly objected. Increasingly acrimonious debates in the next decade brought Presbyterians to the brink of open conflict.[18]

While the synod wrangled with matters of doctrine and faith, it showed more unity on another matter, setting up in 1717 "a Fund for pious uses" to be spent at the synod's discretion and that went primarily toward loans for ministers. Money and subscriptions came in quickly, as the synod encouraged clergymen to "apply their utmost Diligence" in raising funds annually in their congregations. Few individuals received direct aid from the fund, however. Five people—four women and one man—received small sums between 1717 and 1743. Larger sums went to congregations. In 1719 the committee in charge of the fund gave money to a congregation in New York "towards the support of the Gospel among them," and in 1737 it allotted £100 to help a group of Presbyterians build a new meetinghouse.[19]

The vast majority of the Fund for Pious Uses went not into direct aid, but beginning in 1719 to loans. In 1737, for example, the synod recorded that the fund consisted of only £11 in cash on hand for charity, while more than £500 was invested in interest-bearing loans. Between 1719 and 1741 the committee in charge of the fund made thirty-two loans to twenty-eight people, ranging between £1 and £190. Sixty-eight percent of loans went to Presbyterian ministers or elders. Half of the loans were for £10 or less, and all but one were for £50 or less. The single largest loan of £190 went to Joseph Harrison, a Philadelphia carpenter and member of the Presbyterian Church (though not an elder). The religious affiliation of six of the borrowers, one of them a woman, is unknown; these borrowers may have come from presbyteries other than Philadelphia. Two borrowers were definitely not Presbyterian; one was a Quaker and one belonged

TABLE 1
Loans Made by the Fund for Pious Uses, 1718–41

Recipient	Number	Percentage
Presbyterian ministers	16	57
Presbyterian church members	1	4
Non-Presbyterians	2	7
Unknown religious affiliation	6	21
Total	28	100

Source: Book of the Fund, "The Fund for Pious Uses," Day Book, 1718–55, Presbyterian Ministers' Fund, HSP.

to the German Reformed Church. Because of the nature of the records, it is difficult to determine what interest rate borrowers paid or what became of these loans. By 1741 only eleven loans had definitely been repaid (see table 1).[20]

The synod never spelled out the purpose for the "Fund for Pious Uses," but its primary function quickly seemed to be to provide an internal avenue for loans to Presbyterian ministers and lay elders in the presbyteries under the synod's control. These loans, unlike the charity of Quakers, did not go exclusively within the denomination, but they clearly went first and foremost to aid men high up in the hierarchy of the church. Even as they were bickering among themselves over matters like the Westminster Confession, Presbyterian ministers had created a relatively exclusive reserve for small or large loans as they needed them. The loans went to ministers who found themselves on opposite sides of their internal doctrinal dispute. Later, when schism would rend Presbyterian unity, one of the grounds of dispute would be continued access to these funds. It is unclear how the ministers represented the Fund for Pious Uses to their home congregations, which supplied the money for it, but from the beginning its main work was to supply funds for the hierarchy of Presbyterian religious personnel, not to supply the needs of poor relief or education or to give small loans to poorer folks in the denomination, as was true among Quakers.[21]

Even where churches might have liked to arrange for social services for their own members or more broadly, they faced logistical and legal hurdles, the most important of which was the difficulty of holding property in common. Because they were not legally incorporated, churches could not own property, a right inhering in English law only to individuals. Instead, trusted members of the congregation held property in trust on behalf of the church. This strategy, however, could lead to problems when men died or broke from the church, as had happened to the Quakers during the Keithian Schism in the 1690s when one of their trustees, Robert Turner, had left the society for good but still legally shared control of its meetinghouse. Three times between 1705 and 1715 the Pennsylvania Assembly tried to alleviate this problem with legislation to allow religious societies to hold property in common, but British authorities repealed the laws.

One problem was that such legislation gave rights and powers to Pennsylvania religious societies which they did not possess in England.

Something had to be done, however, as became clear in 1731 when the Church of England asserted that it had "a just Right and Title" to the lot and building in which the Baptists met, and tried to seize it. This extraordinary claim rested on the fact that the last surviving trustee of the Baptist meetinghouse had converted to the Church of England before he died, and in his will he conveyed the structure to his new denomination. Philadelphia Baptists protested vigorously, convincing the assembly of their superior claim to the church they had paid for "by voluntary Contributions among themselves." The incident moved the assembly to try once more—and at last successfully—to pass a law "for the better securing the several religious societies in the quiet and peaceable possession of their churches, houses of worship, school-houses and alms-houses and burying grounds." This law, however, merely protected churches from trustees who might try to sell or convey church property against the intent of the original trust; it did not incorporate churches or allow them to hold property in common. In short, once churches managed to establish themselves on stronger organizational and financial foundations, they would continue to face limits in their ability to provide social services in the city.[22]

In the first half of the eighteenth century, newcomers flooded into Philadelphia, piling on top of one another and forever changing the demographics of the town away from Quaker numerical dominance. The mechanisms that had evolved to provide services for the city could not answer the needs of this growing community. State functions remained too dispersed and weak. Most churches, which might have stepped in, were focused on building and strengthening internal denominational organization. None but the Quakers had the wherewithal to offer extensive social services, and they focused their efforts on their own members, a shrinking proportion of the overall population. Even where organizational clout existed among churches, uncertain or cumbersome legal apparatus for joint ownership of property might hinder civic activities. The field remained wide open for other accommodations.

"Intended for a General Benefit": The Invention of Civic Voluntary Associations

Benjamin Franklin was obsessed with Philadelphia's dramatic population increase—and that of America in general—throughout his life. He understood the rising numbers as evidence of the strength of the American political economy and used population statistics as evidence of the increasing power and importance of the colonies. In 1749 Franklin and eleven others took it upon themselves to survey Philadelphia and count all the dwelling houses. They were delighted with the results, publishing them in Franklin's *Pennsylvania Gazette*.

When they remembered that "It is but a few Years . . . since this Country was a Wilderness," they marveled at the alteration "even within the Memory of Man" into a "flourishing City" with 2,076 houses, "Places of Worship and other Publick Buildings, Warehouses, Work shops, and other Out houses, not reckon'd." No government intervention had produced these changes; they had come about through private efforts, the result of liberty and "wholesome Laws with good Government."[23]

The city's growth occurred within the context of colonial population growth generally, but it also participated in a larger British Atlantic trend of urban expansion that affected England, Scotland, Ireland, and much of North America —Franklin's hometown of Boston being one of the rare exceptions of a city that stagnated rather than grew. Urban growth was both effect and cause of economic expansion and diversification as manufacturing and trade flourished.[24]

Urban expansion helped stimulate the rise of voluntary associations in Philadelphia as it did in other British towns and cities. Population growth provided a critical mass of potential members, while in Philadelphia as well ethnic and denominational diversity encouraged new templates other than churches around which to organize. The growing city provided ever more spaces for these new organizations to meet; by midcentury Philadelphia had 101 licensed taverns, one for every 135 city residents, and the number continued to keep pace with the rising population. Soon the center for the wheat and provisions trade in North America, Philadelphia enjoyed mercantile success that spurred economic diversification and craft specialization in the city, which in turn afforded a relatively broad distribution of wealth. Prosperity led to disposable income, which in turn expanded the economy, providing economic opportunities for larger numbers of artisans and shopkeepers and affording them the means to participate in voluntary associations.[25]

At the same time that the physical growth of Philadelphia provided potential members, wealth, and an urban landscape in which to operate, residents began to conceive of their city as a cosmopolitan center of culture, contributing to the British Atlantic world of ideas and refinement. In this Philadelphians participated in a larger English phenomenon of "urban renaissance," in which urban residents asserted a central role for towns and cities as places of fashion and "cultural prestige" contributing to the rise of politeness and civility. "I see no Reason, except our own present Poverty," declared one hopeful Philadelphian in 1737, "why Philadelphia should not (as well as any other place in the West Indies) be the Seat of Literature." Many shared his aspirations for the city. Some hoped Philadelphia would become "the future Athens of America." Others hoped to see Philadelphia become "the Seat of Sciences" and "the Edinburgh of America." Invoking classical Athens or contemporary Edinburgh, Philadelphians consciously sought to craft and represent their city as a cosmopolitan center of learning and refinement surpassing any other city in America and on par with those in Europe.[26]

As a marker of status, club membership fit within the impulses behind the rising trend of consumption and display of luxury goods that accompanied the early modern consumer revolution. Many joiners hoped that the status and prestige connected with voluntary associations would be conferred not only on their city but on themselves as well. Urban density and rising tides of newcomers contributed to "social confusion" in a society very much concerned with rank and status. Participating in voluntary associations, then, advertised not only urban but personal cosmopolitanism, refinement, and gentility. One observer, for example, argued that members of the Library Company of Philadelphia, whatever their occupations or class status, might nonetheless be characterized as "the *better Sort* of People" by virtue of their commitment to reading and self-improvement. Participation in some organizations entailed public displays such as parades or particular markers of dress, such as the distinctive aprons of the Freemasons, which set members apart and proclaimed their participation in exclusive organizations.[27]

Philadelphia's first voluntary organizations founded in the 1720s and early 1730s followed patterns of organization similar to those popular in England, promoting sociability, celebrating ethnic heritage, pursuing sport, and consolidating trade networks. The earliest known formal association[28] in Philadelphia was the Carpenters' Company, founded in 1724, which operated upon the model of old European guilds. Here elite master house builders of the city collaborated together to regulate prices to be charged for all kinds of building work and to support the widows and families of deceased members. Other early organizations followed English club precedents in promoting sociability. The 1729 Society of Ancient Britons had an annual feast to celebrate members' Welsh heritage on St. David's Day in a manner similar to contemporary British feasting and ethnic societies. Beginning in 1728, young, unmarried men formed the Bachelors Club. Scandal and gossip circulated about this group and their secluded clubhouse on the Delaware River, alleging that the seduction of young women occurred there. Other men imported directly a fashionable English organizational structure when the first Masonic Lodge in Pennsylvania was founded in 1731. The Freemasons operated through a federated structure that allowed them to create their own lodges and be incorporated under the umbrella of the larger organization, based back in London. Using the rites worked out by British lodges, Philadelphia Freemasons joined a brotherhood that spanned the Atlantic, gaining them entrée into lodge meetings in distant towns and new contacts in the form of visiting members from abroad—both contributing to the benefit of institutional and personal networks. Finally, in 1732 a group of wealthy Philadelphia merchants and artisans founded the Colony in Schuylkill, a hunting and fishing club. The organization engaged in a comedic parody of contemporary government enacted at feasts at the clubhouse on the Schuylkill River, in which they styled themselves an independent "colony" with its own government, and where no fish or game could be eaten but what had been caught by the members. These local organizations all paralleled forms current in England, participating in a rising trend of sociability under the auspices of clubs and associations, as well as, in the case of the Carpenters' Company, mutual aid.[29]

At the same time, however, a tight-knit group of young men on the make were beginning to rethink the format and possibilities inherent in voluntary association in Philadelphia. These men were members of a secretive organization that began meeting in 1727 called the Junto. Eager to supply by conversation his own lack of a college education, Benjamin Franklin convinced his "most . . . ingenious Acquaintances" to form "a Club for mutual Improvement." The twelve men of the Junto, almost all young men just beginning their careers, met once a week to discuss natural and moral philosophy and to provide one another with practical advice and support that might further any of the members' "honourable Designs." Each meeting began with a number of "Queries," ranging in tone from "Have you lately observ'd any Encroachm[en]t on the just Liberties of the People?" to "Hath any Body attack'd your Reputation lately, and what can the Junto do toward securing it?" Members discussed practical avenues for personal advancement, schemes for civic improvement, history, philosophy, and science. The Junto model had precedent in British forms, as rational and enlightened discourse became an increasing element in informal circles and formal associations alike. More immediately, however, the Junto originated in the ideas and experiences of Benjamin Franklin, who was deeply influenced by neighborhood benefit societies in his native Boston. The Junto was Franklin's earliest formal voluntary association, and it was to have enormous influence on many of the civic organizations that followed, in large part because the ideas and manpower behind many of them originated in the Junto.[30]

Despite the relative secrecy of the Junto, over time, more ambitious men wanted to join, but the original Junto members felt that the discussion was best preserved by limiting the group to twelve. Still, sensible that admitting more men would promote "our particular Interests in Business by more extensive Recommendations" and "Increase . . . our Influence in public Affairs and our Power of doing Good," the Junto members decided that each of them would start subordinate Juntos, and then the original members would report back what had been discussed in the subordinate groups. Franklin noted that "Five or six only were compleated," named "the Vine, the Union, the Band, &c." Together with the original Junto, this network of self-improving young men provided the basis for civic transformation in Philadelphia.[31]

Within four years the Junto moved to extend further its "Power of doing Good" by embarking on the first great civic organization in Philadelphia and arguably British America: the Library Company of Philadelphia. The Junto had been intended to serve as a "School of Philosophy, Morals and Politics," but a short-lived decision to pool together members' libraries ended quickly and with some acrimony. The brief experiment, however, inspired Benjamin Franklin to propose and Junto members to embrace a more comprehensive plan. The Library Company of Philadelphia, founded in 1731, pooled the resources of twenty-five initial subscribers who paid £2 each toward a common stock out of which books would be purchased, a librarian paid, and premises maintained. Each member paid an additional ten shillings toward the stock annually. Overseen by ten coequal directors and a treasurer who were elected annually, the library grew rapidly. The membership had tripled by the end of the decade, despite the fact that the price for a new share rose ten shillings each year. The earliest subscribers were primarily middle-class and elite men, mostly tradesmen and shopkeepers. In the early decades only one woman, Elizabeth North, owned a share in her own right (hers had been inherited from an uncle in 1742, and when she married in 1745 it passed to her husband), but the families of Library Company members enjoyed borrowing privileges, so wives, sisters, and daughters had access indirectly to the collection, though never a voice in governance. Nonmembers too could borrow books for a fee. As the share price rose over the years, newer members tended to come from the elite, who were the only ones who could afford to join. By the 1750s, very few new members bought shares for the related reasons that they had become so expensive and that another library, the Union Library Company, had formed in 1747 with lower prices.[32]

The first subscription library in history, the Library Company was one of the most important cultural institutions in colonial Philadelphia, continually seen by both Philadelphians and visitors as evidence of the intellectual progress of the city, province, and citizenry. It was the first institution in America to make books, still relatively costly and rare, widely available to a broad public. The directors intended their library to provide "a public generous Education" that would otherwise be unavailable in their city. The directors hoped their "valuable" books would "have very good Effects on the Minds of the People of this Province, and furnish them with the most useful kind of Knowledge, that which renders Men benevolent and helpful to one another." The primary objective of the Library Company was practical or "useful" betterment for its members, their families, fee-paying nonmembers, and by extension the larger community. To that end, the collection emphasized books of a serious stamp that the Library Company directors considered "useful." When their London bookseller, Peter Collinson, asked whether they would be interested in a book on metallurgy, for example, the directors declined because they thought that the book bordered on alchemy—the elusive attempt to transmute base metals into gold—and they feared "it's [*sic*] proving injurious to some who might be willing to spend more Time in it than they could prudently afford to spare, & with little Advantage, if any." The Library Company aimed "to propagate Knowledge, and improve the Minds of Men, by rendring useful Science and cheap and easy of Access."[33]

From the foundation of an institution that enriched the city's educational and cultural life, Franklin and his fellow Junto members moved to a more assertive project in 1736 when they tackled a pressing public safety problem that local government could not answer on its own: fire protection. Philadelphia, in common with all urban areas, suffered from devastating fires, which could spread rapidly in the particularly densely settled port city. Technically the municipal corporation ought to have taken the lead in organizing fire protection, as was the practice of local authorities in other American port cities. However, Philadelphia's municipal government simply could not seem to muster the funds or the leadership to do much. As early as 1711 the mayor moved that the corporation provide public fire equipment, including buckets, fire hooks, and a fire engine, but nothing more than the purchase of a single fire engine came of this proposal for twenty years. At last in 1730 the corporation proposed to undertake a public subscription to purchase fire equipment, and by 1731 it had acquired two more fire engines and 250 leather fire buckets imported from England. In keeping with its history, it had no place to house the fire engines and had to rely on churches and private help. The corporation proposed to keep one engine at the Quaker Meeting House, another at the Baptist church, and the last on a private householder's lot at Front and Walnut Streets. After this energetic spate, however, management of the subscription money floundered, and the corporation did little more than keep the existing equipment in repair and buy new buckets for the remainder of the colonial period. Franklin used his newspaper to goad the corporation to organize further, urging even that men be allowed to volunteer for firefighting in lieu of paying part of their taxes, but he met with no success. The corporation, with little power from above and little support from below, had done all it was going to do in an official capacity.[34]

Franklin took advantage of the vacuum to organize the Union Fire Company with nineteen friends and colleagues in 1736. Initially the fire company modeled itself as a mutual aid society. Each member committed to rally to "any of our Dwelling Houses" in case of fire, and to bring with him two leather buckets and four large bags to be used to transport goods out of burning buildings. Union made no provision for fighting fires in general or helping neighbors. Rather, each member kept a list with all fire company members' names posted near his door, specifying whom he was committed to help. Furthermore, Union acted as a kind of insurance policy on behalf of members' families, for members promised fire protection to each deceased member's widow as long as she maintained his buckets in good repair and sent them to fires when needed. The company limited its membership to thirty men on the premise that too large a group would not be efficient or effective, so the benefits of the Union Fire Company, at least on paper, did not extend far through the community. Within two years Philadelphians founded a second fire company on the pattern of the first, and four years after that a third company. The principle of self-help firefighting clearly resonated in Philadelphia.[35]

From the first, however, voluntary companies acted on behalf of the larger community, far beyond the confines of limited mutual aid. Early records indicate that the Union Fire Company fought fires whenever they broke out, not only when fire threatened members' property. By 1743 Union revised its articles explicitly. "This Association is intended for a general Benefit," the members agreed, and therefore "we do further agree, that when a Fire breaks out in any part of this City, though none of our Houses Goods or Effects may be in any apparent Danger, we will nevertheless repair thither . . . and give our utmost Assistance to such of our Fellow Citizens as may stand in need of it, in the same Manner as if they belonged to this Company." All fire companies for which records survive followed Union's example and extended their assistance to all in need, not just members.[36]

Making fire protection a "general Benefit" moved Philadelphia's fire companies firmly into the realm of civic activity, beyond the more sociable purposes of earlier city clubs like the Bachelors Club or the Colony in Schuylkill. The Library Company in 1731 had taken a step in this direction, aiming at the education and improvement of the community through the edification of an expanding reading public. The fire companies, beginning with Union, went further, assuming a public function that they would continue to fulfill until after the American Civil War, when Philadelphia's municipal government finally founded a professional fire department, the last major eastern city to do so.

The fire companies never formally limited their membership to men, but in practice, unlike the Library Company, only men were formal members. However, without ever formally belonging, women also played an important role in firefighting and the fire companies. Wives and widows maintained their husbands' fire equipment (those ubiquitous buckets and bags), sent the equipment to fires when their husbands were not present, and kept up their husbands' membership when they were away. Deborah Franklin, for example, maintained Benjamin's equipment and sent it to fires while he was in England for decades, keeping him a member in good standing in the Union Fire Company. Women even participated in one of the most important aspects of eighteenth-century firefighting: saving as much as possible of the household goods from destruction and helping guard it once it was out of the burning house. Still, though the fire companies relied tacitly on the activity of the female kin of their members, women never enjoyed recognition for their contributions.[37]

The Philadelphia fire company proved to be a readily reproducible template, and men embraced it eagerly. The total number of active companies had tripled by 1749 and then more than tripled again by 1769 to a total of twenty. The numerous fire companies worked together rather than engaging in the brawls made infamous in the nineteenth century. In 1747 for the first time the Union Fire Company proposed that all the fire companies appoint two members to a joint oversight committee that would "Enquire into the Condition of all the Fire Engines in this City." By 1749 the general committee was functioning, with members representing five out of the six existing fire companies. The committee lapsed and then was revived in 1767, now empowered actually to oversee fire engine repairs. Later, fire companies also collaborated on purchasing a fire bell for the city and a fire engine for the Pennsylvania Hospital and House of Employment. For all this cooperation, however, fire companies could not help but engage in a little friendly competition. The members of the Fellowship Fire Company, for example, could not refrain from noting proudly that at one fire where multiple companies had worked together, their fire engine had performed particularly well, "far Exceeding all others there," and eliciting the "Admiration" of onlookers.[38]

In Philadelphia private, voluntary firefighting proved to be the most popular, efficient, and cost-effective strategy to provide a service that would otherwise have gone unmet. Though not the policy initially advocated by Franklin himself, who had urged greater municipal involvement, ceding to private fire companies responsibility for firefighting enjoyed broad public support. Though it meant that private citizens[39] controlled fire protection, it also relieved taxpayers of a cost, and municipal officials of a responsibility, they either could not or did not want to bear.

Philadelphians had by 1736 pioneered two organizational forms that were unique to the city: public libraries and voluntary fire companies. The Union Fire Company modeled itself on the municipal fire companies of other cities, but was the first to organize independently of government authority. The subscription library model was indigenous to Philadelphia and would later be emulated thrice in Philadelphia and numerous times elsewhere.

Both were innovative, moreover, not just in purpose but also in form. The vast majority of contemporary British organizations adopted a hierarchical and often parliamentary organizational structure. The earliest sociable clubs in Philadelphia of the 1720s and early 1730s had adopted similar hierarchical structures. However, both the Library Company and the Union Fire Company, upon which all other fire companies were modeled, chose organizational formats that emphasized equalitarian and consensual governance rather than hierarchy. In this choice they reflected the influence of Quaker religion and institutions in Philadelphia and the number of Quakers who were members. Like Quaker meetings, the Union Fire Company had no officers. The position of clerk rotated among each member in turn, and all members voted on every decision at the monthly meetings. The result often led to confusion and inefficiency —the most extreme example being when one fire company could not locate its own fire engine because in his rotation a previous clerk had moved it and not informed the company. Whatever the drawbacks, all Philadelphia fire companies adopted a similar structure, prioritizing consensus and shared governance over more efficient but concentrated leadership. A larger institution, such as the Library Company, could not function with that model. The much larger scale of the organization—in membership, finances, and responsibilities (including buying books, hiring a librarian, and maintaining a physical space for the library)—necessitated a smaller governing body. Annually shareholders elected a board of ten directors who corresponded in some ways in function to Quaker Monthly or Yearly Meetings. The ten directors were completely equal in authority and responsibility, and they were charged with managing the affairs of the library. Such a strategy recognized the necessity for consolidated leadership and authority but spread it among ten coequal directors, rather than residing in a president and subordinate officers.[40]

Moreover, the library and fire companies relied on a broad base rather than on a single patron founder. Only one local institution was ever attempted through the patronage of an individual, and that was the Loganian Library, which turned out to be an abysmal failure. In the 1740s James Logan built a library near the newly erected State House to be filled with his own extensive collection of Greek, Roman, mathematical, and scientific texts; he intended both the library and the books to be bequeathed to the people of Philadelphia after his death, which occurred in 1751. The library never prospered, despite an annuity for a librarian and new books and the fact that, unlike the Library Company, all comers could use the collections for free. The trustees bickered among themselves, and the collection itself never appealed to the people to whom it had been left: one visitor to the city remarked that the books "mostly consist or treat upon Subjects out of the reach of the generality of people" and as a result "this Library has but few visitors." The Loganian Library limped along until it was shuttered during the American Revolution, only to merge with the Library Company in 1792. By contrast, the Library Company, which started with neither a building nor books, mobilized a broadly dispersed funding strategy that relied on the relatively small contribution of a wide number of members. This approach proved to be an important component of its success. The subscription-based Library Company succeeded in earning community support because it was born out of and responsive to Philadelphians' needs and wishes to a degree never matched by the free Loganian Library. Fire companies also relied on contributions from members, rather than elite patronage: members provided their own buckets and bags. Companies acquired more costly equipment, such as ladders, fire hooks, and fire engines, through the gradual accumulation of dues and fines.[41]

Thus, the two earliest civic organizations in Philadelphia which had an important influence on most subsequent civic voluntary efforts grew out of Philadelphia circumstances and did not conform to mainstream English patterns of organizing. Philadelphians created two organizations that had no immediate precedent elsewhere and that used organizational forms not common outside the Society of Friends. Certainly trends shared in common with the rest of the British Empire were vital—urban expansion, cosmopolitanism, the consumer revolution, the rising fashion of club sociability—but these circumstances by themselves do not explain the innovations Philadelphians pioneered in creating civic voluntary associations. The needs and opportunities of a heterogeneous, growing city with no strong central institutions—governmental or otherwise—served as vital ingredients in the mix.[42]

Both the library and fire companies were able to act so decisively because they enjoyed broad community support. That they would enjoy such support should not be taken for granted. Indeed, in the late 1720s James Logan, faithful supporter of the Penn family, had become deeply alarmed by rumors of Franklin's Junto, fearing that the secretive group was engaged in covert plotting on behalf of ex-governor Sir William Keith (they were not). Authorities like Logan could potentially react to autonomous voluntary association with concern or even hostility.

The Library Company and fire companies elicited no similar concern from formal authorities, but rather support. The municipal corporation probably looked on the fire companies with relief. Rather than contest the fact that the fire companies had usurped the responsibility of firefighting or try to bring them under government control, the corporation let the fire companies act as they saw fit. Indeed, rather than attempt to improve municipal efforts at firefighting, at least thirty-five members of the corporation were content instead to join fire companies themselves.[43]

The Library Company enjoyed more active support from government officials. Proprietor Thomas Penn, son and heir of William, offered the Library Company the rare but helpful instrument of incorporation in 1739, and over the years the Penn family made many valuable donations, including a pair of globes, scientific equipment, and a city lot on which to build a permanent home. The assembly likewise showered support, allowing the Library Company to operate out of rooms in the State House between 1739 and 1772. The directors, meanwhile, carefully maintained for the library a neutral position through whatever conflicts rocked the colony. In 1743, after a period of political discord between the assembly and Governor George Thomas, for example, the directors publicly addressed the proprietors, expressing their "hope [that] these Animosities will cease, and that Men of all Denominations will mutually assist in carrying on the Publick Affairs."[44]

Through the 1730s and 1740s the library and fire companies enjoyed the warm support of the community. On the tenth anniversary of the Library Company in 1741 Benjamin Franklin could boast that, "tho' 'tis compos'd of so many Persons of different Sects, Parties and Ways of Thinking, yet no Differences relating to the Affairs of the Library, have arisen among us." Instead, both within and without the membership of the library, "every Thing has been conducted with great Harmony, and to general Satisfaction." This "happy Circumstance," he hoped, would "always continue." In fact, the goodwill that made the Library Company and fire companies so harmonious depended on a broad public consensus that both types of organizations served a general benefit. It came as something of a shock, then, when soon enough some Philadelphians began to use civic voluntary associations to mobilize toward objectives that inspired no such consensus but instead provoked disagreement.[45]

CHAPTER FOUR

Amidst "Rancour and Party Hatred"

Association by Exclusion

The streets of Philadelphia rang out with unfamiliar sounds in the 1740s. In the beginning of the decade "one could not walk thro' the Town in the Evening without Hearing Psalms sung," the music wafting through the windows and doors of private homes. When not listening to the strains of piety lifted up in song, residents might be arrested in their progress through the streets by thunderous exhortations to eternal grace or perpetual damnation emanating from an impassioned, cross-eyed preacher standing on outdoor platforms and surrounded by thousands—if not tens of thousands—of hushed, eager listeners. By the end of the decade these sounds were replaced by others still more exotic in a city founded and largely influenced by Quakers. Now, a passerby might hear the measured tramp of men marching in unison and the barked commands of officers urging them through the manual of arms. Still more surprisingly, the auditor might hear *cheering* both from and for these drilling companies, an unexpected sound in a city founded and still peopled by pacifists. Accompanying each of these distinctive phenomena were grand concerts of more familiar sounds: hammering, sawing, planing, and the rumble of carts carrying lumber, bricks, and stone, which, by the volume of their din, indicated the furious pace of rapid and large-scale building projects never before seen in the city.[1]

Philadelphia was changing. As early as the 1720s it was no longer the "Quaker

City" of its origins but a mixed, heterogeneous place with residents of many different religious beliefs and ethnicities. Waves of immigrants from England, Ireland, Scotland, and Germany flooded to Pennsylvania, attracted by its religious toleration, peace, and the very real possibility of economic prosperity. They transformed both colony and capital so that the Quaker majority found itself outnumbered numerically—though the descendants of the first founders retained significant political, economic, and social clout. Other changes from afar shaped the city as well. William Penn died in 1718, and administration passed to his widow and executrix, Hannah Penn, until her death in 1727. Thereafter his sons, themselves no longer Quaker but instead converts to the Church of England, would govern the colony. Quakers reacted to these developments by closing ranks politically, forming after 1739 a united political bloc.[2]

The rising diversity intersected in the 1730s and 1740s with the articulation of a relatively new form of civic voluntary association. Though the city's increasing heterogeneity in no way automatically meant that the community would become a more contentious place—after all, the City of Brotherly Love had seen plenty of bitter acrimony in the 1690s, when the vast majority of the population was Quaker—the novel technology offered new opportunities for expressing and acting on difference. Philadelphians who disagreed with one another now had a distinct vehicle to move their differences of opinion out of the realm of words or ideas and into formal organization and concrete action. Unlike the Library Company or fire companies, however, these new organizations did not capitalize on broad public consensus, but used the techniques of civic association to operate in the absence of consensus, answering the ends only of its own constituents.

In the 1740s two civic projects made use of voluntary organizational strategies to pursue limited objectives that, however, only elicited support from part of the community. Each demonstrated the changing demographics of the city away from Quaker dominance, reflecting the needs and desires of other constituencies. The New Building, constructed in 1740, participated in and contributed to religious enthusiasm whipped up by the visits of evangelical preacher George Whitefield. Here was a project in which Quakers had no interest and which many Protestants, suspicious of Whitefield's message, viewed with outright coolness. Seven years later another sort of visitor—French and Spanish privateers threatening local shipping and perhaps even the city itself—provoked much deeper division. In the absence of any state response, unprecedented numbers of Philadelphia men from all walks of life formed the Defense Association, a voluntary extralegal militia. Though no one challenged its right to exist, the association prompted emphatic disapproval from devout Quakers committed to pacifist principles. These two organizations mobilized the technology of civic association in a new way, demonstrating how it could be used for divisive and even unpopular agendas set by constituencies, or even minorities, who were not answerable to anyone else. The circumstances that led to the construction of the New Building and the Defense Association, however, were of finite duration—by 1749 neither remained active, though each left behind major construction projects: a nonsectarian meeting space and two forts. In each case organizers had not consciously acted to shift the operation of voluntary associations from consensual public goods to projects of more limited appeal. Rather, they had pragmatically used the strategies of civic voluntary association toward specific goals.

Afterward, however, when civic-minded Philadelphians moved to found new and more ambitious long-term civic projects beginning in 1749, they found quickly that the level terrain that in the 1730s had facilitated broad public consensus toward civic projects had since then experienced tectonic shifts. Newly contentious provincial politics in the 1750s exacerbated suspicion, rancor, and hostility that spilled beyond purely governmental or political realms into social and civic endeavors. Attempts to found a nonsectarian academy and hospital for the poor, which might before have garnered considerable support, ran quickly aground on newly thrown-up shoals of discord. The strategies the New Building and Defense Association had pioneered as a matter of expediency took on new importance for future organizations, starting with the Academy of Philadelphia and the Pennsylvania Hospital, in navigating the ridges and valleys of a more divided city. Civic voluntary associations in Philadelphia would never again enjoy the kind of widespread support or harmony that had been possible in the 1730s.

Awakening Zeal: The New Building

Philadelphia was abuzz in November 1739, giddy over the arrival of the celebrated evangelical minister George Whitefield from England. Whitefield had a reputation for emotional sermons which had preceded him and aroused a populace eager to hear his words. Within days he preached to "a large auditory" at Christ Church, but found that demand exceeded the capacity of that or any other church. Philadelphians were "very solicitous" that he "preach in another place besides the church; for," Whitefield found, "it is quite different here from what it is in England. There, the generality of people think a sermon cannot be preached well without; here they do not like it so well if delivered within church walls." In less than a week, then, he preached about one hundred yards from the Christ Church pulpit but this time in the open air, "from the Court house stairs to about six thousand people" crowded below in High Street, spilling over north and south on Second Street, and even hanging out of windows, all in the most "profound silence" Whitefield had ever witnessed, hoping to catch his every word. For the remainder of this visit, Whitefield preached regularly both in and out of doors as long as the cold November weather permitted. "Surely,"

Whitefield wrote in reaction to Philadelphians' fervor, "God is favourable unto this people." His visit electrified Philadelphia and the region, provoking evangelical revivals and enthusiasm that captivated not only his own denomination of the Church of England, but Presbyterians and Baptists as well.[3]

Whitefield's visit, however, provoked passionate reactions not only in favor but also intensely against him. He stayed only a short time in Philadelphia on his first visit, traveling on within a few weeks to preach in other parts of America. When he returned to the city in April of 1740, the first news he had was that the rector of Christ Church "could lend me his church no more." The rector understood the power he wielded through access to his church, and he hoped to undermine Whitefield by withholding it. The revivalist had angered the Church of England hierarchy with his critique that its ministry preached too much reliance on the ability of individuals to effect their own salvation through good works. Likewise, Whitefield's visits had proven to be the final straw for the Presbyterian Synod, already straining under the weight of theological differences that had been stewing for a decade. Some Presbyterian ministers, notably the New Brunswick faction that centered on Gilbert Tennent, embraced much of Whitefield's message. In May of 1741 the Presbyterian Synod could contain the debate no longer and split into two rival synods, creating a lasting schism in the Presbyterian Church between "New Light" revivalists and "Old Light" conservatives.[4]

Undaunted by the contention, Whitefield continued to preach out of doors. At the end of his previous visit he had used an outdoor platform or balcony on Society Hill, the highest point in Philadelphia, and there he preached to crowds he alleged numbered as many as twenty thousand people. Now he returned there. As the Presbyterian Synod began to close ranks against revivalist ministers, Whitefield shared the use of his balcony with Tennent and his allies, giving them also the benefit of a platform (literally) from which to spread revivalist zeal. By this means, Whitefield and other revivalist preachers had seized a foothold not in any one church or private space of the city, but, bucking the authority of religious denominations, they had taken their message into the very streets of the city, staking a claim to the public sphere which no religious authority had the power to deny them.[5]

As much as they enjoyed the outdoor sermons, "Great numbers of the inhabitants" wanted a more permanent solution to the problem of churches denying Whitefield access to the pulpit. After all, in his first visit the previous November, the bitter cold had occasionally prevented him from preaching outdoors. They wanted "immediately" to build him "a very large church," but Whitefield demurred. He himself remained a minister of the Church of England, but doctrinally he wanted to de-emphasize sectarian differences and liturgy and instead focus on a community of reborn Christians, regardless of sect. He feared that building a church would provoke sectarian differences among his followers and cause them to "place the Church again, as they have done for a long time, in the church walls" rather than everywhere and in their hearts, where it belonged.[6]

Disregarding Whitefield's concerns, a group of his followers decided to construct a permanent space that would be open to preachers of any denomination and could also be used for a school. Contributors of all religious sects gave money rapidly and "promiscuously," making it possible within months for four representatives in September 1740 to purchase a large city lot on the edge of the city between Sixth and Seventh Streets on Mulberry (Arch) Street for "the use of a Charity School for the Instruction of Poor Children Gratis in useful Literature and the Knowledge of the Christian Religion and also for a House of Public Worship." Manifesting their zeal, the promoters had begun construction even before they had full legal title to the lot, and "the Work was carried on with such Spirit as to be finished in a much shorter time than could have been expected." By November, Whitefield was able to preach there, though the building did not yet have a roof.[7]

The "New Building," as it was called, was at once one of the grandest and yet most troubled spaces Philadelphia had ever seen. With the ambition to provide a space "for the Use of any Preacher of any religious Persuasion," it was the largest building in Philadelphia—larger even than the newly constructed State House. Measuring one hundred by seventy feet, and "sufficiently high for three lofty Stories," Franklin thought its dimensions on par with those of Westminster Abbey in London. Whitefield overcame his scruples and agreed to be one of the trustees of the building and Charity School. The other trustees were carefully selected "to avoid giving a Predominancy to any Sect" and thus included a member of the Church of England, a Presbyterian, a Baptist, and a Moravian.[8]

This intense ecumenical zeal, however, did not long endure. By the next summer, with the roof still missing, the trustees had to advertise, begging for further contributions to finish the building, "either in Money, or any Goods," or in donated labor. Whitefield preached for the last time there in 1746 before he returned to England, and though New Light Presbyterian Gilbert Tennent continued to preach there, the New Building had no regular source of income to pay its debts, let alone deal with upkeep or new expenses. By 1747 creditors petitioned the assembly for immediate repayment of their still-unpaid debts. The trustees could only beg that "the House would indulge them with farther Time," but by 1749 they could maintain their ambitious project no longer. The trustees were forced to sell the building for less than half of the £2,000 it had cost to construct in the first place. However, in the sale, the trustees stipulated that the original intent of the Charity School and space for itinerant preachers still be maintained.[9]

The construction of the New Building altered both the physical and the civic landscape of the city. Whitefield's supporters broke from the previously broadly consensual pattern of Philadelphia voluntary activity by pursuing a project that appealed only to a limited constituency. Founded outside the parameters of either state or church, and harnessing the contributions and energy of diverse individuals, it seemed to fit well within the parameters of projects like the Library Company and fire companies. However, unlike those organizations, the New Building did not enjoy the broad support of the community at large. Rather, it was founded in a moment of religious ferment and even schism. An ecumenical public space to foster revivalist religion did not appeal to many Philadelphians, and some were outright hostile to it. Quakers held themselves aloof from evangelical awakening and engaged little with Whitefield or his ideas, while for their part many Protestant churchgoers rejected his preaching outright as wrongheaded and dangerous. Even those Philadelphians so passionate for the project while Whitefield's preaching held them enthralled turned their attention away from the building after he left, leaving the most impressive edifice in town for a long time without a roof and eventually subject to sale for a fraction of its cost. The staying power of community support which undergirded the library and fire companies by no means extended to the New Building, and those to whom it did (at least initially) appeal were insufficiently organized or motivated to sustain the effort beyond the first enthusiasm.

The New Building represented a shift in the evolution of civic voluntary associations in Philadelphia. For the first time, a particular constituency mobilized the civic technology of voluntary association not for a broadly consensual objective that bridged diverse urban constituencies but for a project with which only one constituency agreed and that elicited the indifference or even hostility of many—maybe most—of the community. If it was a shift, however, it was at this time a subtle one, not easily perceptible. Any civic disruption the New Building caused remained relatively mild. The objectives the revivalists pursued were constrained by interest and by funds to the building itself. Once it had been completed and Whitefield had left the colony, the revivalists abruptly dropped their activities. But they had demonstrated that a committed minority could use the technology of voluntary association to reshape the physical and civic landscape of the city with or without the acquiescence of the majority. Theirs had been an intercession limited both in its objective and in time; the next group to use voluntary association to pursue aims without community consensus would cause far more of a stir.

"An Odd Appearance": The Defense Association

In late November of 1747, worried Philadelphians needed a place to meet—a big place. "Upwards of Five Hundred Men of all Ranks," a quarter of the adult men living in the city, crowded into the largest space in town: the New Building. If the trustees of the New Building had taken the first step in showing Philadelphia how voluntary association could be used by a minority, then the more than five hundred men who gathered in its broad hall that chilly November evening took a second and more controversial step. They formed an organization called the Defense Association, which mobilized as many as half the adult white men of Philadelphia into an extralegal militia to defend the city during the final months of King George's War. Unlike the disinterest or latent coolness the New Building had elicited, however, this organization evoked strongly expressed opposition and operated outside the bounds of the law, with ramifications rippling all the way back to England.[10]

The men filling the New Building had been spurred to meet that night because of the provincial government's stubborn refusal to act despite alarming news accumulating now for months of French and Spanish privateers prowling the Delaware River. The privateers, given license by King George's War, were burning farms, harassing Philadelphia's shipping, and threatening even the rich port city itself. The inhabitants of Philadelphia demanded immediate and decisive action. The majority of Quaker legislators were not unmoved by the danger at hand, but they believed their religious beliefs, including pacifism, to be absolutely inseparable from their political responsibilities. For strict Quakers, government and religious duty could not be divided. Over and above any temporal concerns—even including approaching invaders—they must remain true to the core tenets of their beliefs. To act otherwise would be to betray not only their faith but the founding principles of the colony; it would furthermore, they believed, jeopardize the consciences of all the Quakers in the colony.[11]

The assembly's decision did not correspond with the wishes of most Pennsylvanians, but the assembly refused to reconsider its position. Pennsylvania had been founded on the basis of Quaker belief that power resides with the people and that all the people were bound both to participate in and contribute to the harmonious development of the entire community. However, as the colony grew, Quaker legislators chose to limit the political voice of the new counties extending north and west of the original southeastern core. The original three counties had a total of twenty-four seats in the assembly, but by 1747, despite rapid western settlement, only one new county had been established, and it received only four seats. Between 1749 and 1752 the assembly would set up four more counties but only gave them seven seats total. The city of Philadelphia had gained two seats in the assembly in 1701 when it received its charter, but even though the city's population rose tenfold over the course of the eighteenth century, Philadelphia's share of seats never increased. Philadelphians' voices were drowned out disproportionately by the three original rural counties and then later and to a lesser degree by the new western counties, the latter of which remained themselves underrepresented but still had proportionately more than the capital city. The imbalance resulted in a "paradox of popular and oligar-chic political behavior," in which Pennsylvania's annual elections and relatively widespread franchise were counteracted by a gerrymandered system that gave disproportionate weight and power to Quaker demographic strongholds. Phila-delphians, a majority of whom by 1747 were not Friends, might be seized with "indignation against a Quaker government," but they could not influence or overturn it through the ballot box.[12]

In this critical moment of impasse, with privateers threatening to descend on the defenseless city at any moment, the Quakers' political ally Benjamin Franklin hatched what seemed the perfect solution under the circumstances. He wrote, published, and distributed at his own expense two thousand copies of a pamphlet called *Plain Truth: Or, Serious Considerations on the Present State of the City of* PHILADELPHIA *and Province of* PENNSYLVANIA, a pamphlet calling on "the middling People, the Farmers, Shopkeepers and Tradesmen of this City and Country" to stop relying on either the intransigent Pennsylvania Assembly or the "Great and rich Men, Merchants and others," who had both failed to lead in this time of crisis. Instead, he urged the common men, whom he lauded as "the first Movers in every useful undertaking that had been projected for the good of the City," to unite into an extralegal militia.[13]

Franklin argued that government had not just failed, but had actually refused to live up to its obligations. "Where a Government takes proper Measures to protect the People under its Care," Franklin asserted, the Defense Association would have been "unnecessary and unjustifiable." In Pennsylvania, however, "and perhaps if you search the World through, you will find it in our [province] only," the government refused to defend its citizens from attack. By reneging on that responsibility, the government ceded to its citizens the right to take matters into their own hands. It had become the *duty* of citizens to act on their own. "All we want," he exhorted his readers, "is Order, Discipline, and a few Cannon." By organizing together, "we, I mean, the middling People, the Farmers, Shopkeep-ers and Tradesmen of this City and Country," might become "strong and even formidable." The government's failure became the people's opportunity.[14]

The logic and call of *Plain Truth* resonated profoundly in Philadelphia. With a "sudden and surprizing" response, men answered Franklin's call. Days after its publication a meeting of 150 men, "mostly Tradesmen," adopted Franklin's plan; at another meeting two days later "the principal Gentlemen, Merchants and others" met at Roberts's Coffee House and "unanimously approv'd" it as well. The following day, November 24, Franklin's careful cultivation of different con-stituencies in the town paid off in the mass meeting at the New Building, where more than five hundred men subscribed their names to the "Form of Associa-tion," promising to provide themselves with firearms, form companies, elect officers, and begin drilling. Within weeks the number of subscribers had at least doubled, and historically pacifist Philadelphia was treated to the sight of fully half its adult white male population drilling in companies through the city streets. That spring one thousand men marched in review before the Provincial Council with silk military colors donated by the women of Philadelphia flying proudly.[15]

Defense Association leaders did not stop at raising a militia. They organized two extremely successful lotteries to procure funds that could be used to supply arms for those Associators too poor to provide their own, and to finance the construction of two forts on the banks of the Delaware River. Meanwhile, in urgent need of artillery, Franklin and others opened negotiations with the governors of New York and Massachusetts for the immediate sale or loan of cannon.[16]

That the Defense Association was a novel departure escaped no one. Proprietary secretary Richard Peters recognized as much when he wrote apologetically to Thomas Penn back in England that the Defense Association might appear "singular" and would "no doubt make an odd appearance & occasion divers observations" when news of it crossed the Atlantic. To be sure, it built upon the pattern and strategies of previous civic groups in Philadelphia, particularly the Library Company and fire companies, which Franklin referenced explicitly, in terms of membership appeals, organization, and financial strategies. However, it mobilized an unprecedented number, proportion, and diversity of men Franklin adorned with the title "Fellow Citizens" to form a militia that acted outside (though not actually against) the law or state. Its activities went far beyond churches shouldering much of the cost and care of poor relief or education, local volunteers assuming responsibility for municipal fire protection, or the founding of a library or ecumenical meeting space. A self-created extralegal body had armed and arrogated to itself direction of military defense of the capital of the colony without raising any protest from local authorities.[17]

The three layers of government—legislature, executive, and municipality—allowed or even encouraged the private group to act. The assembly did nothing to hinder its activities, but rather voted itself into recess during the height of activity. Meanwhile, the municipal corporation, which might itself have considered building forts or purchasing cannon and arms, followed instead a now well-established pattern of delegating authority to others. It let the association shoulder entire responsibility for those aims, but helped financially and lent respectability by helping oversee the lottery. The acting governor and council meanwhile gave every support possible to the fledgling group but did not interfere in its organization or choice of leaders, commissioning all the officers the Associators elected.[18]

Only one individual in government raised concerns about what this might mean for government, and he himself was not in Pennsylvania. Proprietor Thomas

Penn, when he came to hear about the association, was deeply alarmed. "The people of America," he fumed, "are too often ready to act in defiance of the Government they live in, without associating themselves for that purpose." Fearful of the implications of an extralegal militia for his government and interests, Penn viewed the Defense Association with deep reservations. In England and far removed from the perceived danger of privateer attack, Penn had the luxury of considering the potential repercussions of the association on government. Those on the ground in Pennsylvania, however, were accustomed to the broad dispersal of powers in local government and accepted the Defense Association, "odd" as it might seem, as the only viable expedient against imminent invasion.[19]

To be sure, not all locals supported the militia, particularly devout Quakers. However, in the debate that ensued, not one printed critique attacked the militia's political legality or legitimacy. Neither critics nor defenders focused on the questions of whether the organization had usurped too much power, or whether an extralegal militia might endanger the structure of legally constituted government or undermine the electoral process. Rather, the angry pamphlets that went back and forth debated the merits of pacifism and whether self-defense was compatible with Christianity. In Pennsylvania promoters and critics alike implicitly accepted the right of the Defense Association to exist; its political legitimacy went without saying.[20]

Indeed, the Defense Association might claim better to represent the people of Philadelphia than did any branch of government. Unlike the assembly, governor, or corporation, it derived its authority directly from the people. Half the able-bodied white men of Philadelphia volunteered in the Defense Association in 1747, a far greater proportion than voted annually for the assembly, the only representative body of government. Probably many of the volunteers possessed limited economic means and did not meet the property requirements to vote. Franklin explicitly noted that fund-raising would enable the purchase of "arms for the poor," indicating that some Associators did not already own and could not afford to purchase arms. The Defense Association not only allowed but encouraged men who had rarely or never participated in the formal political processes of their community now to assume responsibility for defense, one of the most critical functions of the state. They publicly signed their names to "Forms of Association," they voted for their officers, and they served in an organized militia for a period of many months. The Defense Association expanded political participation on two levels: the number of people involved and the time period over which they might exercise that right, extending from a single Election Day to a period of months of active militia service.[21]

Support for the association penetrated deeply through the community beyond the actual volunteers. City residents, including women and even many Quakers, supported its activities by purchasing tickets in two different lotteries designed to raise money for the association. Franklin's Union Fire Company, for example, bought thirty lottery tickets. Three Quaker members resigned in protest, but the vast majority of the Quaker membership of the fire company quietly acquiesced, leading Franklin to conclude that only a few devout Friends sincerely opposed the Defense Association. The lottery, framed as voluntary and patriotic, enjoyed great success. It filled within seven weeks, well short of the several months a lottery usually took. Several publicly minded citizens forbore from collecting their prizes, thus transforming their own lottery ticket purchases into outright donations; the second lottery raised over £600 in this way, "By Presents made by the Adventurers." Opening the two lotteries up to the widest constituency possible expanded the mandate of the association by including numbers of supporters beyond only the volunteers.[22]

Thus, when the formal channels of government and even the ballot box failed to provide Philadelphians with defense in 1747, they voted with their feet, their arms, and their pocketbooks, creating an extralegal, democratic military force that acted, like many organizations before it, outside the bounds of formal government. In the short term Pennsylvania had found a solution to the immediate problem of defense.

The Defense Association never explicitly challenged the state, but acted instead like other voluntary associations and commissions to fill a critical gap left by it. Franklin, as one of the leaders, was always careful to cultivate support on all sides and to blunt critiques of either the Quaker assembly or elite supporters of the proprietary family. The point as he and other leaders saw it was not to apportion blame or to bring down a government that in most cases worked admirably, but to defend the city until the danger passed. Still, the Defense Association contained an implicit threat to the state. Organizers and volunteers had facilitated the creation of an institution that paralleled formal government and took over powers from it but did not answer to it. Thomas Penn was the only one to prophesy danger from a self-created extralegal militia in 1748, but his fears about the "defiance of government" did not come to pass because the militia quickly faded away. He had, it later turned out, identified in extralegal organizing a very real threat, but one that would mature for nearly three decades and beyond his own lifetime before it came to fruition.

For all its zeal, the militia never fired a shot at an enemy attacker. The danger of privateer attack that had inspired the Defense Association dwindled even as the organization began. While Associators formed their companies and began drilling in the streets of Philadelphia, diplomats in Europe were already working out a peace treaty, though the news would not arrive in Philadelphia (or to the privateers) until the spring of 1748. Peace ended abruptly the need for the Defense Association, and within two years it had faded away entirely. However, the two batteries on the Delaware remained, physical reminders like the New

Building of what the initiative of voluntary association could accomplish and the extent to which formal government and public opinion would allow private groups to act.[23]

Like the New Building, the Defense Association made use of but also transformed the civic technology of voluntary associations. Where the construction of the New Building had caused a subtle disruption to the previously broadly consensual context for civic voluntary organizing, the Defense Association jettisoned far more dramatically any pretense of the harmonious or unitary public culture that had been so important to the earliest civic voluntary organizations. Whether or not they personally supported them, the majority of Philadelphians had no quarrel with a public subscription library or men organizing to fight fires and protect property. The New Building trustees had focused on the wishes only of supporters, but their objectives and period of activity were both so curtailed that this caused little concern. The Defense Association, on the other hand, deliberately eschewed broad public consensus. Composed exclusively of men who supported defense enough to join the militia and contribute money toward it, the association could achieve unanimity of purpose impossible in that moment within the broader polity, where an important minority vehemently disagreed. In the association's deliberate exclusion of opposition lay the source of its ability to act so decisively and quickly. Therein too, however, lay the seeds of a decisive shift in the way the technology of civic voluntary association could be used. In this case a substantial percentage—and probably even a majority—of Philadelphians supported the activities of the Defense Association. But in future not only majorities but minority constituencies could avail themselves of the tactics of exclusion it had pioneered and use them to pursue objectives regardless of or directly in contradiction to majority will. The organizers of civic voluntary associations had learned how to operate without broad-based public consensus.

Both the New Building and Defense Association, however, were short-lived and driven by a single objective. When George Whitefield left and the privateers dispersed, both the New Building trustees and Defense Association faded rapidly from the scene, blunting by their brevity their full ramifications for the future use of voluntary associations. Directly after their brief careers, Philadelphians created institutions with far more staying power that shifted in other ways the landscape of possibilities for civic association.

Setting Up for Themselves: Founding the Academy and the Hospital

In 1749, with the Defense Association winding down and more free time thanks to his semiretirement, Benjamin Franklin turned his attention to a matter he had long identified as a glaring need in Philadelphia: an institution that could provide a "compleat Education" for the boys of the city. After cultivating support among his friends for the idea, he published *Proposals Relating to the Education of*

Youth in Pennsylvania in 1749, calling for the establishment of an academy that would promote useful knowledge, with emphasis on practical skills students could use in their work lives: penmanship, mathematics, English grammar, history, rhetoric, natural and mechanical science, and such classical and modern languages as would serve their respective professions.[24]

Franklin's *Proposals* generated considerable enthusiasm, tapping back into the kind of broad public support that had characterized the library and fire companies. He and other academy promoters circulated a subscription that raised £2,000 for the fledgling school, to be paid over the next five years. The first nonsectarian institution of learning to be founded in the colonies, the academy was supervised by a board of twenty-four appointed trustees, consisting primarily of members of the Church of England and Presbyterians, with a few Quakers.[25]

After raising funds, one of the first tasks was to find a place for the academy to be housed. The capacious New Building was a tempting target. Built in a moment of religious enthusiasm, it had witnessed the electrifying preaching of ministers such as George Whitefield and had provided a meeting space large enough for the birth of the Defense Association in 1747. Now, however, it was underutilized with the ebb of ecumenical zeal and the absence of major civic initiatives like the Defense Association. The organizers who had built it were happy to unload the expensive building to the academy trustees for a fraction of what it was worth in February of 1750. Immediately, the trustees began to partition the enormous space into the classrooms the new academy would need. By spring the work was well underway, and the academy was able to open its doors in January 1751.[26]

The first order of business as Franklin saw it was to "apply for a CHARTER, by which they may be incorporated." A charter converted a group into a "body corporate," giving it fictive personhood with all the responsibilities of individuals held in relation to property: the right to sue and be sued, to hold title, and to transfer property in perpetuity—meaning beyond the life span of individual members. Incorporation was relatively rare in British tradition, usually reserved for organizations that served a clear public good, but Franklin and his allies believed they clearly met this criterion. In Pennsylvania, the first step to getting a charter was to go to the proprietor, who had received from the Crown the right to grant charters in his colony. The trustees were confident that Proprietor Thomas Penn would be sympathetic to the academy's aims. After all, Penn had granted a charter to the Library Company just seven years earlier as a testament to its good work in promoting learning in his colony. Furthermore, Governor James Hamilton, who had talked with Penn at his home in England only the year before, assured the trustees of Penn's "great desire . . . to fall on any feasible measures for the advancement of Learning in the Province."[27]

The trustees, then, were shocked at the negative reaction they received from

Penn. He objected in part to elements of the educational program of the institution, but the most important grounds of his concerns stemmed from his
dismay that the academy should have been brought to such a forward state
without obtaining his approval beforehand. He worried that Pennsylvanians
were attempting to "set upp for themselves." In the end, the most Penn would
promise the fledgling academy was not to interfere with it. He refused any active
support.[28]

Not to be deterred, the trustees continued their efforts, attempting to find
suitable teachers for the school and remodeling the New Building. They wres-
tled with the constant problem of shaky finances. It did not help that in 1751,
months after it first opened its doors to students, the academy faced a major
competitor for donations: the newly founded Pennsylvania Hospital. The fates
of these two institutions would be twined for the rest of the colonial period.[29]

The Pennsylvania Hospital was the brainchild of physician Thomas Bond,
who had been impressed by the private charitable hospitals he saw in the course
of his travels and medical training in Europe, and master organizer Benjamin
Franklin. Together the pair began aggressively looking for funds in 1751. Even
as "free and generous" contributions came in, however, it seemed unlikely that
hospital promoters could raise the enormous sums necessary to build and maintain a hospital. Promoters wanted land outside the heart of the city, where they
believed the air would be more salubrious, and they needed a custom-made
building to pursue the modern, scientific medicine that Bond envisioned. The
hospital would thus require property and an entirely new structure to be built;
it could not use a converted building in the city, as had been sufficient for the
academy, and therefore its start-up costs would be higher.[30]

Undaunted, Franklin considered possible strategies for raising sufficient funds
for the hospital. Based on their experiences as trustees for the academy, Franklin and Bond had little hopes of impressing Thomas Penn into charity for yet
another project in which Pennsylvanians "set upp for themselves." Because the
executive branch of government did not seem likely to help, Franklin decided
to approach another branch. The assembly agreed to donate £2,000, if and only
if its promoters could raise £2,000 from charitable contributions first. Franklin remembered that that conditional statement rescued the endeavor. On one
hand, most assemblymen thought that the hospital promoters had no chance of
raising that sum, so they were persuaded to approve the bill, as they "conceiv'd
they might have the Credit of being charitable without the Expence." On the
other hand, the endorsement of the assembly spurred support from the community. Subscribers met in early July 1751 to elect a board of twelve managers
and a treasurer, and that board sent a delegation to the Speaker of the House a
mere eleven days later to say they had raised the necessary sum.[31]

Moreover, the assembly granted the hospital a charter of incorporation, which was something of a departure from tradition. While the assembly had in the past incorporated government commissions, including Philadelphia's workhouse and the Overseers of the Poor, the proprietary family had been the source of charters for all private corporations, including the Society of Free Traders, the city of Philadelphia, the Quaker Free School, and the Library Company. Hospital promoters likely sought incorporation from the assembly not as a political statement but as a practical expediency. With the quantity of funds they proposed to raise, the hospital managers needed charter protections and privileges right away, and they were aware of Penn's refusal to incorporate the academy just a short time before.[32]

Bond and Franklin worked explicitly to mobilize broad-based public support for the hospital on the pattern of previous support for Philadelphia's civic organizations, including by 1751 two library companies, seven fire companies, and the academy. They invited leaders of each of the three major religious groups in the city to sit on the board, including Reverend Richard Peters, rector of Christ Church and avid supporter of the proprietor, Samuel Hazard, an elder of the Second Presbyterian Church, and Israel Pemberton, Clerk of the Yearly Meeting of the Society of Friends. The managers recognized and sought to build on the status and connections of these religious leaders, tasking the three of them with soliciting subscriptions from influential Philadelphians.[33]

Despite these efforts, some critics soon identified the hospital as an institution dominated by Quakers and men opposed to proprietary prerogative. Though Richard Peters, a devoted advocate for Penn, was on the first board of hospital managers, he left after one year as he and other proprietary supporters became concerned about the political uses to which the hospital might be put. Governor Hamilton painted the hospital as nothing more than a political stratagem on the part of Quakers, and he worried about their dominance in the hospital project. "I am persuaded," Hamilton warned the proprietor, that "they will think a very small share either of the Honour or of the direction ought to be lodged with You, or with any in Authority under You."[34]

Why the antagonism? How did a charitable institution devoted to caring for the sick and mentally ill evoke such concern? The answer lay in the fact that the political landscape of Pennsylvania was in 1751 in a state of flux, with lasting ramifications on civic projects. A polarizing series of political fights at the provincial level in the 1750s eradicated common ground and politicized first a charity like the hospital and then a good work like the academy. The previous tactics of appealing to broad public support which had facilitated the libraries, fire companies, academy, and even the Defense Association no longer would work for the hospital or any other civic project afterward.

Pennsylvania politics divided roughly between the Quaker and proprietary factions. Loose coalitions of political allies, rather than modern political vehicles, the two divided over a variety of issues, but at root the Quaker party championed the rights and power of the assembly, while the proprietary party advocated those of the proprietor. From almost the earliest days of settlement, one of the fundamental struggles in Pennsylvania politics had revolved around the executive prerogative of the proprietor versus the power of the elected provincial assembly. The assembly emerged in 1701 as by far the most powerful, but by the early eighteenth century relations between the two factions settled down to be overwhelmingly cooperative and peaceful. When Thomas and Richard Penn inherited the proprietorship of Pennsylvania in 1746, however, Thomas Penn immediately undertook to challenge this status quo by enhancing the power of the executive at the expense of the assembly. Quickly, provincial politics ruptured into newly energized and hostile camps supporting on the one hand the assembly and on the other the proprietor. Religious identity became enmeshed in the dispute, as Quakers overwhelmingly supported the assembly, while non-Quakers, particularly Presbyterians and members of the Church of England, supported the proprietor.[35]

As politics changed, so too did Philadelphia's social world. In 1748 four friends founded the Philadelphia Dancing Assembly, a voluntary association very different from the civic projects championed by Franklin. Male subscribers and their female family members and guests could attend the fortnightly balls during the first four months of the year. As the dancers traced ornate patterns in the movements of their minuets, Philadelphia and its voluntary culture were changing around—and in some part because of—them. Philadelphia had long boasted a thriving culture of sociable clubs, particularly devoted to sport, but these had always been relatively open in their membership. The Dancing Assembly's membership, however, consisted exclusively of elite supporters of the proprietor, men who opposed the Quaker party. The Dancing Assembly, moreover, had exclusion of Quakers built into its very makeup, for Quakers could not, on religious principle, dance. The Dancing Assembly was not the first but the second organization to which Quakers could not belong (the first being the Freemasons, who had established their first lodge in Philadelphia in 1731). However, its timing coincided with the dramatic shifts in local politics and the organization. Indeed, its association with proprietary politics became so strong that at least one historian has used the membership lists of the Dancing Assembly to deduce which politicians were in the proprietary party. At the same time, many men involved in the Dancing Assembly founded the St. Andrew's Society, a Scottish ethnic group named for the patron saint of Scotland. Like the Dancing Assembly, the St. Andrew's Society reflected and contributed to the changing environment of Philadelphia's public culture. All the members were Churchmen or Presbyterians, mostly allied with the proprietary faction in politics. Beginning in the late 1740s, then, as the political landscape hardened into opposing factions, Philadelphia's social world began to diverge, too, separating close neighbors and associates into distinctive social worlds, a process that would continue in succeeding decades with new social clubs.[36]

The atmosphere in which the Pennsylvania Hospital was founded in 1751, then, was one of freshly revived contention between two factions over the rights and power of the legislature versus those of the proprietor, and one in which many important forms of sociability came to mirror political cleavages. Governor Hamilton's misgivings about the new institution and its leadership made clear from its very foundation that at least some partisans understood the hospital to hold political implications in the struggle between two branches of government—the legislature and executive—and the two parties that dominated each: the Quaker and the proprietary parties. The hospital managers did not begin the institution with that intent, but soon enough Hamilton's suspicions turned into a self-fulfilling prophesy. By going to the assembly for money and incorporation, the hospital leadership had aligned the institution with the legislature. Proprietary supporters might interpret the money, and particularly the charter from the assembly, as a usurpation of Penn's prerogative. Soon enough the matter would become explicit as the managers found themselves forced to choose whether to remain loyal to the assembly or to forsake it to conciliate the proprietor.

Within days of their election, the managers petitioned the proprietor to grant the hospital land on which to build. The tone of the petition was humble, but perhaps insufficiently so, for it stressed too the activity and self-reliance of private persons and the Pennsylvania Assembly in achieving a hospital for the province. To a man like Thomas Penn with a high sense of what was due to him as proprietor, with a growing antagonism with the assembly, and having received alarmed reports from the governor about the political implications of the project, such emphasis probably did little to endear him to the hospital. Yet the managers hoped that the proprietor would add his backing to the project by donating land, "so that all concerned in the Province may share in the Honour, Merit & pleasure of promoting so good a Work." That remark was a not-so-subtle reminder that if Penn refused, he would single himself out as the only one "concerned in the Province" who failed to participate—much as he had singled himself out by not contributing to the academy earlier. "The Interest of the Proprietors and People," wrote the hospital managers, "are so nearly connected that it seems to us Self evident that they mutually share in whatever contributes to the Prosperity and Advantage of the Province." Any objections Thomas Penn might come up with as he had with the academy, such as that the province went "too fast" in the development of its cosmopolitan infrastructure, could have no bearing if he considered what was best for the province and, by extension, himself. Here, the managers made support for the hospital an issue of good governance. Any objections born out of partisan concerns would be prejudiced and un-Christian, not to mention shortsighted—not the qualities of good governors.[37]

Penn, with admirable political dexterity, responded with bounty, but not at all the bounty the hospital managers had in mind. He instructed Governor Hamilton to grant the hospital a plot of land and empowered him to incorporate the Contributors to the Hospital. On the face of it, such a gesture complied with all the managers had asked for and more. In truth, Penn's instructions signaled a struggle over the nature of the relationship between voluntary associations and government in Pennsylvania. The offer to incorporate the hospital under proprietary authority, when Penn knew it had already received a grant of incorporation from the assembly, was a direct challenge to the authority of the legislature. Penn could not revoke the charter the assembly had given, but by offering to incorporate the hospital himself, he attempted to undermine the legitimacy of the first charter and the legislature that gave it. His offer underscored a claim to superior authority as the executive branch of government and worked to place the hospital in a position directly subservient to the proprietor rather than to the assembly.[38]

In drafting their reply to Penn's offer of land and incorporation, the managers saw no need—or perhaps no way—to avoid a breach. Penn had placed the managers in the position of having to choose sides. By bundling his offers of land and incorporation together, he made it impossible for the hospital to accept one without the other. If the managers accepted incorporation, they undermined the assembly and acknowledged the proprietor's superior power and authority. Given that most of the managers, as Hamilton had pointed out in his earliest letter to Penn on the subject, leaned to the Quaker party and the assembly, accepting the Penn family's predominance over the legislature was unacceptable.[39]

In no uncertain terms, the managers rejected both incorporation and the land Penn had offered. "The Act of Assembly," they wrote, "is undoubtedly the best grant of Incorporation that we can possibly have." Bestowed upon the hospital by "the representatives of the freemen of this province," the managers would "fail of the respect that is justly due to them, were we to accept of any other." Furthermore, the charter the proprietor offered "confined [the hospital] to stricter limits," to which the managers objected.[40]

The managers also peremptorily rejected the land Penn had offered. On the grounds of health, they alleged that the lot was an improper place to build a hospital as it adjoined pools of standing water, brickyards, and burial grounds. More politically, and echoing past fights between the city and William Penn, the managers challenged the very right of the proprietor to grant that particular lot in the first place. Consulting "Old Maps of the City," the managers reminded

Thomas Penn that the lot he offered had already been given to the city by his father for "publick uses." Penn could not then revoke that gift and redistribute it now to a private corporation. "Our fellow Citizens would Tax us with Injustice to them, if we should accept of this Lott," they explained, "in such Terms as would seem to Imply our assenting to [the proprietor's] having a right" to that land. The managers firmly informed the proprietor that they would prefer to forego a grant of land entirely and spend their limited funds to buy property rather than submit to the terms proposed. However, they hoped Penn would see the justice of their objections. They wrote their go-betweens in London that if the Penn family "regard their own interest in the affections of the people," they would "cheerfully" grant the hospital the plot the managers had originally indicated.[41]

This response infuriated Thomas Penn. "What seems . . . to disgust the Proprietary's," wrote hospital advocates who met with him back in England, "is, your Questioning their Right to the Square . . . and also that you Esteem an Establishment from the Assembly preferable to a Charter from the Proprietary's." Livid at the managers' challenge to his authority, Penn "came to this Resolution not to make any Alteration in what was before granted" and furthermore refused outright any offer from the managers to buy or rent the plot they had originally solicited.[42]

The proprietor and the hospital managers all understood that the political implications of these exchanges extended well beyond merely the management of a local charity. The hospital managers, allied as they were with the assembly, refused to allow the proprietor to assume power over the hospital or diminish what they perceived to be the sovereignty of the legislature, either by a second charter or by land they did not believe the proprietor had a right to bestow. Penn in turn refused to be dictated to by the legislature, and certainly not by the hospital managers. The proprietor would help the hospital on terms that acknowledged his authority or not at all. However, the abrupt break with the hospital caused Penn embarrassment. Not only was he unable to bring the assembly to heel, but, still worse, the very voluntary associations of the provincial capital spurned proprietary input. The hospital's spirited defiance rallied the Quakers and the assembly, precisely the groups Penn was working against politically, and it established the hospital all the more firmly in the orbit of the legislature. Furthermore, the incident cast Penn's enemies as charitable and community minded, while it undermined his claims to those very same virtues.

With a "View to Sect or Party": Politicizing Civic Institutions

All in all, it seemed a propitious moment for the proprietor to reconsider his relationship with the academy. One year after the hospital rebuffed him, Penn sent word out of the blue to the academy that he would now be willing to grant it a charter and also donate £500. True, Franklin, a leader of the Quaker party and an increasingly irritating thorn in the proprietor's side, dominated the board as its president, but the majority of the trustees were proprietary supporters —Churchmen and Presbyterians who opposed Quakers and the assembly. The academy thus seemed to offer an alternative to the hospital as a laudable civic project that could burnish Penn's charitable reputation and at the same time provide institutional cover for factional base building.[43]

The proprietors' embrace of the academy began to politicize an organization that had originally sought to avoid factional debates. When it had opened its doors to students in 1751, the trustees carefully admitted students "without any View to Sect or Party." Though the board remained predominantly non-Quaker (indeed, it was dominated by Church of England men), the trustees saw the importance of not becoming completely sectarian; including Quakers and Presbyterians broadened the potential base of support for the school and shielded the academy from charges of "party" or factionalism. The trustees felt so strongly about maintaining this image that when influential Quaker trustee James Logan died in late 1751, the trustees invited his son-in-law, Isaac Norris II, speaker of the assembly and pillar of the Quaker party, to take his place. That appointment meant that Franklin and Norris, the two dominant leaders of the Quaker party, both sat on the board of trustees. Furthermore, while the board was dominated by Churchmen, the teaching staff was mostly Presbyterian. The academy, in those early years, certainly did the best it could to maintain a neutral place within provincial politics by balancing as much as possible sect and party affiliations.[44]

Alongside the pragmatic benefits of a wide base of political support, the academy faced weighty financial obligations and could not afford to alienate any potential contributors or parents who might send their sons to the school. The trustees organized an advertising campaign to bring their school into the public notice, printing their accounts in the local papers and publishing Reverend Richard Peters's inaugural sermon for the school. The school sorely needed cash, and the trustees solicited contributions, organized a lottery, and borrowed £800 from the Defense Association Lottery (of which many of them were also managers). When the news of the proprietors' gift and decision to incorporate it reached the academy, the trustees were extremely grateful.[45]

Quickly thereafter, however, the school moved away from the broad base that had first sustained it. The enterprising young scholar William Smith arrived from England, where he had become extremely friendly with Thomas Penn, and secured a post as a teacher. Within six months, he proposed that the academy seek a new charter allowing it the right to convey degrees—it would become both a college and an academy. Penn readily agreed to the new charter, which went into effect in 1755, and Smith maneuvered himself into the top job of provost in the newly constituted College of Philadelphia. Meanwhile, Smith entered vociferously into provincial politics, drafting and circulating a petition to the king that all Quakers be barred from Pennsylvania government; ten of the trustees signed that petition. Not long after Smith's circulation of this petition and during the trustees' efforts to secure the second charter, Quaker leader Isaac Norris abruptly stopped attending trustee meetings, one of the very few trustees to step down in the colonial period—the vast majority served until they died. The attempt at diversity that had characterized the first years of the academy would have no place in the increasingly politicized college.[46]

Smith did not stop there; during the French and Indian War, he dragged the college into partisan debates over military defense. In his capacity as provost, in 1756 he opened the doors of the college to "a considerable Number" of men who had formed their own extralegal militia in opposition to the assembly. By allowing the proprietary-sympathizing militia to meet multiple times on college grounds, Smith identified the institution with the militia and proprietary party, and in opposition to the assembly and their legally sanctioned militia. On his own account, Smith attacked the assembly and Franklin in print, ending the previous friendship and collaboration between these two leaders of the college. His actions unleashed criticism directed at himself and the college. Detractors argued that Smith appeared to be using the college explicitly to further factional political aims. They charged that he "endeavor[ed] to get the College wholly into the Hands of the Proprietary Faction" with one clear and sinister aim: "that high Notions of Proprietary Power may be early inculcated in the Minds of the Youth of this Province."[47]

Meanwhile, the trustees moved to isolate Franklin on the board. In May 1756 the trustees took advantage of Franklin's absence from town to end his presidency of the college, voting proprietary supporter Richard Peters into the post in his stead. Franklin participated less and less in college affairs after this slight and as he became increasingly marginalized on the board. Though he technically remained a trustee until his death, he was not an active member after 1756. Three years later he seethed that "the Trustees had reap'd the full Advantage of my Head, Hands, Heart and Purse, in getting through the first Difficulties of the Design, and when they thought they could do without me, they laid me aside."[48]

Thus, by 1755, two institutions founded for charitable and broadly popular aims, health care and education, came to be associated with opposing sides of the political rift. On one side, the hospital allied with the assembly; on the other, the college and academy allied with the proprietary family. The college always remained the more politically divisive of the two, for the simple reason that it provided a rare institutional base around which proprietary sympathizers could organize. The proprietary cause was espoused most strongly only by a relatively small core of elite men whose interests were served by advocating strong executive authority and reaping personal rewards from the Penns in the form of lucrative appointments and favors. Though the proprietary party proved adept at manipulating the frustration of key segments of the population against the Quaker party, it could not formulate a political program that rallied widespread support. The only political institutions it controlled, the Provincial Council and, by midcentury, the Philadelphia Corporation, boasted little political clout. The former acted only to advise the governor and had no independent power; the latter was extremely weak, meeting irregularly, conducting little business, and sharing power with various assembly-appointed commissions. By contrast, the college, especially under the leadership of William Smith, offered a vibrant and active institution around which the non-Quaker elite could organize, albeit outside of formal state auspices. Furthermore, the continuing nonsectarianism of the institution, reflected not only in the diverse religious persuasion of trustees but also in the student body and the teaching staff, aided the proprietary party tremendously. The college, fraught with sectarian tension though it might sometimes be, represented a bastion of proprietary support and a catalyst for non-Quaker interdenominational political cooperation.[49]

The Quaker party–dominated assembly recognized the importance of the college to its enemies and moved against it twice in the 1750s. First, on questionable legal grounds it jailed Provost William Smith in 1757 for libel. He continued to teach his classes, however, from his jail cell, where his students came to visit him, until he was freed at the end of the legislative session. Then the assembly attempted to undermine the college's funds by going after its one local source: lotteries. Because so many viewed the institution as partisan, the college never did well in its fund-raising efforts in Pennsylvania after 1756. "Whatever its original Design," one detractor wrote, the institution was "at present labouring to disseminate . . . uncharitable Zeal, Violation of Truth, groveling Servility, Disaffection to our Country, Ingratitude to Benefactors, Infidelity to Friends, ill Breeding and Brutality." The college trustees were forced to turn from the contribution model that was still running strong for the hospital and instead pin its hopes on lotteries, but even these brought disappointing returns. In 1759 the assembly took aim at this one remaining source of local revenue when it passed a bill restricting lotteries. Many understood this bill as a move by the assembly to undermine the college and by extension the proprietors. One critic of the college wrote that lotteries "are manifestly no better than public Frauds and Impositions, solely calculated to enrich the Proprietors at the Expense of those who are silly enough to adventure in them." To add insult to injury, all fines collected under this law would be paid to none other than the hospital.[50]

The ban on lotteries moved the college more firmly into the orbit of the proprietor. Penn successfully lobbied the Privy Council in England in 1762 to disallow as politically motivated the act suppressing lotteries, exonerate Smith from charges of libel, and even reprimand the assembly for overstepping its bounds. To tide the college over, Penn sent a large endowment and undertook more fundraising on its behalf in England. William Smith himself toured England in 1762, soliciting more than £1,000 in contributions. As a result, the college became more closely associated with the Penn family and increasingly reliant on support from England, distancing itself still further from local support, financial or otherwise, in Philadelphia.[51]

The hospital, by contrast, flourished in large part because the Quakers did not need the hospital in the way that the proprietary party needed the college. Quakers had safe, common spaces through their religious structure of weekly, Monthly, and Yearly Meetings in which to meet and discuss events and coordinate political activity. The hospital may indeed have served, as Governor Hamilton alleged, in part as a venue to position Quakers as charitable and beneficent, but it was never a central element of Quaker political activism in the way that the college came to be for the proprietary party.

Contemporaries became convinced of the nonsectarian or party aims of the hospital, and people of all denominations, both in and out of the province, donated substantial sums. The proprietor himself continued to ignore the hospital, perhaps further goaded by the fact that the hospital printed in a promotional pamphlet the whole of its correspondence with the Penns relating to the rejected charter and land. Including the letters in the pamphlet was clearly meant to expose the insufficient support of the proprietary family. In 1760 the hospital published a second pamphlet noting that it had bought land and built the first of three projected wings for the hospital. It mentioned in an aside that "Our Proprietaries are Owners of near one Acre on the North," noting blandly that "if obtained, [it] will compleat the Square," meaning that the hospital would own the entire city block and have no impediments to its future expansion. The proprietor took the hint, and whether because he had decided to forgive the hospital its earlier affronts or was trying to save face after multiple pamphlets had pointed out his lack of encouragement to the hospital, Penn granted the hospital the last bit of land in the square and promised an annuity of £40.[52]

The hospital remained, however, very much in the orbit of the assembly. When the hospital became mired in financial straits in 1762, the assembly granted it another £3,000. Because of its substantial financial support, the assembly technically had oversight over the affairs of the hospital. The original Act of Assembly mandated that the hospital's accounts must be open to members of the legislature and anyone else who wanted to see them, to which end the act ordered the hospital to publish its accounts annually in the local newspapers. Assemblymen inspected the hospital every year or so and reported back to the House. Despite this nominal oversight, the assembly never interfered in the slightest with the operation of the hospital, contenting itself merely with approving the decisions of the managers from time to time and ensuring that the hospital financial records were transparent to the public. The hospital in turn remained loyal to the assembly during its contention with the proprietor in the 1750s.[53]

When Thomas Penn worried that the founders of the academy were rushing to "set upp for themselves," his concerns revolved primarily around his own ability to influence or control events in his capital city. As part of his larger project to rein his colony back in, he worried about the independence that characterized Philadelphia projectors and wished to bring them back into a more deferential relationship with the proprietary family. His turn of phrase, however, can be taken in another light. Beginning with the New Building in 1740, proceeding through the foundation of the Defense Association, and continuing in the politicization of the academy/college and hospital, Philadelphians were increasingly turning to civic voluntary associations to set up, not on behalf of the consensus of the larger community, but on behalf only of "themselves," a smaller constituency. Beginning as a matter of expediency, this approach quickly became a matter of necessity as Philadelphia's political and social worlds became more divided. The forces that strained civic harmony were varied and complex and only just unfolding in the early 1750s, soon to erupt to new levels of discord with the start of the French and Indian War in 1754.

CHAPTER FIVE

Lending in Plain Sight
Covert Banks

Mid-eighteenth-century Philadelphia was a growing, bustling place, but it was not for everyone. William Maugridge, for one, wanted to give up his trade as a joiner in Philadelphia, buy land outside the city, and settle down as a farmer. Unfortunately, he lacked the capital to achieve this goal, so beginning in 1753 he did what most people did when they were short of cash: he approached old friends for loans to help him realize this dream. But Maugridge's friends failed him; they were unable to provide him with enough credit to purchase his coveted farmland. Having reached a dead end with private loans, Maugridge would have been out of luck if he had been hunting for capital just a few years before, but in 1753 he had not one but multiple new sources he could try in the form of voluntary civic institutions that had recently begun making large-scale loans. He went to the Pennsylvania Hospital, founded two years before, and asked for a loan of £200. The managers considered his request, but either they were taking too long or they quietly decided against him because within months Maugridge turned to the Philadelphia Contributionship, a mutual aid society that pooled resources to provide fire insurance for its members, founded just the year before in 1752. By February of 1754, he had at last gotten access to the money he needed in the form of a loan for £200 from the contributionship. Shortly thereafter he bought land in Bucks County and moved out of the city.[1]

Unfortunately, in mid-eighteenth-century Philadelphia credit was a shrinking resource. In 1754, the same year that Maugridge secured his hoped-for loan, leading merchant William Allen grieved that capital had become extremely scarce. "We have among us ten Borrowers to One Lender," he lamented. Allen himself was not helping the situation. He moved to invest his own money outside the province, worrying about the potential for depreciating currency, a creditor's worst nightmare. Without institutional banks where customers could invest and borrow money, Philadelphians found it extremely difficult to secure lines of credit, dampening expansion, innovation, and investment.[2]

Philadelphia was, by the middle of the eighteenth century, the largest city in British North America, a trade entrepot linking the mid-Atlantic interior to markets in the Caribbean and Europe. The city needed ever more financial services, most notably credit, but the one institutional resource available—the state-backed General Loan Office—fell victim to imperial and provincial politics in 1755, closing off one of the few avenues for small to medium loans. Part of the problem stemmed from the fight between the proprietor and assembly over control of the colony's finances, but more deeply, the difficulty in facilitating institutional banking was rooted in British policy. In the wake of the South Sea Bubble of 1720 and in order to promote mercantilist policies, the British Board of Trade remained extremely conservative about what financial activities it would allow in the colonies. With the demise of the credit-granting capabilities of the General Loan Office in 1755, the Pennsylvania legislature found itself powerless to take any measures to help stimulate the circulation of desperately needed capital. It could not charter a new bank, either public or private. Parliament and Thomas Penn together blocked that avenue.

Pennsylvanians found an innovative way to work around the problem. They organized not banks, but a different kind of corporate body, explicitly opposed to the stock-jobbing projectors who had so ignominiously wreaked havoc on the British economy in the early eighteenth century. These colonial projectors banded together in voluntary associations aimed to improve the public weal through libraries, hospitals, and mutual assistance. They pursued these objectives in good faith, but under cover of their publicly stated aims, some organizations in addition quietly took on some of the lending functions of banks. As they accrued capital, they invested their money by loaning it out to borrowers, thus providing another kind of public service in an economy desperate for loans. Unable to charter banks, Pennsylvania authorities could and did charter these kinds of organizations, doubly benefiting the local community: first through the stated aims of the organization, and then again through the work many of them, such as the hospital and contributionship, did in providing the loans that made new economic activities possible for men like William Maugridge.

Ten Borrowers to One Lender: Limited Avenues for
Credit in Colonial Philadelphia

The British Empire reeled from the effects of its first financial bubble in 1720. In that year the South Sea Company followed closely on the heels of its French counterpart, the Mississippi Company, first expanding in a speculative frenzy and then bursting as company shares turned out to be worthless, bringing down the national economy with it. The bubble wreaked havoc on England's economy and financial development and provoked a strong backlash not only against corporations and "stock-jobbers" but against speculation and indebtedness. Even before the landslide in share prices had begun, the British Parliament passed the Bubble Act to limit drastically the formation of corporations. That act hampered the growth of the stock market and the evolution of business corporations in England until it came off the books over a century later. A generation of thinkers derided the stock-jobbers who had brought on the crisis. Prime Minister Robert Walpole summarized the position of many when he called it "never to be forgotten or forgiven."[3]

John Trenchard and Thomas Gordon were inspired by the folly of the South Sea Bubble to write *Cato's Letters*, commentaries that were published weekly from late 1720 to 1723 and eventually would become a primer for American revolutionaries. In their commentary they considered the larger structural problems that had allowed the bubble to happen in the first place. Selfish passions had produced corruption; avarice had temporarily prevented the populace from exercising sufficient vigilance. *Cato's Letters* urged a rebirth of civic virtue grounded in private self-interest and a system of checks and balances to monitor government. The South Sea Bubble helped shape for decades the social, economic, and political consciousness of early modern Britons—at both the center and the periphery.[4]

British creditors were careful to remain especially vigilant of currency stratagems that might lead to another inflationary bubble. They were particularly attentive to the activities of the colonial legislatures. Intent on maintaining the supply of gold and silver in England, British policies drained the American colonies of specie. By the early eighteenth century, the volume of trade in the colonies far exceeded the volume of specie in circulation, and colonial governments turned to paper currency as a necessity. By 1740 almost every colony formed a land bank (also known as a loan office) that circulated paper money in the form of notes issued on loan to borrowers with mortgaged property as security. Those notes then circulated as currency.[5]

Because of the clear necessity, the Board of Trade tentatively allowed the practice despite the protests of British merchants, who remained wary of paper currency after the South Sea debacle. By the 1740s, however, the Board of Trade was persuaded to extend the Bubble Act of 1720 to the colonies as well, eliminating the possibility of any private banks and restricting severely even the state-sponsored ones. Parliament restricted New England monetary emissions with the Currency Act of 1751, extending those restrictions to all the colonies in 1764. Legislators worried that an excess of paper money would lead to inflation and hurt British creditors. American colonies were forced to defer overwhelmingly to London-based finance for their needs, especially for credit.[6]

Philadelphians, then, found themselves forced to rely for the most part on personal avenues for credit. Historians have identified three major sources: book credit, loans from friends or family, and loans from wealthy merchants. Pennsylvania, moreover, stood out among the colonies as having one of the most stable and successful of the colonial land banks, the General Loan Office, which extended loans from 1723 to 1755.

Book credit entailed allowing a customer to purchase goods and pay the balance at some future point. It was a widespread and necessary practice in the colonial era, when currency was scarce. Merchants and tradesmen routinely extended credit to their customers. Indeed, in an examination of colonial Philadelphia account books historian Wilbur C. Plummer has found that 90 percent or more of transactions may have been credit based rather than cash based, and that customers of all classes relied on credit. The settling of book debts could be slow, and many debts were never recovered. When Benjamin Franklin wrote his will in 1788, he observed that he was owed unpaid debts stretching back to 1757, and though they had in the ensuing thirty years become "obsolete," they were "nevertheless justly due." He bequeathed the bad debts to the Pennsylvania Hospital in the hopes that those who had failed to pay *him* might be induced to give the money to the charitable purposes of the hospital. On the contrary, after his death in 1790 the hospital found it impossible to collect on the debts and gave them up entirely.[7]

Personal loans were common but could be inefficient. A "lively capital market" existed in colonial Pennsylvania, in which private households loaned small sums, usually no more than £10, spread out among several borrowers. Such a system required a borrower to go to several sources to cobble together larger sums of capital, but it protected lender and borrower alike by spreading risk (in the latter case, reducing the chance that all the money borrowed would be called in at once, before the borrower was able to pay). The drawback to such loans was that it could be very difficult for a borrower to raise large amounts of capital.[8]

Merchants and business acquaintances might loan larger sums, but they required security for the loans that they made, usually mortgages. They were also more likely to charge more interest. Legally, the usury limit was 6 percent, but merchants "probably did not feel well compensated for the risks and trouble of trade if they consistently earned less than 10 percent," and scholarship suggests that 12 percent interest was not uncommon. As with personal loans, individuals had to be personally known to these lenders, keeping the capital within particular social and business networks and limiting access to credit.[9]

The General Loan Office provided another avenue for capital. It acted as a land bank between 1723 and 1755, offering loans up to £100, all at below-market interest rates of 5 percent. The General Loan Office required security and was thus limited to property owners, but it made capital available regardless of risk or personal acquaintance with the borrower. By law, the General Loan Office had to loan to anyone who had security. In practice, the number of potential borrowers exceeded the capital available, necessitating a waiting list. Over the thirty years in which it was active as a land bank, the General Loan Office stimulated the economy of Pennsylvania enormously, extending nearly four thousand loans. By the mid-1750s, however, a pitched battle raged over who would control the interest money of the General Loan Office, the provincial assembly or the proprietary family. From 1755 on, its functions changed and it no longer provided the easy access to credit which had characterized the first thirty years of its history. In short, by the 1750s the only institutional avenue for loans in Pennsylvania no longer functioned, and there was no possibility of replacing it. Imperial policy and proprietary intransigence prevented private or state-operated banks.[10]

Thus far, scholars' understanding of the mechanisms of debt and credit in the colonial period has been restricted to these major avenues. Absent in all these accounts is a previously unstudied source for capital loans: voluntary associations. The colonies were restricted in their ability to charter either public or private banks. However, they retained the freedom to charter voluntary associations that served some stated public benefit. And those voluntary associations could accrue capital and then place it out at interest—providing local loans in an economy desperate for credit.

Money in Hand: Civic Associations and Capital

In Philadelphia, the commercial hub of British North America, merchants and artisans founded civic institutions that also happened to make loans—over £112,000 in the twenty-five years before the American Revolution. The projectors pursued their civic objectives in good faith, but under cover of their publicly stated aims they quietly took on some of the functions of banks. These financial activities were only made possible because these organizations self-consciously constructed themselves not as banks or companies (with all their potential negative connotations after 1720) but as institutions serving the public good through visible, charitable work. The political legacy of the South Sea Bubble meant that for the time being, burgeoning American institutions of finance had to hide their activities behind works of civic altruism.

At least ten of Philadelphia's voluntary associations made loans. Four groups

TABLE 2
Philadelphia Voluntary Association Loans, 1750–76

Association	Amount loaned* (in £)	Percentage of all loans
Pennsylvania Hospital	35,058	31.18
The Corporation for the Relief of Poor and Distressed Presbyterian Ministers . . . (Presbyterian Ministers' Fund)	32,553	28.95
College of Philadelphia	21,019	18.69
Philadelphia Contributionship	18,365	16.33
Society for the Relief of poor and distressed Masters of Ships, their Widows and Children (Ships Captains Club)	3,160	2.81
Library Company	1,405	1.25
Other (four organizations)	960	0.79
Total	112,443	100

Sources: Pennsylvania Hospital Minutes and Pennsylvania Hospital Cash Book 1756–77 and Ledger 1752–77 (bound together), Pennsylvania Hospital Archive; Waste Book, 1761–98, Presbyterian Ministers' Fund, HSP; Journal A Belonging to the Trustees of the Academy of Philadelphia, 1749–64, and Day Book of the Academy of Philadelphia, 1749–89; University Archives and Records Center, University of Pennsylvania; Minutes of the Philadelphia Contributionship, Treasurer's Journal, 1752–68, and Treasurer's Journal, 1768–99, Philadelphia Contributionship Archives; Articles of the Sea Captains Club And Treasurers Account, 1765–77, HSP; Library Company Minutes, Library Company of Philadelphia; Minutes of the Cordwainer's Fire Company, HSP; Minutes of the Union Fire Company, 1736–85, HSP; Friendship Carpenter's Company Minutes, 1770–75, American Philosophical Society; Minutes of the Proceedings and Transactions of the Corporation for the Relief of Widows and Children of Clergymen in the Communion of the Church of England in America, 1769–1842, HSP.
*All totals rounded up to the nearest pound, Pennsylvania currency (pounds).

predominated—95 percent of all such loans came from (in descending order) the Pennsylvania Hospital, the Corporation for the Relief of Presbyterian Ministers, the College of Philadelphia, and the Philadelphia Contributionship. The Society for the Relief of Poor and Distressed Masters of Ships, their Widows and Children and the Library Company of Philadelphia together made just over 4 percent of the remaining loans. Finally, another four groups collectively made less than 1 percent of the loans: these were the Cordwainers and Union Fire Companies, the Friendship Carpenters' Company, and the Corporation for the Relief of Widows and Children of Clergymen in the Communion of the Church of England in America (see table 2).[11]

All the organizations that loaned £1,000 or more shared one very important characteristic: they were all incorporated. Groups of individuals had no inherent legal standing in court, so they could not hold property in common. They could not collectively sue or be sued, inherit, or pass along property, which made the accumulation or loaning of capital extremely risky. As discussed elsewhere, incorporation protected common funds by transforming a collective of individuals into one fictive person, for example, "the Library Company." Incorporation was a necessary prerequisite to the extensive loans made by the six lenders of more than £1,000. Having been granted fictive personhood, a corporation had all the rights and responsibilities of any other individual respecting property: it could sue and be sued, hold title, and transfer property. Corporations also enjoyed limited liability, which meant that members' personal assets could not be seized to pay the corporation's debts.[12]

The four major lenders all needed to finance major undertakings and all intended that lending their capital at interest would be their principal investment strategy. Accordingly, all but one sought incorporation early in their histories to protect their assets. The only exception was the Philadelphia Contributionship, founded in 1752. For reasons that are obscure and possibly had to do with the political climate of the 1750s, the contributionship did not get around to petitioning the Pennsylvania Assembly for incorporation until 1768. By that time the harried directors were desperate. They complained that "great inconveniencies have Arisen in lending the Stock of the Company for want of a Law by which we may be incorporated." Reminding the legislature that the group's activities had been "Advantageous to the Publick," the directors requested a charter of incorporation, which they received. The contributionship's lending activities immediately picked up. Between 1752 and 1768 it loaned £6,520. In the remaining eight years before the American Revolution, it loaned nearly double that amount.[13]

The Pennsylvania Hospital was the earliest group to gain incorporation, and it was the lender for the longest period and of the most money. Physician Thomas Bond and master organizer Benjamin Franklin conceived of the plan for a hospital and began assiduously looking for funds in 1751. Even with "free and generous" contributions pouring in, however, it seemed unlikely that they would be able to raise the enormous sums necessary to build and maintain a hospital. Franklin, an old hand by this time at organizing civic projects, approached the provincial legislature for help. He convinced the tight-fisted assembly to grant the project £2,000 to match private contributions of the same amount. The province's money came with conditions, however. It was intended to be a "capital Stock," and the hospital managers were limited to "applying its annual Interest or Rent, towards the Entertainment and Care of the sick and distempered Poor." That is to say, the managers could not *spend* the £2,000. They were legally obliged to lend it out at interest, giving the hospital a source of perpetual income in the form of annual interest payments. The assembly, meanwhile, had essentially set up a fund of £2,000 that would be permanently employed in loans in the local economy—loans, moreover, that would be overseen by trustworthy men of standing in the community, but not by assemblymen themselves, who were thus spared the concern.[14]

Thereafter the hospital attracted substantial charitable contributions, which the managers added to the capital stock from which they made loans and earned interest. However, the costs of the institution were high, and in 1762 the assembly granted the hospital another £3,000 to add to the capital stock, again assisting the institution with interest from loans that thereby benefitted the hospital and the local economy at once. The hospital received a further boon in 1760 when the British Parliament passed an act transferring all unclaimed assets of the moribund Pennsylvania Land Company to the hospital. After a ten-year waiting period, the hospital began to receive those funds, totaling in all over £12,000—31 percent of all the money the hospital loaned between 1750 and 1776. Because of that parliamentary grant, on the eve of the Revolution the hospital was for the first time on a strong financial footing.[15]

Almost exactly equaling the hospital in funds lent was an organization with no sense of brevity in naming: the Corporation for the Relief of Poor and Distressed Presbyterian Ministers and of the Poor and Distressed Widows and Children of Presbyterian Ministers—hereafter referred to as the Presbyterian Ministers' Fund. Francis Alison, a Presbyterian minister who arrived in Philadelphia in 1755, proposed a fund that would act essentially as life insurance. Presbyterian ministers would make annual payments (called "subscriptions"), and their surviving family members would receive annuities after the minister's demise. The Presbyterian Ministers' Fund received a charter in 1759 and began aggressively seeking to build up a capital fund. The small annual payments of the ministers themselves would not build up a stock sufficient to pay survivor benefits, so organizers solicited charitable donations, especially from Presbyterian congregations locally and in Scotland and England. In 1760 organizers took the momentous step of sending Reverend Charles Beatty to Great Britain to raise funds. He collected over £3,800 by 1761, and the board of managers loaned it out as soon as they could. The fund grew very quickly, thanks largely to church collections. The enormity of the Presbyterian Ministers' Fund's fund-raising can be gauged by the fact that it loaned only slightly less than the hospital, despite having no state support and starting a full ten years later.[16]

The next largest lender, the College of Philadelphia, was founded in 1749 as the Academy of Philadelphia, another project of the enthusiastic Benjamin Franklin. It gained incorporation in 1753 as the Academy and in 1755 as the College. The first nondenominational college in the colonies, the College of Philadelphia within a few years jettisoned a disgusted Franklin and became a focal point for Churchmen and Presbyterians, particularly those with close allegiances to the proprietary family. Indeed, the Penns donated generously to the college, the only one of the four major lending institutions to receive eager support from that family. However, because so many Pennsylvanians viewed the institution as partisan after 1756 (about the time Franklin left), the college never did well in its fund-raising efforts in Pennsylvania. It turned to lotteries, but these too brought in disappointing returns. The college then relied on contributions first solicited in England by Thomas Penn himself and later assisted by Provost William Smith, who traveled especially to Britain for the purpose.[17]

The last of the largest lenders was the Philadelphia Contributionship for the Insuring of Houses from Loss by Fire. Founded in 1752, once again largely through the energies of Benjamin Franklin, the contributionship provided fire insurance. Like the life insurance of the Presbyterian Ministers' Fund, this service was seen as deriving from motives of mutual assistance rather than profit. Subscribers paid premiums according to the rate assigned them by contributionship inspectors who assessed risk of fire. In case of loss of a member's property through fire, the contributionship would indemnify the member. The Deed of Settlement of 1752 explicitly laid out the conditions under which the directors could loan money, indicating an expectation from the beginning that they would do so in order to augment the stock. The contributionship relied entirely on the payments of its members; it had no charitable contributions similar to those of the other groups.[18]

All four of the major lenders, then, accumulated capital in part by bringing together many local small or middling subscriptions and donations from numerous members and/or benefactors. Many small payments of £5 and £10 came from throughout the British Atlantic world, but the vast majority came locally. In this way, civic-minded Philadelphians benefitted their community twice: first by supporting the stated goals of the lenders (health care, education, mutual aid), and then again by creating a pool of private funds that would be made available for loans far larger than those commonly found on the market— and at rates consistent with the law but actually below market values. The large lenders, then, acted like the opposite of microfinance lenders in the twenty-first century. They bundled together hundreds of small contributions to make available very large loans that were otherwise difficult to come by, recycling the funds of tradesmen and shopkeepers into loans that benefited wealthy merchants and prosperous artisans.

However, the Philadelphia Contributionship was the only major lender to raise money only through its subscriptions. Strikingly, the other three organizations also relied heavily on outside sources. The assembly funneled provincial taxes into support for the local hospital, which in turn stimulated the city's credit market. Another 15 percent (at least) of institutional loans were made possible by funds acquired on the other side of the Atlantic through charitable donation, patronage, or the generosity of the British Parliament. British largesse in the two and a half decades before the Revolution thus played an unheralded role in facilitating large loans in Philadelphia, with all the consequent multiplier effects on the regional economy. Directors were eager to get this money to Philadelphia, rather than invest it abroad where it had been obtained. "Our

Exchange is low," the Pennsylvania Hospital managers admitted to their agents in England, "yet we can place it out here on good and sufficient Securities, and terms more advantageous than in your fluctuating Stocks in London." Britain's charitable impulses saved the hospital, college, and Presbyterian Ministers' Fund from failure and at the same time injected money into Philadelphia's credit market. Board directors recognized the double advantage of bringing those funds into their city: it helped their local civic objectives, and it provided a pool for loans that helped the local economy.[19]

A Borrower and a Lender Be: Loans

All of the major lenders tended to loan their money only in large amounts. One of the earliest decisions by the Board of Managers of the Pennsylvania Hospital was that they would not make loans out of the capital stock which were for less than £100. For the most part the other groups followed suit: the average for all loans was £317. Restricted to just the largest four lenders, the average loan was £447 (table 3). The median loan for the four largest lenders was £300; the most common size of a loan was £200. Nineteen of the 310 loans voluntary associations made were for under £100 (ranging from £10 to £75, and all but three coming from the Presbyterian Ministers' Fund). Twenty were for £1,000 or more, with the single largest loan coming from the Pennsylvania Hospital: £3,000 to John Bull in 1772—a loan he successfully repaid in 1776.[20]

These loans represented substantial sums. To put them in context, one gentleman estimated in 1759 that "to live but meanly, and maintain a Horse" in Philadelphia cost seven shillings a day, or more than £125 annually. Fifteen years later, unskilled laborers earned three shillings a day, while masters at the top of their craft might earn as much as nine shillings—yielding an annual income of between £47 and £140 if they had full-time employment. A journeyman printer might make £54 a year, while a professor of Greek at the College of Philadelphia earned £200. In terms of property, a category separate from annual wages or income, the wealthiest 10 percent owned substantial property—with median personal wealth valued at more than £2,900. The median personal wealth of the next wealthiest 30 percent was £560; the 30 percent below them had a median wealth of £113, and the poorest 30 percent of Philadelphia households had a median wealth of £24.[21]

The fact that board directors consciously chose mainly to lend sums over £100 was significant. The primary example of institutional lending in Philadelphia before midcentury was the General Loan Office, which had been very successful making loans of no more than £100. Its loans had been repaid, and substantial interest had been collected. Furthermore, by making numerous (nearly four thousand) small loans, the General Loan Office spread out the risk of borrowers defaulting. The board directors would have been well aware of how

TABLE 3
Number and Average Size of Loans of Philadelphia Voluntary Associations, 1750–76

Association	Average amount loaned (in £)	Number of loans	Number of borrowers
College	589	38	44
Ministers' Fund	278	117	100
Library Company	200	7	7
Hospital	638	56	60
Contributionship	296	62	55
Ships Captains Club	143	22	19
Other	88 (estimate)	8 (at least)	10 (at least)
Total	317	310	269*

Sources: See previous table (p. 109). These totals count only once borrowers who borrowed multiple times.
    *If this column is added, the total number of borrowers would be 295. However, 26 men borrowed from multiple institutions—the total number of borrowers across all 10 organizations is thus 269.

the General Loan Office functioned; many had served on it. Indeed, the hospital's first treasurer, Charles Norris, had also been the treasurer for the General Loan Office. But the boards consciously decided not to follow the lead of the General Loan Office and offer primarily small loans. That decision cannot have been based solely on a clear-eyed calculus of cost-risk benefit because, again, the General Loan Office had been a profitable, flourishing, and popular institution.

In deciding to focus on very large loans, the major lenders were perhaps more concerned with the efficiencies of large loans, or perhaps they were making a social statement about who would be their clientele and how they wanted to shape Philadelphia's economy. The board members themselves were older, prosperous, well-established men. The loans their institutions would make would go to men like themselves and would be invested in relatively large-scale endeavors. Their loans, then, would do very different work and serve very different populations than their institutions. The hospital would assist impoverished Philadelphians through free health care, but it would not give them low-cost small loans. The college would offer education to young men, but it would not help them out with small starter loans when they left school. The Presbyterian Ministers' Fund provided life insurance for "poor distressed" families, but not capital to help those widows or orphans set up a small business.

The decision to loan large sums did provide a central location for borrowers to go when they needed substantial capital for large projects. It was more efficient than forcing borrowers to cobble together many smaller loans to come up with the larger amount they really needed. This decision, moreover, was more efficient for the lending institution, which had fewer borrowers to monitor. The board directors thus provided a valuable economic service to the city, one that may even have had multiplier effects that rippled through the larger economy and ultimately helped some of the impoverished poor, recent college graduates, and distressed widows that their institutions desired to serve. But ultimately, the directors' decisions tended to benefit primarily their own class and age group.

To assess what proportion of Philadelphia's entire credit market these groups' loans represented is difficult. Probably it was extremely small in comparison to book credit. English merchants were generous in extending this kind of commercial credit to wholesale merchants in the eighteenth century, and they in turn passed on similar credit to their storekeeper customers, who in turn passed it on to their customers, creating a chain of consumers all relying on book credit. This kind of credit, Thomas Doerflinger has pointed out, was practically as ubiquitous as sunlight—it was "an expandable resource, transferable through a simple entry in a ledger." No actual wealth changed hands until the final link in the chain began repaying his debts, allowing the storekeeper to repay the merchant, the merchant his English creditor. This kind of commercial credit was vital not just to Pennsylvania's but all the colonies' economies. However, it was substantially different from the kind of credit offered by Philadelphia voluntary associations, which in many if not most cases were placing cold, hard cash in the hands of their borrowers. The quantity of these associations' loans may have been considerably smaller than the commercial credit originating with English merchants and extending through Philadelphia's economy, but they also represented a very different kind of loan that could be used much more flexibly—indeed for any activity where ready money was necessary or advantageous.[22]

Not enough research has been done to allow easy comparison with other private cash loans. While historians on the subject widely agree that private loans tended to be small, the probate records of very wealthy Philadelphia merchants suggest that some may have been loaning amounts comparable to the hospital, college, contributionship, and Presbyterian Ministers' Fund. Doerflinger found that thirty-six merchants with median assets of £6,112 generally had less than £700 on hand in cash, with the remainder tied up in loans, though he remarks that "most of them [were] fairly small." Wealthy merchant Jonathan Mifflin's loans, however, do not seem to have been small. When he died in 1781, he was worth £11,600, but £11,280 of that was out in loans to thirty-five separate individuals, meaning the average size of his loans would have been £322, just over the average for all voluntary associations (£317). Brewer Anthony Morris appears to have loaned £1,600 on thirteen mortgages over a period of forty years; five of these ended up defaulting, bringing him various properties. Another brewer, Reuben Haines, loaned £1,250 to five borrowers. Finally, Hugh Roberts, prosperous, but not in the same echelons as Morris or Mifflin, made two loans in 1748 and 1749 equaling £585. In short, anecdotal evidence suggests that the size and volume of private loans in Philadelphia may have been larger than historians have generally assumed, but currently no reliable figures allow for comparison.[23]

If wealthy men were indeed making loans available, they did not do so on the same terms as Philadelphia's voluntary associations. Though the legal usury limit in Pennsylvania was 6 percent, historians estimate that this rate of return discouraged most private lenders, and they either charged higher rates under the table (as high as 12% Doerflinger has estimated) or found other avenues to invest their money. The hospital, college, Presbyterian Ministers' Fund, and Philadelphia Contributionship were incorporated bodies and could not flout the legal limit. Indeed, the hospital, by the terms of its charter, had to publish its annual accounts and submit to an audit by the Pennsylvania Assembly. Even groups under less intense scrutiny appear to have followed the limit as well. Across the board, all ten groups that loaned money charged 6 percent interest. Such loans attracted potential borrowers easily; they represented lines of credit at very competitive rates in a city where these appear to have been scarce.[24]

In general, lenders had no difficulties locating men, and in a very few cases women, to borrow the money. Shortly after acquiring the hospital's first funds, Treasurer John Reynell reported to the board that he had been inundated by "several Applications . . . for borrowing Sums of the Hospital Money." He had only £265 in hand, but borrower Isaac Greenleafe anxiously insisted he wanted £300. The hospital managers agreed that Greenleafe could have all their current cash, and, as soon as they had collected it, the remaining £35. In short, demand for hospital loans exceeded the speed with which managers could collect from contributors.[25]

This fast-paced demand for loans remained the norm. As soon as money came in, whether because a borrower repaid his loan or through some other infusion, institutions turned it around into another loan as quickly as possible. The college trustees acted typically when they learned that the proprietor had raised £1,000 in donations on August 19, 1763. That very day they loaned half that sum, and by September 7 the remaining £500. Across town, the hospital managers were likewise anxious to get their money loaned as quickly as possible. They fretted daily that "our loss of the Interest arising from the Money [not yet lent] is a great disadvantage." The rapid pace at which new funds and paid-off debts entered the credit market reflected both the organizations' desire to maximize the profits from lending their money and the intense demand in the local economy for such loans. With such high demand, the directors of these funds had to be careful which individuals they chose to loan to.[26]

Board members looked to "put out the money . . . on good & sufficient Securities," which in most cases meant that the borrower had to be a property owner. Prospective borrowers had to provide a legally binding promise called a bond and a mortgage that gave "clear Security of at least double the Value" of the loan. The treasurer held these documents until the borrower repaid the loan, or until it became necessary to take legal action, including seizing the mortgaged property. The hospital and contributionship, both dominated by Quaker directors, additionally required that borrowers "shall likewise make a Declaration upon Oath or Affirmation that the Mortgage promises are to the best of their knowledge free from all Incumbrances." Quickly, however, directors recognized that accepting a borrower's word was unwise. One of the most time-consuming aspects of serving on the board of directors for any of the four major lenders turned out to be looking into the proposed mortgages to make sure the borrower owned the property in full without any liens or disputes marring his or her right to post it as collateral. As a further precaution, when part of the value of the property lay in buildings, many boards required that their borrowers get fire insurance.[27]

Sometimes it took negotiation to decide what amount to lend. In 1759 when Abraham Bickley offered as collateral the mortgages on four lots and tenements on Front and Market Streets, the managers of the Pennsylvania Hospital decided that the properties were worth more than double the £500 he wanted to borrow. After a "Conference" with him, they convinced him to "take the further Sum of Two hundred & two pounds," for a total of £702. The hospital managers presumably congratulated themselves on finding a reliable borrower for their funds; Bickley was a prosperous and well-connected merchant, and he ended up paying back the money in less time than he had negotiated for. Merchant Richard Waln, on the other hand, applied for £1,000 from the hospital, offering as security his "Dwelling house" on Delaware Street and thirty acres of land in the Northern Liberties. On inspection, the hospital managers decided that the property only warranted a loan of £750, and Waln was forced to lower his expectations.[28]

It appears that the majority of loans were backed by property—indeed the bylaws of two of the major lenders, the Pennsylvania Hospital and Philadelphia Contributionship, required it. However, for the college and Presbyterian Ministers' Fund, in some cases a man's bond or warrant appeared to be sufficient. The sum might be small, as when Reverend Francis Alison, a professor, borrowed £30 "as p[er] his Note," or quite sizable, as when Philadelphia merchant Richard Stevens borrowed £500 with only "his Bond Dated this Day."[29]

Even mortgages and bonds were insufficient in some cases to secure a loan. Sometimes directors required yet one more layer of security: the joint signature of another creditable person. This was the case with artisan John Rouse. He borrowed £300 in 1752 and gave as security a mortgage on his shop and lot in town, as well as his farm in Pequa. When these mortgages still proved insufficient security, Rouse obtained prosperous baker John Hughes's promise to be his joint security for repayment of the loan. When a borrower lived outside of Philadelphia, it was often customary to require that someone in Philadelphia cosign the loan. The hospital managers only agreed to loan money to John Burgess of Bucks County "if he procures Daniel Williams or some other Person of Creditt in this City to engage for the Punctual Payment of the Interest annually."[30]

Once a loan was made, 6 percent interest came due annually on the date the loan was made. Record keeping of these interest payments varied, but it does seem that most borrowers, most of the time, were relatively punctual by the standards of colonial Philadelphia in meeting their obligations—which is to say, give or take a few months. Occasionally, a borrower might skip a year, or sometimes more, and pay the accumulated interest later. Merchant James Coultas, elected an officer of the county militia, commissioned a justice of the peace, and in 1765 appointed judge of the Orphan's Court, Quarter Sessions, and Common Pleas, was such a powerful man that the Philadelphia Contributionship made no quibble when he neglected to pay his interest for a full three years between 1766 and 1769. He resumed payments in 1770 and 1771, but did not pay again for another six years until 1778. The contributionship never made any official complaint.[31]

Though James Coultas might count on his status and apparently secure finances to shield him from pestering from the contributionship managers, not everyone could get away with this kind of behavior. Other men were less high ranking or less trustworthy in the eyes of the directors. In some cases, if the interest payments added up for too long, the board of directors might decide to begin charging interest on those back payments as well. Samuel House took out a loan of £800 from the Presbyterian Ministers' Fund in 1762 and then proceeded to miss his interest payments each following year until finally in 1765 he owed £96 in back interest. The directors of the fund paid him an extra £4 and put the loan down on their books as a new loan for £100. In the end, this may have been no more than fancy accounting to disguise House's negligence and balance the books. Whatever it said on paper, however, House continued to fail to pay his interest, and eventually the Presbyterian Ministers' Fund unloaded his loan onto someone else.[32]

Refinancing was not successful in Samuel House's case, but it was in others. Many men took out additional loans from the same lender or renegotiated the terms of their standing loans to absorb missed interest payments, and then did manage eventually to pay off the entirety. Refinancing could represent distrust then, as with House, but it could also be an act of good faith. It bought a borrower more time to pay off his or her loan.[33]

If boards of directors allowed some men to try to refinance their debt, with others they had reached the end of their patience. The treasurer of the Pennsylvania Hospital, "representing to the Board the pains he has taken to obtain payment of Samuel Flower and George Taylor . . . without success," was at last instructed "to take speedy legal measures to secure the Payment of the Money [£500] due from them." In the end, the treasurer appears to have come to some settlement outside of court, because Flower eventually paid back the money. Very rarely did loans from Philadelphia's voluntary associations end in a courtroom. Only eight suits were brought out of 310 loans, though legal action was threatened in four other cases. The Presbyterian Ministers' Fund was the most litigious; it brought all but two of these suits, suing seven men for six loans. The fund directors moved relatively quickly to seize assets—waiting less than five years on average. The other two organizations that finally took their borrowers to court, the Pennsylvania Hospital and Philadelphia Contributionship, delayed much longer. The hospital waited a full seventeen years before moving against Jacob and John Naglee. The contributionship only brought suit against William Young in 1788, twenty-one years after he had taken out his loan. It is unclear why the Presbyterian Ministers' Fund had such bad luck in its loans. Though it was less stringent than the hospital or contributionship in its requirements, all the borrowers taken to court had given mortgages as security. Perhaps fund borrowers were no more likely to be bad risks than other borrowers; the higher incidence of suits may instead reflect a greater willingness on the part of the Presbyterian Ministers' Fund to sue tardy borrowers.[34]

Once boards decided to take borrowers to court, events seemed to move smoothly in their favor. The hospital treasurer noted matter-of-factly that he had "received from the Sheriff of the County of Philad.a Five hundred and ninety Pounds in full discharge of the Principal and Interest due on the Mortgage of Jacob Naglee." The Presbyterian Ministers' Fund directors preferred to take personal control of the mortgaged property and sell it directly, rather than use the sheriff as an intermediary. Despite the fact that mortgaged property was supposed to be equal to twice the value of a loan, the evidence all seems to indicate that the hospital and Presbyterian Ministers' Fund resold it for the original sum borrowed plus whatever interest was owing on it—a very advantageous deal for the new buyer.[35]

The combination of factors that led a board of directors to be patient with one man and act against another is unfortunately a calculus that failed to inscribe itself into the dry columns of figures that tell most of the story of these loans. It is easy to guess why a powerful man like James Coultas received forbearance, but what precisely moved the Presbyterian Ministers' Fund to wait only three years before bringing suit against unfortunate Moses Erwin is less easy to unravel. Erwin was a well-respected (German?) farmer of comfortable means in Lancaster County, entrusted by his neighbors to certify county elections in 1757 and 1759 and to represent them at a provincial meeting of deputies in 1774. What the directors of the fund knew or suspected about him that inspired them to drag him to court will probably never be known. Perhaps in 1764 he had met with economic reversals that worried the directors. Then again, maybe their motives were more political in an election year that pitted Presbyterians against Quakers and their German supporters.[36]

Fortunately for the good works of the voluntary associations, most borrow-

TABLE 4
Status of Loans for Presbyterian Ministers' Fund, 1761–76

Status	Number	Percentage
Paid	63	58
In good standing as of 1776	19	18
Transferred	8	7
Suit	6	6
Unknown	12	11
Total	117	100

Source: Waste Book, 1761–98, Presbyterian Ministers' Fund, HSP.

ers do appear to have paid their interest reasonably regularly and either paid their debts or intended to in good faith. Unfortunately, however, the Revolution disrupted what might have otherwise been orderly repayments. Between war, British occupation, and confused or lost records, the fate of many loans outstanding in 1776 is difficult to determine. The Presbyterian Ministers' Fund has one of the most complete records of what happened to its loans. Just over 70 percent were paid, recovered through suit, or transferred to another lender (in which case the fund recouped the original loan and interest owed). Of the remaining loans, 18 percent were in good standing before the disruptions following 1776 (see table 4).

The Revolution affected repayment dramatically. One treasurer remembered that "troubles came in very fast" after the fall of 1775, and that "Continental Money being very plenty, every body paid off where there was Anything due." His own ability to do his job had been further hampered by the fact that a fire had burned his residence and destroyed many of the vital records of what loans were due. These problems were widespread and not helped by the decision all Philadelphians faced in 1777: whether to stay in the city during British occupation or decamp to the surrounding countryside. In the confusion, many loan records were lost.[37]

The boards of directors scrambled in uncertain times to look out for the financial health of their organizations. The Presbyterian Ministers' Fund directors faced a sudden wave of men repaying their loans as quickly as possible, taking advantage of depreciated currency to settle old debts. While the fund continued to make some loans to individuals, the directors began to turn to other investments, especially land. The Pennsylvania Hospital faced the same problem of repayment in depreciated currency and began actively trying to prevent it. When in 1776 Christian Cauffman indicated that he was going to repay his loan of £1,200, the managers met with him in person and told him they had "no immediate occasion of Money" and in the current uncertain climate "it may be difficult to place it out again," that is, find another borrower. They convinced him to continue the original obligation and to give them at least six months notice before he repaid his loan, and in return released some of the securities he had given for repayment. Cauffman tried again to repay his loan six months later, but the managers were firm: "we do not intend to receive it but agreeable to that Contract," they sternly declared.[38]

To guage how much longer many borrowers would have continued their loan obligations if currency depreciation in the 1770s and 1780s had not allowed for more rapid repayment is impossible. The average time it took to repay a loan was around six years, but the most commonly repeated pattern (statistical mode) was ten years. A number of very short term loans balanced out others that were very long. Occasionally borrowers held the money for only a matter of months; more often, for a period of years. The longest loan taken out and repaid within the colonial period was Jonathan Rouse's, who borrowed £300 from the hospital in 1752 and finally repaid it in 1776. Some of the loans not repaid by 1776 appear to have stretched on for quite some time; borrowers were still paying interest into the 1780s and beyond.

The directors of the lending voluntary associations kept a watchful eye on all these matters because, after all, these loans were meant to underwrite the stated objectives of each organization. The interest from the biggest lenders supported the building and maintenance of a hospital for the poor, the education of young men, annuities for widows and orphans, and indemnities against loss of property by fire. Because of differences in record keeping, it is difficult to compare how much money the organizations made from their loans. The hospital provides the best picture of the profit made from loans because it was legally obligated by the terms of its charter to publish its annual accounts. All but the last column of figures in table 5 are drawn from the numbers the hospital itself published. The final column, "Percent return on loans," was calculated based on the figures given.

In the twenty-five years before the Revolution devalued currency and otherwise disrupted its finances, the Pennsylvania Hospital earned nearly £7,900 off of interest alone. Throughout the period, the hospital usually earned near the 6 percent returns that the legal usury limit allowed. Probably the other major lenders enjoyed a similar rate of return; they were careful to take securities against default and to lend to men who were good credit risks.

The Borrowers

In 1771 the Library Company appointed a committee to decide where to loan £200 at that time "in the hands of the Treasurer," Samuel Morris Jr. The committee deliberated and returned to the directors to inform them that they thought they should lend the money to . . . Samuel Morris Jr. The rest of the directors agreed, and so Treasurer Morris was empowered to loan the money to himself. He was now in the position of being the party responsible for making sure that

TABLE 5
Pennsylvania Hospital Loans Made on Bonds and Mortgages, 1753–76

Year	New loans (in £)	Number of new borrowers	Total amount lent (in £)	Total number of borrowers	Interest paid (in £)	Principal paid (in £)	Percent return on loans
1753			1,850		67		—
1754			1,850		160		8.65
1755			1,850	6	61		3.30
1756	1,100	3	2,860	9	105		5.68
1757			2,860	9			?
1758			2,860	9			?
1759			2,850	8			?
1760			3,252	8			?
1761			3,252	8			?
1762	600	1	3,852	9	195		6.00
1763	1,500	2	6,963	14	312		8.10
1764	500				288	1,050	4.14
1765	700	1	6,429	13	368	688	?
1766	1,457	2	7,176	13	421	647	6.55
1767	150	1	7,326	14	441	250	6.15
1768			6,726		411	600	5.61
1769	400	1	7,126	14	444		6.60
1770	640	3	6,266	14	410	1,500	5.75
1771	600		6,766	16	446		7.12
1772	800	2	6,766	16	446	1,800	6.59
1773	11,827	12	17,493	25	324	1,100	4.79
1774	1,250	3	17,686	24	1,018	1,057	5.82
1775	2,600	4	17,186	26?	809	3,100	4.57
1776			16,886	24	1,162		6.76

Sources: PHM, 1751–76; *Some Account of the Pennsylvania Hospital . . .* (Philadelphia, 1754); *Continuation of the Account of the Pennsylvania Hospital . . .* (Philadelphia, 1761).

Notes: There are no records in either the minutes or printed materials for 1751 and 1752, and the account keeping was not uniform throughout the period. Percent return on loans is calculated by dividing interest received in a year by the amount out on loan the previous year.

he paid the annual interest and of course repaid the loan at all. Not until 1773, two years later, did it occur to the directors that they really ought to have Morris execute a bond, a legal document promising to repay his debt.[39]

The extant records rarely mention borrowers who were unsuccessful in obtaining loans, so we can surmise little about who directors turned away and for what reasons. The patterns of who directors did choose to loan to show that these organizations were still rooted in the personal connections and networks that characterized other private loans, but that boards of directors were at the same time making significant steps in a new direction, increasingly lending to men not personally known to them—even using intermediaries and brokers to negotiate those loans.

As we have seen, the loans made available by voluntary associations came in large sums and hewed to the legal limit of 6 percent interest, which was below market rates. These facts made them attractive loans, and the first men to take advantage were the directors themselves. The first loan made by the Pennsylvania Hospital in 1751 for the whopping sum of £1,000 went to board member Israel Pemberton. The board of directors almost certainly received many requests for all or part of that sum, but it was Pemberton who was able to secure it.[40]

Pemberton was far from the last board member to take advantage of the ever-deepening hoard of cash to be loaned. Directors almost certainly had first priority if they cared to get a loan. James Pemberton, board member and brother of Israel, got his own loan of £1,200 from the hospital; Treasurer John Smith borrowed £150 from the Philadelphia Contributionship; William Smith, provost and political champion of the college, got one or possibly two loans from that institution; the Presbyterian Ministers' Fund gave William Allen, an influential lay supporter and board member, four loans totaling £1,025. Francis Alison, however, took borrowing to a whole new level. A professor at the college, he got a loan there for £500, and at the Presbyterian Ministers' Fund, which had been his idea in the first place, he got no fewer than nine loans totaling £610. He seems to have treated the fund as a source for ready cash when he needed it on short notice. Though most of its loans were for well over £100, the fund seems to have made exceptions for Alison, allowing several loans between £10 and £30. He frequently took out small loans, apparently as the need arose in his personal finances. Alison was an outlier. In practice, few of the men who served as directors took advantage of the opportunity to borrow money from their institutions. Indeed, some explicitly went to a different institution when they wanted to borrow.[41]

If they did not borrow money for themselves, board directors sometimes used the connection to help their friends or relatives. Abel James, on the board of the Philadelphia Contributionship, acted as go-between and negotiator for a loan for his friend Edward Brooks Jr., while the Presbyterian Ministers' Fund only consented to loan Robert Taggart £100 on the "advice of Dr Alison and Rev.d Mr. Ewing." Benjamin Franklin appears to have been approached by many potential borrowers in the early 1750s before he went to England, and he brought their requests to two of the boards he served on: the Pennsylvania Hospital and Philadelphia Contributionship (he was also on the college's board, but it did not accumulate enough capital to make loans until the early 1760s).

If it helped to have a friend on the board of directors, that connection by itself was not always enough, as William Maugridge found. Maugridge was a joiner, and Benjamin Franklin thought him "a most exquisite Mechanic, and a solid sensible Man." Their friendship stretched back to the formation of the Junto in the late 1720s, and when Maugridge needed a loan in 1753, he asked Franklin for help, which evidently his old friend was happy to provide. Franklin first approached the Pennsylvania Hospital with Maugridge's request: £200 in return for a mortgage on land in Berks County. Franklin added his own personal guarantee that Maugridge's "Inter[es]t shall be punctually paid." Three of the hospital managers (not counting Franklin) were also old Junto members and friends of Maugridge, so one might think that the loan would sail through, but they took seriously their responsibility to find a safe haven for the hospital's capital. They and the other hospital managers agreed that Maugridge could have the loan if, upon inspection, his "Title is clear and the Value appears to be at least double the said Sum." But something went wrong. A mere two months later Franklin brought the same proposal to the Philadelphia Contributionship board, asking again for £200, offering the same Berks County land as security, and once again presenting himself as the guarantor for the annual interest payments. What had happened? It appears that the loan with the hospital fell through for some reason. Whether the managers found his property insufficient security for a loan of £200 or something else intervened is unclear. But Franklin persevered on his friend's behalf. Fully one-third of the board members at the hospital also served on the board of the contributionship, so the latter surely knew about Maugridge's previous application to the hospital and whatever had held up its completion. Here again four members of the twelve-man board were former Junto men (two of them, like Franklin, serving on both boards). Whatever had prevented Maugridge's loan at the hospital, the contributionship approved the loan. Perhaps in this case Franklin had done more to lay the groundwork and persuade his colleagues that Maugridge was a good bet.[42]

If personal connections did not always work with board members, another possible route was to use a more formal intermediary. Beginning in the 1770s, two men mediated several loans for the Pennsylvania Hospital. One was William Parr, the official recorder of deeds for Pennsylvania and a man important and wealthy enough to be labeled "Esquire" by 1770. By virtue of his job, he knew the property and aspirations of Philadelphians better than anyone, and the hospital managers frequently relied on his advice. They agreed, for example, to lend widow Ann Croston £500 in 1772 "if the Security She Offers be in the Opinion of William Parr Esq.r. Good and clear of Incumbrance." But Parr not only advised; more often he advocated. When the hospital was flush with money from the British Parliament in 1772, Parr applied within five months for no fewer than eight loans on behalf of other men. He even gave his own personal bond in one case, promising that the interest money would be paid on time each year. Six of the men Parr represented did not live in the city, but in the surrounding counties. Parr was taking on the functions of a broker, negotiating loans on behalf of clients, many of whom lived at a distance from the hospital, and who presumably paid him for his services.[43]

Lewis Weiss acted as an intermediary between the hospital and the German community. Weiss was a lawyer who had arrived in Philadelphia from Prussia by midcentury. He was a respected man in Philadelphia, who had the trust of the German immigrant population and the hospital managers. And crucially he spoke both English and German. He brokered two loans in 1773 for three men who were probably German, all living outside the city. When the borrowers of one of those loans proposed to repay it, Weiss approached the managers and asked "to have the preference given him when that mony is again let out, he being applied to by a person [from Lancaster County] who has a good Security to give." The managers happily consented. Later, when the managers had dif-ficulty with borrower Caspar Zenger, they consulted with Weiss about how to proceed. Finally, Weiss shows up in the Philadelphia Contributionship records making the annual interest payments for Reinard Kamer, probably another Ger-man who lived outside the city. Whether Weiss was a paid intermediary or an unremunerated go-between assisting members of the German community, he was taking on the functions of a broker, finding and negotiating the terms of loans on behalf of others. His actions likely helped the German-speaking population have access to loans they otherwise might have missed because of language problems and distance.[44]

Historians of credit and financial markets in the colonial period have painted a picture of prerevolutionary private lending as "arranged in an informal person-to-person atmosphere with few intermediaries." In most cases, this assessment is probably accurate, but the hospital for one was beginning to move toward a form of lending that went beyond personal connections alone. Friendships and networks clearly continued to be important. However, with large sums available to loan and a concern to see the money in the hands of dependable borrow-ers, the hospital managers looked beyond their own circles and perhaps even slighted old friends to place their institution's capital in the best position to earn reliable interest. The lenders had not become impersonal institutional banks open equally to all comers, but, within a certain socioeconomic class, they were also not ruled entirely by cliquish interests. By 1773 the hospital managers had to agree to a new policy: "in future," they mandated, all "the Titles of all Estates . . . *with which they are unacquainted,* shall be examined by John Dickinson Esq.r and certified by him to be good and sufficient before the Money is lent." What a long way the hospital managers had come from that first loan in 1751 to one of their own.[45]

If brokers represented one form of intermediation in the loan market, another very important one worked alongside it: commonly individuals and organizations traded in someone else's debt. Thomas Gordon's loan is an example of this practice. Gordon was an established Philadelphia merchant and a manager of the Pennsylvania Hospital from 1758 to 1766. When he needed a loan in 1759 for £200, however, he went instead to the Philadelphia Contributionship to get it. In 1761 he came back to the contributionship to repay his debt, but not by giving the treasurer the cash he had originally borrowed. A man named John Johnston by this time owed Gordon £200, so Gordon assigned the contributionship Johnston's debt to him. In practical terms, this meant that the treasurer returned to Gordon his mortgage and took in its place Johnston's (which Gordon as Johnston's creditor had in his possession) for the same amount. Now Johnston owed annual interest of £12 to the contributionship rather than to Gordon, the man he had originally borrowed from, and when Johnston went to repay his own debt, it would be to the contributionship. Johnston never asked for a loan from the contributionship; he nevertheless found his debt now transferred to it and away from Gordon. In this case, the contributionship made Gordon guarantee Johnston's repayment, so he remained involved until Johnston finally repaid the debt the following year. However, in most situations, once a debt had been transferred to cover a borrower's debt, that borrower was free and clear. The debt was now the responsibility of the assignee.[46]

Trading in debt did not always work out so well for the organizations. The bond of James Claypoole and David Chambers for £100 was assigned to the Presbyterian Ministers' Fund in 1773. It appears that the pair had not paid their original lender (whose name is lost because of damage to the document) any interest in four years, nine months, and three days (the accounting in these matters could be very exact!). The fund treasurer refinanced their loan to include the interest owed, but Claypoole and Chambers still could not be prevailed on to pay their debt. Only in 1777, in vastly depreciated currency, did they finally repay the fund. Whoever had assigned this debt was the winner; the fund certainly lost. Why the fund agreed to take Claypoole and Chambers's debt is unclear, but they surely regretted the decision.[47]

The lending organizations themselves sometimes met their own financial obligations by transferring debt. In 1767 and 1772 the hospital managers found themselves in dire financial straits and agreed that the treasurer should "sell off any of the Securities taken for Money lent" that would equal the sum they needed (£500 in 1767, £300 in 1772). In both cases, the treasurer was quickly able to find others willing to take the loans and give the hospital the cash it so desperately needed. In at least one case the Presbyterian Ministers' Fund did not have enough cash on hand to give a borrower all the money he wanted, so it assigned him one of their outstanding debts instead. In 1774 John Waugh wanted £230, and the fund gave him £180 cash, but made up the difference with Robert Alison's debt to the fund dating back to 1767. Alison had made one single interest payment in all that time, so the fund directors were presumably relieved to unload it; now it became John Waugh's problem to collect.[48]

This shuffling of debt, however, raises questions about the interest rates charged by voluntary organizations versus private lenders. Scholars of credit in colonial Philadelphia have posited that the 6 percent legal interest rate was below the market rates covertly charged by private lenders. The transfer of debt between private lenders and voluntary associations—all of which definitely did charge 6 percent interest—suggests either that private lenders *were* adhering to the legal limit or that some other financial adjustments had been quietly worked out that did not make it into the public records.

Major lenders in this period took some halting steps away from the patterns associated with private lending by using brokers and through the trading of borrowers' debts. People not personally known to the boards of directors became their borrowers, either through choice or by having their debt traded around.

Between 1750 and 1776, 269 individuals took out 310 loans from the ten lending voluntary associations. The borrowers themselves tended to be merchants or shopkeepers (39% of all individuals where profession is known), artisans (32%), or professional men (16%). The merchants borrowed across the board, but the professional men tended to get their loans from the Presbyterian Ministers' Fund, while the contributionship furnished the most loans to artisans—many of them carpenters, which made sense since the contributionship worked closely with men in the building trades to assess fire risk and rebuild ruined property. Over time, the borrowers came from further afield, increasingly outside of Philadelphia in the surrounding Pennsylvania counties, with occasional properties being mortgaged in Delaware or New Jersey. Those newer borrowers may have been farmers. Not enough is known about the religious or ethnic affiliations of the borrowers to indicate any clear patterns, though it does seem that Presbyterians were very likely to borrow from the Presbyterian Ministers' Fund.[49]

Eight women were named as borrowers. In most cases, women were named alongside men, often their husbands, as was the case of "Will: Garrett & Wife." Presumably in cases like these the husband required the wife's signature to sign over a mortgage as collateral for the loan. In two or possibly three cases, a woman alone was the borrower. Ann Croston and Susannah Morris were both widows in 1772 and 1773 when each woman received a loan from the Pennsylvania Hospital.

To say exactly what borrowers used their money for is difficult. The organizational records are silent on the matter, and frustratingly no borrower's papers that I have yet seen state explicitly how he or she used the money. From the extant financial papers of many of the borrowers, however, we can hazard some educated guesses about how they might have used the money.

On average, borrowers were in their early or middle forties when they got their loans. These loans, then, were not being used primarily by young men just setting up, but by more established men who had over time accrued the collateral necessary for very large loans. Only 5 of the 269 borrowers were in their twenties at the time they took out a loan, and most of those young men borrowed money in conjunction with another, older partner.

Some borrowers probably used their loans to buy more property. As we have seen, William Maugridge used a £200 loan from the Philadelphia Contribution-ship in 1754 to buy a farm in Bucks County. Others may have gotten loans to make improvements to their existing property. At the time that John Dickinson got a loan from the Philadelphia Contributionship in 1773, for example, he was renovating Fairhill, his estate. Dickinson was an extremely wealthy merchant and lawyer, so it is possible that he took out the loan not so much to finance the repairs as to have ready cash on hand to pay the workers. If the 6 percent interest rate charged by the contributionship really was below market values, Dickinson may have preferred to keep his capital tied up in more lucrative investments and borrow the £500 he needed for immediate expenses.[50]

Others used their loans to facilitate investments. Richard Waln applied for a loan from the Pennsylvania Hospital the same month that he purchased a mill. It took about two months for the loan of £750 to come through, but the money came just as he needed it. Waln complained that the purchase had "drained me intolerably" and "take[n] all my present Cash." Other investments by borrowers are plausibly but less directly tied to their loans. John Gibson, a Scottish mer-chant, insured a vessel bound for Antigua and Jamaica in 1767, perhaps using some of the £1,000 he had borrowed from the college to cover that investment. Robert Callender, on the other hand, was oriented westward, as he involved himself deeply in the Indian trade. He collaborated with and financed the trad-ing activities of traders George Croghan, John Baynton, and George Morgan. Almost certainly, his loans went toward those activities. John Houston, on the other hand, had "made a Discovery of a small vein of Lead ore" that he hoped to exploit. His application to borrow money from the College of Philadelphia alerted trustee William Allen, who himself invested in mining activities, to the possibility of a new source of lead in the area. Allen collaborated with Houston, perhaps before but certainly after Houston applied for a loan from the college board on which Allen served.[51]

Some of the names that appear among the list of borrowers are frankly sur-prising. William Allen had the highest tax assessment in the city at midcentury, and yet he borrowed over £1,000 from the Presbyterian Ministers' Fund in four loans between 1761 and 1775. The names of other similarly wealthy men dot the list. Why were they borrowing money? One possibility, already mentioned, is that they were taking advantage of the low interest rate, borrowing money and reinvesting it at a higher rate elsewhere. Another is that, for as much money as they had on paper, these wealthy men had a shortage of cash. They found the loans available from voluntary associations useful for these reasons.[52]

William Allen's son James suggests another use for the borrowed money. James Allen borrowed £200 from the Presbyterian Ministers' Fund in February 1771, another £200 in March, and another £50 in May. On December 30 of the same year, he repaid the entire amount plus £21 13s. 6d. interest. These were probably working capital or bridge loans to provide him with the necessary cash flow to cover his day-to-day costs of business until outstanding debts or investments paid off, which apparently they did within ten months of his taking the first loan. Nearly 10 percent of all prerevolutionary loans were repaid in less than one year, while another 4 percent were paid in less than two. Such financial instruments helped keep merchants and artisans solvent between payoffs.[53]

Finally, one last group of borrowers took advantage of voluntary association credit: other organizations. The Commissioners of the Lighthouse borrowed £310 from the Society for the Relief of . . . Masters of Ships in 1766; the Contributors to the Relief of the Poor borrowed £400 from the Library Company in 1770; the county commissioners borrowed £500 from the hospital and £300 from the Library Company in 1774 to build Walnut Street Prison; and "ten Principall Members of ye Dutch Lutheran Congregation," presumably the Church's directing board, borrowed nearly £900 from the hospital in 1762. The loans of voluntary associations represented a line of credit utilized not only by individuals but also by other voluntary associations, governmental bodies, and churches.[54]

The economic relationship between credit-extending associations and their borrowers benefited both. The borrower gained necessary capital and (insofar as it mattered to him or her) could feel civic pride that the interest money went to a good cause. The associations promoted the economic development of the city by investing thousands of pounds in local enterprise, while at the same time growing their own capital stock and extending their ability to provide health care for impoverished Philadelphians, educate young men, support widows and orphans, and rebuild property destroyed by fire.

Philadelphia voluntary associations were not unique in accumulating large amounts of money to fund their activities and lending their capital at interest. The practice dated back at least to the late fifteenth century in England. However, by the eighteenth century, British societies did not tend to loan to individuals. Rather, they put their money in public funds, in British government securities, in the Bank of England, and occasionally in property. The choices British organizations had about where to invest their funds reflected an entirely different realm of financial possibilities. The infrastructure of Britain in general, and London in particular, offered institutional avenues for investment that simply did not exist in the more restricted colonies.[55]

In contrast, the voluntary associations of Philadelphia became themselves the institutional avenues for many financial services—imperfect vehicles that operated in the absence of a true banking system. With the declining activity of the General Loan Office after 1755, these organizations partially filled a void, making available much-needed credit for Philadelphia's growing commerce with the western hinterlands and Atlantic world. How the activities of Philadelphia compared to other British American cities such as New York, Boston, or Charleston is a question that can only be answered through further research, but the evidence strongly suggests that voluntary associations in other colonial cities played a similar role. Furthermore, to assess what proportion of Philadelphia's entire credit market these groups' loans represented is unfortunately difficult if not impossible because we know so little about the volume of interpersonal lending.[56]

What is clear is that these organizations provided necessary financial services for Philadelphia. They made available over £112,000 in low-cost cash loans to borrowers in the city and its surrounding counties; they offered flexible time frames, which some borrowers used for short-term bridge financing and others used as long-term capital; and they provided large loans from one source, creating efficiencies where otherwise borrowers might have had to cobble together loans from many sources.

The memory of the South Sea Bubble, combined with British mercantilist policies, hampered the evolution of American financial infrastructure. Fighting suspicions of corporations, worried about speculative bubbles, and constantly overseen by a conservative ministry, American legislators had to fight to implement even the most basic financial institutions. The fight over land banks and currency has garnered considerable attention. Ignored until now has been the more covert work of civic institutions, which, chartered by and condoned by the legislature and proprietor, quietly went beyond their stated public works functions to fill a void in the local economy.

CHAPTER SIX

Private Men Interfering with Government
Taking Over from the State

A visitor first approaching Philadelphia by water in midcentury would have seen one of the most impressive skylines in British North America: a bustling waterfront in the foreground, beyond it houses and shops crowded together, and, towering over them all, a remarkable number of steeples puncturing the sky. Churches were going up everywhere. Quakers built two new meetinghouses and replaced their main meetinghouse at Second and Market with a larger structure. Across the street Church of England parishioners replaced their original small church with a handsome brick building and began by midcentury a subscription to build a grand steeple to tower over all others. The steeple engaged civic as well as religious pride, and some contributions even came in from nonmembers anxious to see improvement and beautification in their city. Meanwhile, the expanding membership of the Church of England necessitated the construction of two new large churches in other neighborhoods in the 1760s. Presbyterians too built rapidly. At midcentury they enlarged the original Presbyterian Church, "Old Buttonwood," and by 1770 they had built three more churches not only to host growing numbers of congregants but also to accommodate differences between "Old Light" and "New Light" believers. Catholics, meanwhile, first built a chapel in the 1730s, then enlarged it, and finally supplemented it with a larger church. A newer sect, the Methodists, opened their church in 1769. The

city swelled with people of many faiths, and the skyline grew crowded with the steeples under which they worshipped.[1]

One of the more popular activities undertaken by first-time visitors to the city was to attend these various houses of worship and comment on the services. William Black visited Philadelphia in 1744, and on his first full Sunday in town he went to three churches. He attended Christ Church in the morning, where he admired the quantity "of Fine Women in one Church, as I never had heard Philadelphia noted Extraordinary that way," and in the afternoon to hear the New Light preaching of Presbyterian Gilbert Tennent, whose zeal manifested itself as he "turn'd up the Whites of his Eyes . . . Cuff'd his Cushion . . . and twist'd his Band." The theatrics did not appeal to Black, who snuck out of the service before it ended and went instead to the Quaker Meeting, where he found a Friend "Labouring Under the Spirit very Powerfully" and ranting so quickly that Black could hardly follow him for fear "of his Choaking." Thirty years later, John Adams, busy as he was as a delegate to the Continental Congress, also found time within his first few weeks in Philadelphia to visit various churches. He thought the Presbyterian meeting sparse and not "very polite," but found Christ Church "a more noble Building," with "a genteeler Congregation." He found the rich surroundings and music of the Catholic chapel so affecting that he could not help but wonder how "the Reformation ever succeeded."[2]

The sectarian diversity represented by this crowded skyline and this popular tourist activity indicated more than religious pluralism in Philadelphia; they were manifestations of tremendous demographic and civic change, which opened pressing questions about governance—specifically *who* would or should govern. Quakers traditionally had ruled, even in the second quarter of the century when they no longer dominated demographically but continued to enjoy broad-based approval for their policies. Their hegemony crumbled almost overnight, however, with the outbreak of violence on the Pennsylvania frontier in 1754. The coming of the French and Indian War provoked deep problems surrounding war, pacifism, the responsibility of the state, the inviolability of conscience, and the place of Quakers in the public arena. In the midst of the war, one constituency, influenced by the partisan rift between the so-called Quaker and proprietary factions, challenged Quakers' right to rule if they refused to take defensive measures to protect the province. Despite the passage of a militia bill, these partisans used the technology of civic voluntary association in a new way: not to accomplish something that the state was not doing, but to impose themselves in arenas and policy making in which the state *was* involved.

Quakers ultimately could not survive the onslaught of calls for them to quit the helm, at least for the duration of the war, and for the first time found themselves largely outside the corridors of formal power. Not content, however, to cede power over policy to others, Quakers also adapted civic voluntary association to usurp policy prerogatives away from formal channels of government and into their own hands. Mobilizing through organizations that were not answerable to the larger public, Quakers first inserted themselves in Indian diplomacy and thereby influenced the course of the war. Next they took over all public poor relief in Philadelphia in an attempt to continue to shape the policy and culture of their city.

Chapter 4 demonstrated how the new civic technology of voluntary association, which had enjoyed broad public consensus, became embroiled in the 1750s with political posturing between proponents of the proprietor on the one hand and of the assembly on the other, permanently eradicating easy common ground for voluntary associations, no matter how laudable their projects. This chapter examines another facet of what this critical period of change meant for local governance and popular mobilization. It looks at how constituencies blocked from formal power dealt with being on the outside. First non-Quakers but then more enduringly Quakers themselves would appropriate the mechanisms of voluntary association to take over from the state.

Acting without Law: The Independent Companies

By midcentury profound shifts in the demographics and culture of Philadelphia were clear to every observer. Long gone were the days when Quakers had been a majority. Newer immigrants crowded into the already densely packed city and brought with them their own religious, cultural, linguistic, and political forms and ideas. Though the days of Quaker dominance had by no means been characterized by harmony, this new diversity brought with it different ways of drawing lines through the community, different matters over which to quarrel. Coinciding with the rise of the civic technology of voluntary associations, moreover, newly formed constituencies could now make use of new and increasingly potent ways to express and act on differences of opinion. By the 1750s political questions divided elites into increasingly clear political factions but had little spillover into the world of ordinary Philadelphians, who continued overwhelmingly in provincial politics to support the Quaker Assembly, which championed freedom of conscience, kept taxes low, enacted minimal laws and regulations, and ensured economic productivity through sound fiscal policy, relatively equitable land distribution, and careful regulation of the quality of Pennsylvania's main export, flour.[3]

One problem, however, had plagued the province from its very inception: the Quaker insistence on pacifism, even in cases of self-defense. Pennsylvania politician James Logan expressed the problem succinctly: "Ever since I have had the power of thinking, I have clearly seen that government without arms is an inconsistency." That "inconsistency" provoked problems on at least three levels.[4]

First, the absence of a militia weakened the political community. Eighteenth-century political theory emphasized the importance of freemen bearing arms in defense of their community. The militia served a dual purpose: it provided a route for freemen to express their masculine civic virtue and claim full membership (and rights) in a polity, and it acted as a bulwark against the encroaching tyranny of a government that might otherwise overreach itself. Bearing arms, then, was at once a right and a duty with multiplier effects for the individual and the larger community. The absence of required military service in Pennsylvania presented a problem in that it prevented the enactment of these virtues and benefits, but it may also have been an attraction to newcomers to the colony, especially Quakers and migrants from Germany, eager from principle or from experience to eschew compulsory military service. The military utility of militias had, by the eighteenth century, declined in most of early America, but nevertheless musters continued to serve important social functions knitting together the community. Pennsylvania lacked this social and civic common ground. To be sure, the Quaker founders offered other routes to civic participation, but the enthusiastic response of Pennsylvania men (including many Quakers) to the first extralegal militia in 1747 and subsequent iterations suggests that these nonmilitary avenues were not entirely satisfactory.[5]

Second, the refusal of the assembly to organize military defense abdicated one of the core responsibilities of the state to its inhabitants: defense of life and protection of property. Frustrated by Quaker intransigence on defense during the privateering crisis in 1747–48, Benjamin Franklin, who was otherwise a stalwart political ally of the Quaker political elite, had articulated the stance of many when he declared that "*Protection* is as truly due from the Government to the People, as *Obedience* from the People to the Government." In Pennsylvania the government not only failed but actually refused to live up to its obligations. In that case, Franklin and others concluded that Pennsylvanians not only retained the right but became impelled by duty to act on their own, which they did in forming the Defense Association, an extralegal militia.[6]

Finally, the "inconsistency" of government without arms placed Pennsylvania in a precarious position vis-à-vis the British Empire, which on multiple occasions considered changing fundamentally the provincial constitution, either to bring the colony under royal control or to bar pacifists from holding government office. William Penn himself had concluded that in order to protect the political sovereignty of the colony, Quakers must compromise on the matter of a militia—advice his fractious colonists declined to take. As long as Pennsylvania had no provision for military defense, it not only failed in its responsibility to its own residents, as Franklin pointed out, but imperiled its position in an empire engaged in frequent imperial contests and bent on territorial expansion.[7]

Pennsylvania had for the most part been able to avert the problem of military defense up to now because no pressing and immediate danger had compelled government action. The wars that plagued the British Empire beginning with the Glorious Revolution largely bypassed both the territory and the shipping of the Quaker colony. Pennsylvania's fortuitous placement, sandwiched in the middle of the mainland North American colonies, allowed it to reap the benefits while others bore the brunt of attack. In tandem with a strong British navy and its own successful Indian diplomacy, Pennsylvania remained not only free from immediate threats for the first half of the century but quite successful in westward expansion, which in turn enhanced its agricultural production and prosperity. It elided the costs of war and enjoyed the benefits of peace and expansion. To be sure, both the imperial and other colonial governments called on Pennsylvania to shoulder its fair share of American defense, but aside from occasional grants of money to the monarch's use, the assembly ignored such calls. Governor John Evans had attempted to raise a militia in the early 1700s, provoking a storm of protest and acrimony. His impolitic blundering disgusted friend and foe alike and, in combination with Pennsylvania's relative safety, had hobbled further concerted moves for state-directed defense.[8]

Quakers might take deep satisfaction in their continuing ability to remain true to pacifist principles, but in reality the stability and relative harmony that characterized Pennsylvania in the first half of the eighteenth century masked deep-rooted problems and unanswered questions. What responsibilities did the layers of government from proprietor to assembly owe to the colony's founding principles, its defenseless population, and its parent empire? What civic roles could or would inhabitants play? What loyalty could be expected of an increasingly ethnically, linguistically, and religiously diverse population touched only lightly by the laws or administration of government and without strong institutions or civic rituals (like a militia) to unite them? And would the ever more dominant non-Quaker population be content to let Quaker legislators continue to decide these matters?

The French and Indian War erupted suddenly and violently in western Pennsylvania in 1754, bringing these questions to the fore. Mayhem engulfed the ter-rified backcountry settlements, which could expect no help from Pennsylvania's government, as it had taken no measures to defend its population. Indeed, by 1754 the political landscape made the defense question even thornier than it had been in 1747. To the misfortune of the settlers in the line of fire, the war came at a time when the elected assembly and Proprietor Thomas Penn were locked in a contest for political dominance. The assembly remained unwill-ing to take explicit military measures, but in the midst of crisis it did pass legislation, as it had in the past, to make funds available for military purposes. Determined to assert more control over "his" colony, however, Penn instructed the governor to veto all money bills—even those that would have given money for defense—until the assembly acceded to his demands for greater control. Defense had become entangled with an abstract fight over proprietary versus legislative power, with neither side willing to back down. While Penn and the assembly bickered, the frontier burned.[9]

Once again in a moment of impasse, it was Benjamin Franklin who saw a way forward: simply use the same stratagem that had succeeded in 1747, a voluntary militia. Proprietary supporters, however, stonewalled this idea. They refused to countenance an extralegal force this time. Sensing an opportunity to embarrass their political enemies and drive them from office, they demanded a formal militia law they believed the "quaking Assembly" could never produce. They had not counted, however, on the ingenuity and political dexterity of Franklin.[10]

Undeterred, Franklin worked to mobilize the might of Pennsylvania's provin-cial government to provide defense. Now himself an assemblyman representing his adopted city of Philadelphia, Franklin introduced and got passed Pennsylva-nia's first and only colonial militia bill in November 1755. In framing the Militia Bill, however, Franklin drew on the institutional and cultural patterns forged by the extralegal Defense Association of 1747. The central provision of the bill was that military service would be voluntary, not mandatory as was the norm in every other colony, thus preserving Quakers from having to participate against their consciences. As in 1747, volunteers would elect their own officers, and even more, they would have voice in drawing up a military code of conduct and only be asked to commit to serve if they agreed to the terms of that code. In its structure, then, the legal militia reflected its earlier extralegal parent. It took as a given that some men would serve while others would not.[11]

As in 1747, the militia quickly drew many volunteers. Within weeks of the passage of the Militia Act, companies had formed, drilled, and elected officers. By February 1756 Philadelphia's "City Regiment" marched in review through the city streets with great pageantry and discipline. Supporters claimed that one thousand men in the city alone had joined, including a substantial German contingent. Critics sneered that the Philadelphia militia was not so impressive, consisting rather of "between 6 and 700 Men and Boys, a great part of who had never appeared at any former Muster."[12]

From a pragmatic standpoint, Franklin's strategy worked, but it was far from a complete triumph, for it also had the effect of passionately dividing Philadelphians. The Militia Bill had been designed to find a compromise that would satisfy both Quakers and those urging militarization. However, as compromises usually do, it failed to satisfy extremists in either camp. Strict Quakers excoriated any legal countenance for a militia. Proprietary supporters were even more outraged. The grounds of their scorn rested primarily on the very fact that the law was voluntary. Opponents to the Militia Bill believed that "no Man would willingly bind himself while his Neighbours are free." Disregarding the recent example of the Defense Association and their own eager participation in it, proprietary critics complained that "not one fiftieth Part of the people can be brought to act" under the Militia Bill. "The very Spirit" of the plan was "odious" because it put those who did volunteer on an "unequal and slavish Footing" with all those free riders who did not serve. They railed against the "iniquitous Exception of ye Quakers" implicit in the bill. They saw Franklin and the assembly's compromise as dangerous. Drawing on republican notions of citizenship, they argued that where the good or the defense of the whole community was at stake, all men ought to serve. Civil society and civic duty should not—*could not*—be divided between those who did all the work and those who reaped all the advantage. Arguing that it was "highly unjust to think that the Burden of Defence should fall upon a few Individuals," they bluntly refused to participate. Their opposition, however, stemmed from motives other than high-minded republican spirit. Siding with Thomas Penn in his fight with the assembly, proprietary partisans wished to eject Quakers from government, and even petitioned the king to bar them from serving in office. They could hardly support a measure like the Militia Bill which might help the assembly.[13]

Unable to prevent the "iniquitous" Militia Bill from coming into operation, proprietary supporters organized on two fronts to combat it. In England they petitioned the Privy Council, the final arbiter of all colonial legislation, to disallow the law. In Pennsylvania critics took advantage of the very element of the law they found most offensive—that military service was voluntary—and in the winter of 1756 decided to form their own extralegal militia, outside both the parameters of the Militia Bill and the assembly. Four or five extralegal "Independent Companies" quickly formed in the city, with another nine in the surrounding countryside. Unfortunately, no muster rolls survive, so it is impossible to gauge how it compared to the estimated one thousand who had joined the legal militia in Philadelphia. The governor, although technically bound in his role as executive to support the legal "City Regiment," instead encouraged the Independent Companies in their defiance of the assembly and its militia.[14]

Franklin and others urged the extra-legal Associators instead to add their energies to the legal militia, arguing that the Independent Companies split and therefore weakened the defensive posture of the colony and moreover "affront[ed] in express Terms the Laws and Legislature of their Country." The members of the Independent Companies defended their right to organize extralegally. The law might legalize one form of militia, "yet it no where says that it shall be illegal to follow any other Mode." The Independent Companies might act *without* law, but that clearly was different, as they pointed out, from "acting *contrary* to positive Law." The appropriate functions and boundaries of sovereign power in Pennsylvania belonged not just to the state but to private individuals, who, the Independent Companies argued, retained the right to undertake any activity that was not explicitly prohibited.[15]

The men in the Independent Companies thus took civic voluntary association one dramatic step further than had anyone before. In 1747 Philadelphians had argued that when government failed to meet its responsibilities, citizens retained the right to act on their own. The Independent Companies in 1756 undertook defense, even though the state itself had taken measures to fulfill that responsibility. Fundamentally, Pennsylvanians appear to have conceded the point. Even the strongest opponents of the Independent Companies never charged that they acted illegally (only unwisely) and never moved to prevent them from organizing on their own. Collectively, then, proponents and critics alike affirmed the right of individuals to act extralegally, outside, and even *against* the wishes of the government (though not in direct opposition or hindrance to it).

Like the Defense Association of 1747, however, both the legal City Regiment and the extralegal Independent Companies were short-lived. The Privy Council in England, partly at the urging of Thomas Penn, disallowed the Militia Act that had created the City Regiment. The king's councilors deemed the law "improper and inadequate" and thought it "seems rather calculated to exempt persons from Military Services, than to encourage and promote them." The Privy Council disallowed the law in July 1757, but the news did not reach Philadelphia until the fall, shortly before the act was set to expire anyway. The militia quietly disbanded, having done little more than drill and parade around the city since its inception the year before. The Independent Companies were in no way bound by the law and therefore unaffected by the Militia Act's disallowance. However, they promptly set aside all their assertions of right and civic duty and also took the opportunity quietly to fade away. Two years later William Allen lamented that "we have no Militia, nor like to have any."[16]

The City Regiment and Independent Companies contributed to the evolution of civic culture in Philadelphia in three ways. First, by raising seriously the argument that where all were in danger, all must serve, and by trying to undermine the Quaker Assembly, the critics of the Militia Bill politicized as never before the decision to volunteer (or not). Given Pennsylvania's history and political structure, a mandatory militia was never going to be politically feasible; its military forces—however structured—would always have to be voluntary. That very fact conveyed status upon volunteers, whose service could be seen as a marker of civic virtue and patriotic concern for the community. Conversely, for the first time, those who did not volunteer came under suspicion for selfishness or still worse motivations, potentially standing outside—or even opposed to—civil society.[17]

Second, the Independent Companies expanded the political space in which private individuals could organize—not only when there was a gap to be filled, as in 1747, but now also even when there was not a gap. Men retained the right to act when they disagreed with government actions. The independent militia was not the only organization through which Philadelphians asserted this right at this time. Within months another group, in some ways still more controversial, would build on this precedent.

Finally, the Independent Companies laid bare the tensions between the rights of Associators and the rights of everyone else. On one hand, the Independent Companies, like the Defense Association of 1747 before them, demonstrated the vigor of self-representational culture in Philadelphia. Men were able to collect together and act for themselves in the way they saw fit—the ultimate expression of their own agency. On the other hand, the Independent Companies represented a shutting down of the democratic process for everyone else who was not a member. The companies acted outside the law, which in a republican system had to be understood as acting outside, even against, the will of the people expressed through and by their chosen representatives. Answerable only to its own constituents, the independent militia operated without any check, such as public elections. The extralegal militia could take actions that had ramifications for members of the whole community, but it never had to answer to or worry about their wishes, as ideally a republican government would.

The same had been true of the Defense Association of 1747 as well, of course. Indeed, its independence of action was the wellspring of its efficiency. It could mobilize like-minded men only and ignore the concerns of men who disagreed. The minority of strict Quakers who opposed its activities were left powerless to stop the association because the militia did not answer to them, the elected assembly, or anyone else. The same tensions were present, then, for the Defense Association as for the Independent Companies. However, the much broader consensus enjoyed by the Defense Association in 1747–48 masked the ways in which it acted to undercut the democratic process of others because only a minority sincerely opposed its activities. The Independent Companies in 1755–56 differed only in degree. Formed in the context of the poisoned politicking of the 1750s, they sparked virulent and vocal opposition, exposed and contributed to a greater rift in the community, and acted in direct opposition to a legally constituted group (as opposed to the Defense Association, which acted against a vacuum of government response). On one hand, it spurred direct participation in the most fundamental sense; on the other hand, it constrained the democratic participation or oversight of nonmembers. Contemporaries seem to have concluded that the former consideration outweighed the latter because the principle of the Independent Companies' right to organize was never seriously challenged.

"A Separate Body of People": The Friendly Association

In the midst of competing militarization schemes, another organization formed with the opposite intent—to promote peace with warring Indians—but with similar ramifications in recalibrating the relationship between state and private actors. In 1756 Quakers founded the Friendly Association for Gaining and Preserving Peace with the Indians by Pacific Measures, with the explicit intention to shape Indian diplomacy, a matter that took on additional urgency not only because of the violence of the conflict but because Quakers had that year resigned from provincial government. They founded and used the Friendly Association as a way to assert continuing influence on provincial and even imperial policy, freed now by virtue of their private foundation from answering either to a voting public that preferred Indian killing or to an imperial British hierarchy that could no longer rein them in through the Privy Council or other formal government channels. Quakers here tread the path earlier beaten by the Defense Association of 1747 and the Independent Companies of 1756, using a private organization, answerable only to its own constituency, to shape or even take over policy, not only at the municipal but at the provincial and imperial level.[18]

The French and Indian War provoked a crisis for Pennsylvania Quakers, who had for some time struggled with what their faith would mean amid the comfort and prosperity of their New World home. By the 1750s Quakers had dominated Pennsylvania government for seventy years. Since the founding of Pennsylvania, many Friends had become less committed to the radical core values of the sect; they had become increasingly "secular" in their approach to government, less strictly tenacious of the beliefs they had held when their denomination had been a persecuted minority in England in the seventeenth century. Many were far removed from the radical beliefs that had inspired their forebears. By midcentury a small group of reformers had had enough. They called emphatically for spiritual renewal and a severe crackdown against backsliding Quakers to restore the religious purity of their sect.[19]

In the midst of this movement, the first real war Pennsylvania had ever faced sorely tested Quakers' commitment to pacifism and became a flash point between reformers and their more secular brethren. Pacifism stood apart from other Quaker values as a "symbol of morality in politics, the position to be held at all costs to preserve the good name of their church." Those Friends calling for spiritual renewal were appalled in 1755 at the Militia Act and other legislation passed by the assembly to raise funds for defense. They began intensely lobbying Friends in the assembly to step down and dissociate themselves and by extension the Quaker sect from such shameful proceedings.[20]

Quakers were under considerable pressure from multiple sides to leave Pennsylvania government. Reformers' calls coincided with those of partisans opposed to continued Quaker political dominance. Proprietary supporters began a campaign to discredit the Friends in government with authorities in England, seeking to bar them from serving in the legislature. The Privy Council came very close to doing so, but English Friends "moved heaven and earth" to prevent this extremity. They brokered a deal with Lord Granville of the Privy Council whereby Quakers would voluntarily leave office and not stand for election while the war continued. Meanwhile, in Pennsylvania reform-minded Quakers were working toward the same end, successfully convincing most of their brethren that holding governmental office was incompatible with their religious beliefs. By the end of 1756 most Quakers—and all who retained strict notions about pacifism—had left government.[21]

For the first time since the colony had been founded, Quakers did not control Pennsylvania's legislature, leaving serious questions about what the future of Quaker political engagement would look like. What role should Friends, convinced as they were that they held the moral and spiritual high ground, play in these difficult and trying times? They had pressured their leaders to leave government to avoid compromising Quaker principles, most importantly the peace testimony, but that did not mean they wanted to stop influencing policy. They had no intention of sitting by and watching others mobilize the engines of the state they and their ancestors had built for a war they disagreed with so much that they had given up power rather than countenance it.

Conscience had been powerful enough to give up government; it impelled now a new kind of action as Quakers became private citizens. Many radicals took an individual stand, vowing not to pay taxes that would go toward the war. Purist John Woolman hoped such principled behavior "may tend to put men a thinking about their own publick Conduct" and thereby encourage both private and public men to reform their ways. Others advocated a more vigorous collective response, rather than individual action. They could not, however, organize as they had frequently in the past and act directly through the powerful Society of Friends meeting structure. The Society of Friends was a tightly linked transatlantic British institution, connecting meetings not just in Pennsylvania but throughout the empire. Already in a sensitive position during a war that seemed to threaten British interests and Pennsylvania security as never before, the Society of Friends preferred caution. British Friends had saved their Pennsylvania brethren from being barred from government; they would not, however, countenance direct institutional action that might suggest that Pennsylvania Quakers were anything but loyal Englishmen. Likewise, the local Monthly Meeting sought publicly to adopt a neutral stance vis-à-vis the "Proprietors, Governor & others in Authority." Unlike their campaign to combat poverty through their own almshouse or to foster education through the Free School, Quakers would have to find another vehicle independent of the Meeting through which to organize.[22]

Concerned Quakers turned to the only option available to them now that they could use neither their church nor their state: private civic organization. A private Quaker association might have the ability to shape policy unhindered either from above by British authorities or from below by angry voters. Likewise formally unbound from their denomination, these passionate men could act without reflecting directly on all their coreligionists. A voluntary organization could harness the fervor, funds, and efforts of many committed Friends, making for much more powerful and concerted action than was possible through the refusal to pay taxes, an act that, though laudable, occurred outside the public eye, was individual, and was limited in both its duration and its impact. Through voluntary association Quakers, outside of government for the first time and acting without the formal structure of their Meeting, could apply sustained, collective pressure to influence policy.[23]

Quakers did not come immediately to this end point, but moved there gradually, acting increasingly in concert before fully realizing the benefit of organizing formally. As early as 1755, convinced that fort building and militia drilling would do little to bring peace, various Quakers in Philadelphia began trying to improve their contacts with Indian diplomats and go-betweens visiting the city. After the 1756 declaration of war on the Delawares, several Quakers met to discuss the calamitous breach with the Indians. These men, led by wealthy Quaker merchant Israel Pemberton, were convinced "that some Dissatisfaction respecting their Lands, had tended to the alienating their Friendship from us" and that "the only Method to save the Province from Ruin was to endeavour for a Peace with them by pacific Measures." They began immediately by meeting with some Indians who happened to be in the city, and they "had some Conversation on the happy State of the first Settlers of this Province and the unhappy Rupture which had lately happened." Conrad Weiser, acting as interpreter, expressed astonishment at how receptive the Indians were to the Quakers' overtures.[24]

Friends tried to move formal government to pursue peaceful negotiations with the Indians. They petitioned both the governor and the assembly toward that end, urging that "tho' they are Savage, and inexpressibly cruel," Indians had yet "in many Cases clear Sentiments of Justice and Equity." These Quakers were willing, moreover, to put their money where their mouths were. They informed Governor Morris that they intended at their own expense to send messengers to various tribes, informing them that "there are those in the Province some of the Descendents of those who came over with the first Proprietor who are principled against War," who wished to mediate between them and the governor. Though they originally obtained the governor's permission to take this step, Morris changed his mind. "Not liking it [that] any private men should interfere with matters of Government he put an End to all the Quaker affairs" and sent an official government messenger to call a conference at Easton, Pennsylvania, to which, pointedly, the Quakers who had initiated it were not invited.[25]

Excited by the prospect of peaceful talks and undeterred by Morris's refusal to include them, Quakers began meeting in Philadelphia in an increasingly formal way to prepare for the conference. They met in July to subscribe funds to buy gifts to grease the peace negotiations. Not yet explicitly organized, these men clearly understood their project to be a long-term collaboration, for they decided that they would use only the interest from the funds they gave toward purchasing gifts, leaving the principal intact for future projects. The eager participants subscribed "upwards of twelve hundred Pounds," and Israel Pemberton hurried off to tell the decidedly unenthusiastic governor that the Quakers would be making a "small present" to the Indians at the conference.[26]

The Quakers who had initiated the conference were not invited to it, and legally they had no right to be there, but they inserted themselves aggressively into the proceedings anyway. At least forty Quakers went to Easton. Immediately the governor forbade them to speak separately with the Indians and placed a guard to see that his order was enforced. The Quakers disregarded this mandate almost from the moment they arrived. Enraged, Governor Morris barked that "he should treat them as his Majesty's Enemies if they held any Conference with the Indians on any Matter relating to the Government." For all his wrath, however, Morris was forced into the embarrassing position of having to present the Indians with the gifts bought by the Quakers, because the government's were insufficient. Richard Peters, no friend to the Quakers, assured Thomas Penn that "if the Quakers had not been Complying & added their large Present to that provided by the Assembly we should have been ruind, the Indians woud have gone away disatisfied and the matters made infinitely worse." The Quakers had successfully elbowed their way into Indian negotiations. Their perseverance had caused the conference to be called in the first place, and their private subscription for gifts had saved it from failure.[27]

Their intervention continued through the fall, eliciting suspicion and hostility from government officials and particularly from proprietary supporters. Fifty Quakers attended a second conference at Easton that fall, this time with the permission of the newly arrived governor, William Denny. They surpassed their earlier present of around £120 in gifts to the Indians with a second round of gifts worth £500, but their presence and their generosity provoked misgivings from many who saw only political motives behind their largesse. Conrad Weiser, an interpreter and longtime intermediary between Indians and Pennsylvania, objected strongly to their presence at the conference. He believed that the Quakers put words in the Indians' mouths and urged them to rehearse complaints that they would not have otherwise raised. He thought Israel Pemberton in particular "manifestly endeavoured to ruin the Proprietaries Intrest and Character." At this treaty, the Delawares brought up grievances against the government for fraud in the 1737 "Walking Purchase" of Indian land. Richard Peters maintained that this idea had never independently entered Indians' heads, but that the Quakers had planted it there. He regretted, however, that "the Quakers have, by this Declaration, gaind great Cause of Triumph, thinking they have fairly shifted off the Cause of the War and Bloodshed from themselves, to . . . the Proprietors, by cheating the Indians." Proprietary supporters like Peters saw Quakers' actions as motivated by a desire to shift blame for frontier violence away from their own refusal to defend the frontier and onto the Penn family for alleged shady land dealings.[28]

As they lodged themselves ever more firmly as a thorn in the side of the governor and other Indian negotiators, the Quakers involved thus far took steps at last to organize formally. In the fall of 1756 they agreed that they would form an association with trustees and a treasurer. However, busy preparing for the approaching second conference at Easton, for the time being they appointed interim leaders who would draft rules for the new organization, and then hurried off to the conference. Finally, in December they drew up official parameters to organize their collective activity, founding what would henceforth be known as the Friendly Association for Gaining and Preserving Peace with the Indians by Pacific Measures.[29]

The founders of the Friendly Association modeled it closely on the existing voluntary associations in Philadelphia, but unlike earlier groups, the founders took conscious measures to insulate it as a Quaker institution. Its organization was similar to that of the library companies and hospital—indeed, many of the men who drew up the rules and served as the first trustees were themselves on the boards of those institutions. Like the libraries and hospital, anyone who donated a certain amount, in this case the relatively low contribution of £2, could vote for the ten trustees and treasurer, though whether the women who donated money also voted is unclear. The group did not restrict itself to Quakers but did mandate that officers must "be a Member in Unity with the People called Quakers" and have contributed at least £10.[30] Another rule that aligned the group with the Society of Friends was that nine of the ten trustees had to agree in order for anything to be done, not strictly the consensus that governed a Quaker Meeting, but very close to it. The trustees' main responsibility was to purchase goods to present to Indians at treaties and other occasions; secondarily, they might provide for the education of a few Indian children to train them in Christian religion and as interpreters. The general membership, the vast majority of whom came from Philadelphia, was not actively involved in day-to-day decisions, but manifested their support by showing up en masse at Indian treaty conferences and attending association general meetings, where they voted on the trustees' actions.[31]

Almost immediately, the Friendly Association stepped in to aid government or even usurp it in matters of Indian diplomacy. The legislature, though no longer Quaker dominated, still opposed proprietary prerogative and entertained no qualms about turning to Quakers and their extralegal organization for help. The assembly informed the Friendly Association in the winter of 1757 that "the Publick Treasury of this Province is much exhausted." The association immediately loaned the assembly £100 and donated another £100 to defray the cost of sending messengers to the Shawnee and Delaware Indians. George Croghan, the leader of the mission, asked for another loan of £150, which he received. Altogether, in less than a year, the Friendly Association expended just over £1,300 in direct gifts to the Indians and loans to officials at a time when government was scrambling to make ends meet.[32]

Imperial officials viewed these developments with considerable alarm. The Earl of Halifax, head of the Board of Trade, stormed at Thomas Penn when he heard that private men had been allowed at the treaties of 1756. He thought it

> the most Extraordinary procedure he had ever seen in Persons, who are on the same footing only with all Others of the Kings private Subjects to presume to Treat with foreign Princes. And further that as the suffering any one part of the King's Subject's, whether of a different Profession of Religion, or however else distinguish'd to Treat or Act as Mediators, between a Province in which they Live, and any Independent People, is the highest Invasion of His Majesty's Prerogative Royal and of the worst consequence as it must tend to divide the Kings Subjects into different parties and Interests.

He ordered the proprietor to order the governor to prohibit any further meddling. Governor Denny accordingly forbade the Quakers to go to the next conference that summer of 1757, an order they serenely disobeyed.[33]

The Friendly Association defended its past efforts and its current decision to attend the Indian treaty as "conducive to the Publick Interest." The well-meaning Quakers grieved at the reproof from the Earl of Halifax and Governor Denny, but believed that their actions had been misrepresented in England. They had no compunctions about disregarding the imperial and gubernatorial instructions entirely. "Nothing less than a Regard to the Publick Interest," its members averred, "would Engage us to decline fully complying with the Governor's Advice." Of course, the governor had not offered "advice," but given a direct order. The association ignored it, deciding that a few members would go to the treaty immediately, but as a small concession, they would not bring gifts worth £500 with them. Those would remain behind, to be sent up at a moment's notice when the time was right.[34]

Like Governor Morris before him, Denny found himself powerless to stop the Friendly Association's active participation in the Indian conference. If he entertained ideas of ejecting Quakers the moment they arrived, he was immediately controverted by the Delawares themselves. Teedyuscung, their leader, insisted that he wanted the Quakers there. Moreover, he demanded one of them be allowed to act as his clerk to take minutes of the treaty. This request represented a radical innovation, one that Teedyuscung hoped would better protect the interests of his people, whose words he believed had in the past been misrepresented by the representatives of the English and colonial governments who took official treaty minutes. Proprietary supporters thought they knew who had originally suggested this idea, and saw confirmation of their suspicions in the "hearty welcome" Teedyuscung gave Friendly Association representatives. The governor and proprietary representatives only grudgingly acceded to the Delawares' request and did nothing to eject the Friendly Association, though interpreter George Croghan thought that this meddling by "a separate Body of People" would have "fatal Consequences to all the rest of his Majesty's Subjects." The governor even allowed the association to bring up and distribute its gifts.[35]

The year of 1757 and the spring of 1758 marked the high tide of the Friendly Association's activities, which were about to go into rapid decline. It continued to present gifts to the Indians, encourage understanding between them and Pennsylvanians, and offer loans to the cash-strapped government to proceed on these good works. The basis of the association's power, however, lay in its connection with the Delawares, whose power in turn stemmed in part from their ability to act as mediators and bring the Iroquois and other tribes to the treaty circle. The Delawares made good on that promise in 1758, helping engineer a conference that more than five hundred Indians, including Iroquois representatives, attended. Dwarfed in numbers and having performed their service, the Delawares lost their importance and bargaining power. They found themselves and their interests eclipsed by and made subservient to the Iroquois. Teedyuscung, who Friendly Association members had hoped would become a moral, upstanding Christian leader, sank rather into alcoholism and despair. Proprietary supporters, on the other hand, celebrated the Easton conference of 1758, for it ended discussion of earlier fraudulent land deals (the Iroquois having been central parties to the deal in question themselves and just as loathe as the proprietary party to revisit it) and brought a halt to Indian raids on the frontier. It also, to proprietary delight, ended the influence of the Friendly Association on Indian diplomacy. After 1758 the Friendly Association continued to attend treaties, present gifts, and meet with Indians who visited Philadelphia. Without success it continued to push the matter of the Walking Purchase. Effectively, however, the group accomplished little after 1758, though it could claim to have contributed around £5,000 in gifts and loans.[36]

In 1762, the Friendly Association's pacific influence ended abruptly at the business end of a sword. In a treaty that year Teedyuscung, dispirited and battling alcoholism, disavowed all claims of dishonesty in the Walking Purchase of 1737 in exchange for a substantial present. Israel Pemberton, a leader of the Friendly Association, became so upset that he tried to intervene. Sir William Johnson, longtime ally of the Iroquois and the imperial representative who had convened the conference, jumped to his feet, drew his sword, and offered to kill Pemberton unless he backed down. Thus ingloriously did the activities of the Friendly Association come to a halt. The Friendly Association had built all its work around the influence it had with Teedyuscung and the Delawares, angry over fraudulent land practices. Now that the Delawares were overshadowed by the Iroquois, with whom the Friendly Association had no connection, and the Walking Purchase matter had been effectively closed, the Quaker group had lost its allies, its cause, and its influence.[37]

The Friendly Association built on the foundation begun by the Defense Association in 1747 and the Independent Companies in 1756 to extend still further the ability of privately organized actors to take over government responsibilities. The Defense Association had claimed the right to act when government did nothing. The Independent Companies expanded that claim to the right to act even when government *did* act, but individuals happened to disagree with the means or the extent of official policy. They acted without law but stopped short of acting contrary to it or in opposition to the government.

The Friendly Association claimed that its work was "conducive to the Publick Interest," but it consistently participated—critics would have said "interfered" —in an arena normally the responsibility of state officials alone. Moreover, it blatantly and repeatedly disobeyed the direct orders of the provincial executives and imperial authorities, though it did enjoy the countenance of the assembly, which relied on its financial intervention. William Allen, a proprietary supporter, raged that the association's activities were actually treasonous. "Many persons have been ordered home, from America, for more trifling matters, than what they have been guilty of," he fumed. The Friendly Association members tried to defend themselves. "We do not intend nor desire to frustrate nor delay such Measures which may be pursu'd" by the government, they claimed, "nor do we aim at any Right or Power" that competed with those of officials or rulers. However, "in the Transaction of Matters so immediately relative to the Lives, Liberties and Properties of the People in General," Friendly Association members claimed the right of private individuals acting collectively through civic organizations to act even in matters of state, and even when some representatives of the state explicitly forbade it.[38]

Moreover, the Friendly Association members asserted that they alone had the ability to negotiate peace because of their historical connection with William Penn and the pacifist founders of the 1680s. Israel Pemberton thought it vital "to use our Endeavours to revive in the Minds of the Indians those happy Impressions which had been formerly made" and demonstrate that at least some men in the province still cherished "those principles which had at first procur'd their Regard and Esteem." Quakers alone could build on the early successes of William Penn, and therefore they held a sacred trust. Only they could accomplish peace.[39]

Where the Defense Association had provoked disapproval and the Independent Companies had represented a minority, the Friendly Association acted directly in opposition to the will of the vast majority. Most Pennsylvanians found it incomprehensible that Quakers would encourage and nurture murderous "savages" while pitilessly leaving their Christian neighbors to suffer and die on the frontier. The £5,000 so proudly contributed toward diplomacy and gifts might better have been spent, many thought, toward the protection or succor of the wounded backcountry inhabitants. The Friendly Association might try to negotiate with Indians, but it competed against strong popular opinion advocating the immediate and violent expulsion of all Indians from Pennsylvania's borders. Quakers faced not only disapproval but hostility and even accusations of treason for their activities.[40]

So out of step with broader public will was the Friendly Association that in February 1764 a party of armed frontiersmen known as the Paxton Boys marched on Philadelphia, calling, among other things, for violence against Israel Pemberton, its most prominent leader. Outraged at the lack of adequate defense or equitable representation for the frontier counties, the Paxton Boys marched on the city to air their grievances and to punish the culprits they blamed for frontier violence: the Quakers who had aided and abetted Indians and a party of Indians themselves—Moravian Indians sheltering in the city in fear for their lives. The anger manifested by the Paxton Boys stemmed from inadequate frontier defense and the unequal representation of the western counties, but it also reflected the impotence many Pennsylvanians felt in the face of the actions of the Friendly Association. Despite accusations that it succored "secret enemies," the Friendly Association was a private, voluntary association, and no one—not a series of furious governors, irate imperial officials, or even the population at large—could restrain its activities.[41]

Frightened by what they saw as an invasion by backcountry ruffians who threatened not just Quakers but their city and their very government, Philadelphians mobilized overnight to form yet another military association for defense. New governor John Penn requested that the assembly frame a new militia law, but everyone knew that this could not be accomplished in time. Instead, city residents gathered in the pouring rain outside the State House on February 4, where they "entered into an Association, and took Arms for the Support of Government, and Maintenance of good Order." Benjamin Franklin organized them quickly into six companies, which were to remain assembled at the market overnight despite the bitter cold. Alarms in the night, however, roused Philadelphians from their beds. Expecting fire, instead they heard "the old militia drums with solemn dubb beating to arms, and saw the inhabitants running from all quarters to obey the summons. By sunrise . . . [the Associators] had got themselves officers" and resurrected the old artillery companies. The crisis seemed to abate, only to be reanimated by rumors of impending invasion by the Paxton Boys, now said to be at Germantown. In response to one such rumor, one resident was astounded "with what alacrity the people flew to arms; in one quarter of an hour near a thousand of them were assembled." For a short time, supporters of the proprietary party and even (it was said) Quakers associated and took up arms for the defense of the city. Most did not do so out of love for the Indians or the Friendly Association Quakers who were threatened, but because they saw the Paxton Boys as a threat to the city's "liberties and laws." Their immediate response, facilitated by previous experiences with extralegal militias, helped dissuade the Paxton Boys from entering the city, and the crisis was diffused through negotiation.[42]

The Friendly Association, then, laid bare the problem with voluntary civic associations: they formed to answer objectives defined by one constituency and did not answer to the larger community, which had no power to stop them. In the face of overwhelming public hostility and opposition, the Friendly Association bravely adhered to its position and forced itself into Indian treaty negotiations to try to stop a bloody conflict. Admirable perhaps, but the fact remains that it acted in direct contradiction to the consensus of the rest of the community. The Friendly Association Quakers asserted that, as the heirs of William Penn's legacy of friendship with Indians, they were better prepared to understand and gain the trust of the Indians, better positioned than provincial or military leaders to bring about peace. The organization's attitude, in short, was not democratic but paternalistic, both toward the Indians it wanted to help and toward the rest of the colony that disagreed with it. Government officials found themselves dependent on the money the Friendly Association raised and hostage to the demands of Indians themselves, and so could do nothing to stop the Friendly Association from participating in Indian diplomacy, leaving the rest of Pennsylvania no choice but to suffer the organization to act as it saw fit, with no regard for popular opinion.

"This Disagreeable Service of the Publick": The Contributors to the Relief of the Poor

In 1766, ten years after the Independent Companies had dispersed and four years after the treaty that finally undermined the Delawares' and thus the Friendly Association's importance, another private civic association that in no way answered to the public explicitly took over government functions. The Contributors to the Relief of the Poor were empowered by the legislature to take over all public poor relief in Philadelphia and its surrounding townships. In many important ways the contributorship resembled the earlier extralegal militias and Friendly Association: it took over government functions that affected the entire local population, but it answered only to its own members, and its actions prompted outrage by vocal Philadelphia constituencies. Like the Friendly Association, moreover, the Contributors to the Relief of the Poor provided an avenue for Quakers to continue to shape policy even as many left formal government, seeing it as incompatible with their religious beliefs. However, the contributorship differed in several important ways from earlier groups taking over state functions. First and foremost, it was not extralegal. It operated not only with the permission but with the blessing of the state. Moreover, in contrast to the extralegal militias or Friendly Association, the contributorship did not disband after a short time, but lasted until the Revolution dissolved the Pennsylvania government altogether.

Philadelphia officials found themselves overwhelmed by the problem of poverty after the French and Indian War, as the city's most vulnerable residents were hard-hit by postwar depression. Old structures of poor relief proved unable to cope with the problem. Responsibility for public poor relief in Philadelphia had long been complicated by being dispersed among various bodies, public and private. The private efforts of the Society of Friends, which had proven so efficacious in the first quarter of the century, made less of a dent now in a city that was not majority Quaker and therefore not eligible or perhaps desirous of their aid. New organizations attempted to address the needs of more recent immigrants: for example, the Scottish St. Andrew's Society extended aid to Philadelphians of Scottish ancestry. However, none of these private efforts made up the gap between the need and public resources. The pressures on the poor relief system caused by population growth, diversity, and difficult economic times were further exacerbated in the 1760s by a string of exceptionally cold winters that left many without the means even to afford firewood.[43]

The Philadelphia Overseers of the Poor, though charged with dealing with poor relief, found its powers inadequate. In 1749 the legislature incorporated that body and gave it control of the city's almshouse, but still the overseers struggled to meet the needs of the city. In 1764 the overseers petitioned the legislature to expand its powers still further to meet the growing needs of the population. The overseers wanted to be allowed to build a workhouse. At that moment they had 220 persons in their care and estimated that three-quarters could be put to work, rendering them "capable as earning as much in Summer as would maintain them through the Winter." Though a workhouse would allegedly cut costs in the long run, it was an expensive proposition in the wake of a costly war. The legislature therefore did nothing.[44]

Meanwhile, private citizens organized separately to assist the poor, attempting to fill the gap left by public measures. In the brutal winter of 1761–62 several "Inhabitants of this City comiserating the distress of the Poor" met, elected a treasurer, and went door-to-door to raise money for firewood and other necessaries such as blankets and warm clothing. They distributed the goods to "those who are real objects of Charity." The group became active again in the bitterly cold winter of 1764–65. By that time, many of the men, predominantly Quakers, began advocating a radical new approach to poor relief.[45]

Convinced that they could work more effectively than could the Overseers of the Poor, these men wanted the legislature to give them, even though they were private citizens, control of public poor relief, promising in return that the cost of poor relief would be dramatically reduced. The assembly accepted the proposal and in 1766 incorporated the Contributors to the Relief of the Poor. Anyone who contributed £10 or more would be considered a "Contributor" and would be eligible to elect or serve as a manager. Once the contributorship had raised £1,500, the city of Philadelphia would convey the almshouse to it to use as collateral for loans of up to £2,000. The contributors intended to use the contributions and loans to build a new, modern bettering house. One wing would be the almshouse, for those too sick or old to work; the other would be the House of Employment, in which the healthy poor would be put to work to pay for the cost of their maintenance.[46]

The law made two more innovations in Philadelphia's poor relief. First, instead of applying to the city alone, it would encompass as well all the surrounding townships of Southwark, Passyunk, Moyamensing, and the Northern Liberties. This move was intended to end time-consuming and costly disputes among the city and townships over the residence of poor people, because the town of their residence was responsible for providing them with poor relief.

Combining the city and suburban poor relief would put a stop to arguments among officials as to which locale was responsible for an individual's poor relief and create economies of scale in the House of Employment.[47]

Second, despite the fact that the Contributors to the Relief of the Poor was a private body, elected by no one and never accountable to the public, it would have the right to levy taxes on the inhabitants of not only Philadelphia but also Southwark, Passyunk, Moyamensing, and the Northern Liberties. Taxation was a loaded issue in the heady days of 1766, on the heels of the British Parliament's passage of the Stamp and Declaratory Acts. Philadelphians as a group lagged behind many other British Americans in their protests of the Stamp Act, but they too objected to imperial taxes to which neither they nor their representatives had consented. The incorporation of the Contributors to the Relief of the Poor at precisely the same moment gave a local group the same power of taxation without the input of elected officials, but it raised no comparable outcry. To be sure, the Overseers of the Poor in both Philadelphia and the affected suburbs protested loudly, but the larger population took little notice of the fact that a private group, which was not answerable to the public, would have the power to levy taxes. The managers, for their part, understood to whom they answered and were careful to act in a way that "will justify us to our Constituents," by which they meant contributors, not taxpayers.[48]

Not only did the contributorship not answer to the public, but it dictated what the state-instituted Overseers of the Poor in Philadelphia and the surrounding townships would do. The contributorship did not hesitate to bully the overseers, converting the commission from a body with control over taxation, poor relief, and the almshouse to little more than a group of lackeys at the command of the contributorship. The wealthy men who ran the contributorship were convinced that they knew best: that the poor must be reformed by forcing them into the House of Employment and that the old system of giving "outdoor" relief must be ended. The overseers, by contrast, wanted the power to give out pensions to the "deserving" poor, but the contributorship refused, systematically stripping the overseers of most of their power. When the overseers balked, the managers of the contributorship complained to the assembly and received swift judgment on their side. The assembly removed any doubt about the subservient position of the overseers, passing in 1768 a law that compelled the overseers to collect and pass along any taxes assigned to them by the managers of the contributorship. The overseers' ongoing complaints and recalcitrance would not be tolerated. The overseers retained a few small separate sources of income independent of taxation, and they were empowered to distribute that money as they saw fit until 1771, when new legislation took away even that power from them. Thenceforth the overseers would collect taxes and be in charge of removing any pauper who was not a resident of Philadelphia (and therefore not legally entitled to poor relief there).[49]

The Philadelphia Overseers of the Poor recognized that they had been made largely irrelevant. They registered their disgust in June of 1769 when in their minutes they determined that "as the Overseer's Attendance at the Almshouse seems to answer no good Purpose they will appoint no more Committees for that Service." In future they would limit their activities to referring all petitioners directly to the contributorship and checking up on petitioners' legal residence. As for themselves, they stopped meeting as regularly. They had been made almost entirely redundant, and they knew it. Where they could, however, they did still work to circumvent the contributorship, for example, asking and receiving permission from the municipal corporation to collect firewood from city property to distribute directly to the needy, a form of "outdoor relief" of which the contributorship managers would not have approved.[50]

These changes provoked bitter complaint in the suburbs, however. The taxpayers of Northern Liberties grumbled that their overseers, a separate body from that of Philadelphia, had been divested of all power and "made only mere Collectors of the Tax." They had "no Voice in laying it out, nor (as they are told) so much as a Right of judging of the Quantum of the Tax proper to be raised; but are only to collect it when called upon." It was beginning to be difficult to find "Persons of any Credit" willing to take a job that had turned essentially into a collection agency for the contributorship, with no decision-making power. The overseers of Passyunk complained that the new system was more expensive for their township. They claimed that Passyunk had had on average one person per year needing poor relief and that the costs of providing for the poor accordingly had been very low. The new system of having to pay for the bettering house was more expensive and an unfair burden when so few Passyunk residents were sent there. Moreover, the freeholders of Northern Liberties leveled charges that the entire system was unfair. They pointed out that "only Subscribers of Ten Pounds or upwards have a Vote" for the managers of the contributorship. Such a practice was "unequal" to the taxpayers. "Those whose Estates are thus chargeable," they asserted, should have an equal voice. The assembly not only ignored these complaints but acted to buttress the contributorship, despite the fact that it was declining quickly into debt and disillusionment.[51]

Despite its ambitious vision, by any assessment, including its own, the Contributors to the Relief of the Poor performed poorly. Its efforts did not reduce poverty in the city, and the costs of caring for those on public poor relief skyrocketed. Constructing a new building proved more expensive than the organization had anticipated, and poor people resisted coming to or working in the House of Employment. Beginning in 1768, the contributors began to levy multiple three-penny taxes every year, finding that a single annual tax did not net funds sufficient to its needs. One author concluded that the entire "Experience has proved to be chimerical."[52]

The contributorship began to borrow heavily. Its 1766 charter had permitted it to borrow up to the staggering sum of £6,000, but within one year it petitioned the assembly and received the ability to borrow a further £3,000. The loans would be repaid first by selling off the old almshouse lot and building and any remainder through direct taxation of the residents of the city and suburbs. However, the managers soon admitted that they found it "impracticable" to sell the almshouse in the poor economic climate of the late 1760s. The assembly came to its rescue once more in 1769, essentially by printing money and lending it to the contributorship. The assembly would "emit" £14,000, which the managers were to use to repay their outstanding debts. The managers were then responsible for finding a way to raise £1,000 a year for fourteen years. That money would be used to "redeem" (that is, buy back) the circulating currency and burn it. The act helped the contributorship through a substantial loan, but the assembly was spurred not only by altruism. It noted that "trade and commerce of this province are carried on with the greater difficulty from the want of small change." The emission of £14,000 through small bills ranging in sum from four pence to twenty shillings (equal to £1) would, it was hoped, help grease the wheels of local commerce.[53]

The contributorship, however, had no way to pay back this money. It had at its disposal the sale or rent of the old almshouse and lot, the income from the products of the House of Employment (low-cost items such as linen, shoes, nails, and oakum, much of it used by the inmates themselves), taxation, and charitable contributions, which were slowing down after the initial rush of enthusiasm. In 1770 the contributorship had sold or rented enough of the old almshouse lot to net £710, nearly £300 short of its expected repayment of £1,000 for that year. Moreover, while it valued its remaining saleable property at nearly £7,000, that would still fall short of fulfilling its debt to the province of £14,000. It found it necessary to raise more and more money through taxes. The assemblymen, who by law had to review the contributorship's finances, put the best gloss possible on the situation, noting the numbers of poor cared for by the institution and attributing to it many good effects on the community at large, including a drop in alcohol abuse, the increased health of the poor, and even a decline in crime rates. Still, spin it how they would, by 1775, in the managers' own judgment, the contributorship was in "a very embarrass'd State." It simply could not keep pace with its debts and responsibilities.[54]

The managers grumbled about the growing complaints by their neighbors. "We chearfully and voluntary give up our time, to this disagreeable service of the publick," they protested, "without Reward or Emolument; yet are frequently so unhappy to hear ungenerous and illiberal Reflections and Insinuations against our Management and OEconomy." The unthinking masses were to blame, for "we know that to serve the publick, in any manner, more especially Gratis, it is but too frequent and general to be found fault with, however cautious and circumspect the proceedings." Of course, the public might have preferred that their service not be "Gratis" but directly answerable to the taxpayers.[55]

The assembly, which *was* answerable to those taxpayers, however, never intervened, and in fact strengthened the contributorship in 1771 and even made it perpetual in 1776, ending any possibility of reverting to the older model. Why? On a merely pragmatic level, the legal and logistical complications of extricating the public from the private would have been too great for legislators who were preoccupied in 1776 with other matters. Other overarching reasons probably played a factor as well, however.[56]

Entangled in the decision in the first place to undercut the Overseers of the Poor and put public poor relief in Philadelphia into the hands of a private civic voluntary association were class and political considerations. The managers tended to be much more elite and Quaker, while more overseers worked or had worked as artisans, came from a variety of religious backgrounds, and came from the middle class. The overseers, having been or still being closer in economic status to the people they helped, may have felt more sympathetic to the resistance most poor people exhibited toward being forced into the Bettering House. The managers, who had little personal contact with the lived experience of poverty, focused more on the economic and reform opportunities inherent in an institutional response to poor relief and less on the preference of the poor for "outdoor relief" and independence. From now on a more elite group of men would control policy decisions about poor relief.[57]

The incorporation of the contributorship must be understood, moreover, in the context of renegotiations about who would shape policy—and how— once Quakers no longer controlled the formal mechanisms of local government. Dating back to 1701, the Philadelphia Overseers of the Poor had been appointed by and responsible to the Philadelphia Corporation, but after the first quarter of the eighteenth century the corporation came to be dominated by non-Quaker men who tended to support the proprietary party. The bruising fights of the 1750s and 1760s demonstrated that at the provincial level Quakers not only were outnumbered demographically but could no longer command the political clout they had once enjoyed. Through the Friendly Association from 1756 to 1762 Quakers had found an avenue to shape policy toward peace with Indians but without having to answer to the public. The Contributors to the Relief of the Poor gave them another way to control as they saw fit another vital aspect of public policy and community life. They could use the Bettering House to shape their fellow Philadelphians into the sober, industrious community members they wanted them to be. This time, however, instead of baldly usurping power as they had done in 1756, Quakers found an ally in the assembly, which incorporated their civic association. In one stroke the assembly siphoned a vital public service and policy control from the Overseers of the Poor and the proprietary-party-controlled Philadelphia Corporation and into its own ambit. The contributorship answered only to the assembly and to its own contributors. It gave civic-minded Quakers new scope and powers to shape Philadelphia even as they lost demographic or local political dominance.[58]

In the 1740s and 1750s, in times of panic and amid great controversy, two extra-legal militias and the Friendly Association usurped state functions of defense and diplomacy, respectively. In important ways they seemed to operate as desperate measures in desperate times, but in fact they drew on a longer culture of decentered governance in which the state relied on various governmental, quasi-governmental, and nongovernmental institutions to provide necessary services. First the Independent Companies and then the Friendly Association took voluntary association to a new level, however, when they used their organizations not to provide a service unmet by government, but to interfere in matters where the government was acting. The Independent Companies asserted they did not act contrary to but only outside of the law; the Friendly Association could make no such claim but repeatedly ignored direct orders to cease and desist their activities. The Corporation for the Relief of the Poor in 1766 did not emerge as a response to desperate times, but, like the Friendly Association, as a vehicle for elite Quakers to control policy even as they no longer controlled the formal levers of municipal government.

The operations of these three civic associations that took over matters of state lay bare the difficulties of discussing a monolithic "state" in eighteenth-century America (or, indeed, in just about any other time or place). Each association was able to function in part because, although it angered one part of government, it enjoyed the support of another. The Independent Companies were the darling of the governor, who, like their organizers, was sympathetic to the proprietary interest. He countenanced the Independent Companies and gave them clout even as partisans of the assembly objected. The Friendly Association never received such clear approbation from the assembly, but even as the governor fussed and the imperial government fumed, the Pennsylvania legislature leant the organization credibility by continually relying on it for financial assistance to continue Indian diplomacy. The Corporation for the Relief of the Poor enjoyed the most tangible support of all these groups from one branch of government—the assembly—at the expense of the local municipal institutions of the Philadelphia Corporation and the Overseers of the Poor for Philadelphia and the surrounding townships.

Multiple, separate, sometimes overlapping layers of government held sway over colonial Philadelphia, a fact that had long allowed many entry points for various constituencies to shape their community. The dispersed character of government, not only at the local but at the provincial level, now had the added effect of assisting some private entities to take over responsibility for public functions altogether at the expense of other branches of government. Thomas Penn had worried in 1748 that Philadelphians might act "in defiance of government," a scenario that in fact never came true because always they had found some branch of government supportive of their aims. But in 1775 all that was about to change.

CHAPTER SEVEN

Mars Ascendant
The Military Association and the
Reconstitution of Government

A singular body of newcomers arrived in Philadelphia in the fall of 1774: delegates from twelve of Britain's North American mainland colonies gathered together in a Continental Congress to discuss joint protests to the Boston Port Bill and other so-called Coercive Acts. Many of the delegates had never been to Philadelphia before and marveled at the city they found. Philadelphia in 1774 was "in a most flourishing state," the largest city in British North America with over twenty-four thousand residents. More houses were built in Philadelphia in 1774 alone than had been built in Boston in the preceding decade. Alongside "the great Increase of Stores and Shops for the Sale of every species of Merchandize," the built environment of the city and suburbs by now extended for two full miles along the Delaware River, creating a bustling and thriving riverfront, "the great mart of America," one observer called it. At its midpoint, the city had also edged slightly farther west, now as much as half a mile into the interior, anchored by the market on High Street, which was "scarcely to be equalled by any single market in Europe." Numerous public buildings provided "great ornament" to the city's appearance; observers frequently singled out for particular mention the State House with its newly enclosed square behind, the hospital, the college, and the House of Employment. Meanwhile churches of all denominations found "happy asylum" in the city, "and such is the Catholick spirit that prevails," one writer found, "that I am told, they have frequently and chearfully assisted each other in erecting their several places of worship." One local lamented that William Penn's "Original form in Laying out the City is not nor cannot be altered," and a visitor noted that "the uniformity of this City is disagreeable to some," but others applauded the "beauty and regularity" of the old grid, with roads well tended by the inhabitants with paving for carriages, brick walkways, evenly spaced lampposts, and patrolling watchmen. All things considered, one visitor celebrated Philadelphia as "the most regular and best-laid out city in the world."[1]

John Adams, delegate and fiercely proud son of Massachusetts, found little in Philadelphia (or indeed anywhere) that compared favorably with Boston, but even he had to concede that the Quaker City's "charitable public foundations" exceeded those of his own city. The Continental Congress held its deliberations in the Carpenters' Company's spacious hall; Adams frequented the "excellent" Library Company (which made its collections available to all delegates for free, and they in turn put it to "great & constant use"), toured the House of Employment built by the Contributors to the Relief of the Poor, visited the Pennsylvania Hospital, and even trekked up the Schuylkill Falls to view the museum of the Welsh fishing club, Fort St. David's. Over meals, he socialized with members of the American Philosophical Society and recommended a new member to them. "In several Particulars," Adams admitted, Philadelphians "have more Wit, than We. They have Societies; the philosophical Society particularly, which excites a scientific Emulation, and propagates their Fame." He vowed to found a similar society in Boston when the present difficulties with Britain were over.[2]

For all his respect for these organizations, it was not until eight months later that Adams's excitement overflowed as he described to his wife on June 10, 1775, "a very wonderfull Phœnomenon in this City—a field Day, on which three Battallions of Soldiers were reviewed, making full two thousand Men." To see a militia review in a pacifist colony was indeed "wonderfull," but Adams was particularly awed because "All this has been accomplished in this City, since the 19th of April," the date of the bloodletting at Lexington and Concord. "So sudden a formation of an Army," Adams concluded in wonder and triumph, "never took Place any where."[3]

But Adams was wrong. "So sudden a formation of an Army" had in fact taken place multiple times, and not just "any where," but in that very city. The roots of military organization in 1775, moreover, delved deep in Philadelphia's civic history, drawing not only on the immediate precedents of militias in 1747, 1757, and 1764, but on the very culture of voluntary organization—the "charitable public foundations"—that Adams had also admired. The Military Association, founded in 1775, would participate in radical change going forward, but in its origins it did not represent a precipitous break. Its tactics, membership, strategies, and indeed the very speed with which it mobilized recalled earlier organizations. More importantly, the militia did not depart from but instead built upon a well-established civic culture that had long authorized and empowered various urban constituencies toward participation and decision making in local matters.

Adams, a stranger to Philadelphia, did not understand this history, these roots. Similarly, scholars who, like Adams, have picked up the story only in the 1760s and 1770s have argued that the Military Association represented something entirely new. One influential historian has called it "the first step in the transition from crowd activity to organized politics" for lower-class Philadelphians. For another, "the very process of the meetings probably augmented the Associators' growing sense of empowerment and greater control over their lives." The association and related organizing thus shattered "a major ideological barrier to their full participation in decisions that affected their lives," giving lower-class Philadelphia men for the first time a sense of their ability and their right to "control their lives." This kind of analysis makes the revolutionary period out to be a time of radical change, laying the groundwork to interpret the period as a time of new sociopolitical engagement by men of middling and lower-class status who had previously been excluded.[4]

The Revolution did act as a catalyst for new, strident politicization, but not because middling or lower-class men organized for the first time. This chapter argues that the Military Association of 1775–76 was not a radical departure but a continuation of Philadelphia's civic and military tradition. Moreover, political radicals chose deliberately to draw on this heritage and create an extralegal militia rather than attempt to use the engines of state. This decision facilitated the creation of a more extreme institution than might have been possible if all constituencies had had to be consulted in its early form and leadership. The Pennsylvania Assembly, presented with a fait accompli and pressured to recognize and support it, could never overcome the militia's extragovernmental origins. The legislature could not overwrite what had already been accomplished; it could neither tame nor control the association, and only feebly did it ever try. Radical leaders successfully used the Military Association first to usurp governmental authority over a critical arena of public policy and then to challenge the very legitimacy of that government. Through the association, radicals built institutional clout and well-organized mass support; on these foundations they challenged the perception of legitimate political participation. After 1775 military service at last came to the center in the discussion of who did—and did not—rightfully belong in the political community. A man's ability or willingness to serve in the militia conferred or denied him full civil rights. Many of the old political elite, particularly but not only Quakers, could or would not themselves take up arms, and they were reluctant to move the gears of state to militarize. Pushed ultimately to adopt measures for defense, the old elites still refused to countenance military service as the litmus test for drawing lines between legitimate and illegitimate participants in civic discourse. Conversely, tying full citizenship at last to military service swung the pendulum of political power to Associators—a group that included men from all walks of life, but, in common with all armies then and now, was composed disproportionately of men of more modest means. Thus did the association—the product of a long civic tradition in Philadelphia—become the wedge that finally collapsed the formal political structures that had been in place since William Penn's day.[5]

However, the transformations of 1775–76 built as well on a correlated and undemocratic aspect of Philadelphia's culture of dispersed governance and reliance on civic voluntary associations, specifically the ability to exclude those who did not agree. Quaker pacifists, Loyalists, and others who did not fully support the new revolutionary government were entirely barred not only from the political process but from the legitimate public sphere. The city's old accreted system that had relied on competing voices and institutions in local governance was swept away in favor of a unitary system that insisted in wartime on total allegiance.

A "Cool, Sensible People": The Calm before the Storm

Up to the very eve of the Revolution, Philadelphia remained eerily quiet, with few crowd actions and relatively little formal protest to British policies. The Pennsylvania Assembly, alone of all major British American colonial legislatures, engaged in no pointed protest with the British ministry over the legislation of the 1760s and early 1770s. During the Stamp Act crisis, other urban port towns saw violent crowd actions, but in Philadelphia the new governor reported that "the giddy Multitude have hitherto been restrained from committing any Acts of open Violence." Philadelphia eschewed "the Mob-Triumphs of a Northern Colony," but instead manifested the "calm Resolution" of a "cool, sensible People." The anomaly went further: in Philadelphia alone, the stamp collector, though not allowed to fulfill his office, was countenanced and even protected by a crowd of artisans who surrounded his house and that of Benjamin Franklin (who had secured his commission) to protect both from the kind of destruction meted out in Boston. The Sons of Liberty, popular in other colonies, resonated with some Philadelphians, but even an insider had to admit regretfully that the group "was not declared numerous." Philadelphia merchants engaged somewhat reluctantly in nonimportation against the Stamp Act in 1765 and the Townshend Duties in 1767, but by 1770 the boycott had petered out. Radicals managed to mount more effective resistance to the Tea Act in 1773, but still in that year a visiting New Englander deemed the colony politically to be "the calmest of any on the continent."[6]

Scholars have explained this calm first and foremost by arguing that in the 1760s both of the major political factions in Pennsylvania were pursuing what one scholar has termed the "politics of ingratiation." In late 1764 the Pennsylvania Assembly, fed up with Proprietor Thomas Penn, voted to petition the Crown to revoke Pennsylvania's charter, which would end proprietary government and bring the province under King George's control as a royal colony. The Quaker party–dominated assembly thus gambled all on overthrowing the proprietor, even if it meant jeopardizing the freedoms enshrined in their beloved charter and ignoring affronts like the Stamp Act which otherwise probably would have provoked complaint. Determined to present a loyal face to the king, the leadership of the party that had in the past always championed popular sovereignty and low taxation thus limited strong protests over offensive imperial policies. The proprietary party found itself oddly in the position of fanning the flames of popular anger at the Stamp Act, but mainly as a short-term ploy to undermine the assembly and Quaker party, not out of heart-felt principle. Ultimately, until it became clear that the king would not grant Pennsylvania a royal charter and relieve the province of the Penn family, neither political party wanted to alienate support in London by vehemently protesting parliamentary taxation. The "politics of ingratiation" provides a convincing explanation of the perspective from the top down, of the motivations that led political elites to stifle their own or others' protests, always with an eye to power brokering at the imperial level.[7]

But politics in Philadelphia did not only happen from the top down. If elites acted primarily through and for their political factions, focused on winning elections and performing loyal subjection to the Crown, Philadelphians outside the corridors of elite politicking had their own forms of collective action, their own history and traditions on which to build, and their own reasons to act.[8] That fact can find no better expression than in the uncharacteristic spectacle of tradesmen defending the homes of stamp collector John Hughes and his patron, Benjamin Franklin, in 1765. Twice crowds began to form with the intent of leveling both houses. The first crowd was riled up by proprietary supporters on September 16 after day-long celebrations in the city over the change of the British ministry. The threat this crowd posed seemed sufficiently imminent to Deborah Franklin, the head of her household while her husband was away in England, that she formed a "Magazin" of two or three guns in one room of the house and prepared "sum sorte of defens up Stairs such as I Cold manaig my self" to deter the assailants. She was, however, shortly assured that eight hundred men were standing by to defend the newly built Franklin house. These men, most of whom were "Mechanicks," did not rally piecemeal, but had in fact "met at the Widow Gray's [tavern] and associated for the Preservation, of the Peace of the City." Faced with the Mechanicks' stout resistance, the threatening crowds melted away. Weeks later when the stamped paper actually arrived in the city, trouble loomed again, once more egged on by prominent figures in the proprietary party who deliberately called together a crowd in the State House yard on October 5. As before, the tradesmen who had associated for public peace turned out and stood down the threat, mustering "ten to their one."[9]

The tradesmen who associated and took to the streets in defense of Franklin and Hughes were not signaling their support for the Stamp Act or its local collector. Indeed, they forced Hughes publicly to resign his commission. Shortly thereafter his fellow tradesmen in the Heart and Hand Fire Company expelled him for having agreed to be the stamp collector. Five years later in 1770, a core constituency among the tradesmen who had protected the Hughes and Franklin homes would lend their support to nonimportation, a cause that appealed to both their ideological and their material interests.[10]

The rapid turnout of the tradesmen during the Stamp Act crisis stood rather as a testament to their long-standing civic history around matters of defense, and specifically with Benjamin Franklin. These men had rallied to Franklin's Defense Association in 1747, again in 1755 with the voluntary legal militia, and most recently in 1764 to defend the city not from privateers or Indians but from fellow Pennsylvanians during the Paxton Boys crisis. Each of these militias had extended the ability of shopkeepers and tradesmen to shape their community not through a ballot box but through their voluntary participation in endeavors that would have failed but for their support. Franklin, a fellow tradesman, had dignified and expanded their participation in civic life. When he was threatened, the "Mechanicks" put aside their concerns about his alleged complicity in the Stamp Act (all too true, as it turned out) and utilized the form he had wielded with such facility on previous occasions: they "associated for the Preservation, of the Peace of the City." Franklin himself might be abroad in England, but the civic technology he had done so much to help establish continued to flourish in his adopted city.[11]

Philadelphia's tradition of civic organization, it was true, stood on a strong foundation, but that did not inherently mean that large-scale organizing could be deployed easily or quickly. Faced with an immediate threat, eight hundred tradesmen for their own reasons rallied to Franklin and his allies' defense. Otherwise, Philadelphia saw little agitation from below. The relative passivity of the city and its inhabitants to the Stamp Act and other British policies demonstrated the absence—or perhaps better said, the failure to coalesce—of a broad-based movement. The Sons of Liberty, "not declared numerous" in 1766, resembled other voluntary endeavors with limited appeal. They were a self-selected core of like-minded men who could perhaps boast a strong internal coherence, but at the same time circumscribed their appeal to a wider constituency. They might be compared to the largely unpopular Friendly Association of 1756–62, trying to shape public policy in ways in which much of the city was uninterested or outright disagreed.

In order for the protest movement against British policies to be effective, it needed broad-based appeal. The Sons of Liberty needed to convince numbers of Philadelphians to espouse its worldview and positions, or it had to shift its positions to accord more with the majority of the population. In fact, both processes happened, producing a continuously revolving binary as each factor exerted gravitational pull on the other. The most radical partisans expanded the realm of the possible by championing extreme positions, but in ongoing negotiation with conservatives and moderates, the actual policy positions adopted in the early 1770s tended to toe a more moderate line. This compromise frustrated radicals, but it also elicited support from more Philadelphians. At the same time, events, particularly British troops firing on Americans at Lexington and Concord in April 1775, convinced many that the radicals' analysis and proposals were either right or at least the best of the available options. Another critical factor that may have pushed more Philadelphians—particularly those of the lower and middling sorts—into a more radical camp stemmed from the worsening economic conditions the city had experienced since the end of the Seven Years' War. Frustrated with the status quo, they turned to new leaders.[12]

To create a strong coalition within the city required careful navigation and compromise, incorporating appeals to and input from diverse constituencies. This took time, personal connections, and recruiting to put into effect. A strong leadership took some time to develop, moreover, because Pennsylvania politics was so confused by the royal colony movement. The men with years of experience, who had long-established trust and authority as expressed through repeated election to public office, were distracted by the question of royal versus proprietary government. One visitor noted that Quaker elites were angered by British taxation but that yet "it was hard to say whether the friends of Government or the other Party at this Period were more attached to a firm dependence on the Mother Country." In the absence, then, of leadership by political elites from either the Quaker or proprietary factions, a new cadre of political activists hoped to step into the void, but needed time to organize themselves and gain the trust and backing of others.[13]

The gradually coalescing new leadership has been taken to represent a class of "new men" or "political novices." Though they did represent a break from the past in formal politics, they emerged out of and reinforced Philadelphia's civic political tradition. They hailed from very different backgrounds than established political elites. The men who served in revolutionary committees in the 1770s came from more humble economic status, were much more likely to be middling than wealthy, and represented greater religious and ethnic diversity—a deliberate strategy to attract as many constituencies to the movement as possible. Scholars have focused on these class differences to argue that the radicalism of Philadelphia's revolution stemmed not only from new policies but from the changeover in personnel, representing a dramatic break from old oligarchic and antidemocratic practices. This perspective can only be borne out, however, with a very limited definition of politics, focusing only on formal electoral politics and office holding. It elides Philadelphia's rich culture of association and dispersed governance. In fact, 70 percent of the 171 men identified as committeemen between 1774 and 1776 were members of at least one voluntary association; 43 percent were in more than one.[14] Of the fifty committeemen who did not belong to an organization that we know of, most served in only one committee. In general, the more committees on which a man served, the more voluntary associations were also in his background. In short, these "new men" were not at all new. They had long experience with precisely the kind of organizing and leadership that gradually moved Philadelphia from its placid response to the Stamp Act in 1765 to its much more radical stance from 1774 onward. They were well versed in organizational culture through participation in a host of civic, social, and cultural organizations.[15]

Finally, with leadership, organization, and a message that resonated with or reflected public will, one more precondition had to fall into place for Philadelphia to have a broad-based movement: there had to be something to do, some active form of engagement through which Philadelphians (at minimum the bulk of white men, and possibly others as well) could participate. Nonimportation might offer just such a means of active engagement. As T. H. Breen has pointed out, nonimportation politicized daily consumption choices and gave colonists up and down the Eastern Seaboard a common means of protest, building shared rhetoric, experience, and eventually a common cause. However, in Philadelphia, the 1767 protests relied on the self-policing of importers themselves, who often had conflicting economic interests in maintaining a strong boycott. Merchants in each seaport nervously watched their counterparts in other commercial centers, worried that their rivals might steal a march on them, resume importing, and rake in profits at the other cities' expense. Never warmly embraced, the Philadelphia nonimportation movement had subsided by 1770. The 1773 protest against tea, when radical activists were much better organized, presented much more opportunity to involve the bulk of the community. The 1774 nonimportation agreements involved Philadelphians still more deeply. For the first time an interlocking committee system oversaw all incoming cargoes and put pressure on importers to cancel existing orders. These committees drew ordinary Philadelphians into concrete action, policing their own and their neighbors' buying and selling. In a similar vein that spring, numerous subscribers founded the American Manufactory, intended as a patriotic and charitable endeavor to employ the poor and produce the textiles that could no longer be imported from Britain. But the organization that would do the most to involve ordinary, white Philadelphia men in revolutionary politics sprang forth one April day on the heels of shocking news from Massachusetts: the British had fired on Americans. The colonies were at war.[16]

"So Sudden a Formation of an Army": The Deep Roots of the Military Association

Pennsylvania—not surprisingly, given its pacifist history—lagged behind all the other colonies in military preparedness. A coalition of conservative politicians and Quakers drew the line at a provincial militia, and though they gave ground in the winter of 1774–75 on nonimportation and other matters, on the central matter of military defense they would not concede. In 1774 in response to the occupation of Boston and (unfounded) rumors of violence that fall, an increasingly vocal group of Philadelphians called for military defense. The assembly met in March 1775, and many hoped that at last it would take measures to arm the colony, but "so great an opposition" manifested inside the State House that the legislature contented itself with "a few harmless resolves" and let the matter rest. "It is happy for us," remarked one disappointed Patriot, "that we have Boston in the front & Virginia in the rear to defend us: we are placed where Cowards ought to be placed in the middle."[17]

Then the news of Lexington and Concord burst upon Pennsylvania, and "the face of things & Men underwent an immediate change." Militant Patriots seized the moment to call for the militia they could not get through legal channels. They capitalized on two necessary conditions: outrage in the aftermath of the shocking news, and the long-existing division of sovereignty which over three decades had allowed militias and other private groups to assume governmental powers and operate outside of formal government. Patriots had no need to innovate here, but instead built confidently upon a well-established pattern. They did not bother to press the assembly to form a militia, as had been the case in 1747 and 1755, but instead pursued the now well-trodden steps to form an extralegal militia, one that radicals could control and eventually use as a counterpoint to established government.[18]

Three times before 1775, the disconnect between the public demand for defense and state intransigence led to creative accommodations that ultimately expanded the civic horizons of ordinary white men and fragmented the popular basis for state sovereignty into ballot box on one hand and muster roll on the other. In 1747 the Defense Association had not worked *against* formal government, but rather preserved the assembly's political power by fulfilling the one need its Quaker legislators could not. In 1756 the extralegal militia formed explicitly to protest and embarrass the assembly, but, again, it offered no threat *to* the government. The short-lived 1764 association had formed to protect Philadelphia from the most imminent threat it had actually faced, but as the danger quickly passed, so too did the militia. These earlier forms of civic extralegal militia had expanded the participation of ordinary men, but had done so within the preexisting structure of government, which left great latitude for independent action. In 1775 the last extralegal militia of the colonial period would take the final step to act in defiance of government, dismantling the Quaker-inflected constitution that had held sway for almost a century.

Just as in 1747, the first step was a mass meeting. Armed confrontation in New England appeared to have transformed public opinion in Philadelphia overnight. A visitor to Philadelphia noted that whereas "from the 1st April . . . they only viewed things at a distance, they now seemed to enter into all the Violence that some time before possesst the Northern Colonies!" The local newspaper summarized it more colorfully: "MARS," it declared, "has established his empire in this populous city." A crowd eight thousand strong—a third of Philadelphia's population at the time and surely consisting not only of adult men but of women and children too—gathered in the State House yard on April 25, 1775, "to consider the measures to be pursued in the present critical affairs of America." Before they had even met, Patriot leaders had begun to circulate a plan for an association, which, perhaps, they had not crafted on the spur of the moment but had been developing to be ready for just such an occasion. The crowd in the State House yard enthusiastically embraced the idea of forming their own militia. They hoped within weeks to marshal four thousand men, roughly the entire adult white male population of the city, "for our own defence or for the assistance of our neighbours." Notably, while they did petition the legislature to allocate substantial sums toward defense, the crowd gathered in the shadow of the State House did not explicitly press it to create a militia. At this stage, Patriots preferred to keep control of so vital a body out of the hands of the much more conservative assembly.[19]

Organizing proceeded rapidly and included diverse constituencies. Within a week of the first mass meeting, Associators met in their respective neighborhoods to form militia companies and elect officers in the manner established in 1747 and reiterated in 1755. Men of all socioeconomic classes, occupations, ethnic groups, and religions quickly joined. Even companies of Quakers formed: some into actual militia companies, and others in a support capacity where volunteers would not bear arms but would put out fires and ferry civilians, among other tasks. Some among the "Tory class . . . renounced their former sentiments" and joined the association, though how heartfelt their commitment was may have varied. Proprietary supporter James Allen confessed that he had joined only because "a man is suspected who does not." He hoped, moreover, that having "discreet people mixing with them, may keep them in Order." Soon between one-third and one-half of Philadelphia's adult white men had associated. One Patriot lauded the "surprizing unanimity [that] prevails here"—unconsciously echoing the exact words used by Benjamin Franklin to describe the effect of the first Defense Association back in 1747. By May 9, when delegates to the Continental Congress began to arrive, they were greeted by a marching band and a company of riflemen and infantry.[20]

Critical to the evolution of the Military Association was that it was voluntary rather than compulsory. Associators had to be convinced to serve and that meant giving privates important concessions. First and foremost, the Military Association, like its voluntary predecessors in 1747 and 1755, gave privates the right to elect their own officers. Furthermore, codes of discipline remained more lenient than many military men might have preferred, an ongoing source of debate and consternation. If the Military Association had begun as a state-directed institution with mandatory service for all adult white men, the clout of the rank and file might have been less powerful. As it was, ordinary men could and did shape the extralegal militia profoundly.

Diverse though its appeal was designed to be, the militia relied heavily on the participation of the "lower sort," the poorest socioeconomic classes, just as had Philadelphia's extralegal militias before and indeed most armies before and since. Through the Military Association these men—who in many cases did not own enough property legally to vote in elections—found a powerful institutional amplifier for their political perspectives and concerns. No longer on the political and civic margins, they found themselves instead assiduously courted and at the center of Philadelphia's most important large-scale voluntary effort in decades. They flexed their muscle early, making clear that they expected all volunteers to be on an equal footing with one another and with their officers. When a committee of officers proposed a uniform for the new association, the rank and file objected on the grounds that even capped at ten shillings it would be too costly. When some officers assured that they were willing to provide uniforms for men too poor to afford them, the privates responded with wounded pride that "there are *hundreds* who could not afford it, yet would never submit to ask *any* man for a coat, neither would they appear in the ranks to be pointed at by those who *had* uniforms." The privates proposed instead that everyone wear hunting shirts, which were ubiquitous, were practical, and, importantly, would "level all distinctions." Furthermore, the offended privates bristled not only at the suggestion of uniforms or charitable handouts but also at the mode by which the officers had come to this resolution, "without the approbation of the people, who are entitled to an equal consultation." They demanded a meeting of all Associators, "that each man may have a voice in what so nearly concerns himself." The officers who had proposed the uniforms were blunderingly learning what Benjamin Franklin had intuited with the 1747 Defense Association:

the rank and file would only participate if they had a real say in the governance of the militia. Privates would exercise the power to choose their own officers, and though they promised to obey them on the battlefield, they demanded an "equal consultation" off of it.[21]

The Military Association, however, differed from the structure of the original 1747 Defense Association in two crucial ways. Where the Defense Association had carefully organized its own funding, relying on individual contributions and public lotteries, the Military Association in 1775 made no clear provision for how it would pay for its activities or material.[22] Moreover, the rhetoric around the militia had changed. In 1747 men had volunteered their time and energy, without any discussion of payment. In 1775, not only did the volunteers believe they should be compensated, especially if they did indeed have to put themselves in harm's way, but they also believed that those who did not volunteer ought to pay an extra tax "equivalent to the Expence and Loss of Time incurred by the Associators." On the surface both had to do with money; at a deeper level, they dealt with what kind of relationship the militia would or should have with the polity and the state.[23]

The 1775 Associators conceived of their role as protecting the liberties, lives, and property of the entire community. As such, they could not—indeed, should not—function as a mere voluntary club, one of many civic projects competing for the loyalty and energies of the people. Rather, they had to create an institution powerful enough to elicit or, if necessary, compel the support of the entire community, all of whom stood equally to gain or lose based on the success or failure of their endeavors. In short, the Military Association needed the powers and scope of a government. Beginning as a self-created, extralegal militia, and staffed by men chosen by the volunteers, not by the government, the Military Association demanded first state recognition, then substantial monetary support, and finally the power to compel all white male Pennsylvanians to participate or pay a fine.[24]

Unlike earlier extralegal militias, then, the 1775 Associators did not want or intend to form a voluntary association, a fact that stood in awkward tension with the fact that the militiamen had gotten their start on a voluntary, extralegal footing. It did not need to be this way. The Pennsylvania Assembly had refused to organize a legal militia in the previous year despite repeated calls, but Lexington and Concord had effected a radical change of public opinion. "So much, have the sufferings of boston excited the resentment & courage of that peace-loving People," one radical remarked, that even many Quakers flocked to the militia, forming two companies exclusively of Friends. Clearly, feelings ran high. In the wake of a similarly horrifying tragedy in 1755—General Edward Braddock's defeat by the French and Indians in western Pennsylvania—the assembly had passed the first ever militia bill in its history. Potentially enough of an impetus existed in 1775 to push the assembly once again to create a legal militia, though if the 1755 example was any indication, the process might take months rather than days. Radicals did indeed petition the House, but only requested that it raise funds in general for defense, not that it found a militia. This decision may simply have had to do with expediency—an extralegal militia, as past experience had shown, could be organized literally overnight, as had in fact happened in 1764. However, the decision may also have reflected the leaders' cognizance that any state involvement in setting up a militia would mean, first, that the conservative assembly would control and direct it, and second, that it would be established legally on a voluntary basis. The Quaker political elite had once before countenanced a militia of "Such as are Willing and Desirous," but it would never agree to one that forced pacifists to act against their consciences. By forming the Military Association on a voluntary basis, its leaders kept control out of the hands of conservatives or moderates, and because its membership consisted of a self-selected group, it could be shaped in ways that might not have been possible if a broader set of constituencies had to be consulted. Later when Patriots demanded universal military service, they intended it to be in their narrowly tailored institution. The assembly, meanwhile, confronted with a strong and numerous militia, could hardly preempt or even do much to modify the preexisting institution, either its officers or its rules. Extralegal organizing thus facilitated a rapid militarization that, whatever its actual defensive capabilities, transformed the city's political and civic landscape. Radicals and ordinary Philadelphians together had created a new, powerful institution, one that was able to agitate for mandatory universal military service precisely because of its own extralegal, voluntary origins.[25]

A month after they had formed their militia, Associators began by lobbying the government to legislate mandatory military service. They argued that their activities "promote[d] the public Security and Welfare," and insisted that the legislature—the same legislature they had deliberately bypassed—ought to shoulder the militia's costs. But money was only part of what the Associators wanted. Again and again they reiterated that "where the Liberty of all is at Stake, every Man should assist in its Support." To allow anyone to dodge this supreme civic duty—the defense of liberty and community—would be absolutely fatal to both the collective virtue and the practical strength of the whole. In the first place, those committed to military organization believed that very few were sincerely opposed to defense on grounds of religious conscience. A steep tax for "Non-Associators" would flush out such shirkers. But even in the case of those of "tender conscience" who could not bear arms, common justice demanded that they contribute *something* to a cause for which others were willing to risk their lives. Any tax or penalty, no matter how high, would always fall short of the supreme sacrifice of those who had joined the association.[26]

The Pennsylvania Assembly slowly acceded to many of the demands of the Associators. However, its cooperation came with a significant price: some degree of oversight. The conservative legislators took two months to recognize the extralegal militia, but from that point on began to appropriate and then print money for defense, and even began to "recommend" to conscientious objectors that they contribute to the cause—though the assembly was not yet ready to compel them to do so, as the Associators demanded. The assembly appointed a twenty-five-member "Committee of Safety" that would become in essence the executive branch of government for the remaining months of Pennsylvania's provincial existence.[27] The assembly tasked the Committee of Safety with making defensive preparations, acquiring and manufacturing sufficient war material, and overseeing the Military Association.[28]

To the surprise and consternation of the Committee of Safety, the soldiers of the association reacted with outrage. Though the membership of the committee reflected the growing strength of moderates and radicals over conservatives, it would nevertheless find its work stymied by the recalcitrance of the Associators themselves, who guarded jealously their autonomy. "The Associators are much alarmed," observed one Philadelphian, "by the power granted to what is Called the Committee of Safety." As much as the Associators had pushed and even bullied the assembly to provide for a plan of defense which knit together the resources of the entire province, they had no intention of ceding to the legislature or any state commission the right to direct their militia. The Military Association had been formed independently, and its volunteers wished it to remain under the control of the men who had first organized and joined it, not the provincial government. The association wanted the extensive powers of the state, particularly in financing and compelling military support, but not accountability to the legislature or the voting public. Like the Defense Association of 1747 and the Independent Companies in 1756, the Associators intended to stand accountable only to their own fellow volunteers and officers. The Military Association thus shared in a strong Philadelphia tradition of promoting active participation within the organization, expanding the civic engagement of its primarily lower-class soldiers, but simultaneously refusing a say to other constituencies or the wider public.[29]

The Committee of Safety nevertheless threw itself into its work, trying to finance the defensive preparations underway, making "earnest" recommendations to the Associators and the larger community alike to prepare for war, and slowly to bring the Military Association under its direction. It aggressively tried to raise funds, by donation or as loans. It asked the city's women to donate old linen for bandages. When the committee moved, however, to try to assert control over the militia, it found itself in a minefield. The trouble began in August when the committee published "Articles of Association" for the Military

Association. Benjamin Franklin, the author of two similar documents in 1747 and 1755, helped draft the articles, which dealt primarily with discipline, providing standards of conduct for soldiers and officers and a mechanism for redress of grievances, courts-martial, and similar matters.[30]

The Associators refused point-blank to sign or accept the articles proposed by the Committee of Safety. Instead, they redoubled their clout by forming a second body within the Military Association, a double layer of organization. By mid-September the Committee of Privates, consisting of three representatives elected from more than thirty of the companies in the city and environs, was meeting regularly. The Committee of Privates refused to accept the Articles of Association. The crux of their protest centered on the fact that the articles exempted Non-Associators from service or financial burden in the defense of Pennsylvania. "We conceive it to be contrary to the true end and intention of legislation," they declared, "for any body of men, claiming legislative authority, to make any laws which shall" place a burden on one part of the community and not on another. Such an unequal law, they concluded, "is destructive of the end and design of civil society." They perceived a devious plot at work, whereby the assembly would rest all the responsibility of defense on the shoulders of the volunteers and ask no sacrifice from men who shared equally in the dangers and benefits of provincial defense. They demanded a militia law that would force all "effective men" to serve or pay. If the assembly passed a military law that applied equally to all men, then Associators would serve in a government-controlled militia. But until the rules extended to all Pennsylvanians, they would volunteer their time only to an organization they themselves controlled.[31]

Moreover, the soldiers rejected outright the idea that the Committee of Safety could make rules for them. "The gentlemen who made the rules," they sneered, "seem to claim to themselves the right of calling out any or all of the present Associators." However, "we know of no right which our Assembly has to invest any body of men with legislative authority, this being an unalienable essential right belonging to the whole body of freemen of which society is constituted." The Committee of Safety had far overreached its authority, exercising "a new and unheard of exertion of power, inconsistent with the trust reposed in them by their constituents, and erecting a dangerous precedent as the body thus Invested is not subject to the controul of, or liable to be called to an account by, the people." This public posturing ignored much of Philadelphia's civic infrastructure, which operated precisely in this manner, "not subject to the controul of . . . the people." For example, at that very moment the Contributors for the Relief of the Poor was assessing the second poor tax of the year on Philadelphia, empowered by the legislature and subject to no input from voters or anyone else. Indeed, the Military Association itself asserted its right to operate without oversight by the legislature or by the legislature-appointed Committee of Safety and therefore ultimately by the voting public. Faced with this overwhelming opposition, the Committee of Safety gave up. Rather than push back, it joined the throng petitioning the assembly for a more effectual military law.[32]

In November the newly elected House at last bowed before intense public pressure and passed several laws that buttressed the Military Association and compelled fines for non-Associators, but asserted little state control over the militia.[33] First, the assembly passed legislation to emit (print) £80,000 for defense. A week later it passed "Rules and Regulations" for the Military Association. The assembly recognized the existing companies, affirmed the officers they had already chosen, and strengthened the present leadership. The rules prioritized association companies, ordering new recruits to join existing units rather than form their own new companies (in which they could have elected their own officers). Latecomers, therefore, would have little ability to affect the leadership of the militia. Moreover, the rules paid considerable attention to the order of command and precedence among the officers. Philadelphia officers would "take Rank or Precedence of all other Officers of equal Dignity, chosen or appointed in any other Part of the Province," and original association officers would have precedence over those elected by later units. Only in the third-to-last regulation did the assembly mention obliquely that its appointed Committee of Safety had the power to call out the association. Otherwise, the law asserted no clear authority for the legislature or any other provincial authority over the militia. Indeed, when the assembly crafted articles of association for the militiamen to sign, it would only "earnestly recommend" but not compel them to do so. Here was the first universal military bill in Pennsylvania's history—the first regardless of religious beliefs to impose a penalty on any able, white man who refused to serve—and yet the assembly asserted little control over its form or its function. By contrast, on four occasions the rules put provincial officials at the service of the association; various state functionaries were charged with supplying arms to those too poor to afford their own, supporting financially the families of poor Associators while the head of the household was away, providing carriages and other conveyances when the troops were called out, and collecting fines for nonattendance.[34]

The legislation represented a significant political victory, a testament to the power of the association to compel the more conservative assembly to actions that directly controverted the wishes of a substantial bloc of entrenched political elites. The militia had emerged rapidly after the news of Lexington and Concord, harnessing the anger and the energies of a substantial proportion of the adult white male population of the city. By organizing outside of state control, the Military Association capitalized on its self-selecting membership to act with a speed and decisiveness probably impossible in a provincial political system characterized by inequitable representation and a divided electorate. The assembly lumbered behind, first recognizing the association and then trying to support and direct it with the Committee of Safety. Efforts at state control, however, proved entirely ineffectual. Instead, the Military Association proved more adept at forcing the assembly to act. In just months it accomplished what had before seemed impossible: it forced the assembly to pass historic legislation that demolished two related pillars of Penn's original vision—pacifism and freedom of religious conscience. Along the way, the association reframed the conversation of what it meant to be a citizen.[35]

The major innovation of the November legislation was that for the first time in Pennsylvania's history it compelled military service for any able-bodied white man.[36] Not only did every man have to serve, but, in common with earlier Pennsylvania militias, he had to supply his own weapons, unless he was too poor, in which case local officials would provide the necessary equipment. Any who failed to attend mandatory muster days had to pay a fine. In addition to that fine for each muster day they missed, Non-Associators had to pay an annual fine of £2 10s. This legislation still fell short of what the Committee of Privates wanted, a steep tax against the estates of Non-Associators which would penalize the wealthy most heavily, but it nevertheless represented a radical departure in Pennsylvania's history.[37]

Despite the lengths to which the Pennsylvania Assembly had gone, for many they had not gone far enough. Associators seriously debated whether to sign the new Articles of Association. They objected to the light fines imposed on Non-Associators, the low rates of pay, and the fact that families of poor Associators called to duty would be assisted by the Overseers of the Poor like common paupers, which they found degrading. Moreover, Associators demanded state compensation not only going forward, but for their past service while an extralegal militia. Ultimately, most Associators did sign the imperfect articles, but only to present a united front, lest the enemy conclude they were "ungovernable," and because the regulations represented "the best thing which can be done at present." Advocates swore to improve the laws as soon as possible. To this end Associators appointed a committee of correspondence to facilitate "friendly correspondence" throughout the provincial armed forces which would "express the desires of the whole body of Associators." As the assembly's political clout was waning, that of the rank-and-file Associators was on the rise.[38]

"The Duty of Every Good Citizen":
Defining Citizenship in the New State

"A question has been lately started," declared the *Pennsylvania Gazette* that May, "which has greatly changed our political ground." One year after Lexington and Concord, the matter of military defense had gradually transformed into the question of independence from Britain. In that year, tectonic transformations had reshaped the political and civic landscape. Two popular institutions vied with one another: the new grassroots association and the old elected Pennsylvania Assembly. Radical and embracing independence on the one hand, conservative and leery of independence on the other, the association and the assembly yet each claimed to speak for "the people." The acrimonious debate about home rule then depended first on answering these questions: Who could decide? Who ruled at home? The contest over independence in Philadelphia unfolded as a struggle over the legitimacy of the two popular institutions claiming to express the sovereign will of the people. Involved in this fight was a critical examination of the civic claims and qualifications of "the people" themselves. Each institution depended for its authority on a different political base: the assembly on voters (which left out men who did not meet property qualifications), the association on militiamen (which left out conscientious objectors and everyone who did not agree with independence). Who, in these troubled times, could claim a voice in public matters: propertied voters or only those men willing to take up arms in defense of their community?[39]

The tense move and countermove between the assembly and Associators progressed through the spring. The assembly attempted to mitigate radicals' call for a new government by finally answering long-standing grievances. It reduced the power of the objectionable Committee of Safety. Still more radically, the legislators added seventeen seats to the House, giving more equal representation to the western counties and the city of Philadelphia, which received four more delegates, bringing the city's total to six (out of fifty-four). Many thought, however, that these reforms did not go far enough. One militia supporter castigated the legislature for a continued "neglect of altering and making such amendments as the Associators have required," and threatened baldly that the Associators had waited patiently "rather than take the matter out of their hands," but that if the assembly did not do as the Associators demanded, the militiamen would "seek . . . redress where they know they can find it."[40]

Public opinion swung ever stronger in favor of independence from Britain, especially after the publication of Thomas Paine's *Common Sense* in Philadelphia early in 1776. The assembly refused, however, to be swayed. It gave specific instructions to Pennsylvania's delegates to the Continental Congress, forbidding them to vote for any measures that would sever its relationship from the Crown. Some "warm members of committee in Philadelphia" were fed up by early March and ready to call a provincial convention to write a new constitution, but public opinion had not yet advanced enough to support so bold a move. "*Absolute necessity* alone," one observer thought, "should give birth to any new powers, and justify an innovation in the constitution." Others disagreed. "It has been urged that the Assembly has done and will do all that a Convention can or may do," one author drily remarked, but then "I ask why have they hitherto neglected it?" Another made it clear that he thought that the assembly's job was to do as the Associators dictated. "No man, or set of men," the author asserted, "have as yet complained against the alterations and amendments proposed by the Associators, the House ought, therefore, to esteem them as the general voice of their constituents."[41]

Of course, there was another means to gauge the "general voice of their constituents," and that was an election. The special by-election scheduled on May 1, 1776, to fill the newly created seats for Philadelphia and the western counties became a referendum on independence. Over eighteen hundred men, one of the highest turnouts in the city's history, cast ballots. The outcome, however, was "bitterly disappointing" to the Philadelphia radicals, who managed to win only one seat; the other three delegates elected to represent the city opposed independence. Thomas Paine attributed the defeat to the absence of many Associators who were serving in Canada, the refusal to allow "a numerous body of Germans" to vote because of property and residence requirements, and temporarily shutting down the polls, which caused confusion. Whatever complaints radicals like Paine raised, a year after blood had been shed in Massachusetts Philadelphia voters had not yet collectively embraced independence.[42]

Unsuccessful at effecting change through the ballot box, Patriots decided that the assembly itself had to go and began to challenge its legitimacy. Thomas Paine, a recent English immigrant and writer, led the charge in a series of newspaper letters penned pseudonymously as "The Forester" in response to a similar series by "Cato," or William Smith, who was a longtime proprietary supporter, provost of the College of Philadelphia, and a minister of the Church of England. Much of these two authors' vitriolic exchange dealt with the merits of independence and the pamphlet *Common Sense*, but in order to talk about independence in Pennsylvania, their conversation pivoted on their definitions of the legitimate basis of government.[43]

Smith opened the salvo with a furious denunciation of the plan to call a convention. "The MAJESTY OF THE PEOPLE OF PENNSYLVANIA," he thundered, "has been grievously wounded in the persons of their legal Representatives, by repeated attempts to intimidate them in the discharge of the great trust committed to them by the voice of their country." Smith accepted and even applauded the work of the various patriotic committees for their work in upholding the nonimportation agreements, founding a manufactory to produce textiles, and assisting those hurt by the cessation of trade, but insisted that these committees could serve only in an "executive" capacity. Here Smith drew on the long civic history of Philadelphia, where a variety of commissions had long operated in a similar manner. "With what face," he asked, could any of these committees supplant the elected legislature? Though many of the patriotic committees had been elected, "they had not two hundred votes" and could not "ever aspire at the powers vested in an Assembly, fairly and constitutionally elected, to represent two or three hundred thousand people." Moreover, these committees were Philadelphia creations and did not reflect the input of rural voters. Without a mandate from "an uncorrupted majority of the good people of this province," he argued, "the Assembly can neither consent to any change of our constitution, or to make the least transfer of our allegiance." He objected that, unlike the constitutional legislature, "no Committees were ever entrusted with any authority to speak the sense of the People of Pennsylvania."[44]

Paine countered that the assembly had become a paradoxical absurdity that no longer had legal force. It derived its authority from the 1701 charter from William Penn, who had in turn received his authority from the Crown. The representatives were thus required to swear allegiance "to serve the same King against whom this province . . . [is] at war." The assembly as an institution was "disqualified . . . unsafe and dangerous" because it "derives it's [*sic*] authority from our enemies." Rather than expressing the will of the people, he maintained, the assembly was "truly unconstitutional, being self created." The committees, on the other hand, were "the only constitutional bodies at present in this province, and that for the following reason; they were duly elected by the people." The May 1 by-election had no bearing on this conversation; rather, "we have stood the experiment of the election, for the sake of knowing the men who were against us," but in this time of threat to life and liberty, "are they so foolish as to think that . . . we, with ten times their strength and number (if the question were put to the people at large) will submit to be governed by cowards and tories?" Paine thus derided the validity of the election that his confederates had just lost, but appealed instead to a theoretical future popular vote, one that would be based on a more legitimate electorate.[45]

Associators and their allies argued that the property requirements for voting excluded many men who had volunteered for the militia, men who were willing to make the ultimate sacrifice to defend their community, and that they deserved a share in public deliberations. The Committee of Privates petitioned that regardless of fortune or length of residence, all Associators "should be admitted to the Enjoyment of all the Rights and Privileges of a Citizen of that Country which they have defended and protected." Paine maintained meanwhile that radicals had lost the May 1 elections largely because many "good citizens" had been called to military duty in Canada, "while the tories by never stirring out remain at home to take the advantage of elections." Tellingly, he sniffed that of the votes cast for one of the conservative new assemblymen, "there will not be found more than sixty armed men," and "perhaps not so many." The opinions of the stay-at-homes did not bear equal weight to those of the "armed men."[46]

Here Paine tapped into an argument gaining wide currency in Philadelphia: if Associators deserved the right to vote regardless of their property because of their virtuous service in arms, perhaps those who "under cloak of conscience, conveniently screen themselves from the hazardous duty which their country calls for" correspondingly had less of a right to vote, or even forfeited that right entirely. "An Elector" made this point clearly: "every citizen who has armed and associated to defend the Commonwealth is, and should be an Elector; *and every non-associator and stickler for dependency on the power that is now in actual depredation of our Rights, Liberties, and all that is dear to us*, should be KEPT FAR FROM OUR COUNCILS." Horrified, "Civis" responded that such a policy would deprive two-thirds of the city's voters of their rights, a move calculated to "give the power to those only who have already fixed their sentiments in favour of independence, without regard to their age, condition, or their knowledge of our constitution." This author imagined that "a great number" of the Associators were minors, apprentices, and newly arrived immigrants—boys and men, in short, who had no stake in or familiarity with the community whose fate they were being given the power to direct.[47]

The Continental Congress, meeting in Philadelphia, was itself edging toward a resolution for independence and recommended that "where no government sufficient to the exingencies of their affairs have been hitherto established," the colonies should "adopt such government as shall, in the opinion of the representatives of the people, best conduce to the happiness and safety of their constituents in particular, and America in general." This recommendation came on May 10, a mere nine days after radicals failed to gain a legislative majority at the polls. Radicals immediately called for a convention "to protest against the present Assembly's doing any business in their House until the sense of the Province was taken," which apparently the recent election had failed to do. Accordingly, around four thousand Pennsylvanians gathered on May 20 in the State House yard in a heavy rain. They agreed that their sitting government was inadequate to their needs, and that because of its linkages to the monarchy the assembly could not legally create a new one. Therefore, the people must act for themselves. They voted for a convention to draw up a new constitution.[48]

Militant patriots used the bifurcation of sovereignty and state power to their advantage. The assembly, even though it derived its authority from annual elections, had lost its legitimacy through its unwillingness to produce a militia law in line with the repeated demands of the Associators, by its "treasonable" resistance to independence, and by the fact that its charter had been granted by "our mortal enemy the King of Great Britain." If the assembly was bad, its creation, the Committee of Safety, was even worse. The old assembly had been "in some measure accountable to their constituents," whereas the "the Committee of Safety . . . has the privilege of secrecy, and the time of their duration is unlimited." By contrast, the officers of the militia, elected by their men, publicly available and known, represented no such threat. "The public seems fully satis-fied, and have a clear confidence" in the militia.[49]

The militia, therefore, and its Associators would become the foundation for the legitimacy of Pennsylvania's Constitutional Convention and, by extension, the new government. One author argued that "the Militia is the natural support of a government, founded on the authority of the people only." Another argued that the new legislators ought themselves to be militiamen. Militant patriots, moreover, appealed to the militia volunteers to take the lead in selecting the framers of the new constitution. The stakes were enormous. "On the Judicious-ness of the Choice which you . . . make," one leader exhorted them, "depends the Happiness of Millions." The expanded franchise that characterized the militia became the principle upon which Patriots determined who could vote for the convention. In framing the constitution, it was a short step to accord the franchise to all men. Pennsylvania, so behind in radical activity through the 1760s and early 1770s, thus sprinted ahead of all the other new states to write what was regarded then and now as the most radical constitution of the revolu-tionary era. The basis for that radicalism lay in the Military Association and in the long-incubating civic culture that had produced it.[50]

Of course, neither the Pennsylvania Constitution nor the process leading up to it had in fact included all Pennsylvania men. By definition, only men who agreed with independence participated in creating and running the new govern-ment. In order to vote for representatives to the convention that would write a new state constitution, a man had to swear or affirm that "I do not hold myself bound to bear allegiance to George the Third, King of Great Britain," and that he would "oppose the tyrannical proceedings of the King and Parliament of Great Britain against the American Colonies." Men ranging from moderates to Loyalists to Quakers were thus left out. Loyalists by definition could not make such a statement. The Society of Friends, meanwhile, had publicly declared in 1775 that their faith demanded that they "demean themselves as peaceable subjects, and . . . discountenance and avoid every measure tending to excite disaffection to the king, as supreme magistrate, or to the legal authority of his government." Strict Quakers, as pacifists, would not formally side with either Patriots or the Crown, but their refusal to countenance independence or defense tarred them as "Hippocrites" who, because they refused to affirm allegiance to the new order, were justified in being excluded from it. The new order would be built without them.[51]

Proponents of the new government, perhaps by necessity in the midst of a civil war, had learned the lesson previous Philadelphia associations offered them: cohesion sometimes works best through the exclusion of nonsupporters. In this respect the Military Association and the new government it did so much to legitimize built upon the previous pattern of the extralegal militias of 1747 and 1756 and Pennsylvania's culture of civic association. Voluntary organizations answered only to their own constituencies, giving them a unity, flexibility, and efficiency that might not have been otherwise possible. They did so, however, at the cost of shutting out everyone else. The Military Association and newly founded Commonwealth of Pennsylvania simultaneously opened up and shut down democratic participation.

Dissent found little tolerance in a polity facing imminent invasion. The convention to create a new constitution celebrated "a growing unanimity among the people of the Province," even as it recognized the ongoing "prejudices of the weak and ignorant respecting the proposed change in our Government." To be sure, the convention urged "forbearance, charity, and moderation" for all inhabitants, but by characterizing opposition as prejudice, weakness, and ignorance, it placed Loyalists and strict Quakers beyond the bounds of legitimate discourse. Already excluded from crafting the new government, these groups also could not voice critiques or opposition without fear of reprisals and, increasingly, state power directed against them.[52]

If the new government did not follow through on one writer's threat that "the rude custom of Tarring and Feathering" ought to "give way to the severer punishment of the gibbet," it did act to curtail severely the rights of the minority. In July 1776 lawmakers passed an ordinance to disarm all Non-Associators, requiring them to hand over all firearms to the militia colonels, who would redistribute the weapons to Associators. Troops seized the large Friends Meeting House on Market Street to house soldiers, a deep affront to pacifist Quakers. In September the tax on Non-Associators was raised dramatically. A year later, with British troops bearing down on the city, Philadelphia authorities arrested forty men, mostly Quakers, because they suspected their loyalty. Twenty of them who refused to take loyalty oaths were deemed dangerous and removed from Philadelphia under armed guard. They were held for eight months in Winchester, Virginia, at their own expense, where two of them died before the group was finally released. Not one of these men ever had the benefit of a trial, nor even formal charges against which he could defend himself. In the fear and confusion of wartime, accusation and conviction became synonymous. When the exiles returned to Pennsylvania, it was to the news that a law, commonly called the Test Act, had just been passed that stripped any Pennsylvania men of full citizenship rights who refused to take an oath of loyalty to the new state—an oath that Friends could and would not take. Freedom of speech and freedom of conscience had no place in wartime Philadelphia.[53]

Historian Carl Becker famously argued that the American Revolution involved two fundamental questions: first, independence or "home rule," and second, "who should rule at home." In Philadelphia, the second question came first. Whether Pennsylvania would join the other colonies in declaring independence was contingent on settling the question of which political leadership, which institutions, and which political base would prevail, with lasting consequences going forward. Dominance depended in part on rhetorical claims to legitimacy, and in part on the mobilization of on-the-ground clout—a fact that in the city gave the well-organized Military Association an advantage. The move for independence in Philadelphia entailed pitting association against assembly and therein a transformative debate about the nature and basis of institutions, governance, and citizenship.[54]

The Military Association represented the final florescence of Philadelphia's colonial tradition of decentralized governance by various commissions and voluntary organizations. Its leaders and members built upon long experience to create a powerful institution that nevertheless worked at first alongside (though always outside) the existing representative government. Because it was voluntary and independent, the association by both necessity and choice developed to be more radical than it would have been under state auspices. When the Associators could not compel the legislature to do as it wished or take over the reins of power through democratic elections, it declared the sitting government illegitimate by virtue of its charter deriving ultimately from the Crown. Likewise illegitimate they declared the sitting political elite—whether Quaker or proprietary—because of their refusal to defend the polity. The association between military service and citizenship became absolute. Before and after 1776 full political rights were accorded to men with a vested interest in the community. The difference hinged on how a man's neighbors determined that he demonstrated that vested interest: before 1776 it was through property holding; in 1776 and for some time after it was through the willingness to bear arms—framed as a duty, rather than a right.[55]

The Military Association acted as midwife to the new political order, altering profoundly the conditions that had made its own genesis possible. More than any other polity in the new United States, Pennsylvania would embrace representative democracy expressed as directly as possible. In 1776 Pennsylvania adopted what scholars and contemporaries alike have regarded as the most radical constitution of the American Revolution, though in fact it reproduced many central tenets of its colonial charter, including a unicameral legislature, weak executive, and annual elections. Pennsylvania's Constitution or Frame of 1776 added to this earlier model by providing for open-door legislative sessions and the abolition of all property qualifications for voting, the first state ever to do so. Meanwhile, in Philadelphia the combination of wartime upheaval and policies enacted by the new government limited the civil rights of Non-Associators and effected the obliteration of the diverse commissions and voluntary associations that before had afforded myriad routes for Philadelphians to policy formation and community action. A desire to present a united defensive front against the invading British army led, moreover, to an emphasis on a unitary public culture that had difficulty imagining opposition in any light short of catastrophe or even treason.[56]

Philadelphia's new political culture, like the one it supplanted, emphasized democratic inclusion and, also like the one it supplanted, enacted it imperfectly and unevenly. The balance of power worked out in the colonial period had allowed both majorities and minorities to influence the texture of local governance and decide what urban services and amenities would be available, how, and to whom. It had never worked through harmony or consensus, but rather by virtue of the reverse—by multiple groups having control over aspects of governance and policy, by contention, by difference. The old model of multiple, competing publics had hardly been a utopia. Elite and middling white men had disproportionate access and power. Moreover, because the system worked through decentralization, governance was inefficient, confused, and sometimes contradictory. In contrast to the byzantine morass of colonial urban governance, the new system emphasized transparency and responsiveness to the electorate through frequent elections, open legislative sessions, and the publication of all proceedings in the local press. Enfranchising (in theory[57]) all adult white men diminished the need and even the right for them to organize independently as they had done in the past. Because of the need for unity in wartime and the mechanisms built into the system for citizens to express themselves through elections, this political culture operated by majority rule. Minorities owed allegiance and obedience to the unitary whole, "the people," even if, because they refused to swear loyalty to the new regime, they were in fact denied civil rights, including the right to vote.

The rise of popular sovereignty championed by the Military Association and the 1776 Frame of Government, in short, was neither universal nor without costs. The parameters for inclusion and exclusion—that is to say, citizenship—and the range of acceptable mechanisms for disagreement which had existed in the colonial era had been overthrown. In the immediate future an insistent unitary civic culture would supersede the polycentric accommodations of the preceding era. What would happen in the longer term when peace returned—how Philadelphians would assert and authorize power over local matters—would take longer to work out.

Epilogue

The City of Brotherly Love struggled to pick up the pieces in the wake of civil war, British occupation, and postwar economic depression. In the 1780s visitors described the city as though it had passed through a natural disaster, leaving behind broken windows, peeling paint, and roads so out of repair that the slightest rainfall turned them to a mire of impassable mud. Public buildings, commandeered for military purposes during the war, still reeked of animal and human excrement. Private homes and shops had been badly damaged or demolished altogether. Peace had brought an end to violence, but not the return of prosperity. Indeed, the end of the war hurt local artisans as cheaper British imports flooded the local market, while the city's export merchants found that their cargos were barred from British ports, stifling the city's trade. Local politics were acrimonious as partisans fought over Pennsylvania's 1776 constitution, a charter for the Bank of America, and the fate of Philadelphia's municipal corporation, dissolved in 1776 and still not re-formed. These local fights received heightened attention because of Philadelphia's national prominence as the de facto and later established capital of the new nation.[1]

Philadelphians struggled to revive or reframe what remained of the vibrant associational world that had done so much to structure not only social but civic life in the city. They found shortly that they could not reconstruct the world they had had before. Pennsylvania, more than any other state in the new union, had overthrown the old political elite and replaced it with a new cadre of men. The new leaders were not eager to return to the dispersed public culture that had characterized the colonial era. Perhaps they recognized how that system had facilitated their own rise to power, and were leery of leaving a similar opening for others. They, like many revolutionaries before and since, emphasized the importance of a unitary public culture similar to the one that had been so vital during the early war effort.

Pennsylvania went from a colony that had welcomed and relied on independent organizing to the state in the Union which was the most alarmed by and wary of two major classes of voluntary organization: groups with overt partisan objectives and corporations. Any organizing that smacked of partisanship became deeply suspect. Like-minded politicians banded together in the halls and back rooms of political institutions, but found it difficult to mobilize popular opinion more broadly in the face of the rhetorical emphasis on a unitary, consensual public culture. When Republicans founded partisan associations that claimed to speak directly on behalf of Pennsylvanians in 1793, Federalists responded with alarm. They saw no place for the mobilization of private citizens in partisan associations, maintaining that opposition could only legitimately be voiced at the polls. Federalist criticism effectively blocked the first attempts at Republican partisan organization, but by the late 1790s Republicans adopted new tactics. They founded the Tammany Society, a fraternal social group with no overt partisan objectives. Through sociability the Tammany Society brought together like-minded men and energized them toward Republican objectives, but without ever claiming to speak for the people as a whole or directly inserting itself into electoral politics. Once out of power, Federalists adopted similar tactics, most notably through their own Washington Benevolent Society.[2]

Only late in the 1790s and more broadly after the election of 1800 did Philadelphia begin to recover anything like the flourishing public culture it had known before the Revolution—inflected now, however, by intense public scrutiny as to objectives and membership and by much sharper limits set by the state. The days when half the adult male population could organize their own extralegal militia were long gone; the broad scope for men of lower classes to influence civic matters beyond the confines of the ballot box diminished in the early Republic, though trade organizations tried to speak for tradesmen and journeymen. Only with the rise of the Jacksonian party system of the 1830s would lower-class men mobilize again in large numbers. Likewise, the capacity for minorities like the Quakers to take over matters of public policy diminished after the Revolution. Though Quakers remained active and influential in matters such as abolition, they never again en masse took over government responsibilities.

Meanwhile, critics alleged that corporations preserved special privilege for a small minority, weakening the sovereign will of the people by conceding special rights to closed combinations of men and property. Many wondered whether incorporation belonged in the new Republic at all or was an anachronism, or even a vice, from corrupt Britain with which they ought to do away. The new legislature fought fiercely over granting new charters and actually revoked the colonial charter of the College of Philadelphia in 1779, on the grounds that if a corporation acted contrary to the public good, as they contended (without much evidence) that the college had, the legislature was fully justified in amending or revoking its charter to require loyalty oaths and legislative oversight. The legislature remained conservative about granting new charters, limiting both public-oriented organizations and other kinds of institutions. Even the municipality did not receive a new charter until 1789, and only then out of fractious contest.[3]

For all critics' reticence about corporations, however, pressure mounted for banks, insurance companies, transportation companies, and business corporations that could expand credit and mobilize capital in new ways. Independence had wrenched away long-standing British constraints that had hobbled the development of American finance, and entrepreneurs seethed for easy credit and secure investment structures. Pennsylvania, an outlier among the states in its suspicion and hostility to chartered bodies, only granted four charters to banks before 1813, but over time banks and other private companies played an increasingly active role in the local economy, superseding the former role of public charitable institutions as lenders of large sums of capital. Gradually, incorporation ceased to be a privilege granted bodies that served the public good and instead became standard operating procedure for large financial institutions, which no longer had any overt public responsibility. Financial and business corporations evolved away from their voluntary associational origins, offering a wide range of financial services to a diverse clientele and engaging less in exclusionary insider lending.[4]

Philadelphia's public culture, then, changed after the Revolution, but the direction of change was not uniformly toward increased participation. Colonial Philadelphia's governance had been predicated upon and thrived off of contention and independent initiative, allowing substantial room for direct participation in policy formation by diverse constituencies among white men. In the short term, the Revolution shut down this dynamic, competitive public sphere with multiple access points. After a quarter-century obsession with a unitary public culture, Philadelphia's public sphere would reemerge with very different contours, shaped by partisan politics, evangelical awakening, reform, the market revolution, a rapidly expanding print sphere, and a new and broader conception of the purposes of incorporation. Previously excluded constituencies, notably African Americans and women, found space to join, shape, and use voluntary association and churches to their own ends, even as poorer Philadelphians found themselves not only shut out but increasingly the object of reform-minded groups' ministrations. Partisans galvanized the masses around the pageantry of party politics, enlarging radically the context in which (still mostly) men articulated and participated in political contests that dealt now not only with the local, but with the national and even international. Violence came to be a more common—if not acceptable—mechanism to express disagreement with other segments of the population, be they African Americans, Catholics, abolitionists, or competing fire companies. Meanwhile, wealthy investors helped reframe the purpose of charters and the definition of public good, moving business corporations away from their original public purposes and introducing for-profit institutions with vast capital into the volatile mix of contending interests.[5]

The definition of the public sphere and which people and institutions constituted it thus expanded and contracted in the early Republic, creating a context that built on but differed substantially from what had come before. It became broader, involving new constituencies, and more constrained, excluding sharply the poor and separating off corporations (along with their interests and responsibilities) as "private" entities no longer responsible for or answerable to some notion of the public good. It became more diverse with so many different political, ethnic, religious, and reform causes to champion, even as it became less particular to Philadelphia, participating in national and global politics and movements less immediately responsive to individual input as had been true when Philadelphians founded groups that operated mostly for and within the context of their own community. Increasingly articulated national political parties absorbed the loyalties and energies of partisans, who in turn framed and contested local matters now at least partly through a national lens.[6]

The emergence of the new United States, then, did not bring into being a vibrant public culture in Philadelphia or foster newly energized participation by ordinary people. The direction of change was more complicated than that. The city had a long history in the colonial period of a robust public sphere; that public sphere arguably faltered in the short term after the war, held hostage to concerns over unity and loyalty, only to pick up again in ways that were not more but only differently participatory or diverse than in the colonial period. The changes reflected the dynamics of the growth of the city and larger trends in which it participated: profound technological, economic, social, and political transformation at the national and international level.

Taking seriously the diverse mechanisms for local governance of the colonial period in a place like Philadelphia reframes the character of the public sphere, the history of political participation, and the relationship between "the state" and its citizens. The power of voluntary association vis-à-vis that of the state has been presented as an either-or phenomenon, a seesaw where when one is up, the other necessarily down. For a time, directly after the Revolution, many Philadelphians espoused this position. They rejected the system of governance without a strong center which had been cobbled together since the city's founding in 1682. In their 1776 constitution and beyond Pennsylvanians called for a republican government as directly responsive to the people as possible, and they looked with hostility upon private initiatives as suspect, even dangerous. The men and women who had lived through civil war, occupation, and political upheaval thus framed the authority of the state and the activities of private actors as a zero-sum game. They put their faith for a generation not in a thriving, competitive civil society, but in a strong legislature, frequent elections expressing the will of the people, and legislators held strictly accountable to their voters, who, between elections, did not agitate but waited until the next electoral cycle to express their sentiments.[7]

Before the Revolution, however, Philadelphians had not framed the relationship between the state and civil society in this way; indeed, it would have made no sense to them. They too valued a strong representative system at the provincial level, boasting a comparatively broad franchise for white men, a remarkably powerful legislature, and annual elections. They fought consistently to champion the clout of their legislature and enhance it by making it more equitably representative. Their deep-seated respect for representative democracy did not diminish but perhaps provided the secure basis through which other—deliberately more exclusive—forms of participation also could flourish, all claiming to work for the public good: libraries, fire companies, schools, advocacy groups, sporting clubs, and even militias. These voluntary combinations derived their power from the commitment and energy of a self-selected (and therefore exclusive) group of people who shared a common vision. They might cohere around a common objective such as fire protection or founding a library; they might instead share a common perspective on policy matters such as Indian diplomacy, poor relief, or the legitimate grounds for military defense. In either case, the power of the private organization derived from the fact that it did not have to answer to the larger public, but as a smaller, self-delimited institution, it could single-mindedly pursue its own ends.

Both representative democracy and voluntary associations were vital institutional avenues for civic participation in early America. They derived from different principles—answering to the whole public or advocating on behalf of a self-selected segment of it. Philadelphians did not turn to private associations simplistically because their government was weak or because they rejected it. Rather, they took advantage of diverse routes to shape civic life—voting with ballots and with their feet; paying both taxes and voluntary subscriptions; signing petitions and articles of association; drinking at election-day "treating" and in tavern-room meetings; debating the issues in closed-door legislative sessions and at mass outdoor meetings; and serving as Overseers of the Poor, tax assessors, church wardens, firefighters, and hospital managers. The delicate balancing act that Philadelphians orchestrated in the colonial period between these two sorts of participation met the needs of the circumscribed scope and small demographic size of the colonial city. The Revolution upended that balance, not because it was a seminal ideological moment or a new unleashing of participation by the masses, but because it was a tense and violent ordeal, a civil war. The war's aftermath coincided with demographic growth, economic transformation, the rise of national partisan politics, evangelical awakening, technological innovation, and reform impulses. Succeeding generations struggled and continue to struggle to negotiate anew the appropriate balance between governance for and by individuals and governance by and through voluntary associations, institutions, and ever-shifting categories of private combinations. Both provided unique avenues to participation. The question was and is at what point one impinges on the efficacy and access of the other.

Abbreviations

AHMM	Alms House Manager's Minutes, 1766–78, Philadelphia City Archives
APS	American Philosophical Society
DBCOP	Day Book of the Academy and College of Philadelphia 1749–89, University Archives and Records Center, University of Pennsylvania
FFCM	Fellowship Fire Company Minutes, 1738–80, Historical Society of Pennsylvania
HSP	Historical Society of Pennsylvania
LCP	Library Company of Philadelphia
LCPM	Library Company of Philadelphia Minutes, Library Company of Philadelphia
MBPPP	Minutes of the Board of Property of the Province of Pennsylvania, *Pennsylvania Archives*, ser 2., vol. 19 (Harrisburg, 1851)
MCC	*Minutes of the Common Council of the City of Philadelphia, 1704–1776* (Philadelphia, 1847)
MCSA	Minutes of the Council of Safety in Assembly, *Pennsylvania Archives*, Colonial Records
MFA	Minutes of the Friendly Association, Historical Society of Pennsylvania
MOPS	Minutes of the Overseers of the Public School, vol. 1, 1712–1770, William Penn Charter School Collection, Quaker and Special Collections, Haverford College
MPC	Minutes of the Provincial Council, *Pennsylvania Archives*, ser. 1, Colonial Records (Harrisburg, 1851)
PFMQM	Philadelphia Friends Monthly and Quarterly Minutes, 1682–1705, Quaker and Special Collections, Haverford College
PHM	Pennsylvania Hospital Minutes, Pennsylvania Hospital Archives
PHS	Presbyterian Historical Society
PMFWB	Waste Book, 1761–98, Presbyterian Ministers' Fund, Historical Society of Pennsylvania
PMHB	*Pennsylvania Magazine of History and Biography*
TJPCA	Treasurer's Journal, 1768–99, Philadelphia Contributionship Archives
UFCM	Union Fire Company Minutes, 1736–85, Historical Society of Pennsylvania
UPM	Trustees of the University of Pennsylvania Minute Books, vol. 1,

1749–68, University Archives and Records Center, University of Pennsylvania

Votes   Votes and Proceedings of the House of Representatives of the Province of Pennsylvania, *Pennsylvania Archives*, ser. 8 (1931)

WMQ   *William and Mary Quarterly*

WPCSC   William Penn Charter School Collection, Quaker and Special Collections, Haverford College

Introduction

1. William E. Lingelbach, "William Penn and City Planning," *PMHB* 68, no. 4 (1944): 398–409.

2. Sept. 1, 1701, Feb. 27, Mar. 2, 1702, PFMQM. Edwin B. Bronner, "Quaker Landmarks in Early Philadelphia," in *Historic Philadelphia from the Founding until the Early Nineteenth Century*, 1965 reprint of *Transactions of the American Philosophical Society* 43, no. 1 (1953): 212.

3. For an opposing view, see Sam Bass Warner Jr., *The Private City: Philadelphia in Three Periods of Its Growth* (Philadelphia: University of Pennsylvania Press, 1968), 10–21, in which he concludes that Philadelphia "functioned as a single community," because of its small size and the face-to-face character of its networks. Gary B. Nash in *The Urban Crucible: Social Change, Political Consciousness, and the Origins of the American Revolution* (Cambridge, MA: Harvard University Press, 1979) assumes a similar unity prior to the economic downturn following the Seven Years' War. My work contributes to the direction indicated by John Smolenski, who highlights the challenge Quakers faced from the beginning to rule a heterogeneous population that did not wholly embrace their ideals or system of governance. Quaker elites' attempt to "creolize" the larger population largely failed; not until the early eighteenth century did stability begin to emerge, and then only because Quakers themselves had adapted their forms and expectations to the new political climate. John Smolenski, *Friends and Strangers: The Making of a Creole Culture in Colonial Pennsylvania* (Philadelphia: University of Pennsylvania Press, 2010).

4. Paul D. Halliday, *Dismembering the Body Politic: Partisan Politics in England's Towns, 1650–1730* (Cambridge: Cambridge University Press, 1998). T. H. Breen and Stephen Foster, "The Puritans' Greatest Achievement: A Study in Social Cohesion in Seventeenth-Century Massachusetts," *Journal of American History* 60 (1973): 5–22. Edmund S. Morgan, *American Slavery, American Freedom: The Ordeal of Colonial Virginia* (New York: W. W. Norton, 1975). Pennsylvania may have afforded some women more public voice than many other places because of the role of women in Quaker meeting structures. See Phyllis Mack, *Visionary Women: Ecstatic Prophecy in Seventeenth-Century England* (Berkeley: University of California Press, 1992). Barry Levy, *Quakers and the American Family: British Settlement in the Delaware Valley* (Oxford: Oxford University Press, 1988).

5. Peter Clark, *British Clubs and Societies 1580–1800: The Origins of an Associational World* (Oxford: Clarendon Press, 2000). On voluntary associations as a technology, see Johann N. Neem, *Creating a Nation of Joiners: Democracy and Civil Society in Early National Massachusetts* (Cambridge, MA: Harvard University Press, 2008), 81–82. He argues for the technological innovation arising in the early Republic, not recognizing colonial precedents.

In Philadelphia, two of the earliest public civic organizations, the Library Company (founded in 1731) and Union Fire Company (1736), had extensive influence on the organizations that followed—not only the three other libraries and at least nineteen fire companies that drew on them directly, but also large institutions such as the Pennsylvania Hospital and even independent militias such as the Defense Association. See, e.g., Jessica Choppin Roney, "'Ready to act in defiance of the Government': Philadelphia Voluntary Associations and the Defense Association of 1747–48," *Early American Studies* 8, no. 2 (May 2010): 358–85.

6. Tocqueville thought that associations had "always existed in America" and recognized their debt to older English models. Alexis de Tocqueville, *Democracy in America*, ed. Richard D. Heffner (New York: Penguin Books, 1956), 95, 97. Neem, *Creating a Nation of Joiners*, 3–4. Quote from John L. Brooke, "Ancient Lodges and Self-Created Societies: Voluntary Association and the Public Sphere in the Early Republic," in *Launching the "Extended Republic": The Federalist Era*, ed. Ronald Hoffman and Peter J. Albert (Charlottesville: University of Virginia Press, 1996), 284.

Scholars of the early Republic have embraced Tocqueville's contention that associations were vital to American democracy, and they have added texture to this insight with analyses of the ways in which group life fostered political, class, race, and gender identities that complicated and challenged notions of citizenship in the early Republic and antebellum periods. The study of corporate life has expanded beyond craft organization, partisanship, benevolence, and reform to examinations of the economic institutions that shaped the physical, financial, and political infrastructure of the new nation. See, e.g., Oscar Handlin and Mary Flug Handlin, *Commonwealth: A Study of the Role of Government in the American Economy: Massachusetts, 1774–1861* (Cambridge, MA: Belknap Press of Harvard University Press, 1969). Louis Hartz, *Economic Policy and Democratic Thought: Pennsylvania, 1776–1860* (1948; repr., Chicago: Quadrangle Books, 1969). Bruce Dorsey, *Reforming Men and Women: Gender in the Antebellum City* (Ithaca, NY: Cornell University Press, 2002). Albrecht Koschnik, *Let a Common Interest Bind Us Together: Associations, Partisanship, and Culture in Philadelphia, 1775–1840* (Charlottesville: University of Virginia Press, 2007). A. Kristen Foster, *Moral Visions and Material Ambitions: Philadelphia Struggles to Define the Republic, 1776–1836* (Lanham, MD: Lexington Books, 2004). Catherine O'Donnell Kaplan, *Men of Letters in the Early Republic: Cultivating Forums of Citizenship* (Chapel Hill: University of North Carolina Press, 2008). Andrew M. Schocket, *Founding Corporate Power in Early National Philadelphia* (DeKalb: Northern Illinois University Press, 2007). Brian Phillips Murphy, "'A very convenient instrument': The Manhattan Company, Aaron Burr, and the Election of 1800," *WMQ*, 3rd ser., 65 (2008): 233–66.

7. On colonial political culture, see, e.g., Richard R. Beeman, *The Varieties of Political Experience in Eighteenth-Century America* (Philadelphia: University of Pennsylvania Press, 2004). Joy B. and Robert R. Gilsdorf, "Elites and Electorates: Some Plain Truth for Historians of Colonial America," in *Saints and Revolutionaries: Essays on Early American History*, ed. David D. Hall et al. (New York: W. W. Norton, 1984), 207–44. Pauline Maier, "Popular Uprisings and Civil Authority in Eighteenth-Century America," *WMQ*, 3rd ser., 27 (1970): 3–35. Thomas P. Slaughter, "Crowds in Eighteenth-Century America: Reflections and New Directions," *PMHB* 115, no. 1 (Jan. 1991): 3–34. Benjamin H. Irvin, "The Streets of Philadelphia: Crowds, Congress, and the Political Culture of Revolution, 1774–1783," *PMHB* 129 (2005): 7–44. Peter Thompson, *Rum Punch and Revolution: Taverngoing and Public Life in Eighteenth-Century Philadelphia* (Philadelphia: University of Pennsylvania Press, 1999). David S. Shields, *Civil Tongues and Polite Letters in British America* (Chapel Hill: University of North Carolina Press, 1997). Benjamin L. Carp, *Rebels Rising: Cities and the American Revolution* (Oxford: Oxford University Press, 2007).

8. Alan Tully, *William Penn's Legacy: Politics and Social Structure in Provincial Pennsylvania, 1726–1755* (Baltimore: Johns Hopkins University Press, 1977). Alan Tully, *Forming*

American Politics: Ideals, Interests, and Institutions in Colonial New York and Pennsylvania (Baltimore: Johns Hopkins University Press, 1994). James H. Hutson, *Pennsylvania Politics, 1746–1770: The Movement for Royal Government and Its Consequences* (Princeton, NJ: Princeton University Press, 1972). Gary B. Nash, *Quakers and Politics: Pennsylvania, 1681–1726* (1968; repr., Boston: Northeastern University Press, 1993).

9. Beeman, *Varieties of Political Experience*, 204, 207–8, 211; Tully, *Forming American Politics*, 320–22, 329. Robert J. Dinkin, *Voting in Provincial America: A Study of Elections in the Thirteen Colonies, 1689–1776* (Westport, CT: Greenwood Press, 1977), 38, 39, 159.

10. On Franklin, see, e.g., Alan Houston, *Benjamin Franklin and the Politics of Improvement* (New Haven, CT: Yale University Press, 2008). Brendan McConville argues that elites sought and suffered from the lack of patronage politics. They yearned for the honor and power accorded through patronage positions, but too few institutions existed to meet their needs, a critical reason ultimately for rebelling. However well the evidence fits this argument in other colonies, it does not describe very well eighteenth-century Philadelphia, where men founded their own institutional structures. Brendan McConville, *The King's Three Faces: The Rise and Fall of Royal America, 1688–1776* (Chapel Hill: University of North Carolina Press, 2006), 145. For more on the Loganian Library, see pages 77–78.

11. My conclusions then rely less on a celebration of the virtue of tolerance in Pennsylvania than on a delicately calibrated civic culture that distributed and balanced power and decision making in the community. For more emphasis on tolerance and toleration, see Sally Schwartz, *"A Mixed Multitude": The Struggle for Toleration in Colonial Pennsylvania* (New York: New York University Press, 1987). Andrew R. Murphy, *Conscience and Community: Revisiting Toleration and Religious Dissent in Early Modern England and America* (University Park: Pennsylvania State University Press, 2001). Ned C. Landsman, "Roots, Routes, and Rootedness: Diversity, Migration, and Toleration in Mid-Atlantic Pluralism," *Early American Studies* 2, no. 2 (Fall 2004): 267–309.

12. Eric Foner, *Tom Paine and Revolutionary America* (London: Oxford University Press, 1976), 64. For similar interpretations stressing a "new" political engagement in the 1760s and especially 1770s by nonelites in Philadelphia, see Charles S. Olton, *Artisans for Independence: Philadelphia Mechanics and the American Revolution* (New York: Syracuse University Press, 1975). Richard Alan Ryerson, *The Revolution Is Now Begun: The Radical Committees of Philadelphia, 1765–1776* (Philadelphia: University of Pennsylvania Press, 1978). Steven Rosswurm, *Arms, Country, and Class: The Philadelphia Militia and "Lower Sort" during the American Revolution, 1775–1783* (New Brunswick, NJ: Rutgers University Press, 1987).

13. Robert F. Oaks, "Philadelphians in Exile: The Problem of Loyalty during the American Revolution," *PMHB* 96 (1972): 298–325.

14. Koschnik, *Let a Common Interest Bind Us Together*.

15. The crucible metaphor comes most enduringly and famously from Gary B. Nash's great work *The Urban Crucible*, about Boston, New York, and Philadelphia in the era of the Revolution. Nash never intended to evoke a melting pot with the metaphor, but to connote the importance of cities at the forefront of change. Nash, *Urban Crucible*, viii.

Chapter 1 · *"Named Before Thou Wert Born"*

1. Charter for the Province of Pennsylvania, 1681, *The Avalon Project: Documents in Law, History, and Diplomacy*, accessed Feb. 16, 2012, http://avalon.law.yale.edu/. Penn's instructions from October 1681 are reprinted in Samuel Hazard, *Annals of Pennsylvania, from the*

Discovery of the Delaware, 1609–1682 (Philadelphia, 1850), 527–31. Gary B. Nash, *Quakers and Politics: Pennsylvania, 1681–1726* (1968; repr., Boston: Northeastern University Press, 1993), 7–42. William E. Lingelbach, "William Penn and City Planning," *PMHB* 68 (1944): 398–409, quotes on 402, 404, 409. Gary B. Nash, "City Planning and Political Tension in the Seventeenth Century: The Case of Philadelphia," *Proceedings of the American Philosophical Society* 112, no. 1 (1968): 54–73. Russell Frank Weigley et al., eds., *Philadelphia: A 300-Year History* (New York: W. W. Norton, 1982), 7, 16. John Oldmixon, *The British Empire in America* (London, 1708), 151–53.

2. In 1684 an estimated eight hundred Quakers were regularly attending Meeting in Philadelphia, a count that does not include the many non-Quakers in the city. James Bowden, *History of the Society of Friends in America*, vol. 2 (London, 1850–54), 16. Nash, "City Planning and Political Tension," 54–55. Nash, *Quakers and Politics*, 56–57. Frederick B. Tolles, *Meeting House and Counting House: The Quaker Merchants of Colonial Philadelphia, 1682–1763* (New York: W. W. Norton, 1948), 38–44.

3. Excellent scholarship treats the contentious first decades of English settlement in Pennsylvania, but these works have focused their attention at the provincial (rather than local or municipal) level, focusing on a three-way struggle for political power. As Quaker elites struggled against Proprietor William Penn on the one hand, they struggled on the other against the political ambitions of lower-class men and non-Quakers who wanted a share in government too. Disputes centered on the respective powers and duties of the executive and the legislative branches, the level of taxation Penn could exact from his settlers, and how land would be apportioned. Though much of the action in these historical narratives occurred in Philadelphia, the city itself as a discrete political community does not play a prominent role. Nash, *Quakers and Politics*. Alan Tully, *Forming American Politics: Ideals, Interests, and Institutions in Colonial New York and Pennsylvania* (Baltimore: Johns Hopkins University Press, 1994). John Smolenski, *Friends and Strangers: The Making of a Creole Culture in Colonial Pennsylvania* (Philadelphia: University of Pennsylvania Press, 2010).

4. William Penn to Thomas Lloyd and others, Aug. 1684, in Robert Proud, *The History of Pennsylvania*, vol. 2 (Philadelphia, 1797), 289. Quote from Francis Daniel Pastorius in Nash, "City Planning and Political Tension," 70.

5. J. Thomas Scharf and Thomson Westcott, *History of Philadelphia, 1609–1884* (Philadelphia, 1884), 1:97–101, 129 (quote on 98). Feb. 1, 1685/86, Apr. 13, 1687, MPC, 1:118, 154. "A Proclamation concerning the Caves of Philadelphia," Feb. 24, 1687, *Pennsylvania Archives*, ser. 2, 19:3–4. For a Swedish perspective on the arrival and settlement of the English in Philadelphia, see Ruth L. Springer and Louise Wallman, "Two Swedish Pastors Describe Philadelphia, 1700 and 1702," *PMHB* 84 (1960): 194–218.

6. Nash, "City Planning and Political Tension," 69. William Rodeney to J. Tyzack, Oct. 14, 1690, and Richard Morris to J. Tyzack, Dec. 12, 1690, *PMHB* 4 (1879): 198, 200. Gabriel Thomas, *An Account of West Jersey and Pennsylvania* (London, 1698), 5–6. Oldmixon, *British Empire in America*, 152. "An Act for Regulating of Streets and Water Courses in the Cities and Towns of this Government" (1700), *The Statutes at Large of Pennsylvania, From 1682 to 1801*, vol. 2 (Pennsylvania, 1898), 65–67. E. V. Lamberton, "Colonial Libraries of Pennsylvania," *PMHB* 43 (1918): 194. Nash, *Quakers and Politics*, 7–42.

7. Jan. 16, 1783/84, MPC, 1:37. Peter Thompson, *Rum Punch and Revolution: Taverngoing and Public Life in Eighteenth-Century Philadelphia* (Philadelphia: University of Pennsylvania Press, 1999), 111.

8. May 4, Sept. 12, 1685, PFMQM. Robert Turner, quoted in Bowden, *History of the Society of Friends in America*, 25. MBPPP, 449. Apr. 7, 15, 16, 18, 1688, MPC, 1:173, 179–81.

9. Hazard, *Annals of Pennsylvania*, 528. Jan. 16, 1683/84, MPC, 1:37. In addition to anger about the city layout, Philadelphia settlers were concerned with the allocation of city lots and the quitrents (a form of tax) Penn expected to receive for them. Nash, "City Planning and Political Tension."

10. Lingelbach, "William Penn and City Planning," 398. The space in the grid closest to the Delaware, the southeasterly park in Penn's plan, was still six blocks from the river and remained surrounded by open countryside well into the eighteenth century, nowhere near the settled part of Philadelphia, which did not advance beyond four blocks west for many decades. Weigley et al., *Philadelphia*, 16–17.

11. Dec. 8, 1701, Feb. 15, 1690, June 30, 1692, Oct. 20, 1712, MBPPP, 210, 23, 88, 532. Nash, "City Planning and Political Tension," 59. The 1690 "Law About Livestock Running at Large" defined the bounds of the city as "the North and South bounds thereof running straight on both sides from the river Delaware to the Center." *Statutes at Large of Pennsylvania*, 1:142.

12. Aug. 16, Dec. 13, 1690, MBPPP, 43, 53. Similarly, Penn had extensive plans for how rural counties and townships would be laid out, but as with his capital city, these plans rarely came to fruition. James T. Lemon, *The Best Poor Man's Country: Early Southeastern Pennsylvania* (1972; repr. (with new preface), Baltimore: Johns Hopkins University Press, 2002), 49.

13. Edwin B. Bronner, "Quaker Landmarks in Early Philadelphia," in *Historic Philadelphia: From the Founding until the Early Nineteenth Century*, ed. Luther P. Eisenhart (Philadelphia: American Philosophical Society, 1953), 211. High Street was often called Market Street throughout the eighteenth century, though the name was not officially changed to Market until the nineteenth century. Weigley et al., *Philadelphia*, 13. Nash, "City Planning and Political Tension," 64. Bronner, "Quaker Landmarks in Early Philadelphia." May 4, 1685, PFMQM.

14. Thompson, *Rum Punch and Revolution*, 27. Scharf and Westcott, *History of Philadelphia*, 1:121. Feb. 26, 1704/5, MBPPP, 449. For a discussion of the role Boston's Exchange played in that city's development, see Martha J. McNamara, "'In the face of the court . . .': Law, Commerce, and the Transformation of Public Space in Boston, 1650–1770," *Winterthur Portfolio* 36, nos. 2/3 (2001): 125–39. Edmund S. Morgan portrays militia service as central to social and political cohesion in the American colonies. Edmund S. Morgan, *Inventing the People: The Rise of Popular Sovereignty in England and America* (New York: W. W. Norton, 1988), 154–73.

15. Concessions to the Province of Pennsylvania, July 11, 1681. *The Avalon Project: Documents in Law, History, and Diplomacy*, accessed Feb. 16, 2012, http://avalon.law.yale.edu/. Hazard, *Annals of Pennsylvania*, 528, 637. Nash, "City Planning and Political Tension," 56–59 (quote on 57). John E. Pomfret, "The First Purchasers of Pennsylvania, 1681–1700," *PMHB* 80 (1956): 137–63.

16. The Charter of the Society of Free Traders is printed in Hazard, *Annals of Pennsylvania*, 541–50. *The articles, settlement, and offices of the Free Society of Traders in Pennsilvania agreed upon by divers merchants and others for the better improvement and government of trade in that province* (London, 1682). Oct. 20, 1712, MBPPP, 532. Nash, "City Planning and Political Tension," 62. Scharf and Westcott, *History of Philadelphia*, 1:119. On dissatisfaction with Schuylkill lots, see the petitions of Barnabas Wilcox and family. Dec. 8, Dec. 20, 1701, Mar. 15, 1690, MBPPP, 210–12, 226–27, 29.

Not all city residents purchased the lots on which they would live. By 1684 about 20% of city lots were rented rather than purchased. Nash, "City Planning and Political Tension," 66. 17. Ibid., 70–73. July 26, 1684, MPC. See note 3 for the historiography of the political fights of the 1680s and 1690s.

18. The bulk of scholarship on early American religion focuses on theology, practice, and popular beliefs, not on dry church financial accounts. However, particularly in the first decades when everything had still to be built, laypeople could assert a powerful voice through their decisions on whether and how much to contribute. Jon Butler convincingly argues that denominations in the Delaware valley reproduced hierarchical, clergy-dominated structures from England. However, this process took many decades to achieve. Jon Butler, "Power, Authority, and the Origins of American Denominational Order: The English Churches in the Delaware Valley, 1680–1730," *Transactions of the American Philosophical Society*, new ser., 68 (1978): 1–85. Jon Butler, " 'Gospel Order Improved': The Keithian Schism and the Exercise of Quaker Ministerial Authority in Pennsylvania," *WMQ*, 3rd ser., 31 (1974): 431–52. On the focus on doctrine and theology in the study of early American religion, see, e.g., David D. Hall, *Worlds of Wonder, Days of Judgment: Popular Religious Belief in Early New England* (Cambridge, MA: Harvard University Press, 1989). Jon Butler, *Awash in a Sea of Faith: Christianizing the American People* (Cambridge, MA: Harvard University Press, 1990). Rhys Isaac took seriously church spaces, but he was most interested in their architecture and interior space, not the process through which they were constructed and paid for. Rhys Isaac, *The Transformation of Virginia, 1740–1790* (Chapel Hill: University of North Carolina Press, 1982).

19. Frame of Government of Pennsylvania, May 5, 1682. *The Avalon Project: Documents in Law, History, and Diplomacy*, accessed Feb. 16, 2012, http://avalon.law.yale.edu/.

In most times and places in English colonization, authorities viewed toleration as disruptive and dangerous to peace and civil order. Andrew R. Murphy, *Conscience and Community: Revisiting Toleration and Religious Dissent in Early Modern England and America* (University Park: Pennsylvania State University Press, 2001).

20. William Warburton, *The Alliance between Church and State, or, the Necessity and Equity of An Established Religion and a Test-Law Demonstrated* (London, 1736). For an overview of religious establishment in the British colonies, see Boyd Stanley Schelnther, "Religious Faith and Commercial Empire," in *The Oxford History of the British Empire*, vol. 2, *The Eighteenth Century*, ed. P. J. Marshall (Oxford: Oxford University Press, 1998), 127–30. Other European powers also emphasized a close connection between church and state. J. H. Elliott, for example, has argued that Spanish colonization was "a joint church-state enterprise" in which Catholic priests and monks played a vital bureaucratic and missionary role. J. H. Elliott, *Empires of the Atlantic World: Britain and Spain in America, 1492–1830* (New Haven, CT: Yale University Press, 2006), 128.

21. Butler, "Power, Authority, and the Origins of American Denominational Order," 6–7, 28. Jane E. Calvert, *Quaker Constitutionalism and the Political Thought of John Dickinson* (Cambridge: Cambridge University Press: 2009), 123. Janet Moore Lindman, *Bodies of Belief: Baptist Community in Early America* (Philadelphia: University of Pennsylvania Press, 2008), 3, 14. Sally Schwartz, *"A Mixed Multitude": The Struggle for Toleration in Colonial Pennsylvania* (New York: New York University Press, 1987), 36–37. Deborah Mathias Gough, *Christ Church, Philadelphia: The Nation's Church in a Changing City* (Philadelphia: University of Pennsylvania Press, 1995), 5.

22. "The Testimony of Richard Townsend, 1727," in Bowden, *History of the Society of Friends*, 17. Butler, "Power, Authority, and the Origins of American Denominational Order." The early Quakers of Pennsylvania were not alone in relying on voluntary contributions. Early New England Puritan churches collected weekly contributions and large-scale donations to pay for the minister's salary, the bread and wine used for the Lord's Supper, and poor relief. See David D. Hall, *A Reforming People: Puritanism and the Transformation of Public Life in New England* (New York: Alfred A. Knopf, 2011), 135–36.

23. July 3, Oct. 2, 1683. PFMQM. Barry Levy, *Quakers and the American Family: British Settlement in the Delaware Valley* (Oxford: Oxford University Press, 1988), 12, 59. John Smolenski and Jane E. Calvert have both argued that Penn sought to mold his non-Quaker settlers to act in Quakerly ways, but without necessarily converting them to his faith or privileging it with the power of the state. Because Penn and the earliest settlers were predominantly Quaker, Quakerism influenced the government extensively, but formally Pennsylvania maintained a separation of church and state. Smolenski, *Friends and Strangers*. Calvert, *Quaker Constitutionalism*. Richard Bauman has argued that in this period "the lines dividing the secular government of Pennsylvania from the Quaker meeting structure were often obscure and at times nonexistent." Richard Bauman, *For the Reputation of Truth: Politics, Religion, and Conflict among the Pennsylvania Quakers, 1750–1800* (Baltimore: Johns Hopkins University Press, 1971), 1.

24. July 3, Dec. 4, 1683, May 6, Sept. 2, 1684, PFMQM. On Monthly Meeting membership, see Butler, "Power, Authority, and the Origins of American Denominational Order," 29–30. Butler argues that Monthly Meetings were small and exclusive, but at least sixty men attended a contentious Monthly Meeting in the spring of 1692. Monthly Meeting proceedings were meant to be closed if not outright secret. See George Keith, *Some Reasons and Causes of the Late Separation* (Philadelphia, 1692), 9, 4, 12.

25. Friends could pay in goods and sometimes through direct labor. They raised subscriptions frequently for construction and poor relief, but also for other reasons—for example, to reimburse printer William Bradford, for a well for the meetinghouse, to found a school, for the redemption of captives in Turkey, and for the relief of Friends in New England. Oct. 7, Nov. 4, 1684, Feb. 9, Mar. 2, Apr. 7, May 4, Oct. 5, 1685, July 6, Oct. 29, 1686, Aug. 2, 1688, Aug. 29, 1690, Mar. 2, 1691, Mar. 6, June 24, 1692, Apr. 30, July 30, 1697, Aug. 26, 1698, PFMQM. On the stress Quakers placed on visiting one another and confronting sinners, see J. William Frost, *The Quaker Family in Colonial America: A Portrait of the Society of Friends* (New York: St. Martin's Press, 1973), 48–54. Jack D. Marietta argues that Friends were more concerned with the reputation of the group than with individual delinquency in their discipline. Jack D. Marietta, *The Reformation of American Quakerism, 1748–1783* (Philadelphia: University of Pennsylvania Press, 1984), 4–10. On "holy conversation," see Levy, *Quakers and the American Family*, 59.

26. Sep. 12, 1685, Dec. 5, Dec. 30, 1687, June 3, 1689, PFMQM.

27. Nash, *Quakers and Politics*, 144–60. Butler, "Gospel Order Improved." Calvert, *Quaker Constitutionalism*, 121–25. Smolenski, *Friends and Strangers*, 149–77.

28. The decision to move meetings back to the Center Meeting House occurred on March 25, 1692. The minutes omitted any discussion or dissent about the matter, but by the next monthly meeting on April 29, the Monthly Meeting "requested . . . that if any freinds have it in their Minds to visit Such freinds as frequent the Seperate Meetting They would Accordingly doe it and tenderly Admonish them in order to bring them to a Sense of their

Condition." The request for the list of subscriptions occurred November 25, 1692, and with uncharacteristic efficiency had been completed two months later, a sign of the urgency with which the Meeting regarded this matter. Jan. 27, 1693, PFMQM. Keith, *Some Reasons and Causes*, 16. Ethyn Williams Kirby, *George Keith (1638–1716)* (New York: D. Appleton-Century, 1942), 65–66. The use of the word "church" in relation to Quakers is tricky because they did not generally use the word themselves to describe either their physical spaces or their larger spiritual community. In this and the next paragraph, however, I follow the lead of Jon Butler in referring to both as a church. Butler, "Power, Authority, and the Origins of American Denominational Order."

29. The Friends Monthly Minutes tersely recorded "the violent pulling down of the gallery in the front meeting house," and for months afterward the minutes deal with the repair of the Public Friends' gallery. Some claim that Keith's followers broke into the meetinghouse and erected a makeshift gallery at the opposite end for Keith and his supporters to rail against the Public Friends in their gallery, and that this too was violently pulled down with axes. Contemporary documents do not clearly corroborate either the construction or destruction of a gallery for Keith. The Monthly Minutes make no mention of other damage or repairs, which the erection and equally violent pulling down of a second gallery would presumably have required. It is also unclear how Keith's followers could have constructed a gallery without anyone seeing or hearing them, although Gary Nash has suggested they did so in the night hours before the Sunday service. In general, historians have relied and built on historian Ethyn Kirby's dramatic description of the destruction of two competing galleries, a vivid metaphor for the confrontation between Keith and orthodox Quakers. Her evidence in turn comes from a pamphlet published in London in 1694 by an author hostile to Keith. Perhaps Keith and his followers did construct a second gallery and then both were destroyed; perhaps the destruction of the Public Friends' Gallery and vitriol against Keith led to embellishment of an already-shocking story. Jan. 27, 1693, PFMQM. Kirby, *George Keith*, 87. Nash, *Quakers and Politics*, 153–54. Thomas Ellwood, *A Further Discovery of That Spirit of Contention & Division Which Hath Appeared of Late in George Keith, &c.* (London, 1694), 49–50.

30. Jan. 27, Feb. 24, Mar. 6, June 5, Sept. 1, Nov. 24, 1693, Mar. 5, 1694, PFMQM. Craig W. Horle et al., eds., *Lawmaking and Legislators in Pennsylvania* (House of Representatives of the Commonwealth of Pennsylvania, 1991), 1:710–12. The other man involved in pulling down the gallery, William Preston, eventually reconciled with Quakers. Dec. 7, 1696, PFMQM. William Penn to Robert Turner, Feb. 27, 1694, in Marianne S. Wokek et al., eds., *The Papers of William Penn* (Philadelphia: University of Pennsylvania Press, 1986), 3:388–89. Aug. 26, 1698, PFMQM. George Keith to SPG, n.d. (ca. 1701). *Collections of the Protestant Episcopal Historical Society for the Year 1851* (New York, 1851), xi–xiii. Feb. 6, 1731, Votes, 3:2081–85.

31. Feb. 22, 1689, Mar. 29, 1689, Jan. 26, 1694, Nov. 30, 1694, June 28, 1695, PFMQM.

32. Sept. 19, 1695, Philadelphia Friends Yearly Meeting Minutes, Special Collections, Haverford College. Butler, "Power, Authority, and the Origins of American Denominational Order," 40.

33. Feb. 24, 1699, PFMQM. This process took time and was by no means complete in 1699. Friends decided, for example, to build a new meetinghouse at Second and High (Market) Streets in 1696 (opened in 1697) and estimated that the cost would be £1,000, to be raised by subscription, not only from Philadelphia residents, but from other regional Monthly Meetings. Jan. 31, Mar. 1, 1695/96, Jan. 29, 1697/98, PFMQM.

34. Contemporaries did not refer to members of the Church of England as "Anglican."

For a brief scholarly discussion of the term "Anglican," see Travis Glasson, *Mastering Christianity: Missionary Anglicanism and Slavery in the Atlantic World* (Oxford: Oxford University Press, 2012), 8–9.

35. The Baptists moved to a brew-house and later shared the meetinghouse of the Keithians (Christian Quakers). Thomas Clayton to the Governor, Nov. 29, 1698, in *Papers Relating to the History of the Church in Pennsylvania, A.D. 1680–1778*, ed. William S. Perry (Hartford, CT, 1871), 14–15. Lindman, *Bodies of Belief*, 18n16. Butler, "Power, Authority, and the Origins of American Denominational Order," 68–69.

36. Col. Quarry and others to Governor Nicholson, Jan. 18, 1696/97, in Perry, *Papers Relating to the History of the Church*, 5–6. For more on the Society for the Propagation of the Gospel, see Daniel O'Connor et al., *Three Centuries of Mission: The United Society for the Propagation of the Gospel, 1701–2000* (London: Continuum, 2000).

37. Col. Quarry and others to Governor Nicholson, Jan. 18, 1696/97, Thomas Clayton to the Governor, Nov. 29, 1698, Edward Portlock to the Archbishop of Canterbury, July 12, 1700, "The State of the Church in Pennsylvania, most humbly offered to ye Venerable Society for the Propagation of the Gospel in Foreign Parts," 1707, in Perry, *Papers Relating to the History of the Church*, 5–6, 15, 16, 32–39. Horle et al., *Lawmaking and Legislators in Pennsylvania*, 1:530.

38. Lingelbach, "William Penn and City Planning," 405. John Edward Daly, "Public Records and Public Policy: Philadelpha, 1681–1770" (PhD diss., University of Pennsylvania, 1983), 25. In 1691 Deputy Governor Thomas Lloyd had signed a charter incorporating the "Town and Borough of Philadelphia," but it was nullified in 1692 when Pennsylvania became a royal colony, and it is unclear whether any government operated under that charter. Judith M. Diamonstone, "Philadelphia's Municipal Corporation, 1701–1776," *PMHB* 90, no. 2 (1966): 186. On Philadelphia's population, see Nash, *Quakes and Politics*, 56–57. On the size of English towns, see Peter Borsay, *The English Urban Renaissance: Culture and Society in the Provincial Town, 1660–1770* (Oxford: Clarendon Press, 1989), 4–10.

In part the slowness of Penn and the other founders of Philadelphia to organize government surely came from distraction. Amid all the other concerns in setting up a colony and its capital, municipal government got lost in the shuffle. The Provincial Council proposed to incorporate Philadelphia, for example, in 1684, but nothing came of it. Then again in 1691 Philadelphians had tried to form a municipal corporation, but again the attempt failed. Adding to the difficulties of setting up urban government were the upheavals surrounding the Keithian Schism, which affected the entire province but were centered in Philadelphia, and the increasingly acrimonious struggle between Penn and his settlers over provincial governance. In addition to all this bickering, Penn briefly lost the right to govern his colony between 1693 and 1695 because the court of new monarchs William and Mary suspected him of misplaced loyalties. In the interim the royal governor of New York, Benjamin Fletcher, acted as governor. He believed that his authority superseded Penn's constitution, and he made some changes but left intact the power of the assembly to initiate legislation. The first two decades of settlement were contentious and difficult on many levels. Still, preoccupation with other matters cannot by itself explain why local governance for Philadelphia fell by the wayside for so long despite increasingly strident demands from residents themselves. Factors other than the enormity of first setting up a colony came into play. July 26, 1684, MPC, 64. Tully, *Forming American Politics*, 35, 69. Judith M. Diamonstone, "The Philadelphia Corporation, 1701–1776" (PhD diss., University of Pennsylvania, 1969), 60–61. Horle et al., *Lawmaking and Legislators in Pennsylvania*, 13. Smolenski, *Friends and Strangers*. Nash, *Quakers and Politics*.

39. Robert G. Ingram, *Religion, Reform and Modernity in the Eighteenth Century: Thomas Secker and the Church of England* (Woodbridge, UK: Boydell Press, 2007), 138–41. Only in Cambridge and London did city magistrates not have direct oversight over parish officials. Phil Withington, *The Politics of Commonwealth: Citizens and Freemen in Early Modern England* (Cambridge: Cambridge University Press, 2005), 181–82. Other colonizing powers relied still more heavily on the church to support state aims. Spanish colonization, for example, was "a joint church-state enterprise" in which Catholic religious personnel played an important bureaucratic role. Elliott, *Empires of the Atlantic World*, 128.

40. "Law about the Registry Keept by Religious Societies" (1690), *Statutes at Large of Pennsylvania*, 1:141. On county government in Philadelphia, see Daly, "Public Records and Public Policy," 25–26.

41. Chap. 37 of The Great Law and "Law Providing for Poor Persons and Orphans" (1682), *Statutes at Large of Pennsylvania*, 1:15, 41. The council tried further to empower the counties in 1690. Mar. 14, June 9, 1683, Jan. 17, 1683/84, Apr. 6, 1688, Apr. 9, 1690, Aug. 8, Aug. 9, 1693, MPC, 1:4, 20, 38, 171, 289, 348–50.

42. Feb. 9, 1684/85, Oct. 7, 1685, PFMQM. Levy, *Quakers and the American Family*, 51, 54. Frost, *Quaker Family in Colonial America*, 68.

43. J. William Frost has called Quaker poor relief an "insurance policy" for members. Frost, *Quaker Family in Colonial America*, 65. Friends in Philadelphia quickly noticed that their burden of poor relief exceeded that of "any Other place In the Province by Reason of Peoples General landing hear," and the Quarterly Meeting mandated that the surrounding Monthly Meetings contribute as well to spread responsibility more broadly. May 4, Oct. 5, 1685, Oct. 28, 1692, Mar. 4, May 31, 1695, Feb. 28, 1696, July 30, Aug. 27, 1697, PFMQM.

44. Aug. 4, 1683, May 31, 1689, Feb. 27, Mar. 27, 1691, Dec. 28, 1694, Mar. 29, 1695, Jan. 31, 1696, Feb. 24, July 28, 1699, PFMQM. Karin Wulf reminds us of the "female character of poverty and poor relief in early America," a statement borne out in internal Quaker relief efforts. Karin Wulf, *Not All Wives: Women of Colonial Philadelphia* (Ithaca, NY: Cornell University Press, 2000), 154. On the importance of keeping children in Quaker families, see Levy, *Quakers and the American Family*, and Frost, *Quaker Family in Colonial America*.

45. The schoolmaster was none other than Minister George Keith, who left the school in 1691 and caused schism shortly thereafter. Part of his disagreement with orthodox Quakers revolved around his insistence that children or young adults should make a full confession of their faith before being admitted as full members of the church. Orthodox Quakers refused. July 26, Aug. 30, 1689, May 29, 1691, PFMQM. Petition to Governor and Council, 1697/98, Charter, 1701, Legal Papers, Box 1, William Penn Charter School Collection, Special Collections, Haverford College.

46. Dec. 26, 1683, Aug. 1, 1693, MPC, 36, 344–45. Frost, *Quaker Family in Colonial America*, 95–96.

47. Quoted in Frost, *Quaker Family in Colonial America*, 93. I. Arrowsmith to Governor Nicholson, Mar. 26, 1698; see also Robert Suder to Governor, Nov. 20, 1698, in Perry, *Papers Relating to the History of the Church*, 6, 9–10. Gough, *Christ Church, Philadelphia*, 10.

48. An example of the reverse would be the rise of the "fiscal-military" English state beginning in precisely this period. John Brewer argues that English military success in eighteenth-century Europe was predicated on and stimulated by the administrative might of a nation

with high taxation and (relatively) efficient bureaucratic structures to collect and distribute those taxes to feed the war machinery of the nation. War acted to enhance and enlarge both the domestic power of the state and national financial institutions. John Brewer, *The Sinews of Power: War, Money and the English State, 1688–1783* (New York: Alfred A. Knopf, 1989).

49. Sept. 3, Nov. 19, 1686, MPC, 142, 148. Apr. 25, 1691, MBPPP, 67.

50. July 11, July 18, 1693, June 2, June 27, 1701, MPC, 1:142, 148, 341–43, 2:23–25. Jan. 31, 1691, MBPPP, 60. "The Law for Regulating Streets & Water Courses in the Citys & Towns of this Government" (1698), *Statutes at Large of Pennsylvania*, 1:257–58. In the case of repairing "common" infrastructure such as landing places, docks, or bridges, funds would be raised from the entire town. Petition from the Inhabitants of Philadelphia, Feb. 1700/1701, Logan Family Papers, Box 3, Folder 9, HSP.

51. June 9, 1683, Apr. 4, 1685, Sept. 5, 1690, MPC, 20, 76, 302.

52. Aug. 29, 1689, Apr. 24, 1690, Sept. 23, 1693, MPC, 257–58, 293, 354. Robert Suder to Governor, Nov. 20, 1698, in Perry, *Papers Relating to the History of the Church*, 10.

53. Feb. 4, 1688/89. MPC, 192–93. Eric Kerridge, *Trade and Banking in Early Modern England* (Manchester, UK: Manchester University Press, 1988), 57. Edwin J. Perkins, *American Public Financial Services, 1700–1815* (Columbus: Ohio State University Press, 1994).

Chapter 2 · Intoxicated with Power

1. Letter of Andreas Rudman, 1700, in Ruth L. Springer and Louise Wallman, "Two Swedish Pastors Describe Philadelphia, 1700 and 1702," *PMHB* 84 (1960): 207. Gabriel Thomas, *An Account of West Jersey and Pennsylvania* (London, 1698), 5. Gary B. Nash, *Quakers and Politics: Pennsylvania, 1681–1726* (1968; repr., Boston: Northeastern University Press, 1993), 208.

2. William Penn to the Board of Trade, Feb. 27, 1699/1700, in Marianne S. Wokek et al., eds., *The Papers of William Penn* (Philadelphia: University of Pennsylvania Press, 1986), 3:589. Nash, *Quakers and Politics*, 215. For Penn's actions on his return to Pennsylvania, see Nash, *Quakers and Politics*, 208–24.

3. In 1700 one observer claimed that there were more than five hundred Churchmen (or Anglicans) in Philadelphia. Edward Portlock to the Archbishop of Canterbury, July 12, 1700, in William S. Perry, ed., *Papers Relating to the History of the Church in Pennsylvania, A.D. 1680–1778* (Hartford, CT, 1871), 16. On the term "Churchmen," see chap. 1, n34.

4. In some records Elfreth is referred to as "Henry" and in others "Jeremiah." Oct. 18, Oct. 19, 1700, Feb. 15, Feb. 18, 1700/1701, May 19, 1701, MPC, 2:9–10, 12, 14, 19. Petition of the Inhabitants of Pennsylvania re. Public Wharf, n.d. (ca. Oct. 1700), Society Miscellaneous Collection, Box 4A-B, Folder 2, HSP. Council Records, Dec. 19, 1700, Logan Family Papers, Box 3, Folder 6, HSP. Debate about public landing place, n.d. [Mar. 1701?], Logan Family Papers, Box 3, Folder 11, HSP. J. Scharf and Thomas Westcott, *History of Philadelphia, 1609–1884* (Philadelphia, 1884), 3:2148. Ultimately Penn left Elfreth in the lurch, referring the matter to the Provincial Council just before he left for England in 1701, asking that they "recommend it to the Town that some care may be taken therein." Oct. 23, 1701, MPC, 54.

5. Apr. 10, 1700, MPC, 1:573. Samuel Hazard, ed., *The Register of Pennsylvania* (Philadelphia, 1830), 5:113. Nash, *Quakers and Politics*, 216.

6. Nash, *Quakers and Politics*, 204–7. Craig W. Horle et al., eds., *Lawmaking and Legislators in Pennsylvania* (Philadelphia: University of Pennsylvania Press, 1991–2005), 1:13–14.

7. Robert Turner quote in Nash, *Quakers and Politics*, 208. Remonstrance of Philadelphia

Inhabitants, Mar. 12, 1697, Anthony Morris and others to William Penn, Mar. 22, 1696/97, in Wokek et al., *Papers of William Penn*, 3:499–506. Griffith Jones et al. to William Penn, Apr. 9, 1697, in Hazard, *Register of Pennsylvania*, 6:257–58. See also Jan. 3, 1699/1700, MPC, 543.

8. *The Governour's Speech to the Assembly, at Philadelphia the 15 September 1701* (Philadelphia, 1701), 1.

9. Charter of Privileges Granted by William Penn, esq. to the Inhabitants of Pennsylvania and Territories, Oct. 28, 1701, in M. Carey and J. Bioren, eds., *Laws of the Commonwealth of Pennsylvania, 1700–1802* (Philadelphia, 1803), vol. 6, appendix, 11–15. Nash, *Quakers and Politics*. Alan Tully, *Forming American Politics: Ideals, Interests, and Institutions in Colonial New York and Pennsylvania* (Baltimore: Johns Hopkins University Press, 1994). Jane E. Calvert, *Quaker Constitutionalism and the Political Thought of John Dickinson* (Cambridge: Cambridge University Press, 2009), 133. John Smolenski, *Friends and Strangers: The Making of a Creole Culture in Colonial Pennsylvania* (Philadelphia: University of Pennsylvania Press, 2010).

10. Each of the three original counties (Philadelphia, Bucks, and Chester) had eight seats in the assembly; the city of Philadelphia had two. Lancaster (added in 1729) had four; York (1749), Cumberland (1750), and Berks (1752) had two each; and Northampton (1752) had one seat. For Philadelphia population statistics, see Gary B. Nash, "Taxable Inhabitants in Boston, New York, and Philadelphia, 1687–1775," in *The Urban Crucible: Social Change, Political Consciousness, and the Origins of the American Revolution* (Cambridge, MA: Harvard University Press, 1979), 407–8. For Pennsylvania population statistics, see James T. Lemon, *The Best Poor Man's Country: Early Southeastern Pennsylvania* (1972; repr. (with new preface), Baltimore: Johns Hopkins University Press, 2002), 23.

11. Sept. 20, 1701, MPC, 2:37–39. Sept. 17, 1701, Votes, 1:284. For a manuscript copy of the petition with signatures, see Petition, Sept. 1701, Logan Family Papers, Box 3, Folder 20, HSP. Committee, Sept. 18, 1701, Logan Family Papers, Box 3, Folder 20, HSP.

12. Sept. 26, 1701, MPC, 41–42. Through his charter from Charles II in 1681 Penn had been designated a lord of the manor and enjoyed rights going back to the feudal era: only he could sell or grant land, and even when he had done so, he was entitled to annual rents. Judith M. Diamonstone, "The Philadelphia Corporation, 1701–1776" (PhD diss., University of Pennsylvania, 1969), 39.

13. Diamonstone, "Philadelphia Corporation," 60–61. Nash, *Quakers and Politics*, 261. Tully, *Forming American Politics*, 35, 69.

14. Robert Suder to Governor, Nov. 20, 1698, in Perry, *Papers Relating to the History of the Church*, 9–10. Churchmen at one point looked to William Penn as a potential ally, but they concluded in the end that he was as bad as the Quaker elites. *A Brief Narrative of the Proceedings of William Penn* (1699), in Perry, *Papers Relating to the History of the Church*, 1–4. "An Account of the State of the Church in North America," n.d. (ca. Nov. 1702). *Collections of the Protestant Episcopal Historical Society for the Year 1851* (New York, 1851), xv–xxi.

For a list of thirty-six prominent Pennsylvania Churchmen, see the letter of Col. Quarry and others to Governor Nicholson, Jan. 18, 1696/97, in Perry, *Papers Relating to the History of the Church*, 5–6. The only name to appear on that letter and in the 1701 petition is Thomas Harris. It is impossible to determine whether the same Thomas Harris signed both documents, or whether two men with the same name signed them. Remonstrance of Philadelphia Inhabitants, Mar. 12, 1697, in Wokek et al., *Papers of William Penn*, 3:499–506. Petition, Sept. 1701, Logan Family Papers, Box 3, Folder 20, HSP.

15. In 1691 Deputy Governor Thomas Lloyd had signed a charter incorporating the

"Town and Borough of Philadelphia," but it was nullified in 1692 when Pennsylvania became a royal colony, and it is unclear whether any government operated under that charter. Judith M. Diamonstone, "Philadelphia's Municipal Corporation, 1701–1776," *PMHB* 90, no. 2 (1966): 186. Charter of the City of Philadelphia, Oct. 25, 1701, and Charter of the Borough of Chester, Oct. 31, 1701, in Carey and Bioren, *Laws of the Commonwealth of Pennsylvania*, vol. 6, appendix, 15–20, 20–23. Penn also at this time signed a charter relating to the Quaker Free School, but this was not a new charter; it was Penn's confirmation of the 1697 charter, granted by Lieutenant Governor William Markham. "A Brief Account of the rise & progress of Friends School in Philadelphia by James Pemberton, 1779," School History, Box 15, WPCSC, Quaker and Special Collections, Haverford College. Charter, 1701, Legal Papers, Box 1, WPCSC, Haverford College.

16. P. J. Corfield, *The Impact of English Towns, 1700–1800* (Oxford: Oxford University Press, 1982), 153–57, quote on 153. Sidney Webb and Beatrice Webb, *English Local Government from the Revolution to the Municipal Corporations Act* (London: Longmans, Green, 1906–8). Jon C. Teaford, *The Municipal Revolution in America: Origins of Modern Urban Government, 1650–1825* (Chicago: University of Chicago Press, 1975), 3–15. Paul D. Halliday demonstrates that the increasing power of the King's (or Queen's) Bench after 1690 to settle internal town disputes helped foster stability in the towns while extending central power over localities. Paul D. Halliday, *Dismembering the Body Politic: Partisan Politics in England's Towns, 1650–1730* (Cambridge: Cambridge University Press, 1998). Phil Withington argues that incorporated towns fostered civic relationships and practices that inculcated new expressions of citizenship in the early modern English state. Phil Withington, *The Politics of Commonwealth: Citizens and Freemen in Early Modern England* (Cambridge: Cambridge University Press, 2005). I am grateful to Tamar Herzog for discussions of English town incorporation generally and for her assistance reading Philadelphia's charter in particular.

17. Charter of the City of Philadelphia, Oct. 25, 1701, in Carey and Bioren, *Laws of the Commonwealth of Pennsylvania*, vol. 6, appendix, 15–20.

18. Charter of the Borough of Chester, Oct. 31, 1701, in Carey and Bioren, *Laws of the Commonwealth of Pennsylvania*, vol. 6, appendix, 20–23.

19. Charter of the City of Philadelphia, Oct. 25, 1701, in Carey and Bioren, *Laws of the Commonwealth of Pennsylvania*, vol. 6, appendix, 15–20. Thomas Hobbes, *Leviathan; or, The Matter, Forme, & Power of a Commonwealth Ecclesiasticall and Civill* (London, 1651), 150. Oscar Handlin and Mary F. Handlin, "Origins of the American Business Corporation," *Journal of Economic History* 5, no. 1 (May 1945): 11.

20. Diamonstone, "Philadelphia Corporation," 260, 270–71, 210. Diamonstone, "Philadelphia's Municipal Corporation," 185.

On the family connections of early mayors, see James Logan to William Penn, Spring 1706, in *Correspondence between William Penn and James Logan . . . 1700–1750*, ed. Edward Armstrong (Philadelphia, 1870), 2:119.

21. Tully, *Forming American Politics*, 35, 69. Diamonstone, "Philadelphia Corporation," 60–61.

22. For a full discussion of nongovernmental accommodations to provide local services, see chap. 1. Oct. 25, 1701, Charter for the Free School, Legal Papers, Box 1, WPCSC. Many but not all incorporated towns and cities provided for local grammar schools. Webb and Webb, *English Local Government*. For more on the Free School, see pages 32–33.

23. Charter of the City of Philadelphia, 1701, in Carcy and Bioren, *Laws of the Com-*

monwealth of Pennsylvania, vol. 6, appendix, 15–20. Dec. 1, 1704, Apr. 29, 1706, *MCC*. Votes, 1:598–603.

Many English corporations received the express power to tax in their charters, either levies directly on households or individuals, or the ability to tax goods or vehicles (carts, ships, etc.) entering the corporation. In other places corporation justices had long levied taxes for the administration of justice and maintenance of jails, a power finally confirmed by Parliament in 1784. Webb and Webb, *English Local Government*, 703n3. In North America New York City's 1730 charter did not give it the explicit power to tax; the New York City Corporation had to gain authorization from the provincial legislature for direct taxation, which it did four times between 1731 and 1750 and more frequently beginning in the 1760s. New York City's extensive rents and fees from other sources, however, brought in substantial revenue and made taxation before the 1760s an infrequent necessity. Hendrik Hartog, *Public Property and Private Power: The Corporation of the City of New York in American Law, 1730–1870* (Ithaca, NY: Cornell University Press, 1983), 31.

24. Charter of the City of Philadelphia, 1701, in Carey and Bioren, *Laws of the Commonwealth of Pennsylvania*, 15–20. Other British cities were able to derive substantial income from similar sources. The Cornish city of Penzance was able to pay for a town watch, water supply, street paving and cleaning, a jail, highway maintenance, a chapel, fire protection, a grammar school, and even the construction of a grand "Coinage Hall" without charging its population of between two and three thousand inhabitants any taxes. It was able to accomplish these ends because its charter gave it control of the town pier, quays, and market; the Penzance Corporation was able to derive a "very substantial income" from the rents it charged for their use. Bristol, the second-largest city in England, earned nearly £3,000 a year from its assets and was able to charge tolls on incoming ships and yet more fees and rents through its monopoly on the marketplace and annual fairs. With its money, it was able to maintain the port and harbor, conserve the river, manage a grammar school and a library, and provide for civic improvements such as street illumination. Webb and Webb, *English Local Government*, 406–10, 443–81.

Closer to home, New York City's 1730 charter gave the city extensive property and a monopoly over the wharves and all ferries coming into or out of Manhattan. The corporation's property gave it a significant degree of independence, both from its residents, whom it never had to tax until the 1750s (and thereafter rates remained quite low), and also from the provincial government, on which it was likewise not dependent. The city's capital could be spent on projects or used as collateral against which to borrow still more money if necessary. Hartog, *Public Property and Private Power*.

25. James Logan to William Penn, Oct. 2, 1702, James Logan to William Penn, Spring 1706, in Armstrong, *Correspondence between William Penn and James Logan*, 1:138, 2:119. Nash, *Quakers and Politics*, 261.

26. James Logan to William Penn, May 25, 1704, in Armstrong, *Correspondence between William Penn and James Logan*, 1:285.

27. James Logan to William Penn, May 26, July 14, Sept. 28, 1704, in Armstrong, *Correspondence between William Penn and James Logan*, 1:287, 299–300, 317–19. July 11, 1704, MPC, 2:151–52. Indictment of William Jolley, Gyles Green, and John Morris, Feb. 1, 1703/4, Ancient Records of Philadelphia (Collected by John William Wallace, 1845), HSP. The Governor's Answer to the Remonstrance of the Corporation, Oct. 3, 1704, Logan Family Papers, Box 3, Folder 91, HSP. Smolenski, *Friends and Strangers*, 189–90. Nash, *Quakers and Politics*, 256–57. On political theory and militias, see note 34 below.

28. Quakers did not believe in oaths, and therefore their judicial system relied on affirmations, a source of deep concern and suspicion to non-Quakers. See page 44.

29. Isaac Norris to Jonathan Dickinson, Sept. 27, 1704, James Logan to William Penn, Sept. 28, 1704, in Armstrong, *Correspondence between William Penn and James Logan*, 1:315, 317–19. Peter Thompson, *Rum Punch and Revolution: Taverngoing and Public Life in Eighteenth-Century Philadelphia* (Philadelphia: University of Pennsylvania Press, 1999), 102–3. Smolenski, *Friends and Strangers*, 64–65.

30. Nov. 2, 1704, MPC, 2:171. Thompson, *Rum Punch and Revolution*, 102–3. Smolenski, *Friends and Strangers*, 64–65.

31. Records survive for three out of the ten city wards. The two women indicted were Katherine Jones and Grace Townsend, both in the Middle Ward. Presumably these women were both heads of their households. It would appear that their local constable thought they should provide a man from their household to fulfill the obligation of city watching, rather than requiring the women themselves to do so—the proclamation had claimed only male participation. Neither of the other two wards whose lists have survived returned the names of female householders, either because no other women were heads of houses that did not meet their city watching obligation or because the other constables did not interpret the law as universally as did Samuel Cresson, constable of the Middle Ward. Report of Constable [High Street Ward], Feb. 4, 1706, Report of Constable, n.d., Report of Constable [Middle Ward], Feb. 4, 1706, Ancient Records of Philadelphia (Collected by John William Wallace, 1845), 31–33, HSP.

32. Aug. 23, Aug. 24, Oct. 4, Oct. 8, 1705, MPC, 204–6. Quoted in Sister Joan de Lourdes Leonard, "Elections in Colonial Pennsylvania," *WMQ*, 3rd ser., 11 (1954): 397. James Logan to William Penn, Spring 1706, in Armstrong, *Correspondence between William Penn and James Logan*, 2:119–20.

33. James Logan to William Penn, June 12, 1706, in Armstrong, *Correspondence between William Penn and James Logan*, 2:130–36. June 26, 1706, MPC, 2:249–50.

34. J. G. A. Pocock, *The Machiavellian Moment: Florentine Political Thought and the Atlantic Republican Tradition* (Princeton, NJ: Princeton University Press, 1975). Tully, *Forming American Politics*, 301. Smolenski, *Friends and Strangers*, 116, 119. John W. Shy, "A New Look at Colonial Militia," *WMQ*, 3rd ser., 20 (1963): 175–85. Edmund S. Morgan, *Inventing the People: The Rise of Popular Sovereignty in England and America* (New York: W. W. Norton, 1988), 153–83. John Smolenski suggests that in Pennsylvania's first decades the courts were the most effective institution for engaging Pennsylvanians in a common civic project, though the power of those forms declined over time. Smolenski, *Friends and Strangers*, 129.

35. Nathan Ross Kozuskanich, "'For the Security and Protection of the Community': The Frontier and the Makings of Pennsylvania Constitutionalism" (PhD diss., Ohio State University, 2005).

36. Dec. 1, 1704, Apr. 29, 1706, Sept. 21, 1705, Feb. 2, 1704/5, *MCC*.

37. Indictment for Grimston Boud and others, Sept. 26, 1702, Indictment for Edward James, Feb. 4, 1702/3, Indictment for Dorothy Cantowill, Feb. 4, 1702/3, Indictment for Sarah Stivor, Feb. 4, 1702/3, Indictment for John Smith, Feb. 4, 1702/3, Indictment for John Simon, Feb. 4, 1702/3, Sept. 28, 1702, Indictments, Nov. 3, 1703, Indictment of Alexander Paxton & his wife, May 6, 1703, Indictments, Nov. 2, 1703, Indictments, Nov. 3, 1703, Ancient Records of Philadelphia (Collected by John William Wallace, 1845), HSP. For a discussion of tavern licensing, see Thompson, *Rum Punch and Revolution*, 24–25.

38. Petition of Enoch Story, Dec. 11, 1704, The Address of the Mayor and Comonalty of the City of Philadelphia to the Lt. Governor, Dec. 11, 1704, Logan Family Papers, Box 3, Folders 103, 101, HSP. Dec. 11, 1704, Feb. 6, 1704/5, MPC, 180, 182. Votes, 1:533, 536.

39. In 1701 the ratio of Philadelphia to rural representatives was 2 to 24, and by 1752, 2 to 35. Leonard W. Labaree, Ralph L. Ketcham, and Helen C. Boatfield, eds., *The Autobiography of Benjamin Franklin*, 2nd ed. (New Haven, CT: Yale University Press, 2003), 200. Ultimately Franklin was able to wheedle funds out of the assembly—see chap. 4. "An Act for Regulating, Pitching, Paving and Cleansing the Highways, Streets, Lanes, and Highways" (1762), *The Statutes at Large of Pennsylvania, From 1682 to 1801* (Pennsylvania, 1898), 6:199. For more on the Pennsylvania Hospital, see pages 93–94.

40. May 22, 1710, June 16, 1713, *MCC*, 69–71, 87–88.

41. "An Act for the Better Assessing and Raising of County Levies" (Nov. 27, 1700) and "An Act for Raising Money on the Inhabitants of the City of Philadelphia" (1712), *Statutes at Large of Pennsylvania*, 2:34–39, 414–19. Historians debate the role of the assessors. Judith Diamonstone concludes that they usurped authority and that their creation represented "a defeat" for the corporation. John Edward Daly, on the other hand, argues that the city assessors asserted little authority and worked hand in glove with the corporation. In the end he writes them off as "a total failure." Diamonstone, "Philadelphia Corporation." John Edward Daly, "Public Records and Public Policy: Philadelpha, 1681–1770" (PhD diss., University of Pennsylvania, 1983), 118, 131–32.

In 1711 an act of assembly created another body that oversaw the assessors in the counties and later in the city. The commissioners were charged with overseeing and enforcing tax collection. The act named the first commissioners, who thereafter appointed their successors. "An Act Empowering Commissioners to Compel the Collecting of All Arrearages of Former Taxes" (1710/11), *Statutes at Large of Pennsylvania*, 2:369–73. Though the county commissioners became vigorous enforcers of tax collection, their city counterparts were less active.

42. "An Act for the Erecting Houses of Correction and Workhouses" (1718), *Statutes at Large of Pennsylvania*, 2:251–54. On Philadelphia poor relief, see Gary B. Nash, "Poverty and Poor Relief in Pre-Revolutionary Philadelphia," *WMQ*, 3rd ser., 33 (1976): 3–30. John K. Alexander, *Render Them Submissive: Responses to Poverty in Philadelphia, 1760–1800* (Amherst: University of Massachusetts Press, 1980). For more on poor relief, see chapter 3.

43. Charter of the City of Philadelphia, 1701, in Carey and Bioren, *Laws of the Commonwealth of Pennsylvania*, 15–20. The fees for purchasing one's "Freedom" were not specified in the charter and appear to have varied widely. Compare, for example, a 1705 list with the membership drive the corporation undertook in 1717, *MCC*, 25, 118–35. For freewomen, see, for example, July 13, 1705, *MCC*.

44. Diamonstone, "Philadelphia Corporation," 260, 270–71, 210. Diamonstone, "Philadelphia's Municipal Corporation," 185.

45. James Logan to William Penn, July 14, 1704, in Armstrong, *Correspondence between William Penn and James Logan*, 1:298–304.

Chapter 3 · For a General Benefit

1. Leonard W. Labaree, Ralph L. Ketcham, and Helen C. Boatfield, eds., *The Autobiography of Benjamin Franklin*, 2nd ed. (New Haven, CT: Yale University Press, 2003), 75–76. For a biography that focuses particularly on Franklin as a civic actor, see Alan Houston, *Benjamin Franklin and the Politics of Improvement* (New Haven, CT: Yale University Press, 2008).

2. On James Franklin's checkered career as a Boston printer, see David Waldstreicher, *Runaway America: Benjamin Franklin, Slavery, and the American Revolution* (New York: Hill and Wang, 2004), 27–54. Labaree, Ketcham, and Boatfield, *Autobiography of Benjamin Franklin*, 92–106.

3. May 30, 1744, "Journal of William Black," *PMHB* 1 (1877): 247. Jan. 9, 1740, *George Whitefield's Journals*, 3rd Impression (Carlisle, PA: Banner of Truth Trust, 1978), 387. *London Magazine* (London, 1749), 334. Population statistics from Gary B. Nash, *The Urban Crucible: Social Change, Political Consciousness, and the Origins of the American Revolution* (Cambridge, MA: Harvard University Press, 1979), 407–8. Sam Bass Warner Jr., *The Private City: Philadelphia in Three Periods of Its Growth* (Philadelphia: University of Pennsylvania Press, 1968).

4. On voluntary associations as a technology, see Johann N. Neem, *Creating a Nation of Joiners: Democracy and Civil Society in Early National Massachusetts* (Cambridge, MA: Harvard University Press, 2008), 81–82.

5. Peter J. Parker, "Rich and Poor in Philadelphia," *PMHB* 99 (1975): 4. "Law for Raising County Levies" (1696) and "An Act for the Relief of the Poor" (1706), *The Statutes at Large of Pennsylvania, From 1682 to 1801* (Pennsylvania, 1898), 1:230–33, 2:251–54. Oct. 18, 1700, MPC, 2:9. Feb. 2, 1704/5, *MCC*, 17. Gary B. Nash, "Poverty and Poor Relief in Pre-Revolutionary Philadelphia," *WMQ*, 3rd ser., 33 (1976): 4–5. Hannah Benner Roach, "Philadelphia's Poor Laws," *Pennsylvania Genealogical Magazine* 22 (1962): 159–69. On the number of houses, see John K. Alexander, "The Philadelphia Numbers Game: An Analysis of Philadelphia's Eighteenth-Century Population," *PMHB* 98 (1974): 314–24.

6. July 29, Nov. 14, 1712, Jan. 28, 1733/34, *MCC*, 80, 83, 330. "An Act for Erecting Houses of Corrections and Work-houses in the respective Counties of this Province" (1718), "An Act for Establishing a Ferry from the City of Philadelphia . . . to Gloucester in New Jersey" (1727), and "An Act for Emitting of Thirty Thousand Pounds n Bills of Credit . . ." (1729), *Statutes at Large of Pennsylvania*, 3:167–71, 4:80–84, 98–116. Votes, 3:1950. Justices of the peace for Philadelphia County tried to take over the workhouse in 1735, only to be rebuffed by the assembly, which reaffirmed the independence of the magistrates of the corporation. Votes, 3:2246, 2249–50. The corporation had not repaid the £1,000 loan for the almshouse ten years later. Votes, 3:2495.

7. Jan. 28, Jan. 30, 1733/34, *MCC*, 330–32.

8. Judith M. Diamonstone, "The Philadelphia Corporation, 1701–1776" (PhD diss., University of Pennsylvania, 1969), 199, 226, 230–31, 257, 260–61. Parker, "Rich and Poor in Philadelphia," 5. John K. Alexander, *Render Them Submissive: Responses to Poverty in Philadelphia, 1760–1800* (Amherst: University of Massachusetts Press, 1980), 92–93.

In a new poor law passed in 1735, the assembly sought to give the corporation a little more oversight, but largely left intact the independence of the overseers. In 1735 the assembly passed a bill that, "for the more easy discovery, certain knowledge, and well management of the affairs of the poor," required the overseers to give the corporation a certified copy of the poor list every time they requested a tax levy, and compelled them to submit their accounts annually. The bill reaffirmed the corporation's direction of the almshouse and vaguely gave it discretion "where it may be needful to direct the receiving into the said almshouse such poor," but did not give a clear grant of power to compel the overseers to end outdoor relief and put the poor into either the almshouse or workhouse. "A Supplement to the Several Acts of Assembly of this Province for the Relief of the Poor" (1735), *Statutes at Large of Pennsylvania*, 4:266–77.

9. Parker, "Rich and Poor in Philadelphia." Carl Bridenbaugh and Jessica Bridenbaugh, *Rebels and Gentlemen: Philadelphia in the Age of Franklin* (New York: Reynel and Hitchcock, 1942), 229.

10. On Quaker poor relief and financial stability from 1682, see chap. 1. Nash, "Poverty and Poor Relief," 4. Carl Bridenbaugh, *Cities in the Wilderness: The First Century of Urban Life in America 1625–1742* (1938; repr., New York: Alfred A. Knopf, 1955), 236. Dec. 30, 1709, Dec. 28, 1716, Jan. 25, 1716/17, PFMQM. The Monthly Meeting distributed small and large sums; it also gave money to the Women's Meeting, which also gave money to women in need.

11. Aug. 25, 1704, PFMQM. Oct. 29, 1714, Apr. 26, June 28, 1717, PFMQM.

12. Bridenbaugh, *Cities in the Wilderness*, 236. J. Thomas Scharf and Thompson Westcott, *History of Philadelphia, 1609–1884* (Philadelphia, 1884), 1:191. Nov. 29, 1706, Feb. 24, 1726/27, Dec. 29, 1727, Aug. 30, 1728, June 27, 1729, PFMQM. Bridenbaugh and Bridenbaugh, *Rebels and Gentlemen*, 229. Scharf and Westcott argue that the Friends almshouse was at first "in general public use," but I have seen no contemporary documents corroborating this claim. Scharf and Westcott, *History of Philadelphia*, 1:191. Edwin B. Bronner, "Quaker Landmarks in Early Philadelphia," in *Historic Philadelphia: From the Founding until the Early Nineteenth Century*, ed. Luther P. Eisenhart (Philadelphia: American Philosophical Society, 1953), 216.

13. PFMQM. Minutes of the Monthly Meeting of Philadelphia, 1715–1744, Special Collections, Haverford College. Quote from Oct. 29, 1714, PFMQM.

14. For the origins of the Quaker Free School, see chap. 1. Charter, 1701, Legal Papers, Box 1, William Penn Charter School Collection, Haverford College, n.d. (ca. 1725?), Overseers' Correspondence, ca. 1725–99, Box 10, William Penn Charter School Collection, Haverford College. Jan. 30, 1701/2, Mar. 27, Sept. 25, Oct. 30, Nov. 27, 1702, Apr. 30, 1703, Aug. 31, 1705, Feb. 27, 1707/8, Feb. 25, 1708/9, PFMQM. May 27, 1725, MOPS. On Quaker theories of education, see chap. 1 and J. William Frost, *The Quaker Family in Colonial America: A Portrait of the Society of Friends* (New York: St. Martin's Press, 1973). Friends were aggressive in encouraging members to contribute to the school through subscriptions and bequests. In one case, the Monthly Meeting withheld a certificate of good behavior from Tobias Dinnock and two of his family members, even though he was a Quaker in good standing, because "he seems not willing to pay a Subscription towards ye School which the Meeting thinks he ought to do." Only when Dinnock had promised to make a subscription would the Monthly Meeting give them certificates. Oct. 31, 1701, Feb. 27, 1707/8, PFMQM. Thomas Woody, *Early Quaker Education in Pennsylvania* (New York: Teachers College, Columbia University, 1920), 62–63.

15. "An Account of the State of the Church in North America," n.d. (ca. Nov. 1702), George Keith to Dr. Bray, Feb. 24, 1703/4, *Collections of the Protestant Episcopal Historical Society for the Year 1851* (New York, 1851), xix, xvi, xxii–xxv. Edward Portlock to the Archbishop of Canterbury, July 12, 1700, Lord Cornbury to the Lord Bishop of London, Aug. 23, 1703, in *Papers Relating to the History of the Church in Pennsylvania, A.D. 1680–1778*, ed. William S. Perry (Hartford, CT, 1871), 16, 17–18. Thomas Bray, *A Memorial, Representing the Present State of Religion on the Continent of North-America* (London, 1701).

16. Charter of the Society for the Propagation of the Gospel in Foreign Parts. June 16, 1701, *Classified Digest of the Records of the Society for the Propagation of the Gospel in Foreign Parts* (London, 1893), 925–28. Jon Butler, "Power, Authority, and the Origins of American Denominational Order: The English Churches in the Delaware Valley, 1680–1730," *Transactions of the American Philosophical Society*, new ser., 68 (1978): 70–74. The first Church of

England bishop in America, William White, would not be appointed until after the Revolutionary War.

17. The Philadelphia Baptist Church had only forty-six full members in 1701; in 1741, only fifty-six. The Philadelphia Baptist Association consisted in 1707 of five churches: two in Pennsylvania and three in New Jersey. By 1763 it would include twenty-nine churches in seven colonies. Butler, "Power, Authority, and the Origins of American Denominational Order," 48–49. Janet Moore Lindman, *Bodies of Belief: Baptist Community in Early America* (Philadelphia: University of Pennsylvania Press, 2008), 4, 22–27, 29, quote from 23. *Minutes of the Philadelphia Baptist Association, 1707–1807* (Philadelphia, 1851).

18. Alexander Mackie, "The Presbyterian Churches of Old Philadelphia," in Eisenhart, *Historic Philadelphia*, 217. Presbytery of Philadelphia to Mr. Davenport, Mr. Webb, Mr. Shove, & Mr. Pouckingham, May 24, 1708, Presbytery of Philadelphia to Edmund Harrison, May 1709, Letterbook from 1708–20, PHS. Sept. 1716, Sept. 24, 1721, Sept. 19, Sept. 22, 1729, Sept. 24, 1734, May 30, 1737, Records of the Presbytery of Philadelphia, From 1706–17, Records of the Synod of Philadelphia, 1717–58, PHS. Butler, "Power, Authority, and the Origins of American Denominational Order," 57, 62–64. Milton J. Coalter, *Gilbert Tennent, Son of Thunder: A Case Study of Continental Pietism's Impact on the First Great Awakening in the Middle Colonies* (New York: Greenwood Press, 1986), 28–53.

19. Sept. 19, 1717, Sept. 18, 1718, Sept. 18, Sept. 19, 1719, May 28, May 30, 1737, May 25, 1738, June 3, 1740, June 2, 1741, May 31, 1743, Records of the Presbytery of Philadelphia, From 1706–17, Records of the Synod of Philadelphia, 1717–58.

20. May 30, 1737, Records of the Presbytery of Philadelphia, From 1706–17, Records of the Synod of Philadelphia, 1717–58. "The Fund for Pious Uses," Day Book, 1718–55, Presbyterian Ministers' Fund, HSP. The surviving accounts were not balanced but merely listed as they came in, so determining what interest rates the synod charged is difficult, particularly because sometimes only the interest repaid was recorded, not the original loan. Interest came in, moreover, at sporadic intervals, not annually. Not counting the one outlier of £190, the average loan was for £16.10 (counting all loans, it was £22).

21. "The Fund for Pious Uses," Day Book, 1718–55, HSP. May 26, 1744, Records of the Presbytery of Philadelphia, From 1706–17, Records of the Synod of Philadelphia, 1717–58.

22. *Statutes at Large of Pennsylvania*, 2:424–25, 3:37–38, 4:208–11. Jan. 3, 1705/6, MPC, 2:221–22. Votes, 3:2068–69.

23. *Pennsylvania Gazette*, May 18, 1749. J. A. Leo Lemay, *The Life of Benjamin Franklin* (Philadelphia: University of Pennsylvania Press, 2009), 3:243, 246. Franklin's most famous thoughts about population growth were contained in his 1751 *Observations Concerning the Increase of Mankind*. Leonard W. Labaree, ed., *The Papers of Benjamin Franklin* (New Haven, CT: Yale University Press, 1961), 4:227–34.

24. P. J. Corfield, *The Impact of English Towns, 1700–1800* (Oxford: Oxford University Press, 1982). Peter Borsay, *The English Urban Renaissance: Culture and Society in the Provincial Town, 1660–1770* (Oxford: Clarendon Press, 1989). Charles S. Olton, *Artisans for Independence: Philadelphia Mechanics and the American Revolution* (New York: Syracuse University Press, 1975), 1–3. Bridenbaugh, *Cities in the Wilderness*. Carl Bridenbaugh, *Cities in Revolt: Urban Life in America, 1743–1776* (Oxford: Oxford University Press, 1955). While cities did not flourish in most of the Chesapeake and Lower South, a number of centers developed that performed the economic function of cities, though without dense settlement. Joseph A.

Ernst and H. Roy Merrens, "'Camden's turrets pierce the skies!': The Urban Process in the Southern Colonies during the Eighteenth Century," *WMQ* 30 (1973): 549–74.

25. Peter Clark, in his study of British associational life, argues that the development of towns and cities was an extremely important element to the proliferation of clubs and societies. Beginning in London and spanning out to smaller cities and market towns, Clark identifies clubs as primarily an urban phenomenon, with only a "sprinkling" of associational activity in rural areas. Peter Clark, *British Clubs and Societies 1580–1800: The Origins of an Associational World* (Oxford: Clarendon Press, 2000), 58, 142–44. Peter Thompson, *Rum Punch and Revolution: Taverngoing and Public Life in Eighteenth-Century Philadelphia* (Philadelphia: University of Pennsylvania Press, 1999), 2.

Philadelphia was a major center of commerce. Beyond shipping it provided the infrastructure for goods processing, shipbuilding and ship repair, communications, and financial services. In addition, with a prosperous hinterland that provided wheat for export, as well as a market for services, goods, and imports, the service and manufacturing sectors of the city became strong. Jacob M. Price, "Economic Function and Growth of American Port Towns in the Eighteenth Century," *Perspectives in American History* 8 (1974): 149. Thomas M. Doerflinger argues for expanding wealth and social mobility among the merchant class of Philadelphia in *A Vigorous Spirit of Enterprise: Merchants and Economic Development in Revolutionary Philadelphia* (Chapel Hill: University of North Carolina Press, 1986). Gary B. Nash demonstrates that the distribution of wealth became increasingly concentrated in favor of the richest 10% as the century progressed, but the middling and upper middling classes retained extensive purchasing power. Dividing Philadelphia into deciles by wealth (poorest 10% through richest 10%), Nash shows that from 1726 to 1735 the third through ninth deciles controlled 42.5% of the city's wealth, 46.1% between 1736 and 1745, 28.4% between 1746 and 1755, 38.4% between 1756 and 1765, and 29.1% between 1766 and 1775. Nash, *Urban Crucible*, 396.

26. Borsay, *English Urban Renaissance*, 311–12. Draft of a letter from Joseph Breintnall to Peter Collinson, Nov. 28, 1737, Smith MSS, HSP, 164. Address of Library Company to Thomas Penn, May 24, 1733, LCPM; quoted in Whitfield J. Bell, "For Mutual Improvement in the Healing Art: Philadelphia Medical Societies of the 18th Century," *Journal of the American Medical Association* 216, no. 1 (Apr. 1971): 127.

27. Clark, *British Clubs and Societies*, 155. "To Mr. OBADIAH PLAINMAN," *Pennsylvania Gazette*, May 22, 1740 (italics in original). On the consumer revolution, see Cary Carson, "The Consumer Revolution in Colonial British America: Why Demand?," in *Of Consuming Interest: The Style of Life in the Eighteenth Century*, ed. Cary Carson, Ronald Hoffman, and Peter Albert (Charlottesville: University of Virginia Press, 1994), 483–697. T. H. Breen, "'Baubles of Britain': The American and Consumer Revolutions of the Eighteenth Century," in *Colonial America: Essays in Politics and Social Development*, ed. Michael Katz et al. (Boston: McGraw-Hill, 2001), 467–96.

28. Philadelphians gathered voluntarily for all sorts of purposes, ranging from tavern sociability to salons to rounds of domestic visiting. I define formal voluntary associations as a distinctive kind of gathering, characterized by regular meetings, codified membership, rules and organizational structure, record keeping, and shared financial commitments. As I have noted elsewhere, in the absence of established religion, churches in Pennsylvania operated as voluntary associations as well, but normally when I use this term I refer to nonsectarian organizations.

29. *Reminiscences of Carpenters' Hall, in the City of Philadelphia and Extracts from the Ancient Minutes of the Proceedings of the Carpenters' Company* . . . (Philadelphia, 1858). *American Weekly Mercury*, Feb. 29–Mar. 7, 1732. *Pennsylvania Gazette*, Feb. 27–Mar. 6, 1734. Daniel R. Gilbert, "Patterns of Organization and Membership in Colonial Philadelphia Club Life, 1725–1755" (PhD diss., University of Pennsylvania, 1952), 156–57. On ethnic societies, see Clark, *British Clubs and Societies*, 291–306. Feasting societies were more popular in England in the seventeenth century and on the decline by 1714 as voluntary organization became more organized and met more often. Clark, *British Clubs and Societies*, 58–59, 69. John F. Watson, *Watson's Annals of Philadelphia and Pennsylvania* (Philadelphia, 1857), chap. 69. Two more Masonic lodges were warranted in or by 1749, and a third in 1757; finally, an "Ancient" lodge was founded in 1761. Wayne A Huss, *The Master Builders: A History of the Grand Lodge of Free and Accepted Masons of Pennsylvania*, vol. 1, *1731–1873* (Philadelphia: Grand Lodge F.&A.M. of Pennsylvania, 1986). Julius F. Sachse, "Roster of the Freemason's Lodge Philadelphia No. 2, of the Moderns," *PMHB* 31 (1907): 19–29. Julius F. Sachse, "Roster of the Free and Accepted Masons Which Met at the Tun Tavern, Philadelphia," *PMHB* 20 (1896): 116–21. Gilbert, "Patterns of Organization," 140–41. Nicholas B. Wainwright, *The Schuylkill Fishing Company of the State in Schuylkill, 1732–1982* (Philadelphia: Schuylkill Fishing Company, 1982). *A History of the Schuylkill Fishing Company of the State in Schuylkill, 1732–1888* (Philadelphia, 1889). David S. Shields, *Civil Tongues and Polite Letters in British America* (Chapel Hill: University of North Carolina Press, 1997), 189–98. Kenneth Cohen, " 'To Give Good Sport': The Economic Culture of Public Sporting Events in Early America, 1750–1850" (PhD diss., University of Delaware, 2008).

30. Labaree, Ketcham, and Boatfield, *Autobiography of Benjamin Franklin*, 116–18, 130, 170–71, 174, 192–93. Benjamin Franklin, Commonplace Book, Dreer Collection, HSP. On the importance of the Boston precedent, see Labaree, Ketcham, and Boatfield, *Autobiography of Benjamin Franklin*, 58n. "Junto" was a common term in the seventeenth and early eighteenth centuries, meaning "a body of men who have joined or combined for a common purpose, especially of a political character." *Oxford English Dictionary*, s.v. "junto," www.oed .com/view/Entry/102116?redirectedFrom=junto.

31. Labaree, Ketcham, and Boatfield, *Autobiography of Benjamin Franklin*, 170–71.

32. Ibid., 118. LCPM, 1731–75; Library Company Record Book A, 1742–89, LCP. "A short Account of the LIBRARY," in *A Catalogue of Books Belonging to the Library Company* (Philadelphia, 1741). The membership of the Junto is not absolutely clear, but four members (including Franklin) certainly helped found the Library Company in 1731, another five Junto members joined the LCP within a year, and six other men who either already were or would shortly become Junto members helped found the library. On Elizabeth North, see May 10, 1742, May 6, 1745, LCPM. Two more women bought shares in their own names in 1769, and a third received one from her brother in 1770. "Articles of the Union Library Company," May 16, 1747, LCP.

33. The Library Company of Philadelphia to Peter Collinson, Nov. 7, 1732, and Address of Library Company to Thomas Penn, Proprietor, May 24, 1733, LCPM. Draft of a letter from Joseph Breintnall to Peter Collinson, Nov. 28, 1737, Smith MSS, HSP, 164. July 20, Nov. 8, 1739, LCPM. For other examples of internal discussions about the "usefulness of books," see Nov. 5, 1735, Dec. 13, 1742, Feb. 14, 1743, Nov. 29, 1769, LCPM. The directors hoped their "valuable" books would "have very good Effects on the Minds of the People of this Province, and furnish them with the most useful kind of Knowledge, that which renders

Men benevolent and helpful to one another." Nov. 24, 1743, LCPM. Later libraries modeled on the Library Company also emphasized "useful" books. See "Charter of the Union Library Company." Oct. 6, 1759, LCP, and "Articles of the Amicable Library Company in Philadelphia," Feb. 8, 1757. Bound into LCPM.

34. Nov. 13, 1711, Apr. 27, Apr. 29, Oct. 12, 1730, Jan. 4, 1730/31, July 21, July 28, 1735, *MCC.* "On Protection of Towns from Fire," *Pennsylvania Gazette*, Feb. 4, 1734/35. On firefighting in other towns, see Bridenbaugh, *Cities in the Wilderness*, 59–61, 209–13. Benjamin L. Carp, "Fire of Liberty: Firefighters, Urban Voluntary Culture, and the Revolutionary Moment," *WMQ* 58 (2001): 781–818.

35. Articles of Union Fire Company, Dec. 7, 1736, UFCM. Union first limited its membership to twenty-five but expanded to thirty in 1737. Fellowship Fire Company was founded in 1738, and Hand-in-Hand Fire Company in 1742. The former, like Union, restricted its firefighting to members' homes and shops; the Articles of Association for Hand-in-Hand are no longer extant. Mar. 1, 1738, FFCM. Thompson Westcott, *History of the Philadelphia Fire Department*, no. 7 (1849). (Bound Volume at the HSP.)

36. "Articles of the Union Fire Company in Philad.a," Jan. 31, 1742/3, UFCM. Fire companies did not record the fires they fought in their minutes but occasionally detailed the loss of equipment at fires. Two of the three fires where the Union Fire Company lost buckets before 1743 occurred at the houses of men who were not members of the company. The third fire was at the house of Joseph Turner, who may or may not have been a member at the time; he joined within a very short time of the fire—and if it was after, perhaps he joined out of gratitude. Dec. 1737, Feb. 1738, June 1741, UFCM.

The fact that all known fire companies also continued strictly to require members to keep up lists of all members' names by their doors and fined those who failed to comply, however, suggests that in the event of multiple conflagrations, company members would get priority, though this happened rarely if ever in practice.

37. See, for example, Mar. 3, 1766, Jan. 4, 1768, FFCM. "Copy of Joan Donovan's Affadavit, sworn before Ralph Asheton, Esq.," *American Weekly Mercury*, Apr. 26, 1744.

38. Dec. 28, 1747, July 30, Aug. 27, Sept. 20, 1750, Mar. 29, Apr. 27, 1752, Nov. 24, 1766, Jan. 25, Mar. 28, May 30, 1768, Jan. 30, Mar. 27, 1769, Jan. 28, 1771, UFCM. Dec. 3, 1759, FFCM. For discussion of all Philadelphia fire companies, see Jessica Choppin Roney, "'First Movers in Every Useful Undertaking': Formal Voluntary Associations in Philadelphia, 1725–1775" (PhD diss., Johns Hopkins University, 2008).

39. Here I borrow the word for city resident used by the Union Fire Company itself in 1743. "Articles of the Union Fire Company in Philad.a," Jan. 31, 1742/3, UFCM.

40. Articles of Union Fire Company, Dec. 7, 1736, UFCM. Articles of Association of the Library Company of Philadelphia, July 1, 1731, LCP. Nov. 6, 1775, Hibernia Fire Company Minutes, vol. 2, 1773–97, HSP.

41. Susannah Wright to James Logan, Dec. 25, 1748, R. R. Logan Collection, 1671–1882, Box 5, John Dickinson Related Families, Folder 37, HSP. James Mease, *The Picture of Philadelphia, Giving an Account of Its Origin, Increase, and Improvements in Arts, Sciences, Manufactures, Commerce and Revenue. With a Compendious View of Its Societies, Literary, Benevolent, Patriotic, & Religious* (Philadelphia, 1811), 319. E. V. Lamberton, "Colonial Libraries of Pennsylvania," *PMHB* 43 (1918): 208–12. Dorothy Fear Grimm, "A History of the Library Company of Philadelphia, 1731–1835" (PhD diss., University of Pennsylvania, 1955), 121–22.

42. As important as British models were to Philadelphia organizing, the connection

should not be taken too far. One historian of British associations, for example, implies an all-encompassing influence flowing westward across the Atlantic. He notes, for example, that Benjamin Franklin was an active club participant during his extended visits to London, and "a number of the societies Franklin established in Philadelphia were clearly influenced by his London experiences." Though Franklin visited at least one club during his stay in London between 1724 and 1726, there is no evidence of its being particularly noteworthy or influential on his later life or organizing. Rather, historians have pointed to the works of John Locke and Daniel Defoe and to Boston's organizational life, particularly the municipal fire companies and Cotton Mather's neighborhood benefit societies, as influential to Franklin. Furthermore, Franklin founded all his projects between 1727 and 1751, *before* his two later extended visits to London, when he was active in the associational life of that city. Clark, *British Clubs and Societies*, 401. Labaree, Ketcham, and Boatfield, *Autobiography of Benjamin Franklin*, 58n. Grimm, "History of the Library Company of Philadelphia," 18. The club Franklin visited in England seems to have been an informal club of literary men, most importantly Bernard Mandeville. Grimm, "History of the Library Company of Philadelphia," 97.

43. Diamonstone, "Philadelphia Corporation," 206–7. Because the records of most fire companies are lost or incomplete, we will never know for certain how many Philadelphia Corporation members were in companies.

44. The Library Company received its charter in 1742. *The Charter, Laws, and Catalogue of Books of the Library Company of Philadelphia* (Philadelphia, 1757). The land donated by the Penns for a permanent building never led to construction. Only after the Revolution would the Library Company build its own space. Jan. 31, 1738, June 21, July 9, Dec. 10, 1739, Mar. 10, 1740, Aug. 10, Oct. 12, 1741, May 3, 1742, May 2, 1743, July 13, 1747, LCPM. "The humble ADDRESS of the Directors of The Library Company of Philadelphia," *American Weekly Mercury*, Nov. 17–24, 1743.

45. "A short Account of the LIBRARY," in *A Catalogue of Books Belonging to the Library Company* (Philadelphia, 1741).

Chapter 4 · Amidst "Rancour and Party Hatred"

1. Leonard W. Labaree, Ralph L. Ketcham, and Helen C. Boatfield, eds., *The Autobiography of Benjamin Franklin*, 2nd ed. (New Haven, CT: Yale University Press, 2003), 175, 176, 179, 183. *George Whitefield's Journals*, 3rd Impression (Carlisle, PA: Banner of Truth Trust, 1978), 341–43, 490. William L. Turner, "The Charity School, the Academy, and the College: Fourth and Arch Streets," *Transactions of the American Philosophical Society* 43, pt. 1 (1953): 179. Benjamin Franklin, "Address to the Associators," Dec. 7, 1747, Benjamin Franklin to James Logan, May 10, 1748, in *The Papers of Benjamin Franklin*, ed. Leonard W. Labaree (New Haven, CT: Yale University Press, 1961), 3:225–26, 287.

2. Alan Tully, *Forming American Politics: Ideals, Interests, and Institutions in Colonial New York and Pennsylvania* (Baltimore: Johns Hopkins University Press, 1994), 145. William Penn's sons John, Richard, and Thomas were coproprietors from 1727 until 1746, when John died. Thereafter Richard and Thomas governed until Richard's death in 1771. Thomas died in 1775.

3. *George Whitefield's Journals*, 341–43. Benjamin Franklin testified to the strength of Whitefield's voice and its ability to carry to as many as thirty thousand auditors in the streets. Labaree, Ketcham, and Boatfield, *Autobiography of Benjamin Franklin*, 175, 179.

4. Gilbert Tennent was inspired to preach what became one of the most famous American sermons of the eighteenth century, *The Danger of an Unconverted Ministry*, in which he

argued that parishioners had the power and responsibility to eject "unconverted" ministers in favor of more "Godly Persons." Tennent's message delivered into the hands of the laity the power and responsibility to weigh in on the synod's long-standing but previously closed debates. *George Whitefield's Journals,* 407. Milton J. Coalter, *Gilbert Tennent, Son of Thunder: A Case Study of Continental Pietism's Impact on the First Great Awakening in the Middle Colonies* (Westport, CT: Greenwood Press, 1986), 58–69. On the revivalism of this period, often called "the First Great Awakening," see Jon Butler, "Enthusiasm Described and Decried: The Great Awakening as Interpretive Fiction," *Journal of American History* 19 (1982): 305–25. Patricia U. Bonomi, *Under the Cope of Heaven: Religion, Society, and Politics in Colonial America* (Oxford: Oxford University Press, 1986). Jon Butler, *Awash in a Sea of Faith: Christianizing the American People* (Cambridge, MA: Harvard University Press, 1990). Nina Reid-Maroney, *Philadelphia's Enlightenment, 1740–1800: Kingdom of Christ, Empire of Reason* (Westport, CT: Greenwood Press, 2001). Thomas S. Kidd, *The Great Awakening: The Roots of Evangelical Christianity in Colonial America* (New Haven, CT: Yale University Press, 2007).

5. *George Whitefield's Journals,* 407–10, 422. Coalter, *Gilbert Tennent, Son of Thunder,* 68–69.

6. *George Whitefield's Journals,* 355, 423.

7. The men entrusted with this task were probably chosen because of their association with the building trades; they included two house builders, one bricklayer, and one other artisan, John Howell, who may have been a tanner or a mariner. These were all men of comfortable economic means but who worked with their hands—men, in short, who could oversee not only the purchase of property but the construction of a building itself. Turner, "Charity School, the Academy, and the College," 179. Labaree, Ketcham, and Boatfield, *Autobiography of Benjamin Franklin,* 176. *George Whitefield's Journals,* 490.

8. Labaree, Ketcham, and Boatfield, *Autobiography of Benjamin Franklin,* 176. Benjamin Franklin to Jared Eliot, Feb. 13, 1750, in Labaree, *Papers of Benjamin Franklin,* Franklin Papers Online. Turner, "Charity School, the Academy, and the College," 180. *American Weekly Mercury,* June 4, 1741.

9. *American Weekly Mercury,* June 4, 1741. Turner, "Charity School, the Academy, and the College," 180. Votes, 4:3135, 3137, 3143–44, 3148. Labaree, Ketcham, and Boatfield, *Autobiography of Benjamin Franklin,* 176. Benjamin Franklin to Jared Eliot, Feb. 13, 1750, in Labaree, *Papers of Benjamin Franklin.*

10. *Pennsylvania Gazette,* Nov. 26, 1747. The total number of taxable inhabitants of Philadelphia in 1751 was 13,720, so as a rough estimate one in fourteen inhabitants (regardless of age or gender) participated in the association in 1747–48. Estimating that free adult males were about one-sixth of the population (based on an average household of two parents and four children and/or servants/slaves), there were about 2,287 adult men in Philadelphia in 1751. Some of those men would have been too old to participate, driving up the proportion of able-bodied adult men involved in the Defense Association. As a rough estimate, then, able-bodied free adult men would have been no more than a quarter of the population and perhaps as little as one-sixth or less. I am grateful to Michael Zuckerman for pointing out this demographic calculation to me. For population statistics, see Gary B. Nash, "Taxable Inhabitants in Boston, New York, and Philadelphia, 1687–1775," in *The Urban Crucible: Social Change, Political Consciousness, and the Origins of the American Revolution* (Cambridge, MA: Harvard University Press, 1979), 407–8.

11. *Pennsylvania Archives* (Philadelphia, 1852), ser. 1, 1:759–60, 763. John Smith, *The doc-*

trine of Christianity, as held by the people called Quakers, vindicated: in answer to Gilbert Tennent's sermon on the lawfulness of war (Philadelphia, 1748). John Churchman, "Journal of John Churchman," *Friends Library* (Philadelphia, 1837–50), 6:200–202. Churchman truly believed that faith in God—not armed resistance—would deliver the province from all foes. His contemporary William Reckitt explained the Quaker adherence to pacifism by arguing that "the weapons of the primitive believers were not carnal, but spiritual, and mighty through God." "Life of William Reckitt," *Friends Library*, 9:55. Richard Bauman, *For the Reputation of Truth: Politics, Religion, and Conflict among the Pennsylvania Quakers, 1750–1800* (Baltimore: Johns Hopkins University Press, 1971), 15.

12. John Swift to John White, July 13, 1747, John Swift Letterbook, HSP. Jane E. Calvert, *Quaker Constitutionalism and the Political Thought of John Dickinson* (Cambridge: Cambridge University Press, 2009), 10–11. Tully, *Forming American Politics*, 321. Quote from Richard R. Beeman, *The Varieties of Political Experience in Eighteenth-Century America* (Philadelphia: University of Pennsylvania Press, 2004), 204.

Philadelphia, Bucks, and Chester Counties had eight seats each in the legislature, dating to 1682. The city of Philadelphia had two (1701), Lancaster County had four (1729), York County had two (1749), Cumberland County had two (1750), Berks County had two (1752), and Northampton County had one (1752). A long scholarly tradition acknowledges the lack of representation in the western counties, but recent historiography stresses the importance of this imbalance to the evolution of Pennsylvania politics. See, for example, Peter Silver, *Our Savage Neighbors: How Indian War Transformed Early America* (New York: W. W. Norton, 2008). Nathan Ross Kozuskanich, "'For the Security and Protection of the Community': The Frontier and the Makings of Pennsylvania Constitutionalism" (PhD diss., Ohio State University, 2005).

13. Benjamin Franklin, *Plain Truth: Or, Serious Considerations on the Present State of the City of* PHILADELPHIA *and Province of* PENNSYLVANIA (Philadelphia, 1747), 18. Labaree, Ketcham, and Boatfield, *Autobiography of Benjamin Franklin*, 183; Richard Peters to Thomas Penn, Nov. 29, 1747, in Labaree, *Papers of Benjamin Franklin*, 3:214–18.

14. While he lambasted Quaker legislators, Franklin was equally if not more scornful of "those Great and rich Men" who opposed them (according to Franklin) from no other motive than political gain. Franklin, *Plain Truth*, 15, 17, 19–20.

15. Labaree, Ketcham, and Boatfield, *Autobiography of Benjamin Franklin*, 183. Richard Peters to Thomas Penn, Nov. 29, 1747, in Labaree, *Papers of Benjamin Franklin*, 3:214–18. *Pennsylvania Gazette*, Nov. 26, 1747, Apr. 16, 1748. In 1749 James Logan wrote to Thomas Penn that in the first flush of organizing, "ten Companies of near one hundred men each in Philadelphia and above one hundred companies in the Province and Counties" had been formed. James Logan to Thomas Penn, Nov. 24, 1749, in Labaree, *Papers of Benjamin Franklin*, 3:185. For a succinct chronology of the events surrounding the genesis of the Defense Association, see Labaree, *Papers of Benjamin Franklin*, 3:180–88, 220–22, 225, 280.

16. Labaree, Ketcham, and Boatfield, *Autobiography of Benjamin Franklin*, 183–84. *Pennsylvania Gazette*, Dec. 10, Dec. 22, 1747, Jan. 19, Mar. 1, June 2, July 14, Sept. 1, 1748. "Proposal to the Associators," in Labaree, *Papers of Benjamin Franklin*, 3:280–81. Richard Peters to Thomas Penn, May 11, 1748, MSS Penn Official Correspondence, vol. 4, no. 93–95. *Philadelphia Lottery Accounts* (Philadelphia, 1752), photostat reproduction from Yale University original, deposited at HSP.

17. Labaree, *Papers of Benjamin Franklin*, 3:214–18. Franklin, *Plain Truth*, 13, 18, 21. For a

full discussion of the ways the Defense Association built on the blueprint of previous organizations, see Jessica Choppin Roney, " 'Ready to act in defiance of the Government': Philadelphia Voluntary Associations and the Defense Association of 1747–48," *Early American
Studies* 8 (2010): 358–85. Richard Peters to Thomas Penn, Feb. 1, 1747/48, MSS Penn Official
Correspondence, HSP, vol. 4, no. 89. Labaree, *Papers of Benjamin Franklin*, 3:186.

18. Rather than assert leadership over the militia, acting governor Anthony Palmer and
the Provincial Council instructed proprietary secretary Richard Peters to inform the associators that "their measures were not disapprov'd of by the Government, and that if they proceeded to chuse their Officers they would readily obtain Commissions." By giving the commissions, the acting governor preserved his prerogative as legal commander-in-chief of the
province. In practice, however, Palmer merely ratified the associators' choices, exercising no
command whatsoever in the matter. Richard Peters to Thomas Penn, Feb. 1, 1747/48, Richard
Peters to Thomas Penn, Mar. 25, 1748, MSS Penn Official Correspondence, vol. 4, nos. 89
and 93. James Hamilton to Thomas Penn, May 10, 1748, MSS Penn Official Correspondence,
vol. 4, no. 107. Labaree, Ketcham, and Boatfield, *Autobiography of Benjamin Franklin*, 184.
The Philadelphia Corporation bought two thousand of the total ten thousand tickets in the
first lottery and donated all its winnings to the association. It also helped oversee the drawing
for the lottery. Dec. 10, 1747, Jan. 18, 1747/8, May 23, 1748, *MCC*, 491–93, 498–99.

19. Labaree, *Papers of Benjamin Franklin*, 3:186. Ironically, Penn could not forge an alliance with devout Friends, the one constituency in Philadelphia which shared his disapproval
of the Defense Association. The grounds of Penn's concerns rested primarily on the threat to
his government and his own authority and prerogative. Strict Quakers, on the other hand,
were concerned more to uphold their peace testimony, and they had moreover begun to
chafe at Penn's attempts to rein in their assembly (also motivated by his desire to assert proprietary privilege). Penn had by this time left the Society of Friends and joined the Church
of England.

20. Supporters of the Defense Association generally pointed to texts in the Old Testament for evidence of God as a warrior and supporter of armies. Furthermore, they stressed
Jesus's admonition to his followers to "render unto Caeser" and obey the government under
which they lived—an ironic position to take, given that the Defense Association, despite its
countenance by the acting governor and Provincial Council, had not been called into being
by any governmental body. Critics relied more heavily on the New Testament and Christ's
abhorrence of all violence, even when his apostles sought to defend him from the Roman
soldiers who came to arrest him. One anonymous author feared that the Defense Association leaders might use the militia to interfere with the democratic process during the next
election in October and place themselves in power. But even this author called no attention
to the fact that the association had no legal basis whatsoever, and no one else picked up on
either his concerns or the legal issue. I rely here on the printed materials circulating about
the association. For the implication that the Defense Association might interfere with elections, see *A treatise shewing the need we have to rely upon God as sole protector of this province
. . .* (Philadelphia, 1748), 18. For arguments of association supporters, see also *Mr. Franklin,
the Absolute and Obvious Necessity of Self-Defense* (Philadelphia, 1748). Gilbert Tennent, *The
late association for defence, encourag'd, or The lawfulness of a defensive war . . .* (Philadelphia,
1748). Gilbert Tennent, *The late association for defence, farther encourag'd . . .* (Philadelphia,
1748). William Currie, *A treatise on the lawfulness of defensive war . . .* (Philadelphia, 1748). For
arguments against the association, see Samuel Smith, *Necessary truth: or Seasonable consider-*

ations for the inhabitants of the city of Philadelphia, and province of Pennsylvania (Philadelphia, 1748). John Smith, *The doctrine of Christianity, as held by the people called Quakers* (Philadelphia, 1748). Benjamin Gilbert, *Truth vindicated, and the doctrine of darkness manifested . . .* (Philadelphia, 1748).

21. In 1737, less than 15% of eligible voters voted. In 1751, the next year for which election returns have survived, just over a third voted. On average, slightly less than a quarter of eligible voters turned out each year between 1725 and 1775. Robert J. Dinkin, *Voting in Provincial America: A Study of Elections in the Thirteen Colonies, 1689–1776* (Westport, CT: Greenwood Press, 1977), 38, 39, 159. Tully, *Forming American Politics*, 329. Benjamin Franklin to James Logan, Dec. 7, 1747, in Labaree, *Papers of Benjamin Franklin*, 3:224. The "Form of Association" that all volunteers signed mandated that each man provide himself with "a good Firelock, Cartouch Box, and at least twelve Charges of Powder and Ball." Provincial Secretary Richard Peters echoed Franklin's attempts to get arms for these men when he wrote to Proprietor Thomas Penn that "Small Arms are exceedingly wanted," suggesting that Penn send some as a gift. "Form of Association," HSP. Richard Peters to Thomas Penn, Feb. 1, 1747/48, MSS Penn Official Correspondence, HSP, vol. 4, no. 89.

22. Jan. 4, Jan. 25, Feb. 29, 1747/48, UFCM. Labaree, Ketcham, and Boatfield, *Autobiography of Benjamin Franklin*, 186–87. Richard Peters to Thomas Penn, Feb. 1, 1747/48, MSS Penn Official Correspondence, HSP, vol. 4, no. 89. *Pennsylvania Gazette*, Jan. 19, 1748. John Swift to John White, Apr. 12, 1748, John Swift Letterbook, HSP. *Pennsylvania Gazette*, June 2, 1748. Labaree, *Papers of Benjamin Franklin*, 3:220–21. *Philadelphia Lottery Accounts* (Philadelphia, 1752). Full records for the first lottery have not survived.

23. The Treaty of Aix-la-Chapelle was finally signed in October 1748. The associators continued to muster through 1748, but by 1749 Franklin remembered that "peace being concluded the Association Business . . . [was] at an End." The association never fired a shot at an enemy attacker, but contemporaries believed that its very formation had convinced the privateers not to attack. Labaree, Ketcham, and Boatfield, *Autobiography of Benjamin Franklin*, 192. Richard Peters to Thomas Penn, June 13, 1748, MSS Penn Official Correspondence, HSP, vol. 4, nos. 95–97.

24. Franklin took employee David Hall into partnership on January 1, 1748, with the understanding that Hall would oversee the day-to-day running of the business. The partnership went into effect January 21, 1748, and lasted eighteen years. Labaree, Ketcham, and Boatfield, *Autobiography of Benjamin Franklin*, 195, quote on 181.

25. The members of the Board of Trustees of the College of Philadelphia were either elected or appointed by the subscribers. For a full analysis of the Academy and College of Philadelphia between 1749 and 1779, see Ann D. Gordon's excellent work, *The College of Philadelphia, 1749–1779: Impact of an Institution* (New York: Garland, 1989). On appointment of trustees, see p. 8.

All the other colonial colleges were explicitly tied to particular religious traditions. Harvard (1636), Yale (1701), and Dartmouth (1769) were Congregationalist. The College of William and Mary (1693) and King's College (now Columbia, 1754) aligned with the Church of England. The College of New Jersey (now Princeton, 1746) was Presbyterian. The College of Rhode Island (now Brown, 1764) was Baptist. Queen's College (now Rutgers, 1766) was Dutch Reformed.

26. Feb. 1, 1749/50, Journal A, Belonging to the Trustees of the Academy of Philadelphia, 1749–1764, University Archives and Records Center, University of Pennsylvania. Benjamin

Franklin to Jared Eliot, Feb. 13, 1750, in Labaree, *Papers of Benjamin Franklin*. *Pennsylvania Gazette*, May 17, 1750.

27. Benjamin Franklin, *Proposals Relating to the Education of Youth in Pennsylvania* (Philadelphia, 1749), 7. Richard Peters to Thomas Penn, July 24, Oct. 25, 1749, quoted in Gordon, *College of Philadelphia*, 26–27; The Library Company received its charter in 1742.

28. The trustees never openly approached Penn with a request for incorporation, but rather directed their queries through the personal letters of such trustees as Richard Peters. See Thomas Penn to James Hamilton, Feb. 12, 1750, and Benjamin Franklin to Samuel Johnson, Aug. 9, 1750, in Labaree, *Papers of Benjamin Franklin*, 4:5–6, 37–40. Gordon, *College of Philadelphia*, 28.

29. UPM. Journal A.

30. Labaree, Ketcham, and Boatfield, *Autobiography of Benjamin Franklin*, 200–201. On the ideal location of the hospital, see Pennsylvania Hospital Managers to Thomas Hyam and Silvanus Bevan, July 6, 1751, PHM.

31. At the end of his life Franklin remembered his "Use of Cunning" in beginning the hospital and confessed, "I do not remember any of my political Manoeuvers, the Success of which gave me at the time more Pleasure." Labaree, Ketcham, and Boatfield, *Autobiography of Benjamin Franklin*, 200–201. July 1, July 12, 1751, PHM. The Speaker noted that in fact the managers had raised no money—only subscriptions to the hospital, which amounted to promises to pay, not actual cash. He demanded that the managers get penal notes for all their subscriptions, which would amount to a legal obligation to pay the promised sum. Of course, in order to collect penal notes from subscribers, the hospital needed the legal status incorporation. The managers had collected the subscribers' notes by August 20, 1751, and at that time the Speaker ordered the first thousand pounds to be paid to them. The second thousand would be paid one year later. Aug. 1, Aug. 20, 1751, PHM.

32. "An Act for the Erecting Houses of Correction and Workhouses in the Respective Counties of this Province" (1718) and "An Act for Amending the Laws Relating to the Poor" (1749), *The Statutes at Large of Pennsylvania, From 1682 to 1801* (Pennsylvania, 1898), 3:167–71, 5:79–86. Gary B. Nash, *Quakers and Politics: Pennsylvania, 1681–1726* (1968; repr., Boston: Northeastern University Press, 1993), 18–23. Charter of the City of Philadelphia, 1701, in M. Carey and J. Bioren, eds., *Laws of the Commonwealth of Pennsylvania, 1700–1802* (Philadelphia, 1803), 6:15–20. Charter, 1701, Legal Papers, Box 1, William Penn Charter School Collection, Haverford College. *The Charter, Laws, and Catalogue of Books of the Library Company of Philadelphia* (Philadelphia, 1757). Ronald E. Seavoy, "The Public Service Origins of the American Business Corporation," *Business History Review* 52 (1978): 31–32.

33. Of the first twelve managers and treasurer, seven were Quaker, three Churchmen, one Presbyterian, one nonsectarian, and one unknown; July 2, 1751, PHM.

34. James Hamilton to Thomas Penn, July 5, 1751, and James Hamilton to Thomas Penn, June 19, 1752, in Thomas G. Morton, *The History of the Pennsylvania Hospital, 1751–1895* (Philadelphia, 1895), 13–15.

35. Though both Thomas and Richard were proprietors, Thomas held a greater share of the land and was much more active in directing policies in the province. He therefore dominated all affairs with the province. For the sake of simplicity, I will refer to him in the singular as "the" proprietor. This decision is borne out by the fact that even though all petitions made by the hospital were addressed to Richard as well as Thomas, the managers knew that Thomas was the one to convince and directed all their personal appeals and visits of

English supporters to him. Alan Tully, *William Penn's Legacy: Politics and Social Structure in Provincial Pennsylvania, 1726–1755* (Baltimore: Johns Hopkins University Press, 1977). Tully, *Forming American Politics*, 83, 145–51. James H. Hutson, *Pennsylvania Politics, 1746–1770: The Movement for Royal Government and Its Consequences* (Princeton, NJ: Princeton University Press, 1972), 6. G. B. Warden, "The Proprietary Group in Pennsylvania, 1754–1764," *WMQ* 21 (1964): 367–89.

36. List of Original Subscribers for the Philadelphia Dancing Assembly, Etting Mss. Large Misc. 9. 19. Etting Collection, HSP. Richard Peters to Thomas Penn, May 3, 1749, *PMHB* 34 (1910): 243–44. Thomas Willing Balch, *The Philadelphia Assemblies* (Philadelphia: Allen, Lane and Scott, 1916). Lynn Matluck Brooks, "Emblem of Gaiety, Love, and Legislation: Dance in Eighteenth-Century Philadelphia," *PMHB* 115 (1991): 63–87. Shippen Papers by Thomas Balch, 1855, vol. 2, HSP. Warden, "Proprietary Group in Pennsylvania," n372. The St. Andrew's Society claims to have been founded in 1747, but its earliest subscription list, rules, and other records all date to November 30, 1749. Minute Book of the St. Andrew's Society, 1749–76. Papers of the St. Andrew's Society of Philadelphia.

37. Robert Middlekauf describes Penn as "a mean and unbending man with a well-developed sense of his own interest." Robert Middlekauf, *Benjamin Franklin and His Enemies* (Berkeley: University of California Press, 1996), 109. Pennsylvania Hospital Managers to Thomas and Richard Penn, July 6, 1751, Pennsylvania Hospital Managers to Thomas Hyam and Silvanus Bevan, July 6, 1751, PHM. All the managers signed the petition except Richard Peters, the faithful partisan of the proprietors who was at the meeting but apparently disagreed with its contents. Peters did write a separate letter to the proprietors recommending the hospital.

38. Copy of Instructions from Proprietors to James Hamilton, entered in July 2, 1752, PHM.

39. June 4, 1752, PHM.

40. July 2, 1752, PHM.

41. Ibid.

42. Thomas Hyam and Silvanus Bevan to Managers of the Pennsylvania Hospital, Jan. 31, 1753. Inserted in PHM, May 5, 1753.

43. Apr. 10, 1753, UPM. The academy received its charter on July 13, 1753. See "Charter of the Academy of Philadelphia," July 13, 1753, in Labaree, *Papers of Benjamin Franklin*. 5:8–11.

44. Feb. 6, 1750, UPM. Gordon, *College of Philadelphia*, 17, 32. Benjamin Franklin to Samuel Johnson, Aug. 9, 1750, in Labaree, *Papers of Benjamin Franklin*. 4:39.

45. Gordon, *College of Philadelphia*, 30–31.

46. There were twenty-five trustees in 1756 when Smith circulated the petition to remove Quakers from government. William Smith to Thomas Penn, Apr. 10, 1755, William Smith to Thomas Penn, July 2, 1755, MSS Penn Official Correspondence, vol. 4, nos. 23 and 81, HSP. Charles J. Stillé, "The Attitudes of the Quakers during the Provincial Wars," *PMHB* 10 (1886): 294–97. Gordon, *College of Philadelphia*, 73–75. To put the weight of Norris's decision to resign in context, he was one of only five men (out of fifty who served before the college was reorganized in 1779) to step down; most served, at least nominally, until death.

47. For more on the 1756 militia, see chap. 6. *Pennsylvania Gazette*, Mar. 4, 1756. Gordon, *College of Philadelphia*, 79–88. Humphrey Scourge, "More Mild Advice," *Pennsylvania Journal*, June 17, 1756.

48. Benjamin Franklin, July 28, 1759, quoted in Labaree, Ketcham, and Boatfield, *Autobiography of Benjamin Franklin*, 196n. When Franklin wrote about the academy in his *Autobi-*

ography, he omitted any mention of his acrimonious departure from the board. But he always referred to the institution as "the Academy," not once as "the College," perhaps a conscious or subconscious wish to erase the college, and the events that ensued after its incorporation in 1755, from his history.

49. The non-Quaker population of Philadelphia suffered religious division on various fronts. The revivalism of the 1740s created schism among "Old Light" and "New Light" Presbyterians. Later, William Smith's machinations to create an American Church of England bishopric drove a wedge between Churchmen and Presbyterians. Warden, "Proprietary Group in Pennsylvania." Tully, *Forming American Politics*, 154.

50. "Scheme of the First Academy Lottery," Oct. 3, 1754, in Labaree, *Papers of Benjamin Franklin*, 435–37. "An Act for the More Effectual Suppressing and Preventing Lotteries" (1759), *Statutes at Large of Pennsylvania*, 5:445–49. Gordon, *College of Philadelphia*, 91–93. David J. Dove, *The Lottery. A Dialogue Between Mr. Thomas Trueman and Mr. Humphrey Dupe* (Germantown, 1758), 5.

51. University of Pennsylvania, Accounts, 1762–63, HSP. William Smith, Account Book, 1762–63, Rare Book & Ms Library Manuscripts, Van Pelt Library, University of Pennsylvania. Gordon, *College of Philadelphia*, 90–93, 95, 98–99.

52. *Some Account of the Pennsylvania Hospital; From its first Rise, to the Beginning of the Fifth Month, called May, 1754* (Philadelphia, 1754). *Continuation of the Account of the Pennsylvania Hospital . . .* (Philadelphia, 1761), 42. The managers learned of the proprietors' gift in May 1762. However, the actual title did not arrive until September 1765. May 17, 1762, Sept. 30, 1765, PHM.

53. May 17, 1762, PHM. "An ACT to encourage the Establishing of an HOSPITAL for the Relief of the Sick Poor of this Province, and for the Reception and Cure of Lunaticks," in *Some Account of the Pennsylvania Hospital* (Philadelphia, 1754).

Chapter 5 · Lending in Plain Sight

1. Ronald Kent Esplin, "Franklin's Colleagues and Their Club: The Junto in Philadelphia's Golden Age" (MA thesis, University of Virginia, 1970), 41–42. Nov. 24, 1753, PHM. Feb. 5, 1754, MPC. Maugridge was relatively good about paying his interest, but never repaid the principal. His executors made good the debt after his death in 1768. Mar. 25, 1769, TJPCA. See page 124.

2. William Allen to John Chiswell in Virginia, Oct. 2, 1754, William Allen to David Barclay & Sons, June 20, 1759, Feb. 9, Oct. 20, 1760, Sept. 11, Dec. 12, 1761, William Allen Letter Book, 1753–70, HSP.

3. Historians debate whether Parliament passed the Bubble Act in June 1720 to limit future damage, to enhance its own prestige and power, or to assist the South Sea Company by limiting competition. George Heberton Evans Jr., *British Corporation Finance, 1775–1850: A Study of Preference Shares* (Baltimore: Johns Hopkins University Press, 1936). John Micklethwait and Adrian Woolridge, *The Company: A Short History of a Revolutionary Idea* (New York: Modern Library, 2003), 31. Margaret Patterson and David Reiffen, "The Effect of the Bubble Act on the Market for Joint Stock Shares," *Journal of Economic History* 50, no. 1 (1990): 163–71. Sidney Homer and Richard Sylla, *A History of Interest Rates*, 4th ed. (New Jersey: John Wiley and Sons, 2005), 149–50. Quote from Micklethwait and Woolridge, *Company*, 32–33.

4. Shelley Burtt, *Virtue Transformed: Political Argument in England, 1688–1740* (Cambridge: Cambridge University Press, 1992), 67–86.

5. Theodore Thayer, "The Land-Bank System in the American Colonies," *Journal of Economic History* 13 (1953): 145–59. Joseph Albert Ernst, *Money and Politics in America, 1755–1775: A Study in the Currency Act of 1764 and the Political Economy of Revolution* (Chapel Hill: University of North Carolina Press, 1973), xvii.

6. Ernst, *Money and Politics in America*, 30. Oscar Handlin and Mary F. Handlin, "Origins of the American Business Corporation," *Journal of Economic History* 5 (1945): 6. Edwin J. Perkins, *American Public Financial Services, 1700–1815* (Columbus: Ohio State University Press, 1994), 203.

7. Wilbur C. Plummer, "Consumer Credit in Colonial Philadelphia," *PMHB* 66 (1942): 390–93, 398–99. Benjamin Franklin, "Will and Codicil," 1788, in *The Papers of Benjamin Franklin*, ed. Leonard W. Labaree, Franklin Papers Online.

8. Mary M. Schweitzer found that two-fifths of Chester County probates included outstanding loans. There were three major sources for small loans: older householders who were liquidating their real assets; legacies and dowries of orphans, widows, and wealthy women, which were put out at interest until needed; and intergenerational transfers of wealth within families. Mary M. Schweitzer, *Custom and Contract: Household, Government, and the Economy in Colonial Pennsylvania* (New York: Columbia University Press, 1987), 142–44, quote on 147. John J. McCusker and Russell R. Menard, *The Economy of British America, 1607–1789* (Chapel Hill: University of North Carolina Press, 1985), 335.

9. Schweitzer, *Custom and Contract*, 116. Thomas M. Doerflinger, *A Vigorous Spirit of Enterprise: Merchants and Economic Development in Revolutionary Philadelphia* (Chapel Hill: University of North Carolina Press, 1986), 127–28, 130, 18.

10. "An Act for the Emitting and Making Current Fifteen Thousand Pounds in Bills of Credit" (1722), *The Statutes at Large of Pennsylvania, From 1682 to 1801* (Pennsylvania, 1898), 3:324–38. James M. Duffin, comp., *Guide to the Mortgages of the General Loan Office of the Province of Pennsylvania, 1724–1756* (Yardley, PA: Genealogical Society of Pennsylvania, 1995). Schweitzer has found records for 3,111 loans, which she estimates represents four-fifths of the total. Schweitzer, *Custom and Contract*, 147. For more on the struggle over provincial financial matters, see page 136.

11. It seems likely that the Carpenters' Company was also making some limited loans (evidence exists for four loans totaling £188 in 1770), but as the documentation is extremely sparse, I am not including them here. See Memorandum Book . . . Concerning the Carpenters' Company's Interest and Buildings &cccc, Dilks Collection, HSP. Many fire company records are also missing. They too may have made small loans, but if they did, the amount loaned probably would not substantially alter the totals here.

12. Handlin and Handlin, "Origins of the American Business Corporation." Pauline Maier, "The Revolutionary Origins of the American Corporation," *WMQ*, 3rd ser., 50, no. 1 (Jan. 1993): 51–84. Simeon E. Baldwin, "American Business Corporations before 1789," *American Historical Review* 8, no. 3 (Apr. 1903): 449–65. Ronald E. Seavoy, "The Public Service Origins of the American Business Corporation," *Business History Review* 52, no. 1 (Spring 1978): 30–60.

13. Jan. 5, 1768, MPC, TJPCA.

14. Leonard W. Labaree, Ralph L. Ketcham, and Helen C. Boatfield, eds., *The Autobiography of Benjamin Franklin*, 2nd ed. (New Haven, CT: Yale University Press, 2003), 200–201. "An ACT to encourage the establishing of an Hospital for the Relief of the Sick Poor of this Province, and for the Reception and Cure of Lunaticks" (bound in with PHM).

15. June 2, 1762, Nov. 8, 1760, May 26, 1766, Oct. 19, 1772, Treasurer's Account, 1773, Treasurer's Account, 1774, PHM. On the Pennsylvania Land Company (related to the Free Society of Traders), see Gary B. Nash, *Quakers and Politics: Pennsylvania, 1681–1726* (1968; repr., Boston: Northeastern University Press, 1993), 21–22, 59, 73, 139–41. Most shareholders lived in Britain, not the colonies.

The hospital also got funds from some other sources. In 1763 the Commissioners to Pave Streets loaned the hospital £4,000 for one year with no interest. The hospital made £360 interest by loaning it out in the interim. The assemblymen also helped the hospital individually. Those men who might have collected a fee for signing all the newly printed Pennsylvania currency instead donated the money owed to them to the hospital. In at least one instance, this money helped the managers out of a tight spot with the impatient workmen building the hospital. July 26, Aug. 22, 1763, PHM. Hugh Roberts to Benjamin Franklin, June 1, 1758, in Labaree, *Papers of Benjamin Franklin*, 8:81–85.

16. This fund grew out of the preexisting Fund for Pious Uses (see pages 67–68). Charter for the Corporation for the Relief of Poor and Distressed Presbyterian Ministers and of the Poor and Distressed Widows and Children of Presbyterian Ministers, 1759, Pennsylvania Miscellaneous Papers, Penn & Baltimore, Penn Family, 1756–68, HSP, 70–73. John Baird, *Horn of Plenty: The Story of the Presbyterian Ministers' Fund* (Wheaton, IL: Tyndale House, 1982), 30–34.

17. UPM. Ann D. Gordon, *The College of Philadelphia: Impact of an Institution* (New York: Garland, 1989), 90–93, 95, 98–99.

18. "Deed of Settlement of the Philadelphia Contributionship," Mar. 25, 1752, in Labaree, *Papers of Benjamin Franklin*, 4:283–94. MPC.

19. Apr. 2, 1770, PHM.

20. Aug. 20, 1751, PHM.

21. *A True and Impartial State of the Province of Pennsylvania* (Philadelphia, 1759), 53; this author also points out that assemblymen earned only six shillings per day to serve in the legislature. Simeon J. Crowther, "Note," *WMQ*, 3rd ser., 29 (1972): 134–35. In my calculations of annual income, I assumed six days of labor per week. These numbers for wages come from the 1770s, a period of economic recession. Gary B. Nash, *The Urban Crucible: Social Change, Political Consciousness, and the Origins of the American Revolution* (Cambridge, MA: Harvard University Press, 1979), 323. J. A. Leo Lemay, *The Life of Benjamin Franklin* (Philadelphia: University of Pennsylvania Press, 2006), 2:567. "Table 6: Median Personal Wealth among Boston and Philadelphia Decedents, 1685–1775," in Nash, *Urban Crucible*, 399.

22. Doerflinger, *Vigorous Spirit of Enterprise*, 69. This kind of credit did not always originate in Britain. James Logan, for example, came to dominate the western fur trade by giving goods on credit to Indian traders, who quickly fell into his debt. By the mid-1720s, Eric Hinderaker has found, "many carried debts of between L.300 and L.650 apiece." Eric Hinderaker, *Elusive Empires: Constructing Colonialism in the Ohio Valley, 1673–1800* (Cambridge: Cambridge University Press, 1997), 23–25.

23. Doerflinger, *Vigorous Spirit of Enterprise*, 130. Craig W. Horle et al., eds., *Lawmaking and Legislators in Pennsylvania: A Biographical Dictionary* (Philadelphia: University of Pennsylvania Press, 1991–2005), 2:732, 3:880, 2:893. List of Debts due Reuben Haines in Huntington & Bedford County, n.d., Accounts, 1757–95, The Wyck Papers, ser. 4, APS.

24. The usury limit was set to 6% in 1722–23. See Schweitzer, *Custom and Contract*, 116. Doerflinger, *Vigorous Spirit of Enterprise*, 127–28, 130, 18.

25. Oct. 12, 1751, PHM. In fact, the funds came in quickly, and Greenleafe got his entire desired sum without much delay.

26. Aug. 19, 1763, DBCOP. June 3, 1771, PHM.

27. Oct. 12, Dec. 16, 1751, PHM. May 30, 1752, MPC.

28. Ironically, having convinced Bickley to take another £200, the hospital found that it did not have that sum on hand. It had to borrow £207 from Manager Israel Pemberton to make up the difference. July 30, Aug. 11, Aug. 28, 1759, Aug. 30, 1763, PHM. Richard Waln: Nov. 7, 1772, Jan. 1, Jan. 27, 1773, PHM. In most cases, the sources state the amount to be loaned with no explanation as to how it was agreed upon.

29. Apr. 9, 1770, PMFWB. Oct. 7, 1763, DBCOP.

30. Rouse was listed in Library Company records as a "smith," though it does not specify what kind of smith he was. 1761, Library Company Record Book A, Library Company of Philadelphia. Oct. 12, Dec. 16, 1751, Feb. 10, Aug. 6, Aug. 20, 1752, June 2, 1762, PHM. Like John Hughes, Williams also happened to be a baker.

31. Mar. 25, 1769, Mar. 1770, Mar. 1771, Mar. 1778, TJPCA.

32. Oct. 14, 1762, Oct. 14, 1765, July 3, 1767, PMFWB. The practice of transferring loans will be discussed in further detail below.

33. For an example of successful refinancing, see Mathew Ingram, June 1, 1774, PMFWB.

34. Quote from July 31, 1769, PHM. See PHM, PMFWB, and MPC.

35. Oct. 4, 1769, PHM. This practice remains typical today in foreclosure auctions.

36. May 22, 1761, Aug. 24, 1767, PMFWB. "Provincial Commissions," *Pennsylvania Archives*, ser. 3 (Harrisburg: Harrisburg Publishing, 1896), 9:197, 343. "Warrantees of Land in the County of Lancaster," *Pennsylvania Archives*, ser. 3, 24:401. William Beidelman, *The Story of the Pennsylvania Germans* (Pennsylvania, 1898), 92.

37. n.d., Corporation for the Relief of Widows and Children of Clergymen in the Communion of the Church of England in America, Correspondence, Financial Papers, Miscellaneous, HSP.

38. PMFWB. Oct. 12, 1776, Mar. 4, 1777, PHM.

39. June 24, 1771, May 10, 1773, LCPM. Organization treasurers were responsible for large sums of money and complicated transactions. Without bank accounts, all that money was physically in their possession, and it seems to have been understood that, as long as they replaced it when called for, they could use it in the interim for their own purposes. It seems to have been customary in neighboring New York and New Jersey for treasurers to pay interest on the money in their possession. Pennsylvania organizations never seem to have required interest of its treasurers, but most did require that treasurers post a bond for double the amount entrusted to their care. See, for example, Committee appointed to examine the Accounts of Jacob Le Roy, Sept. 23, 1785. Corporation for the Relief of Widows and Children of Clergymen in the Communion of the Church of England in America, Correspondence, Financial Papers, Miscellaneous, HSP.

40. Aug. 20, Oct. 3, 1751, PHM. For an interpretation of this act as a disinterested favor on Pemberton's part, see Thomas G. Morton, *The History of the Pennsylvania Hospital, 1751–1895* (Philadelphia, 1895), 27.

41. PHM, Journal A, PMFWB. Compare with the "insider lending" that Naomi R. Lamoreaux identifies as critical to New England banking in the first half of the nineteenth century. Naomi R. Lamoreaux, *Insider Lending: Banks, Personal Connections, and Economic Development in Industrial New England* (Cambridge: Cambridge University Press, 1994).

42. Labaree, Ketcham, and Boatfield, *Autobiography of Benjamin Franklin*, 117. It turned out that Franklin was wrong. Maugridge's loan was still outstanding when he died in 1766, and not until three years later did his executors finally pay it off. Nov. 24, 1753, PHM. Feb. 5, 1754, MPC. Mar. 25, 1769, TJPCA. As late as 1772, Franklin in England was still fretting "whether Mr. Maugridge's Executors have paid off his Mortgage to me, and that to the Insurance Office [Contributionship]." His relatives assured him the executors had. Benjamin Franklin to Deborah Franklin, Dec. 1, 1772, Richard Bache to Benjamin Franklin, Jan. 4, 1773, in Labaree, *Papers of Benjamin Franklin*.

43. *Pennsylvania Chronicle*, Mar. 12, 1770. Sept. 9, Oct. 28, Oct. 31, Nov. 3, Nov. 7, Nov. 30, Dec. 5, Dec. 31, 1772, Mar. 12, 1773, PHM. The hospital managers thought so highly of Parr and his advice that they even held at least one board meeting at his house, even though he was not himself a board member. Jan. 1, 1773, PHM.

44. "An Act the Better to Enable the Persons Therein Named to Hold Lands and Invest Them with the Privileges of Natural-born Subjects of this Province" (1763), *Statutes at Large of Pennsylvania*, 6:270–72. Feb. 19, Oct. 29, 1773, PHM. Mar. 1779, MPC.

45. Perkins, *American Public Financial Services*, 363. Jan. 1, 1773, PHM (italics added).

46. Mar. 27, June 15, 1759, Apr. 1, 1762, TJPCA.

47. Sept. 10, 1773, July 7, 1777, PMFWB.

48. Aug. 31, Oct. 5, 1767, Apr. 27, 1772, PHM. Dec. 1, 1767, Jan. 12, 1773, PMFWB.

49. Profession is known for 40% of male borrowers. "Professional men" includes physicians, ministers, and educators.

50. Esplin, "Franklin's Colleagues and Their Club," 41–42. I do not know for certain what Dickinson used his loan for—this is an educated hypothesis. On Dickinson's remodeling of Fairhill, see "John Dickason In acco.t with Isaac Coats," June 26, 1773, and "Bill of Carpenters Work in House of John Dickenson, by David Evans," n.d. (Dec. 3, 1774?), Logan Papers, vol. 30, Folder 57. Dickenson Estate, Repairs at Fairhill, HSP.

51. Nov. 7, 1772, Jan. 1, 1773, PHM. Richard Waln to Philip Harris, Nov. 30, 1772, May 19, 1773, Richard Waln Letterbook, 1766–94, HSP. Feb. 22, 1765, DBCOP. Insurance Policy, Apr. 18, 1767, James Gibson Papers, 1712–1846, Box 3, HSP. Jan. 30, Mar. 4, 1762, Journal A. Hinderaker, *Elusive Empires*, 41. On the other hand, perhaps Callender used the money to buy (speculate in?) land in Cumberland County in 1763, which he sold soon after in 1764. See "Articles of Agreement between Edward Ward and Robert Callender" (Nov. 1, 1763), in *Pennsylvania Archives*, ser. 3, 10:129–33. For more on Callendar, see Judith Ridner, *A Town In-Between: Carlisle, Pennsylvania, and the Early Mid-Atlantic Interior* (Philadelphia: University of Pennsylvania Press, 2010), 101–2, 109. Oct. 14, 1763, DBCOP. William Allen to Henry Crughar, Oct. 6, 1764, William Allen Letter Book, 1753–70, HSP.

52. Stephen Brobeck, "Changes in the Composition and Structure of Philadelphia Elite Groups, 1756–1790" (PhD diss., University of Pennsylvania, 1973), 102.

53. Feb. 5, Mar. 29, May 15, 1771, PMFWB.

54. Jan. 6, Apr. 8, 1766, Articles of the Sea Captains Club And Treasurers Account, 1765–77, HSP. July 9, Aug. 6, 1770, Alms House Manager's Minutes, 1766–78, Philadelphia City Archives. May 2, 1774, June 2, 1762, PHM. May 30, 1774, LCPM.

55. W. K. Jordan, *The Charities of London, 1480–1660: The Aspirations and Achievements of the Urban Society* (London: George Allen and Unwin, 1960), 26. I am grateful to Amanda Moniz for pointing out this source, and so many others, to me. Peter Clark, *British Clubs and Societies 1580–1800: The Origins of an Associational World* (Oxford: Clarendon Press, 2000), 260–61.

56. See, for example, Margery Somers Foster, *"Out of Smalle Beginnings . . .": An Economic History of Harvard College in the Puritan Period (1636–1712)* (Cambridge, MA: Belknap Press of Harvard University Press, 1962). Nicholas Michael Butler, *Votaries of Apollo: The St. Cecilia Society and the Patronage of Concert Music in Charleston, South Carolina, 1766–1820* (Columbia: University of South Carolina Press, 2007).

Chapter 6 · Private Men Interfering with Government

1. Nicholas Scull and George Heap, "An East Prospect of the City of Philadelphia," 1756, in *Historic Philadelphia: From the Founding until the Early Nineteenth Century*, ed. Luther P. Eisenhart (Philadelphia: American Philosophical Society, 1953). Steeple Subscriptions, 1751, United Churches of Christ Church and St. Peters Records, vol. 4. HSP. Quaker meetinghouses, of course, did not have steeples.

2. "Journal of William Black," *PMHB* 1 (1877): 411–12. Sept. 4, Oct. 9, 1774, L. H. Butterfield, ed., *Diary and Autobiography of John Adams* (Cambridge, MA: Belknap Press, 1961), 2:122, 150.

3. Alan Tully, *Forming American Politics: Ideals, Interests, and Institutions in Colonial New York and Pennsylvania* (Baltimore: Johns Hopkins University Press, 1994). Mary M. Schweitzer, *Custom and Contract: Household, Government, and the Economy in Colonial Pennsylvania* (New York: Columbia University Press, 1987).

4. James Logan to Benjamin Franklin, Dec. 3, 1747, in *The Papers of Benjamin Franklin*, ed. Leonard W. Labaree (New Haven, CT: Yale University Press, 1961), 3:219. Tully, *Forming American Politics*, 257–58, 300; Jane E. Calvert, *Quaker Constitutionalism and the Political Thought of John Dickinson* (Cambridge: Cambridge University Press, 2009), 55. John Smolenski, *Friends and Strangers: The Making of a Creole Culture in Colonial Pennsylvania* (Philadelphia: University of Pennsylvania Press, 2010), 65.

5. J. G. A. Pocock, *The Machiavellian Moment: Florentine Political Thought and the Atlantic Republican Tradition* (Princeton, NJ: Princeton University Press, 1975). John W. Shy, "A New Look at Colonial Militia," *WMQ*, 3rd ser., 20 (1963): 175–85. Saul Cornell, "Beyond the Myth of Consensus: The Struggle to Define the Right to Bear Arms in the Early Republic," in *Beyond the Founders: New Approaches to the Political History of the Early Republic*, ed. Jeffrey L. Pasley, Andrew W. Robertson, and David Waldstreicher (Chapel Hill: University of North Carolina Press, 2004), 251–73. Alan Tully has suggested that the absence of compulsory militia service was a central element of the attractive "civil Quakerism" that dominated Pennsylvania government throughout the eighteenth century. Tully, *Forming American Politics*, 257–58, 292–95. Each time Pennsylvanians organized militias, at least some Quakers joined and were subsequently disowned by the Society of Friends.

6. Benjamin Franklin, *Plain Truth: Or, Serious Considerations on the Present State of the City of PHILADELPHIA and Province of PENNSYLVANIA* (Philadelphia, 1747). 15. Nathan Ross Kozuskanich, " 'For the Security and Protection of the Community': The Frontier and the Makings of Pennsylvania Constitutionalism" (PhD diss., Ohio State University, 2005).

7. Smolenski, *Friends and Strangers*, 189. Gary B. Nash, *Quakers and Politics: Pennsylvania, 1681–1726* (1968; repr., Boston: Northeastern University Press, 1993). Tully, *Forming American Politics*.

8. Fred Anderson and Andrew Cayton argue that Pennsylvania's policies of "peaceable imperialism" from 1682 to the middle of the eighteenth century contained the seeds of its own destruction. Fred Anderson and Andrew Cayton, *The Dominion of War: Empire and Liberty*

in North America, 1500–2000 (New York: Viking, 2005), 56–103. For more on Governor Evans and his attempted militia, see chap. 2.

9. Peter Silver, *Our Savage Neighbors: How Indian War Transformed Early America* (New York: W. W. Norton, 2008), 40–45. Penn insisted that the assembly share with him control over all appropriations and exempt the extensive lands owned by the proprietary family from any tax levies. The assembly defended its long-held legislative prerogative and refused to comply on either point. Tully, *Forming American Politics*, 109–10, 149–50.

10. Robert Hunter Morris to General Braddock, June 4, 1755, MSS Penn Official Correspondence, vol. 4, no. 47, HSP.

11. "An ACT for the better Ordering and Regulating such as are willing and desirous to be united for Military Purposes within this Province" (1755), *The Statutes at Large of Pennsylvania, From 1682 to 1801* (Pennsylvania, 1898), 5:197–201.

12. Robert Hunter Morris to Sir Charles Hardy, Nov. 27, 1755, *Pennsylvania Archives* (Philadelphia, 1853), ser. 1, 2:526. Richard Peters to Thomas Penn, Feb. 17, 1756. *Pennsylvania Gazette*, Dec. 18, Dec. 25, 1755, Mar. 4, Mar. 25, 1756. *Pennsylvania Journal*, Mar. 11, 1756.

13. Critics also argued that the degree of self-determination accorded the militia volunteers was dangerous. "Representation of Citizens to the Assembly," *Pennsylvania Journal*, Nov. 20, 1755, Mar. 11, 1756. William Peters to Thomas Penn, Jan. 4, 1756, MSS Penn Official Correspondence, vol. 8, no. 3, HSP. William Peters to Thomas Penn, Dec. 24, 1755, MSS Penn Official Correspondence, vol. 4, no. 201, HSP. William Smith, *A Brief State of the Province of Pennsylvania . . .* (London, 1755). Tully, *Forming American Politics*, 107.

14. *Pennsylvania Gazette*, Jan. 1, 1756. *The happiness of rewarding the enemies of our religion and liberty, represented, in a sermon preached in Philadelphia, Feb. 17, 1756, to Captain Vanderspiegel's independent company of volunteers, at the request of their officers* (Philadelphia, 1756), 28, 27. *Pennsylvania Journal*, Mar. 11, 1756. *Pennsylvania Gazette*, Mar. 25, 1756. Certified Election Returns for Militia Officers, Apr. 2, 1756, Conarroe Papers, vol. 10, p. 61, HSP.

15. *Pennsylvania Gazette*, Mar. 4, 1756. *Pennsylvania Journal*, Mar. 11, 1756.

16. James Munro et al., eds., *Acts of the Privy Council of England. Colonial Series*, vol. 4, *A.D. 1745–1766* (Hereford: Hereford Times, 1911), 337–39. William Allen to Rev. Dr. Chandler, Feb. 4, 1758, MSS Penn Official Correspondence, vol. 9, no. 5, p. 57, HSP. After 1757 the governor commissioned officers to lead paid provincial enlistees, serving for short periods of time and subject to British rules of discipline. Tully, *Forming American Politics*, 293.

17. For a full discussion of rhetoric asserting the potential treason of Quakers, see Silver, *Our Savage Neighbors*.

18. Historians of the Friendly Association have examined the organization in isolation. They have analyzed it within the context of Quaker culture, religion, and political concerns, seeing it as a radical solution by Pennsylvania Quakers to their new status outside the mainstream of government and an important step toward the activism of postrevolutionary Quakers over slavery and other matters. This approach elides the context out of which the Friendly Association arose. In many ways, the Quaker-dominated group seems diametrically opposed to the Defense Association and the Independent Companies, but in the essential strategy of mobilizing a partial or minority constituency to assume responsibility for activities normally belonging to the state, it built on the work of the extralegal militias. Richard Bauman, *For the Reputation of Truth: Politics, Religion, and Conflict among the Pennsylvania Quakers, 1750–1800* (Baltimore: Johns Hopkins University Press, 1971), 77–101. Peter Silver compares the Friendly Association to ethnic societies. Silver, *Our Savage Neighbors*, 100–101.

19. "An Epistle of tender Love & Caution to Friends in Pennsylvania," Dec. 16, 1755, Jan. 30, Apr. 30, 1756, PFMQM. Sydney V. James, *A People among Peoples: Quaker Benevolence in Eighteenth-Century America* (Cambridge, MA: Harvard University Press, 1963), 142, 145. Nash, *Quakers and Politics*, 98. On the spiritual reformers, or Quaker reformation, see Jack D. Marietta, *The Reformation of American Quakerism, 1748–1783* (Philadelphia: University of Pennsylvania Press, 1984). Bauman, *For the Reputation of Truth*.

20. Apr. 30, 1756, PFMQM. James, *People among Peoples*, 143. After the deal was brokered in England allowing Quakers to remain in government, English Quakers set out for Pennsylvania to convince their brethren to leave office. They arrived to find that reform-minded Quakers had already independently convinced most to leave office. A few Quakers, including Speaker of the House, Isaac Norris, refused to resign despite the repeated calls of their brethren that they do so. In punishment, they were barred from participating in the governance or financial running of the society, though not outright disowned.

21. For the primary attack on Quaker governance, see William Smith, *A Brief State of the Province of Pennsylvania* . . . (London, 1755). Tully, *Forming American Politics*, 113. Marietta, *Reformation of American Quakerism*, 156–58, 161.

22. Though the soon-to-be-founded Friendly Association operated independently of the Society of Friends, it enjoyed its support particularly from the Meeting for Sufferings of Philadelphia and London. Its leadership and rank and file had close ties to the hierarchy of the society. The Friendly Association, moreover, sent copies of its minutes to well-connected Friends in London. Nov. 20, 1756, Dec. 3, 1757, MFA. Jan. 1, 1756, PFMQM. "The Testimony of the Monthly Meeting of Friends," *Pennsylvania Gazette*, Jan. 1, 1756. James, *People among Peoples*, 177–79.

23. As high-minded as some Quakers' motives were in pursuing negotiations with Indians, other concerns also had weight for some, particularly for merchants involved in the fur trade. James H. Merrell, *Into the American Woods: Negotiators on the Pennsylvania Frontier* (New York: W. W. Norton, 1999), 267.

24. MFA, 2, 5–11.

25. Address to Robert Hunter Morris, Apr. 12, 1756, Address to Provincial Assembly, Apr. 12, 1756, MFA. Richard Peters to Thomas Penn, Apr. 25, 1756, Richard Peters to Thomas Penn, Apr. 30, 1756, MSS Penn Official Correspondence, vol. 8, nos. 71–75, 83, HSP.

26. July 19, July 22, 1756, MFA. It appears they spent 10% of those funds on presents. £120 was hardly a "small" present, as Pemberton represented it. Richard Peters to Thomas Penn, Aug. 4, 1756, MSS Penn Official Correspondence, vol. 8, nos. 133–39, HSP.

27. July 25, July 26, July 27, July 30, 1756, "A List of Goods presented to the Indians at the First Treaty at the Expence of the People called Quakers," July 31, 1756, MFA. Richard Peters to Thomas Penn, Aug. 4, 1756, MSS Penn Official Correspondence, vol. 8, nos. 133–39, HSP.

28. Once back in Philadelphia, the Quakers began diligently investigating through provincial records to check the validity of the claims made by the Delawares at the conference about former treaties. Proprietary supporters worked just as diligently to hinder their efforts and keep records from them. "Observations," in Paul A. W. Wallace, *Conrad Weiser, 1696–1760: Friend of Colonist and Mohawk* (Philadelphia: University of Pennsylvania Press, 1945), 461–62. Nov. 2, Nov. 19, Nov. 20, 1756, MFA. Richard Peters to Thomas Penn, Nov. 22, 1756, MSS Penn Official Correspondence, vol. 8, nos. 201–5, HSP. Jan. 4, Jan. 23, 1757, MFA. For a discussion of the "Walking Purchase" of 1737, which had defrauded the Delawares

of their land, see Fred Anderson, *Crucible of War: The Seven Years' War and the Fate of Empire in British North America, 1754–1766* (New York: Alfred A. Knopf, 2000), 205–7.

29. Oct. 28, Nov. 2, Nov. 3, 1756, Dec. 1, 1757, MFA. Israel Pemberton Jr. to Mary Pemberton, Nov. 10, 1756, Pemberton Papers, vol. 11, p. 140, HSP.

30. The Friendly Association documents have conflicting language about the requirement that an officer be in unity with the Quakers and have contributed at least £10. In the minutes for December 1, 1756, the rule applied to the "person [who] shall be chosen a Trustee." MFA. In a separate document, "To the General Meeting . . . ," the rule applied instead to the "person [who] shall be chosen a Treasurer." HSP. Call # Ap. 877. In fact, the trustees and treasurer had already been chosen the previous month, before this rule was adopted. Nov. 2, 1756, MFA.

31. Dec. 1, 1756, MFA.

32. Jan. 8, Apr. 5, Apr. 19, 1757, MFA. The assembly had repaid its loan by 1759. Croghan's loan was repaid much more quickly, by July 1757. It is unclear whether the association charged interest, but I think not. July 5, 1757, MFA. Apr. 19, 1759, Friendly Association Papers (Under Pemberton), Parrish Collection, HSP.

Money was in short supply that winter in all government branches. Richard Peters complained to the Penns that the governor had no cash on hand, and that he, Peters, had had to advance money for public projects. Richard Peters to Thomas Penn, Jan. 10, 1757, MSS Penn Official Correspondence, vol. 8, no. 219, HSP.

33. July 11, July 15, 1757, MFA.

34. July 14, July 15, 1757, MFA.

35. Israel Pemberton Jr. to Mary Pemberton, July 21, 1757, Pemberton Papers, vol. 12, p. 46, HSP. "Extract from Colonel Weiser's Journal," in Wallace, *Conrad Weiser*, 479. July 23, 1757, Minutes of Council held at Easton, Penn Papers, Indian Affairs, vol. 3, p. 20, HSP. George Croghan to Richard Peters, Aug. 18, 1757, MSS Penn Official Correspondence, vol. 8, no. 271, HSP. Israel Pemberton Jr. to Joseph Morris, July 30, 1757, Pemberton Papers, vol. 12, p. 50, HSP. George Croghan to Richard Peters, Aug. 18, 1757, MSS Penn Official Correspondence, vol. 8, no. 271, HSP. William Johnson to William Denny, Sept. 13, 1757, Penn Papers, Indian Affairs, vol. 3, p. 25, HSP. On treaty proceedings, see Merrell, *Into the American Woods*, 253–89.

36. See, for example, 1757–58 and Mar. 25, Apr. 4, 1758, MFA. Friendly Association Papers (Under Pemberton), Parrish Collection, HSP. Anderson, *Crucible of War*, 275–79. James, *People among Peoples*, 187–88, 190–91.

37. Anderson, *Crucible of War*, 275–79, 531. James, *People among Peoples*, 187–88, 190–91.

38. Apr. 19, 1757, MFA. William Allen to Thomas Penn, Feb. 7, 1758, MSS Penn Official Correspondence, vol. 9, no. 9, HSP. "Address of the Trustees & Treasurer of the Friendly Association," Mar. 20, 1760, Penn Papers, Indian Affairs, vol. 3, p. 89, HSP.

39. Mar. 20, 1760, Penn Papers, Indian Affairs, vol. 3, p. 89, HSP. In addition, by stressing that the cause of Indian violence on the frontier came from the fraudulent actions of the proprietors and their servants, the association attempted to shift blame away from Quakers and their former rule in the assembly. According to the Friendly Association, the underhanded dealings of the proprietor and his minions had caused the Indian attacks. The assembly's reticence to take defensive measures was in this version not to blame for the situation on the frontier.

40. In fact, Quakers did donate substantially to the recovery of white captives and to the victims of frontier violence, but their work in Indian diplomacy superseded such efforts in

reality and in public perception. On attacks against Quakers and the Friendly Association, see Silver, *Our Savage Neighbors*; and Benjamin Bankhurst, "A Looking-Glass for Presbyterians: Recasting a Prejudice in Late Colonial Pennsylvania," *PMHB* 133 (2009): 317–48.

41. "Account of the march of the Paxton Boys against Philadelphia in the year 1764. Extracted and Translated from the Journals of the Rev. Henry Melchior Muhlenberg, D.D. . . . by Hiester H. Muhlenberg, M.D., of Reading Pennsylvania," in *Collections of the Historical Society of Pennsylvania*, vol. 1 (Philadelphia, 1853), 74. Silver, *Our Savage Enemies*. Kevin Kenny, *Peaceable Kingdom Lost: The Paxton Boys and the Destruction of William Penn's Holy Experiment* (Oxford: Oxford University Press, 2009).

42. *Pennsylvania Gazette*, Feb. 9, 1764. Letter relating to the Paxton Boys, Feb. 29, 1764, in *Hazard's Register of Pennsylvania*, ed. Samuel Hazard (Philadelphia, 1833), 12:9–13. Col. Shippen to James Burd, Feb. 9, 1764, in *Letters and Papers Relating Chiefly to the Provincial History of Pennsylvania*, ed. Thomas Willing Balch (Philadelphia, 1855), 204. Benjamin Franklin to Richard Jackson, Feb. 11, 1764, in Labaree, *Papers of Benjamin Franklin*, Franklin Papers Online. Kenny, *Peaceable Kingdom*, 151–52.

43. Gary B. Nash, "Poverty and Poor Relief in Pre-Revolutionary Philadelphia," *WMQ*, 3rd ser., 33, no. 1 (Jan. 1976): 12–13. For more on poor relief in the early eighteenth century, see chap. 3.

The St. Andrews Society distributed over £1,300 between 1750 and 1775 in response to 591 successful applications. This figure does not account for repeat applicants. Each individual has been counted once per year (even if he or she made repeat applications in that year), but may be repeated if he or she applied over more than one year. On average the St. Andrew's Society gave £52 per year to an average of twenty-two Scottish men and women. The records of the charity committee indicate that it did not generally inquire too closely into individuals' personal lives, which is to say that there was little investigation of whether petitioners were "industrious" or "idle" poor. It gave Mary Agnew, for example, ten shillings in 1751, "tho' of an undeserving Character." Whenever petitioners were found to be eligible for public assistance, however, the society generally rejected their claims and told them to go to the appropriate authorities. Minute Book of the St. Andrew's Society, 1749–76, Papers of the St. Andrew's Society of Philadelphia, quote from Dec. 18, 1751.

44. "An Act for Amending the Laws Relating to the Poor" (1749), *Statutes at Large of Pennsylvania*, 5:79–86. Jan. 6, 1764. Votes, 7:5506. Nash, "Poverty and Poor Relief," 13–14.

45. Minutes, 1762, Wharton-Willing Papers, Box 1, Folder 1762. Gary B. Nash calls this group the Committee to Alleviate the Miseries of the Poor. Nash, "Poverty and Poor Relief." John K. Alexander, *Render Them Submissive: Responses to Poverty in Philadelphia, 1760–1800* (Amherst: University of Massachusetts Press, 1980), 86–102.

46. "An Act for the Better Employment, Relief and Support of the Poor Within the City of Philadelphia, the District of Southwark, the Townships of Moyamensing and Passyunk and the Northern Liberties" (1766), *Statutes at Large of Pennsylvania*, 7:9–17.

47. Ibid. Some reformers in England had advocated that private corporations take over workhouses, but economic theorists advocated doing away with workhouses entirely and relying on "outdoor" poor relief. A. W. Coats, "Economic Thought and Poor Law Policy in the Eighteenth Century," *Economic History Review*, new ser., 13, no. 1 (1960): 46, 50. For a full discussion of establishing which jurisdiction held responsibility for an individual's poor relief and the complicated system for removing the poor, see Ruth Wallis Herndon, *Unwelcome*

Americans: Living on the Margin in Early New England (Philadelphia: University of Pennsylvania Press, 2001).

48. "An Act for the Better Employment, Relief and Support of the Poor," *Statutes at Large of Pennsylvania*, 7:9–17. May 26, 1766, AHMM. On Philadelphia's reaction to the Stamp Act, see James H. Hutson, *Pennsylvania Politics, 1746–1770: The Movement for Royal Government and Its Consequences* (Princeton, NJ: Princeton University Press, 1972), 180–213. Richard Alan Ryerson, *The Revolution Is Now Begun: The Radical Committees of Philadelphia, 1765–1776* (Philadelphia: University of Pennsylvania Press, 1978), 26–27.

49. "An Act to Amend the Act Entitled 'An Act for the Better Employment, Relief and Support of the Poor' " (1768), *Statutes at Large of Pennsylvania*, 7:159–61, 310, 8:75–96.

50. June 22, June 23, July 13, 1769, Overseers of Poor Minutes, 1768–74. The managers of the contributorship sought some kind of reconciliation, but failed. Sept. 6, 1769, AHMM. Aug. 27, Oct. 4, 1774, *MCC*.

51. *Votes*, 7:6097–99. Feb. 17, 1767, Society Miscellaneous Collection, Box 7a, Folder 1, HSP.

52. *Pennsylvania Gazette*, Jan. 9, 1772. Nash, "Poverty and Poor Relief," 20. The tax was assessed at the rate of three pence to every pound of assessable wealth.

53. "An Act for the Better Employment, Relief and Support of the Poor," "An Act to Enable the Managers of the Contributors for the Relief and Employment of the Poor . . . to Borrow the Further Sum of Three Thousand Pounds, 1767," "An Act to Enable the Managers of the Contributions for the Relief and Employment of the Poor . . . To Raise the Sum of Fourteen Thousand Pounds in Bills of Credit Towards Discharging Their Debts, and To Provide a Fund for Redeeming and Sinking the Said Bills" (1769), *Statutes at Large of Pennsylvania*, 7:143–45, 197–204.

54. *Pennsylvania Gazette*, Jan. 25, 1770. Nov. 3, 1775, AHMM.

55. Nov. 3, 1775, AHMM.

56. Voters in the city of Philadelphia could vote for two assembly representatives; voters in the surrounding townships voted for eight to represent Philadelphia County.

57. Alexander, *Render Them Submissive*, 72–73.

58. Though the legislature no longer included strict Quakers after 1756, it remained in the hands of more secular Quakers and men sympathetic to the aims of the so-called Quaker party. The Philadelphia Corporation, unlike the Overseers of the Poor themselves, voiced no complaints about the change in poor relief and indeed made an early interest-free loan to the contributorship. When the managers were unable to repay the loan, however, the corporation threatened legal action, a move probably prevented only by the disruption of war, because the contributorship had no money to repay debts of any kind. The corporation also continued to assist the overseers to circumvent the contributorship where it could, for example, allowing them to collect firewood from city property to distribute directly to the needy. Jan. 22, 1767, Oct. 6, 1772, Jan. 29, May 1, 1773, Aug. 27, Oct. 4, 1774, *MCC*.

Chapter 7 · Mars Ascendant

1. Jacob Duche, *Observations on a Variety of Subjects* (Philadelphia, 1774), 7–9. Feb. 8, 1775, *Minutes of the Common Council of the City of Philadelphia, 1704–1776* (Philadelphia, 1847), 803. George Cuthbert to Lieutenant-Governor John Dalling of Jamaica, 1775, *PMHB* 61 (1942): 206. Christopher Marshall to Thomas Lowndy, Oct. 12, 1773, Christopher Mar-

shall Letterbook, 1773–78, HSP. "Journal of Josiah Quincy, Junior, 1773," *Proceedings of the Massachusetts Historical Society* 49 (1915–16): 477. Sept. 23, 1774, John Adams Diary, Adams Family Papers, An Electronic Archive, Massachusetts Historical Society. Gary Nash, *The Urban Crucible: Social Change, Political Consciousness, and the Origins of the American Revolution* (Cambridge, MA: Harvard University Press, 1979), 314, 407–8.

2. Sept. 5, Sept. 12, Sept. 17, Sept. 26, Oct. 9, Oct. 14, Oct. 27, 1774, John Adams Diary. Aug. 31, 1774, LCPM. William Bradford to James Madison, Oct. 17, 1774, in *The Papers of James Madison*, ed. William T. Hutchinson and William M. E. Rachal (Chicago: University of Chicago Press, 1962), 1:125.

3. John Adams to Abigail Adams, June 10, 1775, Adams Family Papers, An Electronic Archive, Massachusetts Historical Society.

4. Eric Foner, *Tom Paine and Revolutionary America* (London: Oxford University Press, 1976), 64. Steven Rosswurm, *Arms, Country, and Class: The Philadelphia Militia and "Lower Sort" during the American Revolution, 1775–1783* (New Brunswick, NJ: Rutgers University Press, 1987), 71–72. See also Charles S. Olton, *Artisans for Independence: Philadelphia Mechanics and the American Revolution* (New York: Syracuse University Press, 1975). Richard Alan Ryerson, *The Revolution Is Now Begun: The Radical Committees of Philadelphia, 1765–1776* (Philadelphia: University of Pennsylvania Press, 1978).

5. Rosswurm also identifies this important rhetorical shift but does not recognize its roots in previous extralegal military organization. Rosswurm, *Arms, Country, and Class*, 77.

6. John Penn to H. M. Principal Secretaries of State, Feb. 19, 1766, *Pennsylvania Archives*, ser. 4, 3:311–13. Thomas Coombe Jr. to Thomas Coombe Sr., Nov. 1, 1769, Coomb Papers, Folder 17, HSP. Nash, *Urban Crucible*, 305–7. "Journal of Josiah Quincy, Junior, 1773," 478. Edmund S. Morgan and Helen M. Morgan, *The Stamp Act Crisis* (Chapel Hill: University of North Carolina Press, 1953), 202n72. Ryerson, *Revolution Is Now Begun*, 7, 19–22, 25–38. Rosswurm, *Arms, Country, and Class*, 31. For an account of artisans protecting stamp collector John Hughes's and Benjamin Franklin's houses, see James H. Hutson, "An Investigation of the Inarticulate: Philadelphia's White Oaks," *WMQ*, 3rd ser., 28 (1971): 3–25. Philadelphia did contribute to the rhetorical protest against British taxation through John Dickinson's celebrated *Letters from a Pennsylvania Farmer*, published in the *Pennsylvania Chronicle* in 1767.

7. James H. Hutson, *Pennsylvania Politics, 1746–1770: The Movement for Royal Government and Its Consequences* (Princeton, NJ: Princeton University Press, 1972), 194, 210. Subsequent historians have largely accepted Hutson's argument. See Ryerson, *Revolution Is Now Begun*, 21–22. Nash, *Urban Crucible*, 307–8. Alan Tully, *Forming American Politics: Ideals, Interests, and Institutions in Colonial New York and Pennsylvania* (Baltimore: Johns Hopkins University Press, 1994), 200.

8. By contrast, often scholarship seems to see party politics as controlling Philadelphia politics generally. See, for example, Benjamin L. Carp, *Rebels Rising: Cities and the American Revolution* (Oxford: Oxford University Press, 2007), 190. Steven Rosswurm, who otherwise highlights the independent motive and actions of the "lower sorts," sees them as "subordinate" and generally divorced from the activism of the 1760s. Indeed, they had "little control over their lives" and were held in the thrall of social and political deference until the events of the 1770s. Rosswurm, *Arms, Country, and Class*, 38–42. For the evolution and importance of partisanship to Pennsylvania politics, see Tully, *Forming American Politics*. On Americans' feelings about the monarchy, see Brendan McConville, *The King's Three Faces: The Rise and Fall of Royal America, 1688–1776* (Chapel Hill: University of North Carolina Press, 2006).

9. Deborah Franklin to Benjamin Franklin, Sept. 22, 1765, Deborah Franklin to Benjamin Franklin, Oct. 8, 1765, Samuel Wharton to Benjamin Franklin, Oct. 13, 1765, in *The Papers of Benjamin Franklin*, ed. Leonard W. Labaree, Franklin Papers Online. John Hughes to Governor John Penn, Oct. 8, 1765, John Hughes to John Swift, Alexander Barclay, and Thomas Graeme, Nov. 5, 1765. Mss. Relating to the Non-Importation Resolutions, 1765–66, APS. Hutson, "Investigation of the Inarticulate," 20.

10. John Hughes to Governor John Penn, Oct. 8, 1765. Mss. Relating to the Non-Importation Resolutions, 1765–66, APS. *Pennsylvania Gazette*, Nov. 21, 1765. Jan. 2, 1766, John Adams Diary. Hutson, "Investigation of the Inarticulate." Jesse Lemisch and John K. Alexander, "White Oaks, Jack Tar, and the Concept of the 'Inarticulate,'" *WMQ*, 3rd ser., 29 (1972): 109–42.

11. Hutson, "Investigation of the Inarticulate." Nash, *Urban Crucible*, 306.

12. Ryerson, *Revolution Is Now Begun*. Nash, *Urban Crucible*. Foner, *Tom Paine and Revolutionary America*. Rosswum, *Arms, Country, and Class*.

13. George Cuthbert to Lieutenant-Governor John Dalling of Jamaica, 1775, *PMHB* 61 (1942): 206. The best and most detailed description of the gradual process whereby a new group of leaders came to dominate Pennsylvania politics can be found in Ryerson, *Revolution Is Now Begun*.

14. These numbers, moreover, rely on incomplete membership rosters for numerous voluntary organizations. The totals would probably go up, for example, if we knew more about the membership of all the fire companies or the earlier voluntary militias.

15. On the description of revolutionary leaders as "new men," see note 6 and Ryerson, *Revolution Is Now Begun*, 4. For membership in Philadelphia committees, see ibid., 275–81. In calculating the number of organizations to which a man belonged, I only counted library membership once if a man belonged to one of the library companies (Association, Amicable, and Union), which by 1769 had merged into the Library Company of Philadelphia. For the sources on voluntary association membership, see Jessica Choppin Roney, "'First Movers in Every Useful Undertaking': Voluntary Associations in Philadelphia, 1725–1775" (PhD diss., Johns Hopkins University, 2009).

16. T. H. Breen, *The Marketplace of the Revolution: How Consumer Politics Shaped American Independence* (Oxford: Oxford University Press, 2004). Ryerson, *Revolution Is Now Begun*, 33–34, 38. "Plan of an American Manufactory," in *American Archives*, ed. Peter Force (Washington, DC, 1839), 4th ser., 1:1256, 2:140–44. *Pennsylvania Gazette*, Mar. 15, Mar. 22, 1775. Christopher Marshall to T——n— P——e, Apr. 9, 1775, Christopher Marshall Letterbook, 1773–78, HSP.

17. William Bradford to James Madison, Jan. 4, Mar. 3–6, 1775, in Hutchinson and Rachal, *Papers of James Madison*, 1:131–32, 138–39. Thomas Pryor to Thomas Mifflin, Apr. 13, 1775, Papers of Jonathan Potts, vol. 1, p. 46, HSP. Christopher Marshall to William Marshall, Nov. 17, 1774, Christopher Marshall Letterbook. Ryerson, *Revolution Is Now Begun*.

18. George Cuthbert to Lieutenant-Governor John Dalling of Jamaica, 1775, *PMHB* 61 (1942): 207.

19. Ibid. *Pennsylvania Evening Post*, May 2, 1775. Apr. 25, May 7, 1775, *Extracts from the Diary of Christopher Marshall . . . during the American Revolution, 1774–1781* (Albany, 1877), 17, 23. Apr. 24, 1775, John Pemberton to Henry Drinker, Pemberton Papers, Box 1, HSP. Carp, *Rebels Rising*, 172–212. The assembly allocated a fraction of the money requested. Votes, 8:7230, 7233–34. The population of Philadelphia in 1775 was 24,180. Assuming an average household of six people, one in six residents was an adult male. Nash, *Urban Crucible*, 407–8.

20. At least three hundred Quakers joined the militia. Christopher Marshall to Peter Barker, June 24, 1775, Christopher Marshall Letterbook, 1773–78, HSP. May 1, May 3, May 4, 1775, *Extracts from the Diary of Christopher Marshall*, 17, 22. *Pennsylvania Evening Post*, May 2, 1775. Proposals for a Militia, n.d., Franklin MSS, vol. 5, pp. 31–34, HSP. Oct. 14, 1775, James Allen Diary, 1770–78, HSP. Eliphalet Dyer to Joseph Trumbull, May 18, 1775, in *Letters of Delegates to Congress*, ed. Paul H. Smith et al. (Washington, DC, 1976–), 1:356–57. Ryerson, *Revolution Is Now Begun*, 119–21. Rosswurm, *Arms, Country, and Class*, 50–51. William Bradford to James Madison, June 2, 1775, in Hutchinson and Rachal, *Papers of James Madison*, 1:149. In 1747 Franklin had remarked on the "surpizing unanimity in all ranks." Benjamin Franklin to James Logan, Dec. 7, 1747, in Labaree, *Papers of Benjamin Franklin*, 3:224–25.

21. "To the associators of the city of Philadelphia," May 18, 1775 (Philadelphia, 1775). John Shy, *A People Numerous and Armed* (Oxford: Oxford University Press, 1976). Some compromise must have been worked out. Congressmen observing a review in early June reported the soldiers "all in Uniform." John Adams to Abigail Adams, June 10, 1775, Adams Family Papers, An Electronic Archive, Massachusetts Historical Society. Eliphalet Dyer to Joseph Trumbull, June 8, 1775, in Smith, *Letters of Delegates to Congress*, 1:459. See also the detailed description of the elaborate dress of different companies in J. Thomas Scharf and Thompson Westcott, *History of Philadelphia, 1609–1884* (Philadelphia, 1884), 1:296.

22. An ad hoc public subscription appears to have supplied the first funds, but "Assurances were given to the Subscribers that the said Sums should be repaid as soon as sufficient public Monies were raised by Tax, or otherwise." However, the Associators waited until late September, four months after the militia had been formed, to pursue compensation for the subscribers. Votes, 8:7258–59.

23. June 30, 1775. MCSA, 10:279–82. *Pennsylvania Gazette*, July 28, 1775. "Articles of Association, Passed by the Committee of Safety, August 19, 1775," *Pennsylvania Archives*, ser. 5, vol. 5 (Harrisburg, PA, 1906), 8–12. Votes, 8:7237–40, 7260–63. Rosswurm, *Arms, Country, and Class*, 52–54.

24. For more on the parallels between the 1747 Defense Association and voluntary associations, see Jessica Choppin Roney, " 'Ready to act in defiance of the Government': Philadelphia Voluntary Associations and the Defense Association of 1747–48," *Early American Studies* 8, no. 2 (May 2010): 358–85.

25. William Bradford to James Madison, June 2, 1775, in Hutchinson and Rachal, *Papers of James Madison*, 1:149. "An Act for the Better Ordering and Regulating Such as are Willing and Desirous to be United for Military Purposes Within this Province," Nov. 25, 1755, *The Statutes at Large of Pennsylvania, From 1682 to 1801* (Pennsylvania, 1898), 5:197–201. Votes, 8:7230. May 7, 1775, *Extracts from the Diary of Christopher Marshall*, 23. By way of comparison, John Adams found the deliberations of the Continental Congress "tedious" and proceeding "Not precisely in that Way which I could wish, but in a better Way than We could well expect, considering what an heterogeneous Body it is." Heterogeneity might provide a broader basis for support, but at the cost of delay and compromise. John Adams to Abigail Adams, June 2, 1775, Adams Family Papers, An Electronic Archive, Massachusetts Historical Society.

26. Votes, 8:7237–40, 7245, 7258–63, 7323–25, 7358–61. May 7, 1775, *Extracts from the Diary of Christopher Marshall*, 23. Votes, 8:7258–60, 7262, 7333–43.

27. Governor John Penn, sensing the direction local politics was going, made himself

scarce and never addressed the imperial crisis after May 1775. "Contenting himself with performing his usual executive functions on every occasion the House afforded him, he simply ignored the legislators' unconstitutional seizure of extraordinary executive powers." Ryerson, *Revolution Is Now Begun*, 119.

28. The assembly authorized the emission of £35,000 in late June to pay for defense, and when that still proved inadequate, it authorized another £80,000 in November. These money bills technically provided that taxes would retire the emitted bills, but in essence, the assembly was printing money. Many worried about inflation, and some refused to accept the currency, provoking accusations of inadequate patriotism. Votes, 8:7245, 7247, 7258–63, 7323–25, 7358–61, 7363, 7365. Ryerson, *Revolution Is Now Begun*, 122–24. Steven Rosswurm emphasizes Associators' objections to the low pay they would receive under the assembly's late June resolves. Rosswurm, *Arms, Country, and Class*, 53–54.

29. Quote from Christopher Marshall to S. H., Sept. 30, 1775, Christopher Marshall Letterbook, 1773–78, HSP. Votes, 8:7239–40. Critics of Pennsylvania's legislature then and since point out that the legislature did not afford equal representation to all voters, particularly those in western counties and Philadelphia.

30. Benjamin Franklin to Joseph Priestley, July 7, 1775, and Benjamin Franklin to Jonathan Shipley, July 7, 1775, in Labaree, *Papers of Benjamin Franklin*, Franklin Papers Online. June 30, July 14, July 31, Aug. 19, Aug. 26, 1775, MCSA, 279–82, 286, 295, 308–12, 318–20. *Pennsylvania Gazette*, July 19, 1775.

31. *Pennsylvania Evening Post*, Sept. 14, Sept. 19, Sept. 28, 1775. Votes, 8:7258–60.

32. *Pennsylvania Evening Post*, Sept. 28, 1775. The Contributors to the Relief of the Poor would assess yet another poor tax again that December. Aug. 3, Aug. 12, Dec. 19, 1775, Alms House Manager's Minutes, 1766–78, Philadelphia City Archives. For more on the Contributors to the Relief of the Poor, see chap. 6. The officers quickly fell in line with the Committee of Privates, presenting their subordinates' "Address" to the assembly and adding their own call for proper legislation (rather than committee pronouncements) that would oblige all Pennsylvanians to serve in the militia or pay punitive fines and taxes. Votes, 8:7258–63.

33. After the hotly contested provincial election in October 1775, resistance-minded leaders failed to take over the House, though they did gain ground. The assembly remained in the hands of moderates, with a substantial conservative minority and a bloc of swing voters. Christopher Marshall to S. H., Oct. 31, 1775, Christopher Marshall Letterbook, 1773–78, HSP. Ryerson, *Revolution Is Now Begun*, 135–38, 143. For public pressure as expressed through petitions, see Votes, 8:7311–13, 7323–30, 7333–44, 7348–50. *Pennsylvania Gazette*, Nov. 1, 1775.

34. Votes, 8:7351–52, 7358–61, 7369–84.

35. Tully, *Forming American Politics*, 257–58.

36. Despite repeated concerns about insufficient manpower, African Americans were prohibited from joining the association. Around this time the Committee of Safety questioned David Owen, "a Person Suspected of enlisting Negroes," and threw him into the workhouse (one step above prison) "till further orders." Dec. 14, 1775, MCSA, 427. Apprentices could not join without the written consent of their masters. *Pennsylvania Gazette*, Feb. 7, 1776.

37. Votes, 8:7351–52, 7358–61, 7369–84.

38. "To the Privates of the Military Association belonging to the Province of Pennsylvania," Votes, 8:7412–13. *Gentlemen and Fellow Soldiers* (Philadelphia, 1776). *To the Non-Commissioned Officers and Privates, of the Several* COMPANIES *of* ASSOCIATORS*, belonging to the City and*

Liberties of PHILADELPHIA (Philadelphia, 1775). Petition of the Committee of Privates, Feb. 5, 1776, Petition from the Committee of Privates, Feb. 22, 1776, Petition from the Committee of Privates, Mar. 15, 1776, in Force, *American Archives*, ser. 4, 4:941, 5:662–64, 685. *Pennsylvania Gazette*, Feb. 7, 1776. The Committee of Safety itself petitioned the assembly, calling for immediate change to the militia law because of the "general sentiments" it confronted that the law was "partial and unequal." Feb. 22, 1776, MCSA, 492. Rosswurm, *Arms, Country, and Class*, 61–66. *Pennsylvania Gazette*, Apr. 3, 1776.

39. "To the ELECTORS and FREEHOLDERS of the City of PHILADELPHIA," *Pennsylvania Gazette*, May 1, 1776.

40. "An Act to Increase the Number of Representatives in Assembly for the City of Philadelphia and the Several Counties Named Therein" (1776), *Statutes at Large of Pennsylvania*, 8:456–62. *Pennsylvania Evening Post*, Apr. 4, 1776. Foner, *Tom Paine and Revolutionary America*. The assembly responded to Associators' grievances against the Committee of Safety by assuming from it responsibility for confirming officers elected by privates. Votes, 8:7470.

41. Judge Yeates to Col. Burd, Mar. 7, 1776 , in *Letters and Papers Relating Chiefly to the Provincial History of Pennsylvania*, ed. Thomas Willing Balch (Philadelphia, 1855), 248. *Pennsylvania Evening Post*, Mar. 7, Mar. 9, Apr. 4, 1776.

42. *Pennsylvania Evening Post*, Apr. 4, 1776. Thomas Paine, "The Forester," Letter IV, *Pennsylvania Journal*, May 8, 1776. Ryerson, *Revolution Is Now Begun*, 173–74. Robert J. Dinkin, *Voting in Provincial America: A Study of Elections in the Thirteen Colonies* (Westport, CT: Greenwood Press, 1977), 158–59.

43. "The Forester," Letter III, *Pennsylvania Gazette*, Apr. 24, 1776. "The Forester," Letter IV, *Pennsylvania Journal*, May 8, 1776. Foner, *Tom Paine and Revolutionary America*, 126–27. William Smith, "Cato," Letter I and Letter III, *Pennsylvania Gazette*, Mar. 13, Mar. 20, 1776.

44. "Cato," Letter I and Letter III, *Pennsylvania Gazette*, Mar. 13, Mar. 20, 1776.

45. "The Forester," Letter III, *Pennsylvania Gazette*, Apr. 24, 1776. "The Forester," Letter IV, *Pennsylvania Journal*, May 8, 1776. Foner, *Tom Paine and Revolutionary America*, 126–27. For similar arguments, see "To the Free and Independent Electors of the City of Philadelphia," *Pennsylvania Packet*, Apr. 29, 1776.

46. "To the Honourable the REPRESENTATIVES of the FREEMEN of the Province of Pennsylvania, in General Assembly met, The PETITION of the PRIVATES of the MILITARY ASSOCIATION of the City and Liberties of PHILADELPHIA," *Pennsylvania Gazette*, Mar. 6, 1776. "The Forester," Letter III, *Pennsylvania Gazette*, Apr. 24, 1776. "A Friend to Government by Assembly," *Pennsylvania Evening Post*, Apr. 4, 1776.

47. "To the Free and Independent Electors of the City of Philadelphia," *Pennsylvania Packet*, Apr. 29, 1776. Civis, "To the FREEHOLDERS and ELECTORS of the City of PHILADELPHIA," *Pennsylvania Gazette*, May 1, 1776.

48. *Journals of the Continental Congress, 1774–1789* (Washington, DC, 1906), 4:342. *Extracts from the Diary of Christopher Marshall*, 71. *The Alarm: or, an Address to the People of Pennsylvania* (Philadelphia, 1776). *Pennsylvania Gazette*, May 22, 1776. "Proceedings of the Provincial Conference of Committees of the Province of PENNSYLVANIA," in Force, *American Archives*, ser. 4, 6:951–66.

49. *Pennsylvania Gazette*, May 22, 1776. "To the Honorable the CONFERENCE of the several COMMITTEES of the province of Pennsylvania . . . ," *Pennsylvania Evening Post*, June 22, 1776.

50. It is worth noting as well that colonial Pennsylvania had one of the broadest fran-

chises of any British polity. Historians debate the degree to which the relatively low property requirements had ever been enforced prior to the Revolution. Demophilus, *The Genuine Principles of the Ancient Saxon, or English Constitution* (Philadelphia, 1776), 23. *Four Letters on Interesting Subjects* (Philadelphia, 1776), 23. James Cannon, *To the several BATTALIONS of MILITARY ASSOCIATORS in the Province of PENNSLYVANIA* (Philadelphia, 1776). "Address of the Committee of Conference to the Associators of Pennsylvania, June 25, 1776," *Pennsylvania Archives*, ser. 5, 5:15. June 20, 1776, "Proceedings of the Provincial Conference," in Force, *American Archives*, ser. 4, 6:953. Gordon S. Wood, *Creation of the American Republic, 1776–1787* (Chapel Hill: University of North Carolina Press, 1969), 226.

51. The provision that a man could make an "Oath or Affirmation" recognized that it was against Quakers' religious beliefs to swear an oath. Voters also had to affirm their belief in Jesus Christ and both the Old and New Testament. "Proceedings of the Provincial Conference," in Force, *American Archives*, ser. 4, 6:954. *The TESTIMONY of the People called QUAKERS, given forth by a Meeting of the Representatives of said People, in PENNSYLVANIA and NEW-JERSEY, held at Philadelphia the twenty-fourth Day of the first Month, 1775* (Philadelphia, 1775). Jan. 2 and 24, 1775, *Extracts from the Diary of Christopher Marshall*, 12–13. Christopher Marshall to Peter Barker, June 24, 1775, Christopher Marshall Letterbook, 1773–78, HSP. Quakers in this crisis preferred internal unity at the expense of losing members. They disowned 948 Friends for bearing arms or otherwise participating in revolutionary activity. Thus, while they clearly suffered mass defection, they did not undergo religious schism. Jack D. Marietta, *The Reformation of American Quakerism, 1748–1783* (Philadelphia: University of Pennsylvania Press, 1984), 222–47.

52. June 22, 1776, "Proceedings of the Provincial Conference," in Force, *American Archives*, ser. 4, 6:962. Private reprisals could rise to the level of violence and even riots. For one example of this kind of violence, in 1777 on the anniversary of independence, all "patriotic" citizens illuminated their windows at night with candles. Quakers, who refused to do so (and would not have done so for any other cause, such demonstrations acting against Quaker doctrines), had their windows broken. "All this," drily commented Sally Fisher, whose house had fifteen windows smashed, "for the joy of having gained our liberty." July 4, 1777, " 'A Diary of Trifling Occurrences': Philadelphia, 1776–1778," *PMHB* 82 (1958): 438.

53. "Ordinance for disarming Non-Associators," July 19, 1776, in Force, *American Archives*, 2:6. The ordinance maintained that Non-Associators were to be reimbursed for their arms, but only if they applied for reimbursement within six months. If they refused or neglected to apply, the money would revert to the state. July 16, 1776, in *The Diary of Elizabeth Drinker*, ed. Elaine Forman Craine (Boston: Northeastern University Press, 1991), 1:217. *Pennsylvania Gazette*, Sept. 18, 1776. The new tax was assessed against the entire estate of Non-Associators, thus penalizing wealthy Non-Associators more harshly than others. Robert F. Oaks, "Philadelphians in Exile: The Problem of Loyalty during the American Revolution," *PMHB* 96 (1972): 298–325. "An Act for the Further Security of the Government," Apr. 1, 1778, *Statutes at Large of Pennsylvania*, 9:238–45. The "Declaration of Rights" that preceded the new Pennsylvania Constitution adopted in September 1776 explicitly guaranteed both freedom of speech and freedom of conscience. However, it also stated that "every member of society . . . is bound to contribute his proportion towards the expence of that protection" that was also held to be a common right ("the enjoyment of life, liberty, and property"). While "any man who is conscientiously scrupulous of bearing arms" could not be compelled to do so, he did owe "an equivalent thereto" in the form of a tax. *The Constitution of the Common-wealth*

of Pennsylvania, As Established by the General Convention Elected for that Purpose, And Held at Philadelphia, July 15, 1776 (Philadelphia, 1776), 4–9.

54. Carl Lotus Becker, *The History of Political Parties in the Province of New York, 1760–1776* (Madison, WI, 1909), 22.

55. Both of these definitions, but particularly the latter, acted to exclude women. Nathan Ross Kozuskanich, "'For the Security and Protection of the Community': The Frontier and the Makings of Pennsylvania Constitutionalism" (PhD diss., Ohio State University, 2005).

56. Pennsylvania's 1701 charter provided for a broad franchise with the lowest property requirements in the British Empire. A unicameral legislature was considered radical because it did not provide for a check by an upper house analogous to the House of Lords or Governor's Council in England and other states. The 1776 constitution operated for only fourteen years; opponents managed to overthrow it with a new, more conservative constitution in 1790. *The Constitution of the Common-wealth of Pennsylvania, As Established by the General Convention Elected for that Purpose, And Held at Philadelphia, July 15, 1776* (Philadelphia, 1776). Wood, *Creation of the American Republic*, 226. Terry Bouton, *Taming Democracy: "The People," the Founders, and the Troubled Ending of the American Revolution* (Oxford: Oxford University Press, 2007).

57. In fact, a substantial population of adult white men could not participate at all because they refused to take a loyalty oath to the new regime.

Epilogue

1. Richard G. Miller, "The Federal City: 1783–1800," in *Philadelphia: A 300-Year History*, ed. Russell F. Weigley et al. (New York: W. W. Norton, 1982), 155–205.

2. Albrecht Koschnik, *Let a Common Interest Bind Us Together: Associations, Partisanship, and Culture in Philadelphia, 1775–1840* (Charlottesville: University of Virginia Press, 2007). See also John L. Brooke, "Ancient Lodges and Self-Created Societies: Voluntary Association and the Public Sphere in the Early Republic," in *Launching the "Extended Republic": The Federalist Era*, ed. Ronald Hoffman and Peter J. Albert (Charlottesville: University of Virginia Press, 1996), 273–359.

3. Pauline Maier, "The Revolutionary Origins of the American Corporation," *WMQ*, 3rd ser., 50 (1993): 52. John Majewski, "Toward a Social History of the Corporation: Shareholding in Pennsylvania, 1800–1840," in *The Economy of Early America: Historical Perspectives and New Directions*, ed. Cathy Matson (University Park: Pennsylvania State University Press, 2006), 294–316. Ann D. Gordon, *The College of Philadelphia, 1749–1779: Impact of an Institution* (New York: Garland, 1989). The debate in Pennsylvania about corporations encompassed the college and, more contentiously still, the chartering of the Bank of North America. The college did eventually get its old charter restored, but not until 1791, when the legislature determined that it had overstepped its authority, violating what had been in essence a contract.

4. Terry Bouton, "Moneyless in Pennsylvania: Privatization and the Depression of the 1780s," in Matson, *Economy of Early America*, 218–35. Majewski, "Toward a Social History of the Corporation." Edwin J. Perkins, *American Public Financial Services, 1700–1815* (Columbus: Ohio State University Press, 1994). See also Oscar Handlin and Mary Flug Handlin, *Commonwealth: A Study of the Role of Government in the American Economy: Massachusetts, 1774–1861* (Cambridge, MA: Belknap Press of Harvard University Press, 1969). Naomi R. Lamoreaux, *Insider Lending: Banks, Personal Connections, and Economic Development in Industrial New England* (Cambridge: Cambridge University Press, 1994). Tamara Plakins

Thornton, "'A Great Machine' or a 'Beast of Prey': A Boston Corporation and Its Rural Debtors in an Age of Capitalist Transformation," *Journal of the Early Republic* 27 (Winter 2007): 567–97.

5. The difference between the colonial and the early national period lay not, as some scholars have posited, in the contrast between an earlier hierarchical, unitary public culture and a later pluralistic one. Rather, the difference lay in the scope of the participation possible and the breadth of social, civic, political, and economic activity that could be assumed by groups vis-à-vis the state. Gary B. Nash, *Forging Freedom: The Formation of Philadelphia's Black Community, 1720–1840* (Cambridge, MA: Harvard University Press, 1988). Jacqueline Reinier, "Rearing the Republican Child," *WMQ*, 3rd ser., 39 (1982): 150–63. Susan Branson, *These Fiery Frenchified Dames: Women and Political Culture in Early National Philadelphia* (Philadelphia: University of Pennsylvania Press, 2001). John K. Alexander, *Render Them Submissive: Responses to Poverty in Philadelphia, 1760–1800* (Amherst: University of Massachusetts Press, 1980). Billy G. Smith, *The "Lower Sort": Philadelphia's Laboring People, 1750–1800* (Ithaca, NY: Cornell University Press, 1990). Michael Meranze, *Laboratories of Virtue: Punishment, Revolution, and Authority in Philadelphia, 1760–1835* (Chapel Hill: University of North Carolina Press, 1996). Bruce Dorsey, *Reforming Men and Women: Gender in the Antebellum City* (Ithaca, NY: Cornell University Press, 2002). A. Kristen Foster, *Moral Visions and Material Ambitions: Philadelphia Struggles to Define the Republic, 1776–1836* (Lanham, MD: Lexington Books, 2004). Beverly C. Tomek, *Pennsylvania Hall: A "Legal Lynching" in the Shadow of the Liberty Bell* (Oxford: Oxford University Press, 2013).

6. On participation of Philadelphia voluntary associations in national and global causes, see, for example, Amanda Bowie Moniz, "'Labors in the Cause of Humanity in Every Part of the Globe': Transatlantic Philanthropic Collaborations and the Cosmopolitan Ideal, 1760–1815" (PhD diss., University of Michigan, 2008).

7. Niall Ferguson, *The Great Degeneration: How Institutions Decay and Economies Die* (New York: Penguin, 2013).

Primary Sources

This book is a history of governance in Philadelphia through public, quasi-public, and private institutions and associations. As such, the records of those bodies—their articles of association, minutes, daybooks, and financial documents—make up the backbone of the book. While fortunately some critical collections are available online, tracking down the records of most led me on a wonderful scavenger hunt through archives all over the city, especially as a number of the institutions I study still exist and retain their original records.

The vast majority of records relating to eighteenth-century institutions and voluntary associations are very "clean" documents. That is to say, for the most part minutes and other documents were usually not recorded during the meetings, but afterward entered neatly from notes that were probably more haphazard. Some of the minute books, for example, those of the Library Company, were all neatly transcribed years later by a single hand. Interim records or marginalia were thus entirely lost in pursuit of the neatest entries possible. The records omit almost all conversations or debates, retaining only the results and decisions. For example, very rarely do the records document someone being *rejected* for membership; the recorders only mention successful candidates—making it difficult to assess who wanted to be a member, what criteria were used in selection, and so on. Many of the minutes from individual meetings read as formulaic and dry; one has to read them collectively to get a sense of the mission and passion of the members. Financial records in what were called "daybooks" tend to be less "neat," with entries clearly recorded as payments came in or went out, but with even less commentary or discussion of means and motives.

Many of the papers relating to Pennsylvania government are collected in the published series *Pennsylvania Archives*, available online through www.fold3.com. The Minutes of the Provincial Council and the Minutes of the Council of Safety are in the first series, called Colonial Records. The Papers of the Governors are organized chronologically in series 4. The Votes and Proceedings of the House of Representatives of the Province of Pennsylvania are collected in series 8. *The Statutes at Large of Pennsylvania, From 1682 to 1801*, originally published in 1898, are also available and searchable online at www.palrb.us/stlarge/browse/spselectvolume .php. The Philadelphia City Archives has the Alms House Managers Minutes, 1766–78, and the Overseers of the Poor Minutes, 1768–74. Most of the records of the Philadelphia Corporation are published in *Minutes of the Common Council of the City of Philadelphia, 1704–1776* (Philadelphia, 1847).

Local institutions that still exist, hold their own organizational records, and have archives open to the public include the American Philosophical Society, the Library Company of Philadelphia, the Pennsylvania Hospital, the Philadelphia Contributionship, and the University of Pennsylvania (former College of Philadelphia). I was able to read through the extensive records of the St. Andrew's Society by the generous permission of the secretary in 2005, James St. Bishop. The records at the Presbyterian Historical Society and the Quaker and Special Collections at Haverford College were also essential in discussion of denominational life and early organization in Philadelphia.

Many other institutional records are housed in the Historical Society of Pennsylvania. Some, like those of the Union Fire Company, Friendly Association, or Presbyterian Ministers' Fund, are quite extensive, while others, like those of the Dancing Assembly, contain only a few documents. The American Philosophical Society likewise has collections relating to some voluntary associations, including the Junto and the Friendship Carpenter's Company.

There are many manuscript sources that relate to the activities of voluntary associations and the people in them. At the Historical Society of Pennsylvania, some of the most helpful included the William Allen Letterbook, Ancient Records of Philadelphia, Henry S. Drinker Papers, Jacob Hiltzheimer Diary, 1770–72, Logan Family Papers, Christopher Marshall Letterbook, 1773–78, Mayors of Philadelphia–Dreer Collection, Norris Family Papers, Pemberton Papers, the MSS Penn Official Correspondence, Penn Papers, Private Correspondence, Shippen Family Papers, Smith MSS, and the John Swift Letterbook. At the American Philosophical Society, they included the Jacob Hiltzheimer diaries and Mss. Relating to the Non-Importation Resolutions, 1766–75.

Many organizations printed pamphlets, articles, and advertisements relating to their activities, making the pamphlet collections at the Library Company of Philadelphia extremely important to my research. Newspapers such as the *American Weekly Mercury*, *Pennsylvania Chronicle*, *Pennsylvania Journal*, and *Pennsylvania Gazette* were vital sources. The Library Company also houses numerous images of early Philadelphia. Included in this book are two: Thomas Holme, *A mapp of ye improved part of Pensilvania in America* (London, 1690), and *The east prospect of the City of Philadelphia* (London, 1761).

Printed collections of personal papers that proved particularly important include Edward Armstrong, ed., *Correspondence between William Penn and James Logan . . . 1700–1750* (Philadelphia, 1870); Marianne S. Wokeck et al., eds., *The Papers of William Penn* (Philadelphia: University of Pennsylvania Press, 1986); Leonard W. Labaree, ed., *The Papers of Benjamin Franklin* (New Haven, CT: Yale University Press), also available online; and *Extracts from the Diary of Christopher Marshall . . . during the American Revolution, 1774–1781* (Albany, 1877).

Secondary Sources

I was particularly fortunate to be able to build on a rich scholarly tradition in the history of Philadelphia and Pennsylvania. For a good introduction to the early history of the city and colony, see Alan Tully, *William Penn's Legacy: Politics and Social Structure in Provincial Pennsylvania, 1726–1755* (Baltimore: Johns Hopkins University Press, 1977), and *Forming American Politics: Ideals, Interests, and Institutions in Colonial New York and Pennsylvania* (Baltimore: Johns Hopkins University Press, 1994); Gary B. Nash, *Quakers and Politics: Pennsylvania, 1681–1726* (1968; repr., Boston: Northeastern University Press, 1993), and *The Urban Crucible:*

Social Change, Political Consciousness, and the Origins of the American Revolution (Cambridge, MA: Harvard University Press, 1979); John Smolenski, *Friends and Strangers: The Making of a Creole Culture in Colonial Pennsylvania* (Philadelphia: University of Pennsylvania Press, 2010); and Jon Butler, "Power, Authority, and the Origins of American Denominational Order: The English Churches in the Delaware Valley, 1680–1730," *Transactions of the American Philosophical Society*, new series, 68 (1978). The standard work on the Philadelphia Corporation is Judith M. Diamonstone's "The Philadelphia Corporation, 1701–1776" (PhD diss., University of Pennsylvania, 1969). On Pennsylvania and Philadelphia's economy, see Thomas M. Doerflinger, *A Vigorous Spirit of Enterprise: Merchants and Economic Development in Revolutionary Philadelphia* (Chapel Hill: University of North Carolina Press, 1986); and Mary M. Schweitzer, *Custom and Contract: Household, Government, and the Economy in Colonial Pennsylvania* (New York: Columbia University Press, 1987).

On Quakers, see in addition to the works above Sydney V. James, *A People among Peoples: Quaker Benevolence in Eighteenth-Century America* (Cambridge, MA: Harvard University Press, 1963); J. William Frost, *The Quaker Family in Colonial America: A Portrait of the Society of Friends* (New York: St. Martin's Press, 1973); Barry Levy, *Quakers and the American Family: British Settlement in the Delaware Valley* (Oxford: Oxford University Press, 1988); Richard Bauman, *For the Reputation of Truth: Politics, Religion, and Conflict among the Pennsylvania Quakers, 1750–1800* (Baltimore: Johns Hopkins University Press, 1971); Jack D. Marietta, *The Reformation of American Quakerism, 1748–1783* (Philadelphia: University of Pennsylvania Press, 1984); and Jane E. Calvert, *Quaker Constitutionalism and the Political Thought of John Dickinson* (Cambridge: Cambridge University Press, 2009).

On the French and Indian War and the Revolution in Pennsylvania and Philadelphia, see Eric Foner, *Tom Paine and Revolutionary America* (London: Oxford University Press, 1976); Charles S. Olton, *Artisans for Independence: Philadelphia Mechanics and the American Revolution* (New York: Syracuse University Press, 1975); Richard Alan Ryerson, *The Revolution Is Now Begun: The Radical Committees of Philadelphia, 1765–1776* (Philadelphia: University of Pennsylvania Press, 1978); Steven Rosswurm, *Arms, Country, and Class: The Philadelphia Militia and "Lower Sort" during the American Revolution, 1775–1783* (New Brunswick, NJ: Rutgers University Press, 1987); Peter Silver, *Our Savage Neighbors: How Indian War Transformed Early America* (New York: W. W. Norton, 2008); and Kevin Kenny, *Peaceable Kingdom Lost: The Paxton Boys and the Destruction of William Penn's Holy Experiment* (Oxford: Oxford University Press, 2009).

The starting place for research on voluntary associations and the public sphere in early Philadelphia must be Daniel R. Gilbert, "Patterns of Organization and Membership in Colonial Philadelphia Club Life, 1725–1755" (PhD diss., University of Pennsylvania, 1952); Carl and Jessica Bridenbaugh, *Rebels and Gentlemen: Philadelphia in the Age of Franklin* (New York: Oxford University Press, 1965); and Peter Thompson, *Rum Punch and Revolution: Taverngoing and Public Life in Eighteenth-Century Philadelphia* (Philadelphia: University of Pennsylvania Press, 1999). Recent influential works on voluntary associations and the public sphere in the British Atlantic world include Peter Clark, *British Clubs and Societies 1580–1800: The Origins of an Associational World* (Oxford: Clarendon Press, 2000); and David S. Shields, *Civil Tongues and Polite Letters in British America* (Chapel Hill: University of North Carolina Press, 1997). This work participates in a rich scholarly debate about the character of political participa-

242 Essay on Sources

tion by ordinary people in the colonial era and the importance (or otherwise) of the American Revolution in effecting a change in those political behaviors. The bulk of scholarship recognizes three major categories of political participation by ordinary people (usually men): casting votes in elections, rioting, and engaging in rational-critical discourse in places like taverns or through the press. An excellent recent survey of formal, electoral political structures in early America can be found in Richard R. Beeman, *The Varieties of Political Experience in Eighteenth-Century America* (Philadelphia: University of Pennsylvania Press, 2004); and Joy B. and Robert R. Gilsdorf, "Elites and Electorates: Some Plain Truth for Historians of Colonial America," in *Saints and Revolutionaries: Essays on Early American History*, edited by David D. Hall (New York: W. W. Norton, 1984), 207–44. The most influential account of eighteenth-century riots, or, as she terms them, popular actions, remains Pauline Maier's 1970 article in the *William and Mary Quarterly*, "Popular Uprisings and Civil Authority in Eighteenth-Century America." See also Thomas P. Slaughter, "Crowds in Eighteenth-Century America: Reflections and New Directions," *Pennsylvania Magazine of History and Biography* 115 (1991); Benjamin H. Irvin, "The Streets of Philadelphia: Crowds, Congress, and the Political Culture of Revolution, 1774–1783," *Pennsylvania Magazine of History and Biography* 129 (2005); and Benjamin L. Carp, *Rebels Rising: Cities and the American Revolution* (Oxford: Oxford University Press, 2007).

Rational-critical discourse in taverns, in coffeehouses, and through a shared world of manuscript and printed belles lettres is a critical element in the eighteenth-century creation of a "public sphere" as outlined influentially by Jürgen Habermas in *The Structural Transformation of the Public Sphere: An Inquiry into a Category of Bourgeois Society*, translated by Thomas Burger (Cambridge, MA: MIT Press, 1991). Habermas argued that rational-critical discourse created a "public sphere" distinct from either government or private households. The public sphere, according to Habermas, transformed the participation of citizens from negative (that is to say, merely reacting to government) to positive: contributing proactively in the debate and decisions about state policy and thus making government accountable to them. It was the foundation of democratic self-government. For discussion of the use (and abuse) of the concept of the public sphere, as well as an extensive bibliographical survey on the public sphere, see "Forum: Alternative Histories of the Public Sphere," *William and Mary Quarterly* 62 (2005).

It is the contention of this work, however, that for all its value, this catalogue of activities—voting, rioting, and discourse in the public sphere—describes a relatively circumscribed role for the participation of ordinary people in politics and government. In turn, this limited characterization has led historians to an idea of colonial American political development which misses much about the capacity of ordinary white men to engage in sustained popular mobilization and institution building and has led historians into debates about the nature of hierarchy, class, and political behavior which are premised on an incomplete picture. It leads some historians to see radical change beginning in the 1760s and beyond as many mobilized politically and then militarily to resist Britain in the American Revolution, but this radicalism only makes sense by ignoring the political behaviors that had come before. For representative and influential works from quite different perspectives which, however, argue for emerging radicalism through the 1760s and 1770s, see Gary B. Nash, *The Urban Crucible: Social Change, Political Consciousness, and the Origins of the American Revolution*; Gordon S.

Wood, *The Radicalism of the American Revolution* (New York: Vintage Books, 1991); and T. H. Breen, *The Marketplace of the Revolution: How Consumer Politics Shaped American Independence* (Oxford: Oxford University Press, 2004).

Finally, much of the best scholarship on early American voluntary associations, governance, and the public sphere comes from the period of the early Republic. My thinking was influenced particularly by the following works: John L. Brooke, "Ancient Lodges and Self-Created Societies: Voluntary Association and the Public Sphere in the Early Republic," in *Launching the "Extended Republic": The Federalist Era*, edited by Ronald Hoffman and Peter J. Albert (Charlottesville: University of Virginia Press, 1996), 273–359; Albrecht Koschnik, *Let a Common Interest Bind Us Together: Associations, Partisanship, and Culture in Philadelphia, 1775–1840* (Charlottesville: University of Virginia Press, 2007); and Johann N. Neem, *Creating a Nation of Joiners: Democracy and Civil Society in Early National Massachusetts* (Cambridge, MA: Harvard University Press, 2008).

Academy, Philadelphia. *See* College of Philadelphia: Academy

Adams, John, 132, 159, 160, 232n25

African Americans, 4, 186, 233n36

Alison, Francis, 111, 117, 123

Allen, James, 129, 167

Allen, William, 105, 123, 128, 129, 138, 147

almshouse. *See* workhouses

American Manufactory, 165–66, 176

American Philosophical Society, 159

American Revolution, 2, 3, 4, 5, 8–10, 35, 160, 161, 175, 179, 180–81, 184, 185, 187–88; disrupting lending institutions, 120–21; early organization, 161–66, 168; and eradication of dissent, 179–82; mobilization, 9. *See also* Military Association

Andrews, Jedediah, 26, 27

Anglicans. *See* Church of England

Assembly. *See* Pennsylvania Assembly

Bachelor's Club, 71, 75

banking, 36, 37, 108, 185. *See also* exchange, medium of; exchange, mercantile; lending institutions, capital

Baptists, 26–27, 66, 208n17; and Church of England, 69; Philadelphia Baptist Association, 66, 67; and Whitefield, 83. *See also under* meeting houses

Bettering House. *See* workhouses

body politic, 4. *See also* citizenship

Bond, Thomas, 93, 94, 110

Boston, 59, 61, 70, 72, 130, 158, 159, 161, 166, 169, 192n15, 194n14, 210n30, 212n42

Bristol, 49

British Empire, 78, 106, 135

burial grounds, 18; Quaker, 22, 23, 25

Carpenter's Company, 71, 72, 220n11; Carpenter's Hall, 159

Catholics, 131, 132

Cato's Letters (Trenchard and Gordon), 106

Center Meeting House. *See* meeting houses: Quaker

Center Square, 1, 11, 15, 17

Charleston, 130

charter, English precedent, 45–46

charter, Philadelphia. *See under* Philadelphia Corporation

Charter of Privileges (1701), 42–43, 44, 45

Chester (borough), 45, 46

church, established, 20, 29–30; lack of, in Pennsylvania, 20–21, 29

Churchmen. *See* Church of England

Church of England, 21, 26, 27–28, 131, 132, 198n34, 200n3, 201n14; and Baptist meeting house, 69; in British Empire, 20; desire for American bishop, 66, 207n16, 219n49; education, 33, 65–66; finances, 26, 27–28, 66; hostility toward Quakers, 21, 33, 35, 41, 44, 65; as political bloc, 39, 95; and Whitefield, 82–83. *See also* meeting houses: Baptist

citizenship, 2, 9, 53, 137, 161–62, 174, 175, 177–78, 180, 181, 182, 191n6, 202n16

city lots, 2, 14, 16–19, 29, 34, 194n9, 195n16. *See also* Commissioners of Property

City Regiment, 136, 137, 138, 139

city watch, 2, 35, 50–52, 53, 204n31

Clayton, Thomas, 27

College of Philadelphia, 5, 82, 100–102; Academy, 91–93, 94, 99, 218n43; finances, 92, 93, 101–2, 111–12; incorporation, 92, 98–100, 111, 184; loans, 109, 111–30; and New Building, 92, 93; and T. Penn, 92–93, 98–99, 101–2, 103, 112, 217n28; post-war, 184; and Smith, 99–104, 112; trustees, 92, 99, 216n25, 218n46

Colony in Schuylkill, 71–72, 75

Commissioners of Property, 34

Commissioners of the Lighthouse, 129

Committee of Privates. *See under* Military Association

Committee of Safety, 171–75, 178, 233n36, 234n38, 234n40

Common Council. *See* Philadelphia Corporation

Common Sense (Paine), 175, 176

consumer revolution, 60, 71, 78

Continental Congress, 158, 159, 168, 175, 178, 232n25

Contributionship. *See* Philadelphia Contributionship

Contributorship. *See* Contributors to the Relief of the Poor

Contributors to the Relief of the Poor (CRP), 5, 150–56, 173; finances, 129, 151, 154–55; internal structure, 151–52; origins, 150–51; and Overseers of the Poor, 152–53, 155, 229n50; and Pennsylvania Assembly, 150, 151, 152, 154, 155, 156; and Philadelphia Corporation, 229n58; poor performance, 154–55; and Quakers, 150, 155–56; and suburbs, 151–52, 153; and workhouse, 152, 159

Cordwainers Fire Company, 109

Corporation for the Relief of Presbyterian Ministers. *See* Presbyterian Ministers Fund

Corporation for the Relief of Widows and Children of Clergymen in the Communion of the Church of England in America, 109, 222n39

corporations: fear of, 185, 236n3; for-profit, 186. *See also* incorporation; *names of individual corporations*

court house, 17, 82

credit. *See* loans

Croghan, George, 128, 145, 146, 227n32

currency. *See* exchange, medium of

Currency Act, 107

Dancing Assembly, 95–96

Declaratory Act, 152

defense, 35, 41, 50, 86–87, 134–35, 137. *See also* Militia Bill; *under* Pennsylvania Assembly

Defense Association, 80, 81–82, 85–86, 87–91, 92, 103, 163, 166, 168–69, 213n10, 214n15, 216n21, 216n23; forts, 82, 88, 90–91; lottery, 88, 89–90, 99; as precedent for later organizations, 136, 137, 138, 140, 147, 171

Delaware Indians, 142–50, 226n28. *See also* Friendly Association

Delaware River, 1, 11, 15, 17, 18–19, 34, 39, 52, 60, 86, 158. *See also* ferries

democracy, 6

Denny, William, 144, 145–46

Dickinson, John, 125, 128, 223n50, 230n6

Easton, 143–44, 147

education: of children, 2, 32–33, 84; institutions of self-improvement, 60. *See also under* Church of Englan; College of Philadelphia; Free School; Library Company of Philadelphia; *under* Quakers

elections, 5, 6, 216n21; of 1697, 41, 44; during American Revolution, 176–77, 233n33

Elfreth, Henry (or Jeremiah), 40, 200n4

English cities and towns, 3–4, 13, 45, 49, 202n23, 203n24

Evans, Evan, 27–28

Evans, John, 50–54, 55, 58, 135

exchange, medium of (currency), 36, 105, 106–7, 112–13, 173, 227n32, 233n28

exchange, mercantile: absence of, 35–36; plans for, 11, 17

Federalists, 184

Fellowship Fire Company, 75, 76

ferries, 33, 49, 58; in New York, 203n24

fire companies, 2, 3, 5, 75, 76, 79, 81, 85, 91, 92, 94, 187; as civic technology, 76–77, 78; cooperation among, 76; and Defense Association, 88; internal organization, 77, 78; number active, 76; as template for later organizations, 190n5. *See also specific companies*

fire protection, 60, 61, 74, 76

Forester, The. *See under* Smith, William

Fort St. David's, 159

Frame of Government (1683), 20, 41
Frame of Government (1696), 41
franchise, 6, 9, 168, 175, 177–78, 179, 181, 182, 235n50, 236nn56–57
Franklin, Benjamin: arrival in Philadelphia, 59–60; as civic organizer, 7, 59–60, 212n42; and College of Philadelphia, 91–93, 99, 100, 111, 218n48; and Committee of Safety, 172; and Defense Association, 87, 88, 89, 90, 134, 216n23, 232n20; interest in demography, 69–70; and Junto, 72–73, 74, 78, 124, 210n32; and lending institutions, 107, 123–24, 223n42; and Library Company of Philadelphia, 73–74, 79; and Militia Bill, 136–37, 138; and Pennsylvania Hospital, 55, 93, 94, 110, 217n31; and Philadelphia Contributionship, 112; *Plain Truth*, 87, 214n14; retirement, 216n24; and Stamp Act, 161, 162, 163; and Union Fire Company, 74; and Whitefield, 212n3
Franklin, Deborah, 75, 162
Freemasons, 71, 95
Free School, 32, 48, 65, 94, 207n14. *See also* Quakers: education
French and Indian War, 2, 8, 100, 103, 132–33, 135–6, 140–41, 142, 150, 151
Friendly Association, 3, 6, 133, 140, 141–50, 156, 226n28; and authority with Indians, 148, 149–50; and British officials, 145–46; decline, 146–47; historiography, 225n18; at Indian treaties, 143–44; internal organization, 144–45; origins, 142–45; and Paxton Boys, 148–49; and Pennsylvania Assembly, 145; as precedent for later organization, 150, 156, 164; relationship with Society of Friends, 142, 226n22, 227n30, 227n39; and Walking Purchase, 144, 147. *See also* Indian diplomacy
Friends. *See* Quakers
Friendship Carpenters' Company, 109
Fund for Pious Uses, 67–68, 208n20. *See also* Presbyterian Ministers Fund

General Loan Office, 105, 107, 113–14, 130, 220n10
German Lutheran Church, 129
German Reformed Church, 68
Germans, 81, 119, 125, 134, 137, 176

government commissions, 3, 55, 61; number of, 62; tax assessors, 55–56, 62, 205n41. *See also* Commissioners of Property; Overseers of the Poor
grand jury, 34, 54

Hamilton, James, 92, 94, 96, 97, 102
Hazard, Samuel, 94
Heart and Hand Fire Company, 163
Hobbes, Thomas, 46
hospital. *See* Pennsylvania Hospital
House of Employment. *See under* workhouses
Hughes, John, 117, 161, 162, 163, 222n30

incorporation, 92, 109–10, 186; and Assembly, 94; religious institutions, 69–70. *See also under* College of Philadelphia; Free School; *under* Pennsylvania Hospital; Philadelphia Corporation: 1701 charter; *under* Presbyterian Ministers Fund
Independent Companies, 100, 137–40, 147, 148, 150, 156, 171, 225n18; as precedent for later organizations, 147
Indian diplomacy, 3, 6, 133, 135. *See also* Friendly Association
interest rates: General Loan Office, 108, 221n24; lending institutions, 116, 118, 121, 123, 127, 128; private loans, 107–8; Iroquois, 146–47

Junto, 72–73, 74, 78, 124, 201n30, 201n32

Keith, George, 23–24, 25, 32, 65, 199n45
Keithians, 23–25, 28, 39. *See also under* meeting houses
Keithian Schism, 20, 23–25, 68, 198n38; and contention over meeting house, 24–25, 196n28, 197nn29–30

land office, 106–7. *See also* General Loan Office
legislature. *See* Pennsylvania Assembly
lending institutions, capital, 3, 104, 105, 108–30; and American Revolution, 120–21; borrowers, 119, 122–29; brokers, 124–26; compared to banks, 125, 130; economic impact, 115, 128–29, 130; interest charged, 116, 118,

lending institutions, capital (*cont.*)
121, 123, 127, 128; largest, 108–13; lawsuits,
118–19; refinancing, 118; repayment, 119–21,
122; size of loans, 113–15, terms for loans,
116–18; trading debt, 126–27; treasurers,
222n39; and women, 127. *See also* Fund for
Pious Uses; Quakers: loans
libraries, 76–77, 78, 94, 144, 187; as precedent
for later organizations, 145–46, 190n5,
211n33. *See also* Union Library Company
Library Company of Philadelphia (LCP), 5,
7, 75, 78–79, 81, 85, 91, 92, 210n33; and
Continental Congress, 159; and Defense
Association, 88; founding, 73–74, 210n32;
incorporation, 79, 94, 212n44; internal
organization, 77; loans, 109, 121–22, 129;
members, 71, 77–78; and T. Penn, 78,
212n44; and Pennsylvania Assembly, 78; as
precedent for later organizations, 190n5
Lloyd, David, 44
loan office. *See* General Loan Office
loans, 104–30; avenues of credit, 107–8, 220n8,
221n22; from General Loan Office, 108,
113–14, 130, 220n10; merchants and, 107–8,
112, 115–16, 127, 129. *See also* lending institutions, capital
Logan, James, 7, 49, 50, 52, 57, 77, 78, 99, 134,
214n15, 221n22
Loganian Library, 7, 77–78
lotteries, 101–2. *See also under* Defense Association
lower sorts, 6
Loyalists, 9, 161, 179–80

market, 17, 29, 33
Markham, Ann, 27
Markham, Joanna, 27
Markham, William, 27, 41
Masons, Free. *See* Freemasons
Massachusetts, 88
Maugridge, William, 104–5, 124, 128, 219n1,
223n42
Mayor's Court. *See under* Philadelphia Cor-
poration
meeting houses, 28, 38, 61, 131–32, 159; Baptist,
17, 26–27, 69, 198n35; Catholic, 131, 132;
Church of England, 17, 26, 27, 69, 82, 131,
132; Keithian, 38, 198n35; Methodist, 131;

Presbyterian, 26–27, 66, 131, 132; Quaker,
1–2, 15–17, 21–26, 131, 132, 180, 196n28,
197nn29–30, 197n33
merchants, 13
Military Association, 9, 159–82; articles of
association, 172–74; basis for governance,
179; and citizenship, 161–62, 174, 175,
177–78, 181, 182; Committee of Privates,
172, 174, 177, 233n32; and Committee of
Safety, 171–75, 178, 233n36, 234n38, 234n40;
described, 159–60, 232n21; discipline, 168,
172; funding, 169, 232n22; mandatory service in, 170, 173, 174; membership, 167–68;
and Non-Associators, 170, 172, 173, 174, 178,
180, 181, 235n53; origins, 166, 167–68; and
Pennsylvania Assembly, 160, 166, 167, 169–78,
181, 233n33; privates, 168–69; roots, 160
militia: absence of, 18, 35, 37, 51, 53, 134–35,
166, 224n5; in contemporary political
thought, 51, 53, 137; of J. Evans, 50–54,
58, 135; extralegal, 156, 187; extralegal as
precedent for later organization, 150; in
reaction to Paxton Boys, 149, 163, 167, 170.
See also Defense Association; Independent
Companies; Military Association
Militia Bill, 133, 136–39, 163, 169
militias, extralegal, 3, 8, 9, 150, 156, 166–67,
168, 169, 180, 184. *See also* Defense Association; Independent Companies; Military Association; militia: in reaction to Paxton Boys
Monthly Meeting. *See* Quakers: Philadelphia
Monthly Meeting
Moravians, 84
Morris, Robert Hunter, 143, 146
Moyamensing township, 34, 151, 152

New Building, 81–82, 83–85, 86, 87, 90–91,
103, 213n7; purchased by College of Phila-
delphia, 92, 93
New England, 4, 20, 107
New Jersey, 62, 127, 208n17, 222n39
New York City, 49, 130, 192n15, 203n23,
204n24
New York State, 88, 222n39
Nicholson, Francis, 27
Non-Associators, 170, 172, 173, 174, 178, 180,
181, 235n53
non-importation, 165–66

Norris, Charles, 114
Norris, Isaac, Jr., 99, 100, 218n46, 226n20
North, Elizabeth, 73
Northern Liberties, 18, 151, 152, 153

Old Swedes' Church, 30, 38
oligarchy, 7
Overseers of the Poor (of Philadelphia), 3,
    56, 63, 151, 174; and Corporation for the
    Relief of the Poor, 152–53, 155, 229n50;
    finances, 61; limitations, 62; and Pennsylva-
    nia Assembly, 56, 61, 94; and Philadelphia
    Corporation, 61, 62–63. *See also* Contribu-
    tors to the Relief of the Poor

Paine, Thomas, 175, 176–78
Parliament, British, 105, 106, 107, 111, 112, 124,
    152, 179, 203n23, 219n3
Parr, William, 124–25, 223n43
Passyunk, 151, 152, 153
Patriots. *See* Revolutionaries
Paxton Boys, 148–49
Pemberton, Israel (Jr.), 94, 123, 222n28,
    222n40; and Friendly Association, 142, 143,
    144, 147, 148, 226n26
Penn, Hannah, 81
Penn, John, 149, 161, 233n27
Penn, Richard, 95, 212n2, 217n35
Penn, Thomas, 212n2, 217n35, 218n37; and
    College of Philadelphia, 92–93, 98–99,
    101–2, 103; and Defense Association, 88–89,
    90, 157, 215nn19–20; and Library Company
    of Philadelphia, 78; and Militia Bill, 138;
    and Pennsylvania Assembly, 94–95, 96, 105,
    133, 136, 162, 225n9; and Pennsylvania Hos-
    pital, 93–94, 96–98, 102, 218n37, 219n52;
    religious faith, 81
Penn, William, 13–14, 39, 42, 48; and bank,
    36; charter from Charles II, 201n12; and
    city lots, 16–18; death, 81; debates about
    proprietary rights, 16, 19, 29, 39, 40, 43–44;
    and defense, 50, 135; as historical symbol,
    148; and Pennsylvania government, 41; and
    Philadelphia government, 28, 36, 41–44,
    45, 46, 47, 49–50, 198n38; and Philadelphia
    layout, 1, 11–12, 16–17, 28, 159, 194n12; and
    Quaker meeting house, 21, 23; and religious
    toleration, 20

Penn, William, Jr., 51
Pennsylvania: and American Revolution,
    161–63, 178; colonial government, 6, 135;
    politics, 94–96, 139; post-war, 184; state
    constitution, 179–80, 181, 236n56; state
    government, 9, 178, 180, 181, 187
Pennsylvania Assembly, 6, 47, 89; and Ameri-
    can Revolution, 161–62; and College of
    Philadelphia, 101–2; and Contributors to
    the Relief of the Poor, 150, 151, 152, 154, 155,
    156; and defense, 41, 86–87, 135–36, 169–70;
    and Defense Association, 88, 90, 166; fight-
    ing against proprietary privilege, 41, 42,
    94–95, 96, 105, 133, 136, 225n9; and Friendly
    Association, 145; illegitimacy of, 176, 177,
    178; and Independent Companies, 166; and
    Library Company of Philadelphia, 78–79;
    and Military Association, 160, 166, 167,
    169–78, 181, 232n19, 233n28; and Overseers
    of the Poor, 56, 61, 94; and Pennsylvania
    Hospital, 55, 93–94, 96, 97–98, 100, 102–3,
    217n31; petition to end proprietary govern-
    ment, 162; and Philadelphia Corporation,
    50, 54–56, 57, 58, 61, 62; and religious
    institutions, 69–70; representation in,
    6, 42–43, 55, 86–87, 175, 201n10, 205n38,
    214n12, 233n29; and state house, 18, 78,
    84, 158; supremacy of, 41, 42, 47, 55, 95;
    workhouse, 62
Pennsylvania Hospital, 5, 82, 103, 159; finances,
    93, 102–3, 110–11, 221n15; and fire protec-
    tion, 76; founding, 93–94, 96, 205n39;
    incorporation, 94, 96, 97–98, 110; loans,
    104, 109–30; managers, 217n33; and T. Penn,
    93–94, 96–98, 102, 218n37, 219n52; and
    Pennsylvania Assembly, 55, 93–94, 96,
    97–98, 100, 102–3, 110, 217n31; and Quak-
    ers, 94, 96, 102; as template for later organi-
    zations, 145–46
Pennsylvania Land Company, 111
Peters, Richard: and College of Philadelphia,
    99, 100, 217n28; and Defense Association,
    88, 215n18, 216n21; on Friendly Association,
    143, 144, 227n32; and Pennsylvania Hospi-
    tal, 94, 218n37
petitions, use of, 5, 19, 40, 43, 44–45, 48, 100
Philadelphia: civic culture, 3–10, 35, 36–37, 82,
    90, 103, 156–57, 160–61, 179–82, 183–88;

Philadelphia (*cont.*)
cosmopolitanism, 70–71; as crucible, 10; demographics, 12, 28, 60, 69–70, 80–81, 133–34, 213n10, 232n19; description of, 38, 60, 70, 80–81, 131–32, 158–59, 183; economy, 70, 105, 209n25; founding of, 1, 11–14; government, 28–30, 33–37, 40, 156–57; layout, 1–2, 11, 13–15, 17, 37, 58, 60, 159, 194nn10–11; and Pennsylvania Assembly, 41; post-war, 183–84; record-keeping, 29, 30; representation in Pennsylvania Assembly, 6, 42–43, 55, 86–87, 175, 201n10, 205n39, 214n12, 233n29. *See also* city lots; city watch; streets
Philadelphia Baptist Association. *See under* Baptists
Philadelphia Contributionship: finances, 112; incorporation, 110; loans, 104, 109–10, 112–30
Philadelphia Corporation: 1701 charter, 43–45, 46, 49, 53, 58, 86, 94, 198n38, 201n15; commercial privileges, 57; and Corporation for the Relief of the Poor, 229n58; as defense against proprietary family, 47, 49–50, 57–58; and Defense Association, 88, 215n18; and J. Evans, 50–54, 58; finances, 48–49, 55–56, 62; and fire protection, 74, 75, 78; freemen/women, 56–57, 58, 205n43; governance, 54; internal structure, 47, 89; Mayor's Court, 49, 50, 54, 58; and military defense, 50–54; and Overseers of the Poor, 56, 61, 62–63; and Pennsylvania Assembly, 50, 54–56, 57, 58, 61, 62; and Philadelphia County, 54–55; and proprietary party, 101; and taverns, 54; weakness, 57, 58, 61, 101. *See also* city watch; Philadelphia: government; Philadelphians: agitation for corporate charter; poor relief; workhouses
Philadelphia County, 30, 35, 36, 129; and Philadelphia Corporation, 54–55, 206n6
Philadelphians: agitation for corporate charter, 19, 28–29, 39, 44–45; and American Revolution, 161–66, 168; and Defense Association, 89–90; and founding, 1–2, 11–17, 19; and political practices, 2–3, 5–6, 8; and property rights, 29
Plain Truth (Franklin), 87, 134
polycentric governance, 3, 4, 6–8, 13, 89, 181; demise of, 161, 179–82, 183–84

poor relief, 2, 3, 29, 60, 150–51; contemporary practice, 62, 229n47; in locales with established church, 29. *See also* Contributors to the Relief of the Poor; Overseers of the Poor; workhouses
Presbyterian Ministers Fund: finances and incorporation, 111; loans, 109, 111–30
Presbyterians, 26–27, 28, 66–67, 132; as political bloc, 95; schism, 67, 68, 83, 219n49; in Scotland, 20; and Whitefield, 83. *See also* Fund for Pious Uses; *under* meeting houses
privateers, 81, 86, 87, 90
Privy Council, 101, 137, 138, 140, 141
property rights, 39–40, 42, 43, 48. *See also* city lots
proprietary family (Penns), 5
proprietary party, 90, 94–96, 100–101, 133–34, 137, 144, 146; and American Revolution, 162
proprietors. *See* Penn, Thomas; Penn, William
Provincial Council, 16, 19, 30, 32, 33, 36, 42, 48, 101, 199n41; and city watch, 35; and Defense Association, 88, 215n18; and education, 32; and Philadelphia Corporation, 51; and wharves, 40

Quaker party, 94–95, 96, 101, 102, 133–34, 162. *See also* Quakers: as political bloc
Quakers: almshouse, 64, 207n12; and American Revolution, 160–61, 167, 179–80; beginnings, in Philadelphia, 21–23, 193n2; and Contributors to the Relief of the Poor, 150, 155–56; and Defense Association, 89, 90; deported during Revolution, 9; disowning, 25, 224n5, 235n51; and education, 29, 32–33, 48, 65, 199nn44–45; elites, 6, 42, 44, 50, 54, 58; finances, 22–23, 25–26, 30–32, 63, 66; and French and Indian War, 132–33, 140–41; internal organization, 25, 63, 66; leaving government, 141, 155, 226n20; loans, 31, 64–66; meeting, 132; and oaths, 44, 51, 204n28, 235n51; orphans, 31–32; pacifism, 9, 35, 51, 52, 53, 86, 89, 134, 135, 137, 141, 160–61, 213n11, 215nn18–20, 224n5, 235nn51–53; and W. Penn, 21, 23; petition to remove from provincial government, 100, 137; Philadelphia Monthly Meeting, 22, 23–25, 26, 31, 196n24, 207n10; Philadelphia Yearly Meeting, 25, 26, 94; as political bloc,

39, 81, 102; poor relief, 29, 30–32, 48, 63–65, 199n43; post-war, 184; during Revolution, 9; social services, 61; and subscriptions, 22–23, 24, 25–26, 30, 63, 196n25; visiting Friends, 3, 22, 25. *See also* Free School; Friendly Association; Keithian Schism; *under* meeting houses

radicals. *See* revolutionaries
rational-critical discourse, 5
religious institutions: and property, 68–69; social services, 30, 32, 33, 38, 48, 61, 65, 69. *See also* voluntary associations: religious denominations as; *specific denominations*
religious toleration, 13, 20–21, 42, 192n11. *See also* church, established: lack of
republicanism, 6–7, 137, 139, 187
Republicans, 184
revolution. *See* American Revolution
revolutionaries, 8–9, 106, 160, 161, 164, 166–67, 170, 171, 175–78. *See also* Sons of Liberty
revolutionary committees, 164, 176–77, 179. *See also* Committee of Safety; Military Association
riots, 5
roads. *See* streets

Schuylkill River, 1, 11, 15, 16–17, 18–19, 194n16. *See also* ferries
Seven Years War. *See* French and Indian War
Shawnee Indians, 145
Smith, William: advocating bishopric, 219n49; and College of Philadelphia, 99–104, 112, 123, 218n46; "The Forester," 176–77; and Independent Companies, 100
Society for the Propagation of the Gospel (SPG), 27, 66
Society for the Relief of poor and distressed Masters of Ships (Ships Captains Club), 109
Society of Ancient Britons, 71
Society of Christian Quakers. *See* Keithians
Society of Free Traders, 18–19, 94
Society of Friends. *See* Quakers
Sons of Liberty, 161, 163–64
South Sea Bubble, 105, 106–7, 108, 130, 219n3
Stamp Act, 8–9, 152, 161–63, 165
St. Andrew's Society, 95–96, 150, 218n36, 228n43

state, public sphere and the, 156–57, 187
Story, Enoch, 51, 54
street commissioners, 3, 221n15
streets, 2, 33–35, 43, 200n50
Swedes, 14

taverns, 17–18, 33, 54, 55, 70
Tea Act, 161, 165
Teedyuscung, 146–47. *See also* Friendly Association
Tennent, George, 83, 84, 132, 212n4
Tocqueville, Alexis de, 1, 191n6
Tories. *See* Loyalists
Townshend Duties, 161
town watch. *See* city watch
Turner, Robert, 24–25, 28, 41, 68

Union Fire Company, 74–77, 90, 109, 190n5, 211nn35–36, 211n39
Union Library Company, 73
University of Pennsylvania. *See* College of Philadelphia
urban expansion, 70

Virginia, 4, 61, 166, 180
voluntary associations: in British Atlantic, 4, 60, 71, 129–30, 209n25, 210n29, 211n42; as civic technology, 4, 60, 76–77, 81–82, 85, 91, 133, 142, 156, 160, 187–88, 190n5; definition as formal association, 71, 209n28; in early republic, 4–5, 184–88; and exclusion, 6, 8, 9, 71, 91, 95, 103, 139–40, 149–50, 161, 179–81, 186, 187; influenced by Quaker religion, 60; and joint-stock companies, 4; in Philadelphia, 5, 7, 58, 60–61, 71, 159; religious denominations as, 20–21, 25, 36–37, 69–70; as self-representation, 7. *See also* lending institutions, capital; *specific associations*
voting. *See* elections; franchise

Walking Purchase, 144, 147, 226n28
Walnut Street Prison, 129
war, 135, 200n48; King George's War, 86, 90, 216n23; King William's War, 35; Queen Anne's War, 50. *See also* American Revolution; French and Indian War
Weiser, Conrad, 143, 144
Weiss, Lewis, 125

Weston, Anthony, 15, 16

wharves, 2, 29, 33, 43, 48, 49, 57; fights over, 39–40

Whitefield, George, 80, 81, 82–85, 91, 92, 212n3

widows, 31, 63–65, 75

William Penn Charter School. *See* Free School

women: in Church of England, 27; in Dance Assembly, 95; and Defense Association, 89–90; in early Republic, 186; and fire companies, 75–76; in Library Company, 73; and loans, 127; political exclusion, 4, 236n55; and poor relief, 31, 65, 199n44; Quaker, 190n4

workhouses: House of Employment, 76, 152, 158, 159; Quaker almshouse, 64; before 1765, 56, 62, 94, 206n6. *See also* Contributors to the Relief of the Poor; Overseers of the Poor